STEVE BIRNBAUM

BRINGS YOU THE BEST OF

Walt Disney World ®

STEPHEN BIRNBAUM
EDITOR

WENDY SPRITZER
EXECUTIVE EDITOR

TOM DI NOME
ASSOCIATE EDITOR

PAUL POSNICK
DESIGN DIRECTOR

TONI SACCOMAN
ART DIRECTOR

AVON BOOKS & HEARST PROFESSIONAL MAGAZINES, INC.

CONTENTS

needed to organize a WDW visit right down to the smallest detail: When to Go; Reservations; How to Get There; Answers to the Tough Questions on Budgets and Packages; Hints on Traveling with Children; Hints for the Handicapped, for Singles, and for Older Visitors; plus lots more indispensable information.

AND ACCOMMODATIONS

Similarly, the complex transportation system within the World moves millions of visitors by monorail, bus, and various waterborne vehicles. It's organized to provide swift, efficient, access to all facilities, but it is complicated. Here are all the details.

THE MAGIC KINGDOM

Here is a land-by-land guide to all that there is to see and do, where to shop, and how to avoid the crowds, plus lots of other special tips to make your visit most pleasant and most rewarding.

WORLD AND WORLD SHOWCASE

that offer every visitor the opportunity to be a global and cerebral voyager without ever setting foot out of Central Florida. Here's how to make the most of this unique and fascinating attraction.

THEME PARK

Shops are full of movie memorabilia, movie crews roam Hollywood & Vine, and a surprising number of explosions and floods seem to suddenly occur. We've developed some strategies for seeing this tinseltown theme park, guaranteeing the most fun and the least time standing around.

ELSE IN THE WORLD

sports, shopping, and campgrounds. Whether you want to ride down high watery slides, dance the night away, shop at elegant boutiques, wander among exotic birds, or "go to school" behind the scenes, here's all the information you need to find your way to the wonders.

endeavors with all the rest of the fun that Walt Disney World offers, and this broad spectrum of sports activities is available to help turn your visit into the best sort of well-rounded holiday.

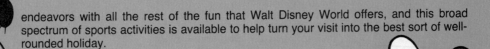

GREAT TIMES

restaurants are where and what specialties they offer. From fried ice cream to special French toast, from foie gras to sushi, we put all the dining choices right on your plate.

For Alex, who went on all the rides.

Other 1990 Birnbaum Travel Guides

Canada
Caribbean, Bahamas, and Bermuda
Disneyland
Europe
Europe for Business Travelers
France
Great Britain
Hawaii
Ireland
Italy
Mexico
South America
Spain and Portugal
United States
USA for Business Travelers

A WORD FROM THE EDITOR

I suspect that my wife may be the most blasé traveler I know. I've actually come home and asked if she'd like to go to Paris for the weekend, only to have her answer that she was planning to wash her hair.

So you can understand why I was a little apprehensive the first time I asked her if she'd like to spend a few days at Walt Disney World. It is perhaps the ultimate tribute to the appeal of this extraordinary place that my otherwise demure and dignified spouse immediately began jumping up and down, screaming, "Can we go on all the rides?"

My wife's reaction was clearly not very unusual, since Walt Disney World occupies the unique position of being the most popular manmade attraction on this planet. On a slow day (admittedly a relative term, and usually the by-product of unseasonable cold, wind, or rain), more than 25,000 visitors still find their way into WDW, while a really busy day in the Magic Kingdom, Epcot Center, and the Disney-MGM Studios can mean more than 150,000 souls streaming onto the premises.

Because I first experienced Walt Disney World as an unescorted, raw tourist, I feel eminently qualified to edit this guide. I believe I'm able to lead readers to and through Walt Disney World because I personally made just about every possible error an unknowing guest could make. Like many other uninitiated visitors before me, I wasted enormous amounts of time queuing up at attractions I should have left for another time, and finally missed a lot of things I really wanted to see because time ran short. I didn't allow enough days to do even a major fraction of all that was available, and I even chose the wrong time of the year to come to the park as a first-timer. I picked one of the most crowded times, when the mass of other visitors made orientation difficult and exaggerated every problem that one encounters at any truly popular destination.

I also committed the ultimate sin where Walt Disney World is concerned: I believed that the Magic Kingdom amusement area was all that Walt Disney World included. So the pleasures of places like River Country, Discovery Island and the trio of first class golf courses were never encountered by me until far later in the course of the research for this guide. The presence of vast, inspiring Epcot Center and the tinsel-touched turf at the Disney-MGM Studios only exaggerates this abundance of riches, as does the expanded spectrum of diversions now playing at places like Pleasure Island, and Typhoon Lagoon.

So what we've tried to do in designing this book is to keep you and yours from making the same mistakes that dogged my own early encounters with Walt Disney World. Even the most willing vacation planner needs adequate information in order to prepare an intelligent itinerary and daily plan, and what we hope we've done is to organize all the information necessary for a productive visit into as accessible and comprehensible a context as possible. Anyone who will take the time to read even the outlines of the pages that follow will find an emerging pattern that fits his or her special tastes; for those unwilling to exert even that much effort, we've compiled specific prospective day-by-day itineraries for several lengths of visits in order to protect you from yourself.

Travel guides of any sort are ultimately reflections of personal taste, and putting one's name on a title page obviously places one's preferences on the line. But I think I ought to clarify exactly what "personal" means with reference to this book. Literally dozens of very talented people have worked on preparing this guide, and what you will read on the pages that follow is the collected wisdom of myself, Wendy Spritzer, and our valued contributors, all amplified and expanded by comments from other knowledgeable editors, friends, and Walt Disney World staff members who gave us unique access to behind-the-scenes operations. We've tried to avoid doggedly alliterative or oppressively onomatopoeic text in favor of simple, straightforward descriptions of what we think is good and bad.

So despite the considerable number of contributors, what follows is as close to the gospel according to Birnbaum as you're likely to find. It represents as much of my own tastes and preferences as possible, and it's likely, therefore, that if you like your steak medium rare, your ice cream served only in a sugar cone, and can't tolerate fish that's been frozen or overcooked, we'll probably have a long and meaningful relationship. Readers with dissimilar tastes may be less enchanted.

This guidebook also owes an enormous debt to one of the most extraordinary groups of executives and operations people ever assembled—the ladies and gentlemen who manage and run Walt Disney World. Despite the designation of *Official Guide*, I should say that the *Walt Disney World staff has exercised no veto power whatever over the contents of this book*. Quite the contrary, they have opened their files and explained operations to us in the most generous way imaginable, so that we could prepare the comprehensive appraisals, charts, and schedules that were necessary to help visitors understand the very complex workings of a very complex enterprise.

I daresay there were times when the Disney folks were less than delighted at some of our opinions or conclusions, yet these analyses all stayed in. Furthermore, we've been flattered again and again by Disney staff who've commented about how much they've learned about some unfamiliar aspects of Walt Disney World from the material in this guide.

But the fact remains that this guide could never have proved as useful as it is without the extremely forthcoming cooperation of Walt Disney World personnel on every level. Both in the park and behind the scenes, they've been the source of the most critical factual data. I can only hope that I'm not omitting any names in thanking Judi Daley, Bill Burns, Reesa Martin, and Roy Young (Operations); Rich Taylor (Entertainment); Cindy McKinney (Guest Relations); Chris Moore and Penelope Baker (Resorts); Dave Venables (Guest Relations); Terri Smith, Patrice Lynch, and Debbie Dobbs (Resorts Marketing); Dwight Dorr (Transportation); John Dreyer (Publicity).

To Norm Doerges, Marty Sklar, Betsy Richman, Charlie Ridgway, Tom Garrison, Linda Warren, and Diane Hancock who did so much to make our job easier (and often possible), more thanks for their extraordinary help.

Most of all, we owe a debt of gratitude larger than we can say to those Walt Disney World executives (past and present) who believed in and nurtured this project, and who allowed us to do it—often against their basic instincts and better judgments. To Vince Jefferds, Bo Boyd, and Tom Elrod, there are no words to say thanks in quite the way we mean it.

Lastly, I should also point out that every worthwhile travel guide is a living enterprise; that is, this book may be our best effort at explaining how best to enjoy Walt Disney World at this moment, but its text is in no way cast in bronze. In each annual revision—you've got the ninth installment in your hand—we expect to refine and expand our material to serve our readers' needs even better. For this revision we've added 8 more pages to the text and a special chapter devoted to the Disney-MGM Studios Theme Park. We've also expanded our index which should make extracting material even easier than before.

We expect to make this guide even better in the future. To this end, no contribution is of greater value to us than *your* personal reaction to what we have written, as well as information about *your* own experiences while you were trying our suggestions. We eagerly and enthusiastically solicit your comments about this guide, and your opinions and perceptions based on your own visit. In this way, we are able to provide the best and most current information—including the actual experiences of individual travelers—and make it more readily available to others. So please write to me at 60 East 42nd Street; New York, New York 10165.

I sincerely hope to hear from you.

GETTING READY TO GO

The key to a successful visit to Walt Disney World is advance planning. This remarkably varied complex is just too vast and diverse to allow a spontaneous visit to be undertaken with notable success. That doesn't mean that even the most casual visitors can't have some significant fun, but they may later find a host of opportunities that were missed because of the pressure of time or an absence of information. The primary purpose of this guide is to eliminate that potential frustration.

What follows, then, is intended to provide a sensible scheme for organizing a visit to Walt Disney World, one that will allow the maximum amount of enjoyment and produce the minimum level of frustration and disappointment. One of the very best ways to judge what there is in the World that is most appealing to you is to have a clear idea of all that is available.

Unless otherwise noted, all phone numbers are in area code 407.

WHEN TO GO

When talk finally turns to the best time to make a trip to Walt Disney World, Christmas and Easter are often mentioned, as well as the weeks that comprise the traditional summer vacation period—especially if there are children in the family. But there are also good reasons to avoid these periods, chief among them the fact that almost everybody else goes then, and that when Walt Disney World is crowded, it can be very crowded indeed. On the busiest days, visitors may wait more than an hour for admission to some particularly popular attraction—at least twice as long as is typical at less crowded times of year.

Considering both the weather and crowd patterns described in the charts below, optimal times to visit WDW are September, October, and early November, the six weeks before and after spring school vacations, and the early part of June. Room reservations in the area are easiest to obtain from September through February, excluding the Thanksgiving and Christmas holiday periods. Youngsters who need to be taken out of school to visit at these times can enroll in WDW's innovative Wonders of Walt Disney World, a day-long educational program that uses the World as a classroom (see page 188). But visiting WDW at the least crowded times does have its own disadvantages: Because of the absence of crowds, the activities tend to close early (7 P.M. in the Magic Kingdom and 8 P.M. at Epcot Center and the Disney-MGM Studios are typical) and there are after-dark attractions (the Main Street Electrical Parade and Fantasy in the Sky fireworks) that do not function at all. So in the end, the choice of time to visit Walt Disney World is a very personal thing.

WDW WEATHER
Temperature

	Average high	Average low	Mean	Average rainfall (inches)
January	70	50	60	2.28
February	72	51	62	2.95
March	76	56	66	3.46
April	82	61	71	2.72
May	87	66	76	2.94
June	89	71	80	7.11
July	90	73	81	8.29
August	90	74	82	6.73
September	88	72	80	7.20
October	82	66	74	4.07
November	76	57	67	1.56
December	72	52	62	1.90

SPECIAL EVENTS

INSIDE WALT DISNEY WORLD: Special festivities are often staged not only to mark holidays, but also to salute special groups by offering discounted admissions to the Magic Kingdom, Epcot Center, and the Disney-MGM Studios Theme Park.

JANUARY: Walt Disney World New Year's Eve Celebration (Dec. 31). There are parties in the hotels and an extra-large fireworks display over the Magic Kingdom, which is open until 2 A.M. for the occasion. The celebration at the Top of the World, the stand-out, sells out first, despite its relatively high cost. The glass-walled room here provides a fantastic view of the pyrotechnics.
Resident Salute. Throughout the month, Florida residents pay special low admission prices to enter the Magic Kingdom, Epcot Center, and the Disney-MGM Studios Theme Park. Held again in May.

FEBRUARY: WDW Village Wine Festival. Sixty wineries from the U.S. and Europe participate. For details, contact Special Events; Disney Village Marketplace; Box 10150; Lake Buena Vista, FL 32830-1000.

EASTER SUNDAY: A nationally televised, promenade-style Easter Parade helps make this holiday celebration special in the Magic Kingdom, during a very busy time of year. The Magic Kingdom, Epcot Center, and the Disney-MGM Studios Theme Park stay open late during the Easter season.

MAY: Armed Forces Days. WDW salutes members of this group with the same special admission fees offered to Florida residents in January. The special prices are offered again in November.
Grad Nites. Top rock entertainment is presented, and the park is open from 11 P.M. to 5 A.M. for graduating high school students, who may buy specially priced tickets. Held on two weekends during the month. Special attire is required. For details, contact the Grad Nite Office; Box 10000; Lake Buena Vista, FL 32830.

JULY 4: Fourth of July Celebration. In the evening fireworks are set off above Cinderella Castle in the Magic Kingdom—as is usual when the park is open until midnight—and over the Seven Seas Lagoon as well. There's a spectacular show at Epcot Center too: IllumiNations, featuring music, lasers, and fireworks. Very busy.

OCTOBER 1 TO DECEMBER 15: Young at Heart Days. During this period, those Florida residents 55 and over receive special low-cost admission values.

OCTOBER: Walt Disney World/Oldsmobile Golf Classic. Top PGA Tour players compete alongside amateurs in this big tourney.

OCTOBER 31: Halloween. Youngsters get dressed up and join Disney villains in the Halloween costume contest at Disney Village Marketplace.

NOVEMBER: Festival of Masters at Disney Village Marketplace. One of the south's best art shows draws exhibitors from all around the country.

DECEMBER: Christmas Celebrations. Some 40 players present a nativity pageant at the Disney Village Marketplace. In the Magic Kingdom, a large, perfect Christmas tree is erected in Town Square; Main Street is decorated to the nines and patrolled by groups of carolers; a special Christmas parade and show are staged. Special tickets are available for Mickey's Very Merry Christmas Party, featuring all of the above—plus more holiday entertainment. The Magic Kingdom stays open late throughout the season, as do Epcot Center and the Disney-MGM Studios Theme Park, where there are also special shows throughout the season.

OUTSIDE WALT DISNEY WORLD: Several major events in the Central Florida communities around Walt Disney World are also worth a visit.

JANUARY: Orlando; Scottish Highland Games. The sizable Scottish population of the area turns out in force for Highland dancing and bagpipe competitions, as well as such traditional field events as tossing of the caber. Scottish shops are also set up. Details: Scottish-American Society of Central Florida; Box 2149; Orlando, FL 32802; 422-8226.

FEBRUARY: Tampa; Gasparilla Pirate Invasion and Parade. Dressed as renegades of the pirate band led by the legendary José Gaspar, members of a local club sail into Tampa Harbor in a full-sized buccaneer ship (accompanied by a flotilla of local boats), claim the city as their own, and then parade through the streets. Among the activities during the subsequent 2 weeks are another raid, this one on Ybor City—Tampa's historic Latin quarter—and a Spanish bean soup day during which this thick, delectable broth is served (along with Cuban bread and Cuban coffee). An illuminated parade winds up the event. Details: Ye Mystic Krewe of Gasparilla; Box 1514; Tampa, FL 33601; 813-228-7338.
Daytona; Speed Week. All the top names in stock-car racing are on hand at the Daytona International Speedway for one week of almost daily competition, culminating in the Daytona 500. Details: Daytona International Speedway; Drawer S; Daytona Beach, FL 32015; 904-254-6767.
Grant; Grant Seafood Festival. Some 75,000 visitors show up on the third weekend in February to eat fresh Indian River seafood at this huge affair staged by a small community on Florida's east coast. Details: Seafood Festival; Box 44; Grant, FL 32949; 723-8687 or 723-0898.
Kissimmee; Silver Spurs Rodeo. This 4-day event, held twice a year since 1944 (it's also held during the July 4th weekend), draws professional cowboys from all over the United States to compete for thousands of dollars in prizes. Details: Kissimmee-St. Cloud Convention and Visitors Bureau; Box 2007; Kissimmee, FL 32742-2007; 847-5000.

Orlando; Minnesota Twins Spring Training. The season at Tinker Field begins late in February and continues through March, with practices and exhibition games until the end of March. The Orlando Twins, a Minnesota farm team, play a full schedule from April through the end of August. Details: Tinker Field; 287 Tampa Ave. South; Orlando, FL 32805 or Box 5645; Orlando, FL 32855; 849-6346.

Kissimmee; Houston Astros Spring Training. The Astros' training season begins in late February and runs through early April. Details: Osceola County Stadium; 1000 Osceola Blvd.; Kissimmee, FL 32743; 933-5400.

MARCH: Orlando; Bay Hill Classic. Held annually early in March; Arnold Palmer hosts this PGA Tour event, one of 8 in the state of Florida, at the Bay Hill Club. Details: Bay Hill Club; 9000 Bay Hill Blvd.; Orlando, FL 32819; 876-2888.

Sarasota; Medieval Fair. Hundreds of entertainers from all over the country and abroad join in a human chess match, jousting, processions, singing, and other medieval merriment at the Ringling Museums complex. Everything from the food and drink served (pot pies, giant turkey legs, and ale) to the crafts sold and the language spoken by participants is authentically medieval. Details: Ringling Museums; 5401 Bay Shore Road; Sarasota, FL 34243; 813-355-5101.

Winter Park; Winter Park Sidewalk Art Festival. Held annually during the third weekend of the month, this display of etchings, pottery, paintings, sculpture, and other artwork and craft items also features concerts, strolling musicians, and a folk sing; it's one of the most prestigious events of its type in the Southeast. The backdrop is a small municipal park full of ancient trees draped with Spanish moss; the town itself is as tony as they come in Central Florida, with an array of chic boutiques and a clutch of first-rate restaurants. Details: City of Winter Park; 401 Park Ave., South; Winter Park, FL 32789; 623-3292.

APRIL: Titusville; Great Indian River Fes.. This community near the Kennedy Space Center makes an annual tribute to the celebrated Indian River with a weekend of arts and crafts, carnival rides, an antique car show, a boat show, live entertainment, food, and the Great Indian River Raft Race, in which only homemade craft can participate. Details: Titusville Area Chamber of Commerce; 2000 Washington Ave.; Titusville, FL 32780; 267-3036.

OCTOBER: Orlando; Pioneer Days. Two days of folk music, and a host of Florida folk demonstrations. Details: Pine Castle Center of the Arts; 6015 Randolph St.; Orlando, FL 32809; 855-7461.

Kissimmee; Florida State Air Fair. The U.S. Army's Golden Knights and the Air Force's Thunderbirds headline a 2-day roster of activities that also includes aerial acrobatic demonstrations, aeronautical displays, and exhibits of war planes on the ground. Details: Kissimmee-St. Cloud Convention and Visitors Bureau; Box 2007; Kissimmee, FL 32742-2007; 847-5000.

NOVEMBER: Orlando Magic Basketball. One of the NBA's newest franchises plays 41 home games at the brand-new Orlando Arena. Details: Orlando Arena; 600 West Amelia; Orlando, FL 32802; 849-2020.

DECEMBER: St. Petersburg; Florida Tournament of Bands. Marching bands from all over the state get together to vie for top honors in a series of competitions that will send shivers up and down the spine of anybody who loves a great parade. Details: Florida Tournament of Bands; Box 1731; St. Petersburg, FL 33731; 813-898-3654.

OPERATING HOURS

Hours of operation of the Magic Kingdom, Epcot Center, and the Disney-MGM Studios Theme Park vary from season to season. This fact should figure strongly in decisions on when to visit. For about a third of the year—in May, September, October, parts of November and December, and all of January—the Magic Kingdom is usually open from about 9 A.M. to 7 P.M. Hours are extended to 10 P.M. during Washington's Birthday week and during spring school breaks; and to midnight for summer and certain holiday periods (Thanksgiving weekend, Christmas, and the two weeks straddling Easter). On New Year's Eve, additional hours are added to the nighttime schedule, keeping the parks open until about 2 A.M.

Epcot Center is usually open from 9 A.M. to 8 P.M.; hours are extended during Thanksgiving weekend, Christmas, Washington's Birthday week, the two weeks straddling Easter, and spring school breaks.

The Disney-MGM Studios Theme Park is usually open from 9 A.M. to 7 P.M.; hours are extended to 9 P.M. or 10 P.M. during special holiday periods and the summer months.

Occasionally, during busy periods, the parks may open earlier or close later. Call 824-4321 for up-to-the-minute details.

HOW BIG ARE THE CROWDS?

Most visitors to Walt Disney World routinely assume that weekends are by far the busiest days on the property. But with the exception of holidays and holiday weekends, Mondays, Tuesdays, and Wednesdays are actually the most crowded days at the Magic Kingdom, Epcot Center, and the Disney-MGM Studios Theme Park. Sunday mornings rank as the most peaceful time to visit, with Fridays running a close second. The chart below offers general information on the density of the crowds during different times of the year. It's very hard to generalize, however, in a property as vast and diverse as Walt Disney World—a crowded day at the Magic Kingdom does not necessarily mean long lines at the Studio—but the chart below does highlight historic trends. Least crowded means that there may be some lines, but by and large most attractions can be visited without much waiting; average attendance refers to those times when there are lots of people around but the lines are still manageable; and most crowded reflects those times when the lines at the most popular attractions can mean a wait of an hour or more.

LEAST CROWDED	AVERAGE ATTENDANCE	MOST CROWDED
	1st week of January	
2nd week of January through 1st week of February		
	2nd week of February through President's Week	
		President's Week
	End of February through 1st week of April	
		2nd and 3rd weeks of April
	Last week of April through 1st week of June	
		2nd week of June through 3rd week of August
	Last week of August through Labor Day	
Week after Labor Day until Thanksgiving		
	Thanksgiving Week	
Week after Thanksgiving through week before Christmas		
		Christmas through New Year's Day

PLANNING AHEAD

Organizing a trip properly takes time, but almost every traveler finds that the increased enjoyment is well worth the effort. The fact is, that planning can become the most pleasant sort of "armchair" exercise, and kids will enjoy their visit to Walt Disney World all the more if they, too, are involved in the planning process.

The best strategy in organizing a Walt Disney World visit is to make a list of the attractions and activities that you most want to see; and assemble all the options from the various sources listed in this guide. Putting these in some practical sequence is the first order of business, and the only additional risk lies in trying to see and do too much in too short a period of time.

SAMPLE SCHEDULES: It's no exaggeration to say that a visitor could spend three weeks in Central Florida and still not have time to see everything there that's worthwhile. Walt Disney World alone requires every bit of four days just to cover the major attractions, and even that doesn't really allow enough time to take in everything. Just the basic inventory of attractions—the Magic Kingdom, Epcot Center, the Disney-MGM Studios Theme Park, Typhoon Lagoon, Pleasure Island, River Country, Discovery Island, Fort Wilderness, the Village Marketplace—only begins to suggest the broad spectrum of nearly irresistible entertainment opportunities, and we haven't even mentioned three fine golf courses, the beaches, and all the other tempting sports facilities.

The schedules that we suggest here should help put you on the right track—and maybe even keep you there. Deviations from the programs we describe should be based on our "Tips from WDW Veterans" (pages 112 and 152). In general, good sense and normal human stamina dictate that a guest can count on visiting seven or eight attractions per day in the Magic Kingdom, about five pavilions in Epcot Center, and most of the major

attractions at the Disney-MGM Studios Theme Park. That leaves some time for shopping, the inevitable lines at some attractions, and some unhurried meals. During less crowded seasons, it may be possible to accomplish significantly more. **Note:** Schedules suggested here are for the periods during the year when extended evening operating hours for the Magic Kingdom, Epcot Center, and the Disney-MGM Studios Theme Park are in effect.

Remember, too, that it's crucial to begin days in the Magic Kingdom, Epcot Center, and the Disney-MGM Studios Theme Park promptly at park opening. It's also wise to recognize that Epcot Center frequently opens a full half-hour before the official posted time.

One-day visit: There is so much to see and do at WDW that we don't really recommend a visit of this frustratingly short duration. But if that's all the time you've got, first decide which of the three prime areas (the Magic Kingdom, Epcot Center, or the Disney-MGM Studios Theme Park) you want to see, and then study all available material in advance so that you're as familiar as possible with your destination's layout and offerings. Be sure to arrive on the property early and move quickly while you're there. For optimal results, follow our schedules to the letter. **Note:** Because 1-day tickets permit visitors to enter *only* one of the three prime park attractions, visitors must concentrate on that park for the day (or pay a second full admission).

• If you choose to tour the Magic Kingdom, be in the parking lot at least 45 minutes before the scheduled park opening, so as to be at the Central Plaza end of Main Street at the official opening time. From there, move rapidly and purposefully from one attraction to the next—first to Space Mountain, then to the Haunted Mansion, Big Thunder Mountain Railroad, Country Bear Vacation Hoedown, Tom Sawyer Island, Pirates of the Caribbean, and the Jungle

Cruise. Plan on lunching at 11 A.M. to avoid meal-time lines. If time remains after the Jungle Cruise, see the Enchanted Tiki Birds and the Swiss Family Island Treehouse before eating; otherwise go to those attractions after lunch. Then begin making a second trip around the area, stopping at American Journeys, It's A Small World, the Penny Arcade, the Main Street Cinema, the shops and entertainment en route, and anything else that catches your eye. Then, having made reservations before leaving home, leave the Magic Kingdom about 4 P.M. for Fort Wilderness and the Hoop-Dee-Doo Revue.

During busy seasons, when all WDW attractions are open late, it may be possible to follow this dinner show with another visit to the Magic Kingdom, where fireworks, the Electrical Water Pageant, and the late installment of the Main Street Electrical Parade combine to make an evening especially memorable.

During other months (or if you could not get reservations for the Hoop-Dee-Doo Revue), head for Pleasure Island and either spend the evening aboard the *Empress Lilly* in one of its restaurants or lounges, or have dinner in one of the new restaurants or clubs there and take in a show.

• If you choose to spend the day in Epcot Center, arrive approximately one half hour before the park's official opening and wait at the gate until the turnstiles are unlocked. Then send the fastest member of your party ahead to Earth Station to make a 5 P.M. dinner reservation at one of the special international restaurants in World Showcase or Future World. Pick up an entertainment schedule while there. That done, visit The Land and then Journey Into Imagination, in Future World, then head quickly for World Showcase and see *O Canada!* in the Canada pavilion and *Impressions de France* in the France pavilion. Then backtrack to *Le Cellier*, in the Canada pavilion, for lunch around 11:30 A.M. Afterward, enjoy the World Showcase entertainment, see the shows at The American Adventure and Norway, and browse through the shops in Canada, the United Kingdom, France, Japan, Morocco, Germany, Italy, and Mexico. Keep an eye on the time so you're out of Mexico at about 3:30 P.M.; then head for Future World to visit The Living Seas (where it's easy to spend at least an hour) before heading for your dining spot at 4:45 P.M. Plan to finish your meal by 6:30 P.M. Spend the time until 9:30 P.M. in the China pavilion (for one of the last showings of the exciting film there); then head for Future World and see Spaceship Earth, Epcot Computer Central, World of Motion, and Universe of Energy.

• If you opt for the Disney-MGM Studios Theme Park, arrive at the park half an hour before the scheduled opening time. Head directly for the Animation Building and its hilarious film starring Robin Williams and Walter Cronkite. Next go directly to the Great Movie Ride. Having decided in advance which of the atmospheric restaurants most appeal to you, stop to make lunch reservations for about 1 P.M. at one eatery, and also dinner reservations for 7:30 P.M. at another. Try the 50's Prime Time Cafe for some old-time television nostalgia, or the Brown Derby for a touch more elegance. Then head for the SuperStar Television Theater (be sure to volunteer to participate on screen) and next for the Monster

Sound Show (also great fun to join on stage). After lunch, go to the Indiana Jones Epic Stunt Spectacular, and then spend some leisurely time browsing through the shops along Hollywood Boulevard, taking time to take in all the Studio's small details. At about 4:45 P.M., head for the Backstage Tour (it lasts about 2 hours and will get you back in time for your 7:30 P.M. dinner reservation). After dinner, you may want to take in another installment of the animation exhibit or do some last-minute shopping. **NOTE:** Because Walt Disney World has eliminated its 3-day passport and greatly expanded its inventory of activities and attractions, we earnestly recommend a stay of three full days and four nights to see just the highlights of the World. The following schedules are predicated on a late-afternoon arrival.

Three-day/four-night visit: This plan is recommended for only the highly energetic, for all the new attractions at WDW make it barely possible to see even the high points during this period. During peak seasons, nothing less than 3 full days and 4 evenings will do the trick. Be sure to check (the night before) on required transportation for early morning hours, and allot plenty of extra time for potential delays. On each day, the idea is to make a quick tour of the premises, visiting the major attractions during the least crowded hours of the early morning, then repeat the circuit of the park once again later in the day.

Steve Birnbaum
BRINGS YOU THE BEST OF
Walt Disney World
THE OFFICIAL GUIDE
includes EPCOT CENTER and the Disney-MGM STUDIOS THEME

How to get there, when to go, where to stay, what it will (and should) cost, how to see and do it all. Get the most for your money . . . and the most fun, too!

AMERICA'S LEADING TRAVEL AUTHORITY LEADS YOU TO AND THROUGH AMERICA'S MOST POPULAR TRAVEL ATTRACTION

1990

• Before leaving home, make reservations for the 5 P.M. seating at the Hoop-Dee-Doo Revue for the evening of the first *full* day of your stay. Then, on the first evening of your arrival at WDW, go directly to Epcot Center (try to arrive before 5 P.M.). Purchase a 4-day All Three Parks Passport for the best value, even though you will not have four full days. Grab a quick bite in one of the restaurants in CommuniCore East or West, then visit the Universe of Energy and the Living Seas. This should take about an hour. Next walk over to Journey into Imagination, where you should count on spending at least an hour-and-a-half. Depending on how much time remains before closing, proceed to Wonders of Life, where the lines for Body Wars should have diminished. Be sure to stick around the World Showcase Lagoon for the evening's presentation of IllumiNations, a spectacular outdoor sound, light, laser, and water show.

• On your first full day, have breakfast as early as possible to allow arrival at the Magic Kingdom turnstiles half an hour before scheduled opening—and to be at the Central Plaza end of Main Street at the official opening time. Once the gates open, make a beeline for Space Mountain, and then head for the Haunted Mansion, Big Thunder Mountain Railroad, Country Bear Vacation Hoedown, Tom Sawyer Island, Pirates of the Caribbean, and the Jungle Cruise in quick succession. When you get hungry, have lunch at the Adventureland Veranda

or the Crystal Palace. Be sure to arrange your meal schedule to have lunch shortly after 11:30 A.M. After lunch, begin making the day's second circuit of the park, visiting American Journeys, It's A Small World, the Penny Arcade, the Main Street Cinema, and anything else that seems appealing. Then, having reserved in advance, leave the Magic Kingdom at about 4 P.M. to head for Fort Wilderness and the Hoop-Dee-Doo Revue. During busy seasons it's possible to follow dinner with a couple of additional hours at the Magic Kingdom to see the fireworks, the Electrical Water Pageant, and the late installment of the Main Street Electrical Parade. During other months (or in the event that Hoop-Dee-Doo Revue reservations were unavailable), head either for Pleasure Island to take in one or more of the unique clubs and restaurants there, or for dinner at the Disney Village Marketplace.

• On your second full day, arrive at Epcot Center about half an hour before the park's official opening, and wait at the gate until the turnstiles are unlocked. Then go directly to Earth Station to make a 1:30 P.M. lunch reservation at one of the World Showcase restaurants and an 8:45 P.M. dinner reservation (when the park is open late) at another. (Note that guests staying at Walt Disney World hotels and Disney Village Hotel Plaza guests can make these reservations up to two days in advance. See *Good Meals, Great Times* for details of the reservation procedure and our dining suggestions). That done,

take in any major attractions in Future World that you missed on your first evening. Then head for World Showcase and see the American Adventure Show, the film at the Canada pavilion, *Impressions de France*, the film at the France pavilion, and the film at the China pavilion. Save shopping for later in the day, when the attractions are more crowded and the shops are not. The hours between 6 P.M. and your dinner reservation time should be spent seeing any attractions that were missed on your two previous circuits. Skip dessert at your dinner restaurant and instead head for the Boulangerie Patisserie in the France pavilion for pastry and espresso. If you couldn't get a reservation in the Epcot Center restaurant of your choice, or if a change of pace is desired, head for Pleasure Island, the Disney Village Marketplace, or the Disney Village Hotel Plaza, where there are many restaurants from which to choose (see *Good Meals, Great Times.*).

● On the third day of your visit, arrive at the Disney-MGM Studios Theme Park about half an hour before the scheduled opening. Head directly for the Animation Building for the very funny and entertaining film starring Robin Williams and Walter Cronkite. Then go to the Great Movie Ride. Having decided in advance which restaurants you'd like to try, make lunch and dinner reservations. (Note that Walt Disney World Resort guests and Disney Village Hotel Plaza guests can make these reservations up to two days in advance by telephone. See *Good Meals, Great Times* for details.) SuperStar Television Theater (where volunteering is a must) should be your next stop, then head for the Monster Sound Show (parents of young children should note that there are no monsters of any sort at this attraction). After lunch, go to the Indiana Jones Epic Stunt Spectacular and then spend some time browsing through the shops along Hollywood Boulevard. Head for the Backstage Tour at about 4:30 P.M. (it lasts about 2 hours and will get you back in time for dinner). After dinner you may want to take in another installment of the animation presentation, do some last-minute shopping, or head for Pleasure Island for an evening of shows and dancing.

Four-day/five-night visit: A stay of this length, while not exactly leisurely, is still the shortest time that can be conscientiously recommended for families with young children, older visitors, or anyone else who wants to visit all the best of Walt Disney World at less than a breakneck pace.

● Before visiting, read as much as possible about the WDW attractions and their locations. This is a must because although the pace of this 4-day program is slower than that required during a 3-day visit, it is still necessary not to waste time in order to cover all the high points. Remember, too, that the first order of business (before leaving home) is to make a 5 P.M. reservation for the Hoop-Dee-Doo Revue for the fourth day of your visit.

● On the evening of the day of your arrival, visit Epcot Center and purchase a 5-day All Three Parks Passport for the best value. Have a quick bite at one of the restaurants in CommuniCore East or West and then proceed as for the first evening of the 3-day visit described above.

● On the first full day of your visit, arrive at the Magic Kingdom 45 minutes before the official park opening. Tony's Town Square Cafe and the Crystal Palace buffeteria on Main Street, begin serving early, so have breakfast at one of these eateries and be at the Central Plaza end of Main Street at the park's official opening time. Then begin circumnavigating the park, taking in just the major attractions described for the first morning of a 3-day visit.

At about noon, leave the park and head for River Country, Discovery Island, or Typhoon Lagoon. Have lunch and participate in the varied activities offered. Golfers may want to take this opportunity to sample one of the trio of first class golf courses. Return to the Magic Kingdom at about 5 P.M. and grab a quick bite at the Tomorrowland Terrace. Then see American Journeys, and if time permits, Space Mountain. By 8 P.M. head for Main Street to stake a claim to a segment of curb for the 9 P.M. Main Street Electrical Parade. Watch the Fantasy in the Sky fireworks after the parade. After the fireworks, see the Electrical Water Pageant on the Seven Seas Lagoon.

● Devote the second day of your visit to Epcot Center. Arrive about half an hour before the official park opening and queue up at the gate. While waiting, choose a restaurant for dinner. When the gates open, send the speediest member of your group to Earth Station to make an early (around 5 P.M. or 5:30 P.M.) dinner reservation. Then begin visiting the Future World attractions you missed on your first evening. Leave Future World at around 10 A.M. and head for World Showcase. First go to France and see the film there, then head to the American Adventure, Norway, and China. Next go to Mexico and have lunch at the pleasant Cantina de San Angel. Afterward, reverse the direction of your route around World Showcase, and stop at the pavilions you missed the first time around. Even if you hate shopping, look into Germany's arts-and-crafts and toy shops and Morocco's brass and jewelry bazaars. Also be sure to look in on the entertainers who perform daily around Italy, the puppeteers on the Promenade, and the street players at the United Kingdom. For a mid-afternoon snack, stop at the U.K. pavilion's Tea Caddy, buy a box of crackers or cookies, and then head for the Refreshment Outpost for a cold drink with which to eat them. Then go back to Future World and explore CommuniCore East and the TransCenter. Remember to allot a full 20 minutes to walk to your dining spot. The uncrowded hours after dinner should be spent visiting any attractions missed on previous circuits.

• On the third full day of your visit, head for the Disney-MGM Studios Theme Park and follow the schedule outlined in the 3-day visit. Go first to the Animation Building and next to the Great Movie Ride. Take in SuperStar Television Theater and the Monster Sound Show before lunch. Feel like you're back in Mom's kitchen at the 50's Prime Time Cafe, have a taste of old Hollywood at the Brown Derby, or try one of the counter service establishments. Then see the Indiana Jones Epic Stunt Spectacular. Spend part of the afternoon hours browsing in the shops along Hollywood Boulevard, and head over to the Backstage Tour at about 4:30 P.M. After dinner, go back to any attraction that you particularly enjoyed or head to Pleasure Island for the shows and/or an evening of dancing. If tired feet prohibit such activity, take in a movie at the multiplex cinema at Pleasure Island.

• On the fourth full day of your visit, try one of the character breakfasts (described in *Good Meals, Great Times*) and then head over to the Disney Village Marketplace for some leisurely shopping. Have a light lunch at one of the restaurants there, or head over to Pleasure Island for a bite and some more shopping. The unusual wares at the Pleasure Island shops are worth a look. For the athletically inclined, try a round of golf, a couple of sets of tennis, a canoe trip, or any of the other varied activities described in our *Sports* chapter. Either

way, at about 4 P.M. head over to Fort Wilderness for the 5 P.M. Hoop-Dee-Doo Revue. Then go back to Pleasure Island for some dancing, comedy, or music, or maybe take in a movie at the multiplex cinema next door.

Five-day visit: Follow our program as outlined for the 4-day visit. On the fifth day, spend the morning in the one park you most enjoyed. Then leave and have lunch at the Grand Floridian Resort, the Polynesian Resort, or the Disney Inn, and then spend the afternoon lounging by the pool, playing tennis or golf, or biking. Try a special dinner at Victoria & Albert's at the Grand Floridian or Portobello Yacht Club at Pleasure Island. Then head for one of the clubs at Pleasure Island, or (having reserved in advance) take in one of the dinner shows like "Broadway at the Top" at the Contemporary Resort or the luau at the Polynesian Village Resort.

For visits of 6 days or longer: In addition to our program described for a 5-day visit, a stay of this length allows guests a chance to sample some of the World's other unique offerings. The Walt Disney World Golf Studio can help improve your stroke (see *Sports*); adult visitors with a yen to go behind the scenes can enroll in a Disney Learning Adventure while children 10 to 15 can participate in a Wonders of the World program (see page 188); Discovery Island offers guided tours that make for a delightful afternoon (see *Everything Else in the World*); or participate in any of the other activities described in our *Sports* and *Everything Else in the World* chapters.

DO YOU NEED A CAR? It used to be that if you were staying at a WDW resort, a car was unnecessary. With the expansion of attractions and the construction of new hotels, this is no longer true. Particularly for guests staying at the Caribbean Beach Resort who plan to spend a lot of time at the Magic Kingdom, a car is a good idea. Likewise for guests staying at the hotels near the Magic Kingdom who expect to spend significant time at the Disney-MGM Studios Theme Park, Epcot Center, or Typhoon Lagoon. It is still quite easy, however, to get around the property without a car. Transportation within the World gets guests from point to point and there's no parking problem. It's also possible to get to WDW resorts from Orlando Airport without a car—Mear's Motor Shuttles operate about every 20 minutes around the clock, serving on-property hotels, as well as Disney Village Hotel Plaza accommodations, Florida Center hotels, and hotels on U.S. 192. (Call for reservations: 423-5566.) Also, visitors lodging outside the World can usually get to and from WDW via their own hotels' bus service (which most hotels offer). Limos and cabs are also available. But a car is a must for taking in Orlando-area restaurants and attractions outside WDW.

INFORMATION SOURCES: For details about other things to see and do in Central Florida, contact the Florida Department of Commerce; Tourism Division; 101 East Gaines St., Fletcher Building; Tallahassee, FL 32399-2000; 904-487-1462. To find out about the area directly around Orlando, contact the Orlando Convention and Visitors Bureau; 7208

Sand Lake Rd., Suite 300; Orlando, FL 32819; 363-5871. For general information about Walt Disney World, write the Walt Disney World Co.; Box 10000; Lake Buena Vista, FL 32830-1000; 824-4321.

Walt Disney World Information/Reservation Center: The best time to make or confirm hotel reservations is *before* you're actually standing at the hotel's front desk. Nobody likes unpleasant surprises, so it's wise to have an assured reservation.

Those driving to Walt Disney World can now arrange that assurance easily because the Disney folks have opened a full-service information facility in Ocala, Florida, at the intersection of Interstate 75 and State Route 200, about 90 miles north of Orlando. Like a welcome center, the facility will help Disney-bound vacationers plan their time, purchase tickets for the Magic Kingdom, Epcot Center, the Disney-MGM Studios Theme Park, and other attractions, and make hotel reservations (or confirm them). And for those heading home from WDW who forgot to buy enough pairs of mouse ears, the center also offers plenty of Disney souvenirs and character merchandise.

Upon arrival at Walt Disney World, a variety of other information sources is available. First, tune into the WDW radio stations after entering the grounds—1030 on the AM dial inbound to the Magic Kingdom and 810 approaching Epcot Center. (Helpful information is broadcast to guests departing from the Magic Kingdom and Epcot Center on 900.)

At check-in, guests at all WDW-owned resorts—that is, the Contemporary Resort, The Disney Inn, the Polynesian Village Resort, the Grand Floridian, the Caribbean Beach Resort, Fort Wilderness Resort, and the Disney Village Resort—are given copies of *Your Guide to the Magic Kingdom*, the Epcot Center guide, and the guide to the Disney-MGM Studios Theme Park at no charge, plus the latest *Walt Disney World Vacation Guide*, detailing a variety of activities inside the World. In addition, all guests except those camping out at Fort Wilderness can tune to Channel 5 on their hotel-room television sets to see a filmed overview of all WDW attractions—a complete orientation tour of the property, which is essential viewing for all first-time visitors. It's broadcast continuously. Guests at Disney Village Hotel Plaza establishments will see a similar program on Channel 7. (The latter gives somewhat more emphasis to the dining rooms and lounges at these lodging places, which, though located on WDW property, are neither Disney-owned nor Disney-operated.) For further information, guests at WDW properties can watch the daily program *Around the World Today*, which provides operating

Channel 5 orientation film; this attempts to give visitors an overview of all Central Florida attractions (WDW among them), rather than concentrating on the World.

For further information about the World, phone WDW Information at 824-4321.

WHAT TO PACK: Walt Disney World is not so casual that all you need to bring is a bathing suit, but with only a few exceptions, comfortable clothing is the rule. Jackets are required for men at the dinner show at the Top of the World, dinner at the Empress Room aboard the *Empress Lilly* riverboat, and for dinner at Victoria and Albert's at the Grand Floridian Resort (ties are also required here). Everywhere else anything from T-shirts and shorts in the daytime to slacks or dresses in the evening is acceptable. This is also true at the full-service restaurants that are found in the World Showcase pavilions at Epcot Center. Bathing suits are a must, and a spare one is useful, as are the right togs for any other sport you might want to pursue. On the tennis courts, tennis whites are appropriate, though not required. Guests should bring lightweight sweaters even in summer—to wear indoors when the air conditioning gets too frigid. From November through March, warmer clothing is a must in the evening. Always pack something to keep you comfortable should the weather turn unseasonably warm or cool. Especially in summer, lightweight rain gear and a folding umbrella come in handy.

The most important item of clothing of all? Comfortable, well broken-in walking shoes.

hours, name entertainers that are currently performing, special events, weather forecasts, and other useful information, on Channel 10. (This program is not shown outside WDW-owned lodging places.) For additional information, guests at WDW resorts should contact Guest Services. To do this, those staying at the Contemporary Resort, the Polynesian Village, the Grand Floridian, The Disney Inn, the Caribbean Beach Resort, and the Disney Village Resort should touch "11" on their room phones or house phones; Fort Wilderness campers should stop at the Pioneer Hall Information and Ticket Window, call extension 2788, or touch "11" from the phones at the comfort stations located at the center of each campground loop area. After 11 P.M., guests at all the WDW resort properties should call their respective front desks.

Day visitors: All day visitors—that is, those staying off the property, as well as those living in the Orlando area—receive a hand-out at the Auto Plaza detailing admission prices and other useful information. When purchasing 1-day admission media at the TTC, at Epcot Center, or at the Disney-MGM Studios Theme Park, guests receive a copy of the the Magic Kingdom guide, the Epcot Center guide, or the Disney-MGM Studios Theme Park guide, depending upon which park they have chosen to visit. Guests who purchase multi-day admission media may receive all three guides upon request. City Hall (in the Magic Kingdom), Earth Station (in Epcot Center), and Guest Services (at the Disney-MGM Studios Theme Park) distribute extra copies of these guides at no charge.

Some hotels off the property—but not all of them—show their own version of the WDW resorts'

RESERVATIONS

Walt Disney World vacations go most smoothly when details are planned well ahead of time. Procrastinators may find no room at the inn, or no space left for a show that they wanted to see. Golf starting times, tennis courts, dinner reservations, and other special affairs should be reserved in advance.

Central Reservations Office: Many arrangements are handled by the Central Reservations Office (CRO); the phone number is 407-W-DISNEY (934-7639) or, for speakers of French or Spanish, 407-824-7900. The office is open 7 days a week from 8:30 A.M. to 10 P.M. The best times to call are after 6 P.M. and on weekends.

When calling, expect the phone to ring for a couple of minutes (up to 5 or even 10 minutes during some very busy periods) before being answered. This is to avoid putting callers, most of whom are phoning long distance, on hold. The telephone system is handled by a computer that automatically puts calls in order, so don't hang up. Have a pencil and paper close at hand (and your credit card) when calling, to jot down dates and the number of your reservation.

Room reservations: It is especially important to book accommodations in advance—up to 1 year in order to have your first choice of dates for visits during the most popular holiday periods, and 4 to 6 months ahead to get your pick of dates for a midsummer visit. During other times of year, it's necessary to call 3 to 4 months before arrival, and even then it may not be possible to get space in the precise resort you've selected, or for the exact number of nights you wanted.

When Central Reservations can't accommodate your first preference, don't despair. Cancellations do come up. There are waiting lists for guests who have managed to reserve at least 1 night of the multinight stay that they had originally requested. Visitors who were not able to arrange for a room at all may sometimes get one by calling later on. There is also a very slim chance of snagging space, left vacant by the occasional early departure, on the day of arrival; contact Central Reservations or get help from Guest Relations (at City Hall, the Transportation and Ticket Center, and Epcot Center; Guest Services at the Disney-MGM Studios Theme Park; or at the hotel's front desk).

Delta Air Lines: As the "Official Airline of Walt Disney World," Delta Air Lines has a substantial number of rooms specifically allocated for its use. Delta is, therefore, a very good means of access to hard-to-book Walt Disney World-owned hotel rooms. These rooms are available as part of Delta Dream Vacation packages, which also have the added attraction of saving visitors some money on air fares as well. American Express and Greyhound offer similar packages.

Reservations for supper seatings, dinner shows, and sporting activities: Some of these are handled by Central Reservations, while others are handled by the individual restaurants and sporting centers. It's always wise to make your plans and reserve your place as far in advance as WDW policy will allow. Just how far in advance may vary depending on where you lodge. (See chart below.)

Package vacationers take note: Your packages cover only the *cost* of dinner shows and activities, *not the reservations that may be necessary to enjoy them. It's up to the individual traveler to make all the specific bookings.*

RESERVATION GUIDE

ACTIVITY	Phone for reservations (area code 407)	Advisability of reservations	Guests in WDW hotels/villas	Guests at Hotel Plaza establishments	Guests at off-property hotels
Sports					
Golf starting times— all courses	824-2270	Necessary from February through April; a good idea at other times	30 days	7 days	
Walt Disney World Golf Studio, The Disney Inn	824-2250	Necessary	.... No limit for any guest		
Private golf lessons, The Disney Inn	824-2270	Necessary	.... No limit for any guest		
Private golf lessons, Lake Buena Vista course	828-3741	Necessary	.... No limit for any guest		
Tennis, Contemporary Resort	824-3578	Suggested	.... 24 hours in advance		
Tennis, The Disney Inn	824-2288	Suggested	.... 24 hours in advance		
Tennis, Village Clubhouse	828-3742	Suggested	.... 24 hours in advance		

How far in advance can reservations be made?

ACTIVITY	Phone for reservations (area code 407)	Advisability of reservations	How far in advance can reservations be made?		
			Guests in WDW hotels/villas	Guests at Hotel Plaza establishments	Guests at off-property hotels
Tennis lessons, private and group, at the Contemporary Resort and at Village Clubhouse	824-3578	Necessary	.... No limit for any guest		
Trail rides, Fort Wilderness	W-DISNEY (934-7639)	Necessary	.... Up to 7 days for all		
Fishing trips, Fort Wilderness	824-2757	Necessary	.... Up to 14 days for all		

Good Meals

ACTIVITY	Phone	Advisability	WDW hotels/villas	Hotel Plaza	off-property
Empress Room, *Empress Lilly* Riverboat, Pleasure Island	828-3900	Necessary	.... 30 days		
Pompano Grill Disney Village Resort	828-3735	Suggested	.... 30 days		
Papeete Bay Verandah, Polynesian Village Resort	824-1391	Requested	.... 7 days....................		
Tangaroa Terrace, Polynesian Village Resort	824-1360	Suggested	.... No limit for any guest		
Garden Gallery, The Disney Inn	824-1484	Suggested; available for dinner only	.... 30 days		
Epcot Center full-service restaurants	828-4000 824-8800 for Hotel Plaza Guests	Necessary	2 days in advance; from noon to 9 P.M.	2 days in advance; from noon to 9 P.M.	Available in person only on day of dining

Great Times

ACTIVITY	Phone	Advisability	WDW hotels/villas	Hotel Plaza	off-property
Top of the World Dinner Show, Contemporary Resort	W-DISNEY (934-7639)	Necessary	.... 30 days for all		
Hoop-Dee-Doo Musical Revue, Pioneer Hall, Fort Wilderness	W-DISNEY (934-7639)	Necessary	Upon receipt of confirmed reservation	45 days*	30 days
Polynesian Revue, Polynesian Village Resort	W-DISNEY (934-7639)	Necessary	Upon receipt of confirmed reservation	45 days*	30 days
Mickey's Tropical Revue	W-DISNEY (934-7639)	Necessary	Upon receipt of confirmed reservation	45 days*	30 days
Breakfast à la Disney, *Empress Lilly*	W-DISNEY (934-7639)	Necessary	Upon receipt of confirmed reservation	45 days*	30 days
Minnie's Menehune Character Breakfast, Polynesian Village Resort	824-1391	Necessary	30 days	30 days	30 days
Chip & Dale's Country Morning Jamboree, Pioneer Hall, Fort Wilderness	W-DISNEY (934-7639)	Necessary	Upon receipt of confirmed reservation	45 days*	30 days
Marshmallow Marsh Excursion, Fort Wilderness (seasonal)	824-2788	Necessary	5 days	.... Resort guests only	

Sunday Brunches

ACTIVITY	Phone	Advisability	WDW hotels/villas	Hotel Plaza	off-property
Character Brunch Papeete Bay, Polynesian Village Resort	824-1391	Necessary	.... No limit for any guest		
Pompano Grill	828-3735	Requested	.... 14 days		
Top of the World, Contemporary Resort	824-3611	Necessary	...................7 days....................		

* only if hotel reservations have been made through CRO; otherwise, 30 days

HOW TO GET THERE

BY CAR

Here are some suggested routes to WDW from the downtown sections of several metropolitan areas.

Figure on driving 350 to 400 miles a day—a reasonable distance that won't wear you down so much that you can't enjoy your stay.

Atlanta: I-75 south, I-475 south around Macon, I-75 south, Florida's Turnpike south, U.S. 27 south, U.S. 192 east to entrance. Total mileage: 455 miles.

Baltimore: I-95 south, I-495 west and south around Washington, I-95 south, I-295 around Jacksonville, I-95 south, I-4 west, U.S. 192 west to entrance. Total mileage: 916 miles.

Boston: I-90 west, I-84 west, I-91 south, I-95 south, I-287 west, Garden State Parkway south, New Jersey Turnpike south to Delaware Memorial Bridge, I-95 south (through Fort McHenry Tunnel in Baltimore), I-495 west and south around Washington, I-95 south, I-295 around Jacksonville, I-95 south, I-4 west, U.S. 192 west to entrance. Total mileage: 1,346 miles.

Buffalo: I-90 west, I-79 south, U.S. 19 south, West Virginia Turnpike south, I-77 south, I-20 west around Columbia (SC), I-26 east, I-95 south, I-295 around Jacksonville, I-95 south, I-4 west, U.S. 192 west to entrance. Total mileage: 1,209 miles.

Chicago: I-94 south, I-90 east, U.S. 41 south, I-24 east to Chattanooga, I-75 south, I-285 west and south around Atlanta, I-75 south, I-475 south around Macon, I-75 south, Florida's Turnpike south, U.S. 27 south, U.S. 192 east to entrance. Total mileage: 1,152 miles.

Cincinnati: I-75 south, I-285 west and south around Atlanta, I-75 south, I-475 south around Macon, I-75 south, Florida's Turnpike south, U.S. 27 south, U.S. 192 east to entrance. Total mileage: 911 miles.

Cleveland: I-77 south, West Virginia Turnpike south, I-77 south, I-20 west around Columbia (SC), I-26 east, I-95 south, I-295 around Jacksonville, I-95 south, I-4 west, U.S. 192 west to entrance. Total mileage: 1,098 miles.

Dallas: I-20 east to Shreveport, S.R. 1 south to Alexandria, U.S. 71 south, U.S. 190 east, S.R. 415 south, I-10 east, I-12 east toward New Orleans, I-10 east, I-75 east, Florida's Turnpike south, U.S. 27 south, U.S. 192 east to entrance. Total mileage: 1,131 miles.

Detroit: I-75 south, I-285 west and south around Atlanta, I-75 south, I-475 south around Macon, I-75 south, Florida's Turnpike south, U.S. 27 south, U.S. 192 east to entrance. Total mileage: 1,193 miles.

FROM THE AIRPORT

Take Route 528 (known as the Beeline Expressway) west (toward Tampa), to I-4 west until you reach the appropriate Walt Disney World exit. The distance is 28 miles.

Indianapolis: I-65 south to Nashville, I-24 east to Chattanooga, I-75 south, I-285 west and south around Atlanta, I-75 south, I-475 south around Macon, I-75 south, Florida's Turnpike south, U.S. 27 south, U.S. 192 east to entrance. Total mileage: 985 miles.

Louisville: I-65 south to Nashville, I-24 east to Chattanooga, I-75 south, I-285 west and south around Atlanta, I-75 south, I-475 south around Macon, I-75 south, Florida's Turnpike south, U.S. 27 south, U.S. 192 east to entrance. Total mileage: 873 miles.

Minneapolis: I-94 east to Madison (WI), I-90 east, I-294 south around Chicago, I-90 east, U.S. 41 south, I-24 east to Chattanooga, I-75 south, I-285 west and south around Atlanta, I-75 south, I-475 south around Macon, I-75 south, Florida's Turnpike south, U.S. 27 south, U.S. 192 east to entrance. Total mileage: 1,545 miles.

New York City: Lincoln Tunnel west, New Jersey Turnpike south to Delaware Memorial Bridge, I-95 south (through Fort McHenry Tunnel in Baltimore), I-495 west and south around Washington, I-95 south, I-295 around Jacksonville, I-95 south, I-4 west, U.S. 192 west to entrance. Total mileage: 1,103 miles.

Philadelphia: I-95 south (through Fort McHenry Tunnel in Baltimore), I-495 west and south around Washington, I-95 south, I-295 around Jacksonville, I-95 south, I-4 west, U.S. 192 west to entrance. Total mileage: 1,017 miles.

Pittsburgh: I-79 south, U.S. 19 south, West Virginia Turnpike south, I-77 south, I-20 west around Columbia (SC), I-26 east, I-95 south, I-295 around Jacksonville, I-95 south, I-4 west, U.S. 192 west to entrance. Total mileage: 1,016 miles.

Richmond: I-95 south, I-295 around Jacksonville, I-95 south, I-4 west, U.S. 192 west to entrance. Total mileage: 761 miles.

Toronto: Queen Elizabeth Way south, I-190 south, I-90 west, I-79 south, U.S. 19 south, West Virginia Turnpike south, I-77 south, I-20 west around Columbia (SC), I-26 east, I-95 south, I-295 around Jacksonville, I-95 south, I-4 west, U.S. 192 west to entrance. Total mileage: 1,302 miles.

AUTOMOBILE CLUBS: Reputable national automobile clubs can offer help with breakdowns en route; insurance that covers personal injury, accidents, arrest, bail bond, and lawyers' fees for defense of contested traffic cases; and travel-planning services—not only advice, but also free maps and route-mapping. Programs vary from one club to the next; fees range from about $25 to $50 a year.

Among the leading clubs:
Allstate Motor Club; Box 3094; Arlington Heights, IL 60006; 800-323-6282
American Automobile Association; 8111 Gatehouse Rd.; Falls Church, VA 22047; 703-222-6000
Amoco Motor Club; Box 9014; Des Moines, IA 50265; 800-334-3300; 800-372-7721 in Iowa

Ford Auto Club; Box 224688; Dallas, TX 75222-4688; 800-348-5220
Gulf Auto Club; 6001 North Clark St.; Chicago, IL 60660; 800-633-3224
JTX Travel Club Inc.; Box 13901; Philadelphia, PA 19101; 800-523-4816
Montgomery Ward Auto Club; 200 North Martingale Rd.; Schaumburg, IL 60194; 800-621-5151
Motor Club of America; 484 Central Ave.; Newark, NJ 07107; 201-733-1234
United States Auto Club Motoring Division; Box 660460; Dallas, TX 75266-0460; 800-348-5058

OTHER MAPS: Those who don't belong to an automobile or travel club can get free maps from state tourist boards. Also excellent is *Rand McNally's Road Atlas* (about $6.95 in bookstores).

BY BUS

Relatively few vacationers come to Walt Disney World by bus. But it makes sense to consider this means of transportation if you're traveling just a short distance or have plenty of time, if there are only two or three in your party, or if cost is a major consideration. Bus travel is usually extremely economical.

Greyhound provides frequent direct service into Orlando; buses deposit their passengers on the very threshold of the Magic Kingdom and at the entrance to Epcot Center (where there are lockers in which luggage can be stored until the end of the day). From there, taxis and limousines provided by the various area hotels and motels provide transportation to the lodging place that you have selected. For further information phone Greyhound at 407-843-7720.

Sample Travel Times

Jacksonville, Florida . . .	about 3½ hours
Tallahassee, Florida . . .	about 7½ hours
Atlanta, Georgia	about 13 hours

BY TRAIN

Amtrak serves the Orlando area twice daily from New York City. The trip takes about 21 hours and costs in the neighborhood of $326 round trip. En route stops are made in Philadelphia, Washington, D.C., Virginia, North Carolina, South Carolina, and Georgia. (Special discounts are sometimes available; it's a good idea to check.)

Amtrak also offers Auto Train service daily in both directions from Lorton, Virginia, 17 miles south of Washington, D.C., direct to Sanford, Florida, just 25 miles northeast of Orlando. Departure time is 4:30 P.M. and arrival time is 9 A.M. in both directions. The fare is $274 per car, $169 per adult, and $100 for children ages 2 through 11. The fare includes two meals and some entertainment. Sleeping accommodations cost extra. Special off-peak fares are often offered, so be sure to inquire.

For reservations and schedule information, send a self-addressed, stamped envelope to Amtrak Distribution Center; Box 7717; Itasca, IL 60143; or call 800-USA-RAIL.

BY SHIP

Premier Cruise Lines, the "Official Cruise Line of Walt Disney World," has made it possible to combine a 3- or 4-day ocean cruise to the Bahamas with a Walt Disney World vacation. Travelers can choose to visit WDW before or after they set sail aboard the Star/Ship *Majestic*, the Star/Ship *Oceanic*, or the Star/Ship *Atlantic*. Cruises leave from (and return to) Port Canaveral, only about 45 miles from the Walt Disney World resort. The ships stop at Nassau and one Out Island en route. Premier's packages include 3 or 4 days at sea (with all meals), 3 or 4 nights' accommodations at a hotel near Walt Disney World, and 3 one-day tickets (allowing admission to all rides, pavilions, and attractions at the Magic Kingdom, Epcot Center, and the Disney-MGM Studios Theme Park). Also included in the package is a Hertz rental car for 7 days with unlimited mileage and a tour of Spaceport, USA, at the Kennedy Space Center, just minutes from the ship's dock at Port Canaveral. Air arrangements to Orlando are available as part of the cruise program. For cruise dates and reservation information contact your travel agent.

BY AIR

The sleek, multimillion-dollar Orlando International Airport is equipped to handle the millions of visitors who flock to Central Florida each year. Shuttle trains transport passengers to and from the central terminal, and there is a WDW information center where arriving guests can find out what's going on during their stay—and departing travelers can buy T-shirts and other Disney merchandise that they may have forgotten to acquire on the property.

There are more than a dozen airlines offering non-stop flights from all parts of the country. Delta Air Lines alone—the "Official Airline of Walt Disney World"—carries more than one million passengers into Orlando annually, on non-stop flights from 26 cities, direct flights (not including a change of planes), and connecting flights from 150 additional cities. Delta offers a special style of service for all passengers, along with special meals and the special Fantastic Flyer™ program for kids.

The airline you decide to fly will depend in large part on where you live, when you'll be traveling, and which airline can get you there when you want to go, for the price you want to pay. Remember, direct flights—those whose lure is that they do not include a change of planes—are not always the swiftest way to get from point to point. If your itinerary requires several stops, it might be wise to investigate all of the possible connection alternatives.

DELTA DREAM VACATIONS®*

As the "Official Airline of Walt Disney World," Delta Air Lines has its own ticket office in the lobby of the Contemporary Resort. In addition Delta has a new attraction in the Magic Kingdom, Dreamflight, offering guests a high-tech view of the history of flight. The close Disney-Delta relationship also means that when guests make a reservation at a Walt Disney World hotel, air arrangements can be made at the same time. In addition, Delta's passengers benefit from the association by being able to fly on the only airline that can offer packages which include lodgings at the Contemporary Resort, the Polynesian Village Resort, the villas at the Disney Village Resort, the Grand Floridian Resort, Fort Wilderness, and The Disney Inn. It is a very significant advantage.

*Dream Vacation is a registered trademark of Delta Air Lines.

DISCOVERING THE LOWEST AIRFARE

Gone are the days when airlines charged a flat rate to get from point A to point B, so it's more important than ever to shop around.

• Find out the names of all the airlines from your point of departure to your destination, then call them all—more than once if your route is complex. Tell the agent how many people there are in your party, and emphasize that you're interested in economy—if that's the case. The more flexible you can be in your dates and duration of stay, the more money you're likely to save. Fares are usually lowest on highly competitive, heavily traveled routes; if you live halfway between two airports—one a major city, the other relatively untraveled—you may do better from one than from the other. Check both.

• Watch the newspapers for ads announcing new short-term promotional fares.

• When it's necessary to change planes en route, it is best to stick with one airline; the agent will know his or her own company's routing—and its discounted fares—better than those offered by other carriers. (For the same reason, smart travelers book all of a trip through the carrier they'll be using most.)

• Fly when most other people don't—at night; on weekends on routes that usually serve business travelers; or midweek to and from vacation destinations.

• Plan ahead. Most carriers guarantee their fares—which means that you won't have to pay extra to use a valid ticket even if fares go up after you buy it. Remember too, that most of the least expensive air fares now assess a penalty for revised flight schedules, and that certain discount fare tickets are non refundable.

WHICH AIRLINE FLIES FROM YOUR CITY?

You can fly nonstop to Orlando from about 50 different cities, on more than a dozen airlines. Schedules do change from time to time, and flights occasionally are dropped or new ones added. This was the operative nonstop service at press time:

City	Airlines
Atlanta, GA	DL, EA, BN
Baltimore, MD	DL, PI
Birmingham, AL	DL
Boston, MA	DL, CO
Charlotte, NC	PI
Chicago, IL	DL, UA, ML, BN
Cincinnati, OH	DL
Cleveland, OH	DL, CO, US
Columbus, OH	DL, BN
Dallas/Ft. Worth, TX	DL, AA, BN
Dayton, OH	PI
Denver, CO	UA, CO
Detroit, MI	DL, NW
Ft. Lauderdale, FL	DL, DL*, PI, TW, ML, BN
Ft. Myers, FL	DL, BN
Gainesville, FL	DL*, PI
Greensboro/Winston-Salem, NC	PI
Hartford, CT/ Springfield, MA	DL
Houston, TX	CO
Indianapolis, IN	US, BN
Jacksonville, FL	DL*, PI, TW
Kansas City, MO	BN
Key West, FL	DL*
Los Angeles, CA	DL
Melbourne, FL	DL*, PI
Memphis, TN	NW
Miami, FL	DL, DL*, EA, BN, PA, PI
Minneapolis/St. Paul, MN	NW
Naples, FL	DL*, PI
Nashville, TN	AA
Nassau, Bahamas	DL, UP, BN
New Orleans, LA	DL, CO
New York, NY/ Newark, NJ	DL, PA, CO, TW, BN
Pensacola, FL	PI
Philadelphia, PA	DL, US
Pittsburgh, PA	US
Raleigh/Durham, NC	AA
St. Louis, MO	TW
Salt Lake City, UT	DL
San Juan, Puerto Rico	DL, AA
Sarasota/ Bradenton, FL	DL
Syracuse, NY	PI
Tallahassee, FL	DL*, PI
Tampa/St. Petersburg, FL	DL, DL*, 6A, BN, EA, UP, AA
Vero Beach, FL	US
Washington, DC	DL, PI, UA, CO
West Palm Beach, FL	DL, DL*, BN, PI

ABBREVIATIONS—AA: American. BN: Braniff. CO: Continental. DL: Delta. DL*: Comair—The Delta Connection. EA: Eastern. ML: Midway Express. NW: Northwest. PA: Pan Am. PI: Piedmont. TW: Trans World. UA: United. UP: Bahamasair. US: USAir or Allegheny Commuter. 6A: Panama Airways.

TOUGH QUESTIONS

SHOULD YOU BUY A PACKAGE?

The sheer number of diverse packages offering vacations in Central Florida is enough to bewilder even the savviest traveler. Still, these packages offer significant advantages. Among them is the opportunity to purchase a vacation that's completely organized in advance, and that will generally cost less than the same package elements purchased separately. (A complete Delta Dream Vacation, for example, can cost less than just the round-trip economy airfare from certain cities, though the package may also include accommodations, a rental car with unlimited mileage for a week, and a 4-day All Three Parks Passport that offers admission to the Magic Kingdom, Epcot Center, and the Disney-MGM Studios Theme Park.)

The main difference among the various package offerings—aside from cost—is the matter of lodging in on-site hotels versus off-property accommodations. Delta Air Lines and American Express packages offer lodgings in Walt Disney World's own on-site hotels, and Walt Disney World itself offers on-site "World Adventure" and "Grand Plan" packages for visitors staying 5 to 10 nights. The Walt Disney World packages are perfect for "top-of-the-line" visitors who don't mind spending a little extra money to obtain a package that includes virtually everything. Delta Air Lines packages, by contrast, are more economical and include the added attraction of low-cost air transportation—plus accommodations at the Contemporary Resort,

Polynesian Village, the Grand Floridian Beach Resort, the villas at the Disney Village Resort, Fort Wilderness, or The Disney Inn.

Appraising the value of any package depends entirely on your specific needs, so check the elements of each package carefully to see how closely they fulfill your requirements. The various sections of this book describe the activities and attractions available in and around Walt Disney World, and once you've determined which of these are most appealing, call Walt Disney World, the airlines that fly between your city and Orlando, or a qualified travel agent to find a package that comes closest to your specific needs and desires.

Don't pick a package that includes elements you don't want or won't use; chances are that you'll be paying for them. And remember that while extras like welcoming cocktails sound attractive, their cash value is negligible. Also note that some packages announce as attractive selling points certain services that are available to *every* Walt Disney World guest.

On the other hand, there's real value in certain other elements, such as transportation to the Walt Disney World property from the airport and discounts on meals. Some of the Delta Air Lines and Walt Disney Travel Company packages also include meals with the Disney characters, tennis lessons, golf greens fees, court rentals or boat rentals, and the like.

SHOULD YOU USE A TRAVEL AGENT?

All of a sudden, our answer has changed from an unqualified "maybe" to an emphatic "probably." The reason for our change of heart is the change in Disney commission policy to travel agents.

Except for the first few months of operation of Walt Disney World, the Disney powers-that-be refused to pay any commissions to travel agents because the Disney-owned and operated hotels were functioning at nearly 100% occupancy—without any bookings from travel agents. The situation changed dramatically in mid-1988.

With the opening of the Grand Floridian Resort in July 1988, the opening of the Caribbean Beach Resort in October 1988, and the addition of the Swan and Dolphin in 1989 and 1990—plus con-

struction of several other new hotels and villa accommodations—the Disney organization now welcomes reservations from travel agents—and pays them an appropriate commission for their bookings. So there is no reason not to use a travel agent; the old agent reluctance to book Disney-owned hotels (due to the absence of compensation) is gone, and there is no better source of complete details on all the varied package offerings and tour options. What's more, all this information is provided at absolutely the right price—free—since all travel agent compensation is paid by the travel supplier. In this case, that supplier may be The Walt Disney Travel Company, Delta Air Lines, American Express, Premier Cruise Lines, or Greyhound.

HOW TO CUT TRAVEL COSTS

Although vacations are not getting any less expensive, scrapping periodic family getaways is no answer. If financial considerations are a primary concern, it's far better to simply prune the vacation budget in 3 main areas:

Food: Eat hot meals in cafeterias instead of waitress-service restaurants. Visit fancier establishments (if you must) at lunchtime rather than dinner. (The very same entrees usually cost less then.) Carry sandwich fixings and have lunches alfresco when possible. Look for lodging places with kitchen facilities: The savings on food, especially for families at breakfast time, may be more than the extra accommodations expense.

Lodging: The chief rule of thumb here is not to pay for more than you need. Budget chains such as Days Inns and Days Lodges, Suisse Chalet Motor Lodges and Inns, Imperial 400 Motor Inns, Passport Inns and Downtowners, Red Roof Inns, Family Inns of America, and Motel 6s can prove economical, though they may not offer many frills. (The best single guide to their whereabouts from coast to coast is the *National Directory of Budget Motels*, revised annually and available for $3.95 plus $1 postage and handling from Pilot Books; 103 Cooper St.; Babylon, NY 11702.)

If swimming pools and other amenities matter, consider the non-budget chain establishments that have them—but remember that cutoff ages (above which there is a charge for children sharing parents' room) do vary. At Howard Johnsons, children age 12 and under always stay free; some properties allow teenagers age 19 and under to stay free, so check at the individual hotels for their specific policy. Quality Inns charge for youngsters over 16; Rodeways charge for young people 17 or older; and Sheratons, Ramadas, and Marriotts charge for kids when they reach age 18. Holiday Inns charge for young people over 12. Get prices for Orlando hostelries in advance, then calculate the exact costs for your whole family.

The Caribbean Beach Resort, located near Epcot Center, offers the first "budget" lodging right on the Disney property. See our *Transportation and Accommodations* chapter for details.

Depending on the number of people in your party, guesthouses and tourist homes may or may not be a good buy. Since these establishments usually levy substantial extra charges for more than two people, regardless of their ages, rooms that are inexpensive for two can prove costly for a family. Consult *Bed & Breakfast America '88-'89* published by Burt Franklin & Co. ($8.95) and *Bed and Breakfast USA* published by E.P. Dutton ($10.95) for locations and prices. Also look into AA Bed and Breakfast of Florida (Box 1316; Winter Park, FL 32790; 628-3233). They represent B & Bs in the WDW area.

Consider sharing accommodations with family or friends. It's often possible to rent a resort condominium or house large enough to accommodate two families for much less than twice what each would pay for a single conventional hotel room. At Walt Disney World, couples can reap savings by this sort of doubling up—with no loss of privacy and some bonus in space. (See the chart "Rates at WDW-Owned Properties" for details.) Finally, remember that rooms at Disney-owned hotels have been designed to accommodate up to 5 guests, with the exception of the Caribbean Beach Resort, where each room accommodates 4.

Transportation: Comparative shopping is vital. Consider transportation needs at your destination, then figure the total transportation cost. Calculate the cost of driving based on your car's mileage, current gasoline prices, the distance you expect to cover, and the cost of accommodations and food en route, then figure what you'll pay by bus, plane, or train. Don't fail to calculate the cost of getting to and from the airport or terminal, and the cost of renting a car (if necessary) in Orlando. And remember that special low fares that are economical for couples can sometimes prove less advantageous for families.

HOW TO GET THE BEST PHOTOS

There are so many wonderful images glimpsed all over WDW that just about any camera in good working order can save them for you—so long as you use the right techniques. Here are some useful hints:

• Don't shoot from closer than 4 feet from your subject, and don't try for a flash picture more than 60 feet away. The former will probably turn out fuzzy, and the latter is likely to come out dark.

• Fill the frame with as much of the prime subject as possible. Especially when shooting people, remember that the larger the subject appears in the picture, the more interesting it will be.

• Hold the camera steady as you *gently* squeeze the shutter.

• Don't shoot into the sun. Instead, position yourself so that light is falling directly on your subject—coming from behind you or from the side.

• Flash photography is not permitted inside any WDW attractions.

• Check the camera's batteries and battery contacts regularly.

• Use film that is fresh. When purchasing film, check the expiration date stamped on the bottom of the box. Keep the film as cool as possible; don't leave it in a hot car for long periods of time.

• Keep the camera clean. Blow dust off the lens and then wipe it with a soft tissue. Blow dust out of the inside of the camera.

• When taking movies or using videotape cameras, note that they'll be more effective if you pick a theme such as "A Walk Down Main Street," "A Stroll Through France," or the like. Pan very slowly and smoothly, and give every scene plenty of time—at least 5 seconds. Don't use the zoom lens too often; it can be distracting.

• If you suspect that your camera isn't functioning correctly, visit the Camera Center on the east side of Main Street near Town Square in the Magic Kingdom, at Epcot Center, the Camera Center near Spaceship Earth or Cameras and Film at Journey into Imagination, or The Darkroom at the Disney-MGM Studios Theme Park.

Rental cameras: Thirty-five-millimeter, disc, and video cameras are available for rental at the Camera Center in the Magic Kingdom; at the camera Center in Epcot Center near Spaceship Earth and Cameras and Film at Journey into Imagination; and at The Darkroom at the Disney-MGM Studios Theme Park. Use of the disc cameras is free, though a $50 refundable deposit is required. The 35mm cameras cost $5 per day to use plus a $145 refundable deposit and video cameras cost $40 per day with a $400 refundable deposit. The required deposits can be charged to American Express, Visa, or Mastercard.

Film processing: Two-hour processing is available at the Magic Kingdom, Epcot Center, the Disney-MGM Studios Theme Park, and the Disney Village Marketplace wherever there is a Photo Express sign. Film is processed right on the premises, using the Kodak Colorwatch System.

WHERE TO BUY FILM

Walt Disney World is one of the largest retail outlets in the world for film.

In the Magic Kingdom
Main Street—Camera Center; Emporium
Adventureland—Tropic Toppers
Frontierland—Frontier Trading Post
Liberty Square—Heritage House
Fantasyland—Royal Candy Shoppe; Kodak Kiosk,

In Epcot Center
Future World—All merchandise locations (best stock at the Camera Center)
World Showcase—At least one shop in each pavilion (film is often stashed under the counter)

At the Disney-MGM Studios Theme Park
The Darkroom
Crossroads of the World
Movieland Memorabilia

In the Hotels
Contemporary Resort—Concourse Sundries & Spirits
The Disney Inn—Gifts and Sundries
Polynesian Village—News from Civilization
Grand Floridian—Sandy Cove
Caribbean Beach Resort—Sundries

At Fort Wilderness
Settlement and Meadow Trading Posts

At Disney Village Marketplace
Guest Services, just outside You & Me Kid

At Pleasure Island
Island Depot

HINTS ON TRAVELING

Tell youngsters that a Walt Disney World vacation is in the works and the response is apt to be nothing less than overwhelming—and the journey to the park is likely to be fraught with "Are-we-there-yets?" recurring like a stuck record.

En route: Certain ploys can quiet this refrain a bit. Get older children involved in planning every leg of the trip, and set up a series of intermediate goals to which they can look forward. Younger children can anticipate discovering the contents of a pint-sized suitcase packed with familiar games and toys, plus a few surprises.

In addition, it's smart to take along snacks to keep things peaceful when stomachs start rumbling and food is miles away. Above all, and especially if the trip is by car, take it easy, and allow time for plenty of breaks en route.

Those who fly should schedule travel for off-peak hours, when the chances are better that empty seats will be available. When the plane is taking off and landing, babies should be given bottles, pacifiers, or even thumbs to promote swallowing and clear ears; a piece of gum or hard candy will provide the same relief for a small child. Newborn babies (those only a couple of weeks old) should not be taken aloft, since their lungs may not be able to adjust easily to the altitude. For finicky young eaters, request special meals when reserving seats. Delta Air Lines offers special meals for kids—juice, cereal, milk, and dessert for breakfast; an all-beef hot dog or cheeseburger, cole slaw, shoestring potatoes, a banana, and a candy bar for lunch or dinner. As the "Official Airline For Kids," Delta features the Fantastic Flyer™ program for children ages 2 through 12. On every Delta flight, kids receive a complimentary Mickey Mouse or Donald

Duck visor with an enrollment card and a copy of the *Fantastic Flyer* magazine featuring games, puzzles, and prizes. Be sure to ask the flight attendant for details.

Budget watchers should pay careful attention to motel rate structures (see page 26 for ideas) when reserving accommodations. Also, some charge for cots, while other motels might bring them in at no charge. Note that some hostelries outside the World *seem* a lot less expensive than the WDW resorts—until the actual costs for everything for a whole family are computed. Sometimes airfares that sound inexpensive actually cost more for a family; sometimes air packages cut costs. The key is to check carefully.

At Walt Disney World: This vacationland ranks among the easiest spots on earth for traveling families with children. Older youngsters don't need to be driven around, and the general supervision is such that kids are hard pressed to get into trouble. All the resorts, plus Fort Wilderness and the Villa Recreation Center at Disney Village Resort, have at least a small room full of pinball machines and video games, much to the satisfaction of kids of all ages; the one at the Contemporary Resort is positively vast. And all the hotels have playgrounds; the one at the Polynesian Village is particularly nifty, with its thatched-roof tree house, climbing rings, and offbeat slide.

And the Polynesian Village, the Grand Floridian, and the Contemporary Resort (but not The Disney Inn) have child-care facilities. In-room babysitters can be summoned to all resort hotels and villas; contact the Guest Services desk. And there is also a center known as Kindercare, suitable for youngsters ages 2 through 12; parents may drop off their children anytime after 6 P.M. For details and availability, phone 827-KIDS.

Nor is there any cause for excessive hand-holding inside the Magic Kingdom, Epcot Center, or the Disney-MGM Studios Theme Park; with older youngsters, it's enough to establish a specific meeting place and a meeting time (allowing a little latitude, just in case). If there are younger children along, it's not a bad idea to stop at City Hall or the Baby Center next to the Crystal Palace to pick up a special name tag to facilitate a reunion in case the family gets separated. Name tags are also available at Earth Station and the Baby Services at Epcot Center, and at Guest Services at the Disney-MGM Studios Theme Park. Aunt Polly's Landing on Tom Sawyer Island is a good bet for lunch; while adults in the party are sipping lemonade, the kids can be bouncing across the Barrel Bridge and exploring every nook and cranny on the island. Gurgi's Munchies & Crunchies in Fantasyland is also a good spot for lunch.

Strollers are available for rent for a nominal fee

WITH CHILDREN

(small deposit required) at Strollers—Wheelchairs on the east side of Main Street at the entrance to the Magic Kingdom; at the Stroller and Wheelchair Rentals Shop on the east side of the Entrance Plaza, and at the France pavilion in Epcot Center; and at Oscar's at the Disney-MGM Studios Theme Park. If your stroller disappears, as often happens while you're inside an attraction, a replacement may be obtained at Space Port (the shop of contemporary decorative gifts) in Tomorrowland; at the Trading Post in Frontierland; at Tinkerbell Toy Shop in Fantasyland; at the France, Germany, and United Kingdom pavilions in Epcot Center, and at Oscar's at the Disney-MGM Studios Theme Park. Stroller renters should be aware that guests only have to pay once a day for a stroller. If you rent one in the Magic Kingdom in the morning and plan to spend the afternoon in Epcot Center, just keep the receipt and present it for a free stroller at Epcot Center.

Baby Services at the Magic Kingdom, Epcot Center, and the Disney-MGM Studios Theme Park can be helpful in many ways to mothers with young children. There are low-lighted rooms with comfortable rocking chairs and love seats for nursing mothers, and a cheerful feeding room. There are highchairs, and bibs and plastic spoons are also available. The baby centers have facilities for changing infants, preparing formulas, and warming bottles. Disposable diapers and nurser bags, pull-on rubber pants, baby bottles with nipples, formula (Similac, Isomil, and Enfamil), teethers, pacifiers, prepared cereal, juices, and strained and junior baby food in a limited selection are available for sale on the spot at a nominal cost. The decor is soothing; the atmosphere is such that it seems a million miles away from the Magic Kingdom, Epcot Center, or the Disney-MGM Studios Theme Park. The guest books in the Magic Kingdom list more wonderful children's names than many a baby name book—as more than one expectant mother has noted. A stop for diaper changing makes a good break for child and mother alike, though changing areas are available in most ladies' and some mens' rest rooms as well. Hours at the baby centers vary, so check at City Hall, Earth Station, or Guest Services.

A variety of other baby-care supplies can be

purchased at Baby Services in Epcot Center, Strollers—Wheelchairs on Main Street, and Oscar's Super Service at the Disney-MGM Studios Theme Park. Disposable diapers are sold, though not displayed, in the Children's Books section of the Emporium on Main Street in the Magic Kingdom, at Gateway Gifts and the Centorium in Epcot Center, and at Baby Services in the Hospitality Building at the Disney-MGM Studios Theme Park.

Lost children: The security forces inside the Magic Kingdom, Epcot Center, and the Disney-MGM Studios Theme Park are far more careful than the happy appearance of things indicates. This is a welcome thought on those rare instances when a child suddenly disappears or fails to show up on schedule. If this happens to you, check the lost children's logbooks at Baby Services or at City Hall in the Magic Kingdom; at Earth Station or Baby Services behind the Odyssey Restaurant in Epcot Center; or at Guest Services at the Disney-MGM Studios Theme Park. Every Disney employee knows where they are—and what to do if a lost-looking child suddenly starts to call for his or her mommy. There are no paging systems in the parks, but in very serious emergencies an all-points bulletin can be put out among employees. The staff at the Guest Relations Windows at the entrances to Epcot Center, the Magic Kingdom, and the Disney-MGM Studios also may have information about lost children.

HELPFUL HINTS

HINTS FOR OLDER TRAVELERS

Walt Disney World can overwhelm an elderly traveler not accustomed to unfamiliar places; Epcot Center encompasses significant distances, and the Magic Kingdom and the Disney-MGM Studios can be disorienting because of the profusion of sights and sounds, nooks and crannies. The heat, particularly in summer, also can be hard to take. Yet with the proper planning and precautions, all of WDW can be just as delightful for older visitors as for kids. Here are a few suggestions:

• Join a tour. Of the several organizations that specialize in group trips for older travelers, only one—the National Council of Senior Citizens (925 15 St. NW; Washington, DC 20005; 202-347-8800)—offers a tour to WDW often enough to mention (and even these are arranged only when interest warrants). Note that visitors who do come with a group bus tour should be sure to allow plenty of time to take the monorail or the ferry back to the bus parking area at the Transportation and Ticket Center, at Epcot Center, or the Disney-MGM Studios Theme Park—usually about half an hour—and should avoid queuing up when time begins to grow short.

Inside the Magic Kingdom and Epcot Center group tours—among the best buys in the World—are offered by Guest Relations. These 4-hour guided walks provide an introduction to the parks; the price is $5 and includes the services of a guide and visits to various attractions. Admission to the parks is an additional cost. For details and availability, phone 560-6233.

• Schedule visits for off-peak seasons and hours when the crowds will not be discouraging. Also, note that special values are available during Young at Heart Days and Florida Resident Days on selected dates in the fall. Call 824-4321 for details.

• Read all Walt Disney World literature carefully before arrival so that things are familiar.

• In the parks, don't be timid about asking for directions or advice. Disney employees are always happy to help out.

• Eat early or late, to avoid mealtime crowds. In the Magic Kingdom, stop in more sedate restaurants such as the Crystal Palace, Tony's Town Square Cafe, or King Stefan's in Cinderella Castle. Or take the monorail to the still calmer Polynesian Village or the Contemporary Resort, to lunch in one of the full-service restaurants there, or make a trip through one of the buffet lines. In Epcot Center, the Odyssey Restaurant in Future World is an especially restful counter service spot for lunch. At the Disney-MGM Studios Theme Park, the Hollywood Brown Derby offers a relaxing sit-down meal.

• Don't try to save money by scrimping on food. Traveling takes energy, and only a good meal can provide it.

• Protect yourself from the sun. Wear a hat, and don't stint on the sunscreen. (And don't forget to cover legs, which are easily sunburned by light rays reflected from pavements.)

• Don't become overheated. Take frequent rest stops in the shade, and get out of the mid-afternoon heat by stopping for a snack in an air conditioned restaurant. Avoid standing in line at Frontierland's Big Thunder Mountain Railroad and at Fantasyland's 20,000 Leagues Under the Sea in midafternoon; parts of these queues are unprotected from the sun and can be very hot. In Epcot Center, spend the hot midafternoon hours in the TransCenter in the World of Motion, in CommuniCore East and West, or the Sea Base Alpha exhibit at The Living Seas in Future World and avoid the uncovered outdoor queues at all the Future World pavilions and at World Showcase attractions like O Canada!, Impressions de France, and El Rio del Tiempo. Don't underestimate the distances at Epcot Center; you may need to walk as much as 2 miles in the course of a day. If taken slowly and in short increments, this is not too ominous. But if you are not strong enough to cover that distance, be sure to rent a wheelchair at the outset of your visit. The buses that circumnavigate World Showcase Lagoon and the launches that make regular crossings can help you cover the distances—but only when there are no long queues. It is better to walk between pavilions, resting frequently en route, than to wait 15 or 20 minutes for a ride in a bus or boat.

• Above all, don't push yourself. Half the fun of Walt Disney World—the part that younger travelers often miss—is just sitting under a tree on a park bench, watching the people go by.

LOST ADULTS

Occasionally, traveling companions do get separated in the press of the crowds or someone fails to show up at an appointed meeting spot. So it's good to know that Guest Relations maintains message books at City Hall in the Magic Kingdom. In Epcot Center, messages are handled by the hosts and hostesses staffing the WorldKey Information Service at Earth Station, and Guest Services hosts and hostesses do the same at the Disney-MGM Studios Theme Park.

FOR THE HANDICAPPED

Walt Disney World gets high marks among handicapped travelers because of the attention that has been paid to their special needs. Special parking is available for guests visiting the Magic Kingdom, Epcot Center, or the Disney-MGM Studios Theme Park; get directions at either of the Auto Plazas

HINTS FOR SINGLE TRAVELERS

Walt Disney World does not exactly attract the young swinging singles crowd, so those on the lookout for romantic encounters probably would do better elsewhere. But those who travel alone for the freedom and the fun of it can have as enjoyable a time at Walt Disney World as they would anywhere else.

WDW employees are generally a friendly and entertaining lot; chatting with a painter about the perpetual repainting of Main Street woodwork, talking to the animal keepers on Discovery Island, or discussing life abroad with one of the young World Showcase employees born and educated in the country the pavilion represents, a single traveler usually learns more about the ways of the World than any group member. Other visitors who might be encountered in the course of a day are away from their own home base as well, and are apt to be just that much less standoffish.

Now that Pleasure Island has opened, the opportunities for single people to meet other similarly unattached folks have significantly improved. The clubs, bars, restaurants, shows—and even the rollerskating rink—can prove to be fertile meeting places. In addition to the other Walt Disney World guests, lots of folks from the Orlando area also patronize the Pleasure Island establishments.

Single women traveling alone will not find the bars and lounges at Walt Disney World hotels off limits. The same relaxed atmosphere prevails in the Rose & Crown Pub in the United Kingdom pavilion and the Matsu No Ma Lounge in Japan, both in the World Showcase area of Epcot Center. Another good way to meet people (albeit a somewhat older crowd) is to sign up for one of Guest Relations' Guided Walking Tours of the Magic Kingdom and Epcot Center. The Biergarten in World Showcase's Germany pavilion and the Teppanyaki Dining Rooms in Japan's Mitsukoshi Restaurant are especially convivial since several parties are seated together at one large table. River Country, Typhoon Lagoon, the hotel swimming pools and beaches, and (for those with the inclination) the Giraffe disco at the Royal Plaza at Disney Village Hotel Plaza are also good places for meeting people.

A note for budget watchers: Rates at all WDW resort hotels and those at Disney Village Hotel Plaza, and at some others in the Orlando area, are the same whether one or two persons occupy a room. Similarly, the villas at the Disney Village Resort are priced per unit, regardless of the number of people who sleep there.

---

upon entering. From the TTC, the Magic Kingdom is accessible either by ferry or by monorail (though the former is preferable, since the slant of the ramp to the monorails makes holding a wheelchair a bit taxing when there are any waiting lines at all). All WDW monorail stations are accessible to wheelchairs except the one at the Contemporary Resort, which can be reached only by escalator. Special "handicap vans," with motorized platforms that lift wheelchairs inside, are available too. To request one, day guests should inquire at the Guest Relations Window at the TTC, at Epcot Center Entrance Plaza, in City Hall in the Magic Kingdom, Earth Station at Epcot Center, or Guest Services at the Disney-MGM Studios Theme Park. Resort guests should also contact Guest Services in their hotel. Count on at least 20 minutes between the request and pick-up.

In the Magic Kingdom, wheelchairs are available for rent at Strollers—Wheelchairs on the right-hand side of the souvenir area, just past the turnstiles. In Epcot Center, the rental area is just inside the turnstiles on the left as you enter. Oscar's Super Service rents wheelchairs at the Disney-MGM Studios Theme Park. A "Guidebook for Disabled Guests" will prove beneficial throughout your visit and may be obtained at wheelchair rental locations, City Hall in the Magic Kingdom, Earth Station in Epcot Center, and Guest Services at the Disney-MGM Studios Theme Park. Most restrooms in the parks have extra-wide cubicles with wall bars for people in wheelchairs. Furthermore, most attractions are accessible to guests who can be lifted to and from their chairs and many can accommodate guests who must remain in their wheelchairs at all times.

Outside the Magic Kingdom, Epcot Center, and the Disney-MGM Studios Theme Park, all WDW resort hotels are easily explored by wheelchair. The Polynesian Village is the most convenient for vacationers in wheelchairs. The monorail is easy to get to, and there are 3 special first-floor units with grab rails next to the bathtubs and wider automatic entrance doors. In the Oahu, there are even Braille characters on the elevators. The Oahu and Moorea longhouses have some specially equipped bathrooms for handicapped guests.

At the Disney Village Resort some two-bedroom units are accessible to wheelchairs and some are not; the best bets are the planned-for-the-purpose units facing the Lake Buena Vista golf course. The Fleetwood Trailers at Fort Wilderness would be difficult to manage because of their stairway access and their narrow interior spaces.

In River Country and at Typhoon Lagoon, life jackets are available for the handicapped. (No other flotation devices are permitted.)

For blind guests, a tape recorder and cassette that describes the Magic Kingdom, Epcot Center, and Guest Services at the Disney-MGM Studios Theme Park in terms of smells and sounds is available. A small refundable deposit (about $5) is required for cassette use. Seeing-eye dogs are permitted in the parks. In Epcot Center, personal translator units that amplify attraction sound tracks for the benefit of the hearing impaired are available at Earth Station. The $5 deposit is refunded upon the return of the unit. Guests who use telecommunications devices for the deaf (TDDs) can call 827-5141 for WDW information. TDDs are available for guest use at City Hall in the Magic Kingdom, Earth Station in Epcot Center, and Guest Services at the Disney-MGM Studios Theme Park at no charge.

Tours: The Society for the Advancement of Travel for the Handicapped (5014 42nd St.; Washington, DC 20016; 202-966-3900) has a number of member travel agents who are knowledgeable about tours for the handicapped and can help arrange individual and group tours. Send a self-addressed stamped envelope to receive a copy of their listings. Among the organizations that sponsor trips for the handicapped and offer tours to WDW are:

• Flying Wheels Travel; Box 382; Owatonna, MN 55060; 800-533-0363, 800-722-9351 in Minnesota

• Evergreen Travel Service; 19505 L 44th Ave. West; Lynnwood, WA 98036; 206-776-1184

• Happy Holiday Travel; 2550 NE 15th Ave.; Ft. Lauderdale, FL 33305; 305-561-5602

All of these organizations can also arrange trips for individuals.

Books: One of the best books we know for general hints on travel by the handicapped is *Access to the World* by Louise Weiss (available from Facts on File; 460 Park Ave. South; New York, NY 10016; $16.95).

Traveling by car: Hertz, Avis, and National all have a limited quantity of hand-control cars for rent in the Orlando area; it's a good idea to call well in advance to reserve them.

Traveling by plane: Airlines have not always been as helpful in dealing with handicapped travelers as they are now. Occasionally, vacationers can go into the aircraft in their own chair—provided the chair is narrow and the plane's aisles are wide; more often, travelers transfer to a narrower airline chair at the door of the aircraft, while their own chair is sent down to the luggage compartment. Wheelchair passengers are usually preboarded and then deplaned after other passengers. If you are not taking your own wheelchair along and have a tight connection to make, be sure to advise the airlines' attendants well in advance. Similarly, if a passenger wishes to utilize an airline's wheelchair at a connecting point or destination, that wheelchair service should be ordered at the time that flight reservations are being made.

Allow plenty of time to make all your arrangements, and don't fail to alert all airline personnel to your special needs.

Policies on motorized wheelchairs vary, depending on the airline and the type of chair; check with carriers in advance. Seeing-eye dogs are always allowed aboard aircraft (though some carriers may require them to be muzzled), but arrangements should be made at the time reservations are made so that a bulkhead seat may be requested.

For general information on traveling by air, get a copy of "Fly Rights: A Guide to Air Travel in the United States" (available for $1 from the U.S. Government Printing Office, Superintendent of Documents, Washington, DC 20402-9325; include the stock number 050-000-00-513-5; to order by phone call 202-783-3238).

Traveling by train: Whether riding with or without reservations, it's wise to phone in advance to arrange for one of the special seats that Amtrak maintains for handicapped travelers. Wheelchairs are available at major Amtrak stations, some 500 in all, including Orlando. New cars have special seats and specially equipped bathrooms and sleeping compartments; older equipment has also been refurbished to accommodate handicapped travelers. Blind and handicapped passengers get a 25 percent discount on one-way tickets though companions must pay full fare. Seeing-eye and hearing-ear dogs may ride with passengers at no extra charge.

Battery-powered, standard-size wheelchairs are permitted in coaches. Fuel-powered and oversized chairs must be stored in the baggage car for the duration of the trip. Always be sure to phone the train stations and reservations center well before your departure date to arrange for any special facilities or services you may need.

Traveling by bus: Greyhound has implemented plans that allow a handicapped vacationer and a companion (to help with boarding and disembarking) to travel together on a single adult ticket; all that's required is a doctor's written statement of the necessity of such aid. Greyhound carries non-motorized folding wheelchairs at no additional charge. Motorized wheelchairs are not accepted.

And remember to plan in advance. Allow plenty of time, and at each step of the way, inform air, bus, train, and hotel personnel of your special needs.

OTHER INFORMATION

BARBERS: The most amusing place to get a haircut is the old-fashioned Harmony Barber Shop (824-6550), tucked away at the end of the flower-filled cul-de-sac just off the west side of Main Street in the Magic Kingdom; the Disney books on hand are terrific, and the "Dapper Dans," the park's own barber-shop quartet, can often be heard here. Moustache cups and other nostalgic shaving items are for sale.

Outside the Magic Kingdom, visit the Captain's Chair on the third floor of the Contemporary Resort (824-3411) or the Alii Nui Barber Shop on the first floor of the Great Ceremonial House at the Polynesian Village (824-1400).

BEAUTY SHOPS: Shampoos, sets, coloring, waving, manicuring, and wig-setting are available at the Pretty Wahine Beauty Shop in the Polynesian Village (824-1396) and the American Beauty Shoppe on the third floor of the Contemporary Resort (824-3413). The manicurist at the Contemporary Resort's shop has held the hands of many a Walt Disney World executive, and can provide some fascinating insights into the workings of the park.

CAR CARE: Auto and travel club members probably will want to call their local club-sponsored towing service in the event of problems. The Disney Car Care Center (824-4813), located on Floridian Way near the Magic Kingdom Auto Plaza, has a service garage which is open Mondays through Fridays from

7 A.M. to 5:30 P.M. Emergency road service and gas are available from the Car Care Center during park operating hours. Though routine maintenance work is probably best done by mechanics who know your car well—before leaving home—the Disney Car Care Center is a good place for gas and repairs in a pinch. Disney personnel here will chauffeur guests to their day's WDW destination, and arrange for later pickup when requested.

It's also reassuring to know that WDW breakdowns don't mean disaster. All WDW roads are patrolled constantly by security vehicles equipped with radios which can be used to call for help.

RELIGIOUS SERVICES: Vacations are a good time to broaden the family's religious experience. A variety of services are held around Walt Disney World.

Protestant: 9 A.M. on Sundays at Luau Cove at the Polynesian Village.

Catholic: 8 A.M. and 10:15 A.M. on Sundays at Luau Cove at the Polynesian Village. Call Holy Family Catholic Church (876-2211) for specific information, or check with Guest Services at any of the Disney hotels.

The closest Catholic church off the property is Mary, Queen of the Universe Catholic Shrine, 2½ miles north of Lake Buena Vista on the I-4 service road. Call 239-6600 for mass times. In Orlando, there are services at St. James Cathedral (215 North Orange Ave.; 422-2005) at 4 P.M. and 6 P.M. on Saturdays and on Sundays at 7:30 A.M., 9 A.M., 10:30 A.M., noon (in Spanish), and 6 P.M.

In Kissimmee, there are services at the Holy Redeemer Catholic Church (1603 North Thacker Ave.; 846-3700) on Saturdays at 4 P.M. (winter only), 6 P.M., and 7:15 P.M. (in Spanish), and on Sundays at 7:30 A.M., 8:45 A.M., 10:30 A.M., and noon. Daily masses are said at 7:30 A.M. and 9 A.M.

Jewish: Conservative services are at 8:15 P.M. on Fridays and 9 A.M. on Saturdays at the Congregation Ohev Shalom (5015 Goddard Ave.; 298-4650) in Orlando. Reform services are at 8:15 P.M. on Fridays and 10:30 A.M. on Saturdays at the Congregation of Liberal Judaism (928 Malone Drive; 645-0444).

Kosher dinners are available at any time at the Contemporary Resort, the Polynesian Village, The Disney Inn, Fort Wilderness, the Grand Floridian, the Caribbean Beach Resort, and all waitress-service restaurants in the Magic Kingdom, Epcot Center, the Disney-MGM Studios Theme Park, and the Disney Village Marketplace. Guests should call 560-6233 at least 24 hours in advance to order breakfast (cheese or vegetable omelet), lunch, and dinner (beef brisket, salmon steak, veal, lasagna, or roast chicken). Cost is $14 for breakfasts and $17 for lunches and dinners.

Note also that most airlines also offer special meals conforming to dietary codes. Order them when making reservations.

MAIL: Postcards are for sale at many spots in the resorts and around the Magic Kingdom, among them Main Street Stationers on the west side of Main Street.

Postage stamps can be purchased at the front desk at any of the WDW hotels, at the trading posts at Fort Wilderness, at City Hall on Main Street, at Earth Station at Epcot Center, and Guest Services at the Disney-MGM Studios. The old-fashioned, olive-drab mailboxes that punctuate Main Street are no longer official U.S. post boxes, but letters can be mailed there for pickup by Disney employees and subsequent transportation to the Lake Buena Vista post office. Postmarks read "Lake Buena Vista," *not* "Walt Disney World." All window services are available at the Lake Buena Vista post office, including postal money order and stamp sale, registry, and certification. The post office is located at the Crossroads of Lake Buena Vista shopping center.

Personal Message in the Disney Village Marketplace sells attractive stationery and note pads. Postage stamps also are available here as well as at Village Guest Services.

Mail may be addressed to guests c/o their hotel at Walt Disney World; Box 10000; Lake Buena Vista, FL 32830-1000.

Don't forget to arrange for mail at home to be held by the post office.

LOST AND FOUND: The extensive indexing system maintained by Walt Disney World's Lost and Found department is impressive, especially when a prize possession turns up missing, whether it's false teeth or a camera. (Both have been lost in the past; the dentures were never claimed.) To see just how it works, the first thing to do is to report the loss on the proper forms at City Hall, at the Guest Relations window on the east end of the Transportation and Ticket Center, at the Epcot Center Entrance Plaza, Earth Station, or the Guest Services desks at the Disney-MGM Studios Theme Park, in the first floor lobby at the Contemporary Resort, or the main lobbies at the Polynesian Village, The Disney Inn, the Grand Floridian, and the Caribbean Beach Resort; at Fort Wilderness, phone ext. 7-2726 from a comfort station telephone; from outside the campground, phone 824-2726; at Walt Disney World Village phone 828-3384.

Items lost in the Magic Kingdom can be claimed on the day of the loss at City Hall, and thereafter at the main Lost and Found station at the Transportation and Ticket Center. Articles found at Epcot Center remain at the Epcot Center Lost and Found for one day before being delivered to the main Lost and Found. At the Disney-MGM Studios Theme Park, claim or report lost items at the Guest Services building on the day of your visit. To claim or report lost items after your visit, call 824-4245.

Articles not claimed by the owner may be claimed by the finder—an added incentive for visitors to turn over valuable items to Lost and Found.

POCKET PAGERS: Two types of devices are available to WDW guests to signal a telephone call or message. They are available at all WDW hotels, Fort Wilderness Outpost, the Lake Buena Vista reception center, and the Royal Plaza.

GIFT CERTIFICATES: Available at Guest Services at WDW Village and the Disney-MGM Studios Theme Park, Guest Services desks at all WDW hotels, City Hall, Earth Station, and at Guest Relations windows in the Magic Kingdom and Epcot Center.

DRINKING LAWS: In Florida, drinking is legal at 21. There are many bars and lounges all over the World; minors are permitted to accompany their parents, but are prohibited from sitting or standing at the bar. There's no drinking in the Magic Kingdom (where even the piña coladas are nonalcoholic), but alcoholic beverages are available at restaurants in Epcot Center, the Disney-MGM Studios Theme Park, Pleasure Island, and WDW Village.

By the bottle: Liquor is sold in full-size and mini-bottles at Village Spirits at the Disney Village Marketplace, at Trader Jack's on the second floor of the Great Ceremonial House at the Polynesian Village, at Gifts and Sundries in the lobby at The Disney Inn, at Concourse Sundries & Spirits in the Contemporary Resort, and at Sundries at the Caribbean Beach Resort. Liquor may also be purchased from Room Service at the Polynesian Village Resort, the Contemporary Resort, The Disney Inn, and the Grand Floridian Resort.

LOCKERS: There are coin-operated lockers underneath the Main Street Railroad Station in the Magic Kingdom and at two locations at the Transportation and Ticket Center—next to Lost and Found on the west end and beside the bus parking lot on the east side. Lockers are also available at Epcot Center at the Bus Information Center in the bus parking lot, just outside the main Entrance Plaza, and in an area to the right of Earth Station as you face World Showcase Lagoon. At the Disney-MGM Studios Theme Park, lockers can be found next to Oscar's near the main entrance. Cost is 50¢ per day for the regular size, 75¢ for the larger ones. Items too big to fit into the latter can be checked at the Guest Relations windows at the TTC, at City Hall inside the Magic Kingdom, in the package pickup area or in the storage area at Epcot Center, and at Guest Services at the Disney-MGM Studios Theme Park.

PLANT-SITTING: Plants do not fare well in the heat of a closed-up car for a day. Those who have purchased greenery at Disney Village Marketplace or brought a favorite fern from home will be grateful to know that their horticultural wonders can be accommodated at the kennels at Fort Wilderness, Epcot Center, the TTC, or the Disney-MGM Studios Theme Park. There's no charge.

MEDICAL MATTERS: For travelers with chronic health problems, it's a good idea to carry copies of all prescriptions and to get names of local doctors from hometown physicians. However, Walt Disney World is equipped to deal with many types of medical emergencies. In the Magic Kingdom, next to the Crystal Palace, there's a First Aid Center staffed by a registered nurse; there is another at Epcot Center, located in the Odyssey Restaurant complex (during holidays and summer months, at the TTC and River Country as well). At the Disney-MGM Studios Theme Park, the First Aid Center is in the Guest Services Building at the main entrance. For resort guests, as well as guests staying at other area hotels, a service known as House Med is available. Call 648-9234 and a physician will report directly to the guest's room. Serious emergencies can be reported to the nearby Sand Lake Hospital, 351-8550.

The most common malady? Not sensitive stomachs upset by rides, but simple *sunburn*. So be forewarned. Wear a hat, and slather on sufficient sunblock or sunscreen, especially during the spring and summer.

For diabetics: Walt Disney World resorts provide refrigeration services for insulin; the villas and the Fleetwood Trailers at Fort Wilderness have their own refrigerators.

Prescriptions: The Buena Vista Walk-In Medical Center (828-3434) offers shuttle service from the First Aid Center and

Epcot Center. The clinic is open daily from 8 A.M. to 8 P.M. for basic medical, diagnostic, and treatment services for non-critical injuries and illnesses. A pharmacy is available at the clinic Mondays through Fridays 9 A.M. to 8 P.M., Saturdays 9 A.M. to 6 P.M. Delivery to any WDW resort hotel can be arranged. The Gooding's supermarket at the Crossroads shopping center also has a pharmacy. On Sundays, Loomis Drugs (in Orlando) will deliver from 9 A.M. to 9 P.M.

MONEY: Cash, traveler's checks, personal checks, American Express (the official credit card of WDW), MasterCard, and Visa are accepted as payment for all admission media. Checks must bear the guest's name and address, be drawn on a U.S. bank, and be accompanied by the proper identification—a valid driver's license and a current major credit card such as American Express, Visa, MasterCard, Diners Club, or Carte Blanche. Fast food restaurants in the Magic Kingdom, Epcot Center, and the Disney-MGM Studios Theme Park operate on a cash-only basis.

For charges at sit-down restaurants and shops inside the theme parks, however, and for all other charges throughout Walt Disney World, American Express, Visa, and MasterCard credit cards are accepted. WDW resort guests may use the WDW resort IDs that each member of a party receives upon check-in to cover purchases in shops, lounge and restaurant charges, and recreational fees incurred inside WDW (but outside the Magic Kingdom). At Epcot Center and the Disney-MGM Studios Theme Park, guests can use IDs to charge meals at table-service restaurants. These cards are not valid for charges made past check-out time on the last day of the guest's stay.

Wiring money: Friends and relatives at home can send money to WDW guests through Western Union offices at WDW in the Contemporary Resort (824-3456), in Kissimmee (847-4838), as well as in the city of Orlando (841-4733).

The Sun Bank: This institution (which has an old-fashioned branch on Main Street inside the Magic Kingdom, a branch in Epcot Center to the left of the turnstiles as you enter, another in Disney Village Marketplace, and one at the Crossroads shopping center) can:

• Give cash advances on MasterCard and Visa credit cards, with a $50 minimum in amounts as large as a guest's credit limit will permit.

• Cash and sell traveler's checks and provide refunds for lost American Express and Bank of America traveler's checks.

• Cash personal checks of up to $1,000 for American Express cardholders upon presentation of their cards (part payable in cash and the rest in American Express traveler's checks).

• Cash personal checks for up to $25 upon presentation of a driver's license and a major credit card for other guests.

• Help with wire transfers of money from a guest's own bank to the Sun Bank.

• Exchange most foreign currency for dollars.

The Sun Bank branches in the Magic Kingdom and Epcot Center are open from 9 A.M. to 4 P.M. daily; phone 824-5767 for further information. The Sun Banks in Disney Village Marketplace at Lake Buena Vista and at the Crossroads shopping center are open from 9 A.M. to 4 P.M. on weekdays (until 6 P.M. on Thursdays); drive-in teller windows are open from 8 A.M. to 6 P.M. on weekdays. Phone 828-6100.

Traveler's checks: Even the most careful of vacationers occasionally loses a wallet, and traveler's checks can take the sting out of that loss. Which type a traveler should buy is not so much a function of which is most easily refunded (because in the U.S., and at Walt Disney World in particular, all the major traveler's check offerers can come through with emergency funds in a pinch) as of which costs less. It's a good idea, therefore, to look for special promotions by banks at home in the months preceding a vacation, and check to see which of the six major brands—American Express, MasterCard, Visa, Thomas Cook, Citicorp, and Bank of America—are available for free.

While at WDW, American Express checks can be purchased at the Sun Bank and at the American Express cardmembers' check dispenser located there as well. The machine automatically vends traveler's checks when you feed it an American Express card and punch in an identification number which has been obtained from the company in advance.

Don't fail to sign checks in the proper place as soon as they are purchased. And stash the receipt bearing the check numbers in a separate place from the checks themselves, along with one piece of identification such as a duplicate driver's license or spare credit card. These will speed the refund process should your checks get lost.

Foreign currency exchange: This can be done at the Guest Relations windows at all three parks, or at City Hall, Earth Station, Guest Services, or, from 9 A.M. to 4 P.M. daily, the Sun Bank in Town Square inside the Magic Kingdom or at the Epcot Center branch. Currency can be exchanged at WDW resorts, except The Disney Inn, at other times. The Sun Banks in Disney Village Marketplace and at the Crossroads shopping center also exchange foreign currency.

SHOPPING FOR NECESSITIES: Almost all everyday needs can be satisfied right on the property. Concourse Sundries & Spirits in the Contemporary Resort, Village Gifts & Sundries on the second floor of the Polynesian Village, Gifts and Sundries in the lobby of The Disney Inn, Sandy Cove at the Grand Floridian, Sundries at the Caribbean Beach Resort, and the Meadow and Settlement trading posts at Fort Wilderness all stock a limited number of brands of a wide variety of toiletries; a broader selection is available at the Disney Village Marketplace at the Gourmet Pantry. In addition, a number of over-the-counter health aids, plus many other useful items, can be purchased in the Books and Records section of the Emporium on Main Street in the Magic Kingdom; they're kept behind the counter, so it's necessary to ask for the supplies you want. Aspirin and suntan lotion are also available at Mickey's Mart in Tomorrowland.

In Epcot Center, sundries are available in at least one shop in each of the World Showcase pavilions and at all the retail outlets in Future World (except the Kodak camera sales kiosk at Journey into Imagination). Here, too, you'll have to request what you need.

At the Disney-MGM Studios Theme Park, sundries are available at the Crossroads of the World and Movieland Memorabilia shops.

Reading matter: Newspapers, magazines, bestsellers, and paperbacks are available in a limited selection at Concourse Sundries & Spirits in the Contemporary Resort, at News from Civilization on the first floor at the Polynesian Village, at Gifts and Sundries in the lobby at The Disney Inn, Sandy Cove at the Grand Floridian, Sundries at the Caribbean Beach Resort, and at Personal Message at the Village Marketplace. Most carry the daily papers from Orlando and Miami, *The Wall Street Journal*, and, on Sundays, *The New York Times* and the *Chicago Tribune*.

A larger stock of paperbacks and hardcover books is available at Personal Message in Disney Village Marketplace. The Emporium in the Magic Kingdom has a good selection of children's books. Epcot Center offers an interesting selection as

well. Books related to the themes of Future World pavilions are available in the Centorium and at Epcot Outreach. In World Showcase, the United Kingdom's Toy Soldier and Der Bücherwurm in Germany stock children's books.

Comic books and magazines are available at Lakeside News at the Disney-MGM Studios Theme Park. Books on the subject of animation are on sale at the Animation Gallery.

Cigarettes: Smoking items are widely available all over WDW, and Market House on Main Street stocks tobacco items as well.

Cigarettes can also be purchased inside the Magic Kingdom at Tropic Toppers in Adventureland, at the Trading Post in Frontierland, at the Royal Candy Shoppe in Fantasyland, at Heritage House in Liberty Square, and at Mickey's Mart in Tomorrowland. In addition, there are cigarette vending machines in the Columbia Harbour House in Liberty Square; at King Stefan's in Cinderella Castle and the Pinocchio Village Haus in Fantasyland; in Tomorrowland Terrace; and in the Mile Long Bar in Frontierland.

In Epcot Center, cigarettes are available in Future World retail locations and in at least one shop in each World Showcase pavilion. In addition, His Lordship in the U.K. pavilion stocks a selection of British tobaccos, the Galerie des Halles area in the France pavilion offers French cigarettes, and Der Bücherwurm in the Germany pavilion sells their German counterparts.

At the Disney-MGM Studios Theme Park, cigarettes are sold in most shops. They are kept behind the counter so guests have to request them.

In the hotels, you can buy cigarettes at Concourse Sundries & Spirits in the Contemporary Resort, at News from Civilization on the first floor of the Great Ceremonial House at the Polynesian Village, at Gifts and Sundries in the lobby of The Disney Inn, at Sandy Cove at the Grand Floridian, and at Sundries at the Caribbean Beach Resort. In addition, there are vending machines in all the hotels. At Fort Wilderness, they are for sale in the Meadow and Settlement trading posts. At the Disney Village Marketplace, cigarettes are sold at Village Spirits and the Gourmet Pantry.

PETS: No pets are allowed in the Magic Kingdom, Epcot Center, the Disney-MGM Studios Theme Park, or at the WDW resorts. Travelers who bring pets along can lodge them in one of 4 attractive air conditioned Pet Care Kennels, presented by Gaines Foods, Inc.: near the Transportation & Ticket Center; to the left of the Epcot Center Entrance Plaza; at the Disney-MGM Studios Theme Park entrance; and at the Fort Wilderness Campground Entrance, next to a huge field where pet owners can take their animals out for a run. In busy seasons, it's best to arrive before the 9 A.M. to 10 A.M. morning rush hour. Be sure to note that the kennels close an hour after the Magic Kingdom, Epcot Center, and the Disney-MGM Studios Theme Park.

Bears, cougars, and ocelots have all been accommodated by the WDW kennels, and exotic pets may be accepted—if a bit reluctantly. However, owners themselves must put the more unusual animals into the kennel's cages; and snakes, rabbits, birds, turtles, hamsters, and other animals unsuited (because of size) to cat- and dog-size cages must be accompanied by their own escape-proof accommodations.

Advance reservations are not accepted. WDW resort guests and guests at Disney Village Hotel Plaza may board their pets overnight in the TTC Kennel or until 8 P.M. in the Fort Wilderness kennel. Cost is about $6 for overnight stays, including food; $4 for a day stay, without food. Only pets of WDW resort guests may board overnight.

Never leave pets in your car.

Also, bring along your pet's certificate of vaccination, since Florida law requires proof of immunization for animals involved in biting accidents.

Outside Walt Disney World: A number of hotels in the Orlando and Kissimmee area permit pets. For specific information phone the Greater Orlando Chamber of Commerce, 425-1234.

TIPPING: Walt Disney World is not one of those places where bellmen stick out their hands even before they put down your luggage. Instead, they seem genuinely glad to help out. Oddly enough, this pleasant attitude seems to discourage tipping at the same time it arouses the sentiments that make most travelers want to reach for their wallets.

Lack of ostentatious need does not mean that tips are any less valued at WDW than they would be at any other good resort hotel—the standard 50¢ to $1 per bag is appropriate for lugging luggage. Gratuities of 15% to 18% are also customary at full-service restaurants all over WDW. At the posh Empress Room, a service charge of 20% of the food and drink bill is automatically added.

Gratuities are not required in fast-food restaurants or at the attractions, but in the beauty shops, it's usual to leave a tip of about 15% of the total bill.

Cabdrivers in the Orlando area expect a 15% tip. Baggage handlers at bus and train stations and at the airport expect at least 50¢ per bag.

TELEPHONE: The folks at home can reach resort guests at the following numbers (all are in area code 407): 824-1000 for the Contemporary Resort; 824-2200 at The Disney Inn; 824-2000 at the Polynesian Village; 824-3000 at the Grand Floridian; 934-3400 at the Caribbean Beach Resort; 827-1100 at the Disney Village Resort; and 824-2900 at Fort Wilderness.

Public telephones in the Orlando area and in Walt Disney World cost 25¢.

TIME AND WEATHER PHONE: In the Orlando area, the number is 422-1611.

TRANSPORTATION AND ACCOMMODATIONS

Misconceptions about Walt Disney World (like the impression that it's located in the middle of downtown Orlando), and about the surrounding region (like the idea that the park is located on one or another of Florida's coasts), seem to abound. The fact is that Walt Disney World is situated virtually in the center of Central Florida, and, despite perhaps the most prevalent of nonresident misconceptions, nowhere near Miami or Miami Beach.

But the popularity of Walt Disney World has made the region around Orlando one of the world's major tourism and commercial centers, and everything from new airline facilities to a very efficient network of roads and highways brings visitors to the area literally by the millions.

There's no doubt, however, that confusion about getting to and around the Walt Disney World region is prevalent and may be exceeded only by the dilemma concerning which sort of specific accommodation is most appropriate for a given family's needs. Just the accommodations facilities that are

operated by Walt Disney World itself range from futuristic high-rise towers to treehouses buried deep in piney woods. In between are resorts echoing images of the South Pacific and old Florida and efficient trailer-type facilities in an almost perfectly maintained campground. And that doesn't include villas that provide extraordinary space and luxury, at surprisingly affordable prices. What follows should help any traveler sort out all the available options and preferences.

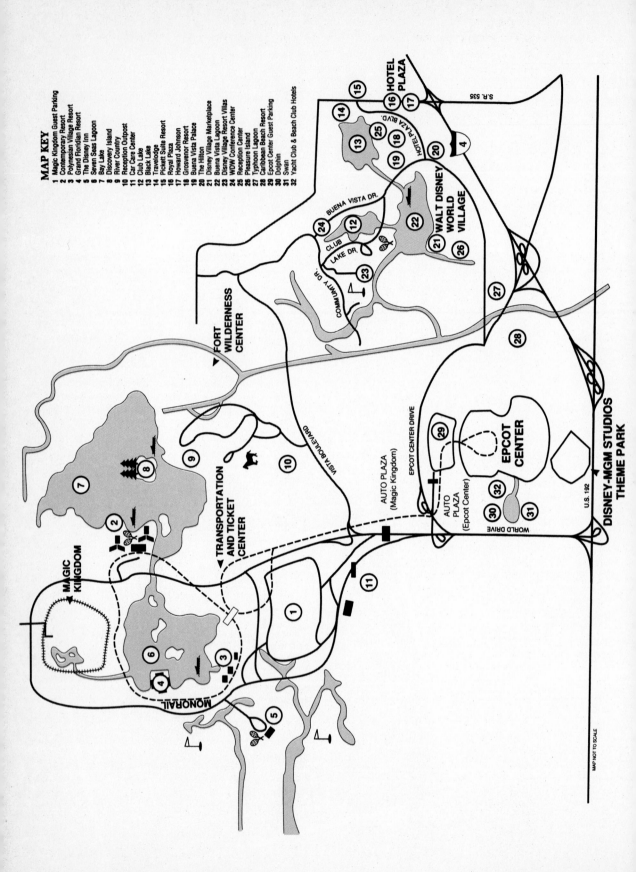

MAP KEY

1 Magic Kingdom Guest Parking
2 Contemporary Resort
3 Polynesian Village Resort
4 Grand Floridian Resort
5 The Disney Inn
6 Seven Seas Lagoon
7 Bay Lake
8 Discovery Island
9 River Country
10 Reception Outpost
11 Car Care Center
12 Club Lake
13 Black Lake
14 Travelodge
15 Pickett Suite Resort
16 Royal Plaza
17 Howard Johnson
18 Grosvenor Resort
19 Buena Vista Palace
20 The Hilton
21 Disney Village Marketplace
22 Buena Vista Lagoon
23 Disney Village Resort Villas
24 WDW Conference Center
25 Reception Center
26 Pleasure Island
27 Typhoon Lagoon
28 Caribbean Beach Resort
29 Epcot Center Guest Parking
30 Dolphin
31 Swan
32 Yacht Club & Beach Club Hotels

HOTEL PLAZA

S.R. 535

HOTEL PLAZA BLVD.

WALT DISNEY WORLD VILLAGE

BUENA VISTA DR.

CLUB LAKE DR.

COMMUNITY DR.

FORT WILDERNESS CENTER

MAGIC KINGDOM

MONORAIL

TRANSPORTATION AND TICKET CENTER

VISTA BOULEVARD

AUTO PLAZA (Magic Kingdom)

EPCOT CENTER DRIVE

AUTO PLAZA (Epcot Center)

EPCOT CENTER

WORLD DRIVE

U.S. 192

DISNEY-MGM STUDIOS THEME PARK

MAP NOT TO SCALE

GETTING ORIENTED

Orlando, the Central Florida city of over 161,000 residents, is the municipality with which Walt Disney World is most closely associated. It is not, however, the closest urban community to WDW. That distinction belongs to Kissimmee, a far smaller community of 27,000 people, located just southeast of WDW. Many newish motels are located here, though there are far more in Orlando proper, to the north.

Most of the area's better restaurants are found in Orlando, or in adjacent communities like Winter Park (on its northeastern extremity), Maitland (west of Winter Park), and Altamonte Springs (west of Maitland).

ORLANDO-AREA HIGHWAYS: The most important Orlando traffic artery is I-4, which runs diagonally through the area from southwest to northeast, cutting through the southern half of Walt Disney World, then angles on toward Orlando and Winter Park, ending near Daytona Beach at I-95, which runs north and south along the coast. All the city's other important highways intersect I-4. From south to north, these include U.S. 192 (aka Irlo Bronson Memorial Highway), which takes an east-west course that crosses the WDW entrance road and leads into downtown Kissimmee on the east; S.R. 528 (aka the Bee Line Expressway), which shoots eastward from I-4; S.R. 435, also known as Kirkman Road, which runs north and south and intersects International Drive, where many motels catering to WDW visitors are located; U.S. 17-92-441 (aka Orange Blossom Trail), which runs due north and south, paralleling Kirkman Road on the east; and U.S. 50 (aka Colonial Drive), which runs due east and west.

WALT DISNEY WORLD ROADS: The 43-square-mile tract that is Walt Disney World is roughly rectangular. I-4 runs through its southern half from southwest to northeast; there are 3 highway exits within WDW. The Magic Kingdom, the Polynesian Village Resort, the Contemporary Resort, The Disney Inn, the Grand Floridian Resort, and Fort Wilderness are all located in the property's northern third. They are located off the Main Entrance Road, a route accessible via I-4. This route is also suggested for Disney-MGM Studios Theme Park guests. The Main Entrance Road is about a mile from the I-4 exit, and the parking lots are about 4 miles from there. Disney Village Marketplace, the hotels of Disney Village Hotel Plaza, Pleasure Island, and Typhoon Lagoon also have their own exit off I-4 (marked "Lake Buena Vista"), 4 miles before

GETTING AROUND WDW

The internal transportation system at Walt Disney World was in the process of being completely revamped as we went to press. The reorganization is a byproduct of the immense expansion of WDW attractions and accommodations and the need to efficiently connect new hotels and diversions to the older areas. Accurate details were not available, but plans call for the Walt Disney World Resort to be divided into five areas: one is composed of the Magic Kingdom, the Transportation and Ticket Center, the Contemporary Resort, the Polynesian Village Resort, the Grand Floridian Resort, and The Disney Inn; a second area consists of Fort Wilderness, including River Country and Discovery Island; the third area takes in the Disney Village Resort, the Disney Village Marketplace, the Disney Village Hotel Plaza, Pleasure Island, and Typhoon Lagoon; a fourth area consists of the Disney-MGM Studios Theme Park; and the fifth area includes the Caribbean Beach Resort, Epcot Center, and the new Dolphin and Swan hotels. All bus stops are clearly marked with operative routes, and all guests receive detailed information upon arrival.

the one for the Main Entrance. The Disney Village Marketplace parking lots are located about a mile from I-4. The newest exit off I-4 (between the 2 described above) leads to Epcot Center, the Caribbean Beach Resort, and is another route to the Disney-MGM Studios Theme Park. Note that many off-property hotels offer free shuttle-bus service to WDW.

There are also a number of roads *inside* the World. In some cases, it is possible to drive from place to place on them. Bus transportation is also provided between most points, and is available without charge to most guests. At the northernmost end of WDW, an elevated monorail train operates along a circular route, making stops at the Polynesian Village, the Grand Floridian Resort, the Contemporary Resort, and at the Magic Kingdom and the TTC; a separate extension of the monorail system also goes to Epcot Center. Motor launches and cruisers from the Contemporary Resort and the Magic Kingdom call at Fort Wilderness and Discovery Island.

TRANSPORTATION ID REQUIREMENTS

Within WDW there are several different types of identification and/or admission media that are required for use of the various forms of transportation. This list explains what sort of card, ticket, or All Three Parks Passport permits use of each:

- WDW-owned resort identification card allows a guest unlimited use of any part of the WDW transportation system (including buses, monorails, and watercraft)
- Disney Village Hotel Plaza hotel identification card allows unlimited use of the bus transportation system.
- Valid 1-day Magic Kingdom ticket permits a guest to use the ferries and monorails running between the TTC and the Magic Kingdom entrance. (**Note:** Valid 1-day Epcot Center or Disney-MGM Studios Theme Park tickets do not allow guests to use the WDW transportation system.)
- 4- and 5-Day All Three Parks Passports and 1-Year Passports allow guests unlimited use of the WDW transportation system.
- River Country, Discovery Island, and Pioneer Hall tickets allow guests the use of buses from the TTC, watercraft from the Contemporary Resort, and watercraft from the Magic Kingdom to and from River Country, Discovery Island, and Pioneer Hall. Guests with these tickets also may take buses from the Polynesian Village and Contemporary Resort to the TTC and then transfer to other buses. For further information call 824-4321.

A WDW Transportation Ticket (around $2.50) allows unlimited use of all WDW transportation systems for 1 day.

ACCOMMODATIONS

Orlando and its environs have literally thousands of hotel and motel rooms. Few of these, however, whether inside or outside the World, are of a design much beyond the standard Anywhere, USA motel/modern decor, usually with 2 standard double beds, shag carpeting, simulated wood paneling, color television, and private bathroom.

The biggest differences between accommodations seem to be in the power of the showers, the sizes and thicknesses of the towels, the dimensions of the rooms and the adjacent bathrooms, the furnishings, the recreational facilities, the landscaping of the surrounding grounds, and the locations.

Basically, Walt Disney World-area accommodations fall into 2 main categories: those owned and those not owned by WDW.

All of the former are located inside the World. Rates are higher than at most other motels in the area (with the exception of the Caribbean Beach Resort), but the convenience is so much greater and the additional benefits available to an on-property guest so extensive—guaranteed park admission when parks are full, closed circuit TV announcing WDW events, a free copy of Walt Disney World News, and the best possible access to Guest Services personnel—that the extra expense is not at all unreasonable. Resort guests, for instance, can make dinner reservations at Epcot Center and Disney-MGM Studios Theme Park restaurants 1 or 2 days in advance by telephone, a not inconsiderable convenience. They can also reserve tee-off times on the golf courses up to 30 days in advance, and assure places at most of the dinner shows as soon as their on-property room reservations are confirmed. They have access to transportation within the World. The cost of Typhoon Lagoon, River Country, and Discovery Island tickets, and greens fees are a bit lower for guests at resorts on WDW property. The benefits for guests are so extensive that you should be wary of anyone who encourages you to stay elsewhere for reasons other than a major difference in price.

Locations of the non-Disney-owned properties are quite scattered. Some are located within the WDW boundaries at Disney Village Hotel Plaza and near Epcot Center. The rest occupy sites completely off the property, primarily in Kissimmee, along U.S. 192 (which runs east and west) intersecting the WDW entrance road, and along International Drive (off S.R. 435 at the Orlando city limits). The U.S. 192 establishments are closer to the WDW main entrance—usually only a few miles away, depending on the individual hostelry. But International Drive, some 10 miles from the WDW main gates, is a more pleasant place to stay, thanks to its array of sidewalk-connected lodging places, restaurants, and other minor attractions. Its proximity to still more of the same in Orlando, just a few miles farther

north, constitutes an additional benefit.

In choosing a place to stay, decide first just how much money you want to spend. If your budget permits, try to get a reservation at one of the Disney-owned properties. Remember that there are now Disney-owned accommodations in varying price ranges. If not, select accommodations outside the World based on what you can afford and on the guidelines given in this section.

Remember, when examining rate sheets for the best buy for your family, to check the cut-off age at which children accompanying you (and staying in the same room) will be billed as extra adults. Those with large families should note that the Disney villa-type accommodations, which may seem more expensive at first glance, can actually prove less costly in the long run—by eliminating the necessity of hiring an additional hotel room and providing cooking facilities that can mean big savings on meals.

WDW-OWNED RESORT PROPERTIES

With the addition of the moderately priced rooms at the Caribbean Beach Resort, we find it difficult to recommend staying off the property. Be sure to plan far enough ahead to be sure to get a room here, or keep trying in hopes of getting a cancellation if you don't secure a reservation the first time around.

In general, rooms at the 5 conventional hotels—the Contemporary Resort, the Polynesian Village Resort, The Disney Inn, the Grand Floridian Resort, and the Caribbean Beach Resort—are quite large and can accommodate up to 5 guests in a single room without difficulty (except at the Caribbean Beach, where rooms hold up to 4 people). Most rooms have patios or balconies. And considering the incredibly high occupancy rate here, it's astonishing that things look so fresh. Even the rooms without views have views, if only across the gardens at masses of lovely flowers.

The villa accommodations at the Disney Village Resort, which can accommodate larger groups, are especially good for families, especially those who want to cook some of their own meals "at home." Like the hotel accommodations, the villas aren't pretentiously luxurious, but the basics are all there. At Fort Wilderness Resort there are both campsites and fully equipped Fleetwood Trailers set on 780 acres of quiet woods.

Each resort and villa complex has its own character, and one may hold more appeal for you than another. The Contemporary Resort, the Polynesian Village, and the Grand Floridian are set right along the monorail route and are the most bustling; youngsters love them because there are always other kids around. The Disney Inn, off the monorail and just a bit off the main WDW track, offers a quieter atmosphere and only a slightly less convenient location. Fort Wilderness is quieter still. The villa accommodations near Disney Village Marketplace are remote enough from the heart of things that guests will probably want a car in which to get around, but there are also WDW buses to get from place to place. The Village Clubhouse, with its golf course and tennis courts (described in *Sports*), the *Empress Lilly* riverboat restaurants, and the Pleasure Island restaurant and entertainment complex are just a short distance away. The Caribbean Beach Resort is particularly convenient to Epcot Center and the Disney-MGM Studios Theme Park.

CONTEMPORARY RESORT

Watching the monorail trains disappear into this hotel's enormous, 15-story, A-frame tower never fails to amaze onlookers. The sleek trains look like long spaceships docking as they slide inside, or the sight may bring to mind the story of Jonah being swallowed by the whale. (Note that wheelchair guests cannot board the monorail here, but they can at the Polynesian Village Resort or at the Grand Floridian Resort.)

Passengers, for their part, are impressed by the cavernous lobby, with its tiers of balconies and, at its center, designer Mary Blair's huge 90-foot-high, floor-to-ceiling tile mural depicting Indian children, stylized flowers, birds, trees, and other scenes from the Southwest. (Look carefully and you may be able to spot the 5-legged goat.)

The imposing establishment has more than 1,050 rooms in its Tower and the 2 Garden Wings that flank it on either side. The hotel has 6 shops, 3 complete restaurants, 2 snack bars, 2 lounges, large meeting rooms, a marina, a beach, a health club, and more. The larger of the hotel's pair of swimming pools, measuring a generous 20 by 25 meters, is a delight for lap swimmers—the best in WDW for that purpose. And the Fiesta Fun Center—a vast room full of pinball and other electronic games that's open around the clock—is lively until the wee hours of the morning. For many youngsters, the presence of this room is reason enough to lodge here. The activity that these installations generate gives the place an urban feeling that is not found elsewhere in WDW. Certainly, the place can be a bit intimidating, and the hotel is not to everyone's taste. But you can't deny the Contemporary Resort's vitality, and the sense it gives of being right in the heart of things can prove irresistible.

A new concierge package is available for guests who choose to stay in the hotel's 14th-floor suites. Special services include free valet parking, special check-out service, complimentary fruit and juice in the morning and wine and cheese at night, and nightly turn-down service, complete with cookies and milk. Other amenities include a special concierge on duty from 8 A.M. to 9 P.M. and the opportunity to purchase tickets and Passports in advance, have them charged to the guest's room account, and have them waiting upon check-in.

The telephone number of the Contemporary Resort is 824-1000.

ROOMS: The hotel's guestrooms are almost evenly apportioned between the Tower and the North and South Garden Wings, which flank it on either side. Rooms in the Tower boast exciting views of Bay Lake or the Magic Kingdom and cost more than the rooms in the Garden Wings. From rooms on the Bay Lake side, guests can watch the sun rise through the eerie early-morning mists; in the evening, they can watch the Electrical Water Pageant (described in *Good Meals, Great Times*) from their own terraces. Rooms on the Magic Kingdom side, on the other hand, have fine views of the sun setting behind Cinderella Castle (Central Florida sunsets are dazzlers) and of the fireworks exploding around

the Castle just after 10 P.M. on nights when the park is open until midnight. Access to Tower rooms is by speedy elevators—ones that "talk."

All rooms can accommodate up to 5 (plus 1 additional child under 3). Some units have king-size beds; the rest have 2 queens, and all rooms have a day bed. Adjoining and/or connecting rooms may be requested, though they can't be guaranteed.

Bathrooms in the Contemporary Resort are particularly well laid out. Not only are they extremely large, but they also have double sinks and a bathtub with a shower head (some even have a separate shower stall).

Suites: Several varieties are available. In the Tower, they come with a Bay Lake or Magic Kingdom view, either with 1 bedroom (and 2 queen-size beds and 2 double sleep sofas, to accommodate up to 8), or with 2 bedrooms (to accommodate up to 12). Garden Wing suites are available in 3 types—second- and third-floor Bay Lake view, with either 1 or 2 bedrooms. Each bedroom has a queen-size bed and there is a Sico bed (similar to a Murphy bed) in the parlor which can sleep 2. There are also junior suites, with a king-size bed, providing spacious accommodations for 2. (For price information, see the chart "Rates at WDW-Owned Properties" in this chapter.)

MEETING AND CONVENTION SPACE: Most meeting facilities are located on the second floor of the Tower. The 11,968-square-foot Ballroom of the Americas, at the north end of the hotel, is the largest single facility, accommodating up to about 1,400 seated theater-style, or about 1,000 for a banquet. It can be divided into 2 smaller rooms, each with a capacity of about half the above numbers. The 8,777-square-foot Grand Republic Ballroom holds slightly fewer people; it can be split into 3 rooms ranging in size from 2,080 to 4,290 square feet. In addition, there are 5 other rooms nearby of 800 to 1,160 square feet each; and on the 15th floor there

are 2 others measuring 697 square feet and 1,247 square feet. Both have wonderful panoramic views over the rest of the World.

WHERE TO EAT: Most of the hotel's restaurants are located on the Grand Canyon Concourse on the 4th floor, but there is a restaurant on the 15th floor, and snack spots beside the marina and in the 1st-floor Fiesta Fun Center. Special children's menus are generally available at these restaurants. The meal-by-meal specialties of these facilities are described in some detail in the *Good Meals, Great Times* chapter. Here is a brief synopsis:

Character Cafe: On the Grand Canyon Concourse. Features a character breakfast daily and a bountiful, all-you-can-eat Italian buffet character dinner every evening; one of the World's best buys. No reservations.

Pueblo Room: On the Grand Canyon Concourse. Breakfast, lunch, and dinner are served here, and offerings include eggs and pancakes for breakfast, soups, salads, and burgers for lunch, and chicken, fresh fish, steak, and ribs for dinner.

Top of the World: This lovely room boasts superb views from the hotel's 15th floor. There's a bountiful, all-you-can-eat buffet for breakfast and brunch (on Sundays), and a dinner show, *Broadway at the Top*, where diners can choose from an à la carte menu. For lunch, there's an unlimited salad bar and assorted entrées. The setting is unique in the World. After dark, the golden spires of Cinderella Castle glitter under the floodlights, and the white lights edging the rooflines of Main Street wink and twinkle like distant fireflies. Reservations are required for the dinner shows; phone Central Reservations at W-DISNEY (934-7639). For Sunday brunch reservations, call 824-3611.

Fiesta Fun Center Snack Bar: On the first floor; serves light fare 24 hours a day.

Dock Inn: The snack stand at the marina behind the hotel. Open during peak seasons only.

WHERE TO DRINK: The no-liquor policy in the Magic Kingdom notwithstanding, enjoying a drink is one of the pleasantest pastimes at Walt Disney World, thanks to the settings of many of the bars and lounges and the array of specialty drinks. The Contemporary Resort is no exception.

Outer Rim Cocktail and Seafood Lounge: On the Grand Canyon Concourse, with a lovely setting overlooking Bay Lake. Serves sandwiches, seafood appetizers, and cocktails and specialty drinks. The appetizers can be a meal in themselves. Open from 11:30 A.M. to midnight.

Top of the World Lounge: Adjoining the Top of the World Restaurant, this spacious, high-ceilinged room offers superb views over the Magic Kingdom. While listening to the dinner show's entertainment, just out of sight, it's possible to gaze across the night toward Cinderella Castle. This is a good spot to watch the sunset and, when the park is open until midnight, the fireworks. Dash out onto the more easterly of the 2 observation decks nearby at 10:05 P.M. to see the Electrical Water Pageant blipping and bleeping and glittering on Bay Lake far below.

Sand Bar: Beside the marina, serving a variety of mixed drinks. The specialty here is a nifty piña colada made with ice cream. Open during peak seasons only.

ROOM SERVICE: A wide range of offerings suitable for breakfast, lunch, dinner, and snacks can be ordered; consult room service menus for serving times. Room service, which had been notoriously slow in recent years, has improved considerably. But it's still a good idea to pre-order room service breakfasts the night before, using the card hanging from the doorknob. For other meals, count on phoning in an order 30 to 45 minutes before you want to be served. When the food arrives, it comes with a smile and, in the morning, with a local newspaper.

WHAT TO DO: All by itself, the Contemporary Resort boasts more activities and recreational facilities than many large resorts; it would not be difficult to have a first class holiday without ever leaving the premises.

Boat rentals: Sailboats, pedal boats, and flote boats, as well as the zippy little motorcraft known as Water Sprites, are all available for rent at the Contemporary Resort marina, near the beach. (See *Sports* for details.)

Water Skiing: Boats with driver and skis can be hired at the hotel marina. (For details, see *Sports*.)

Swimming: There are 2 main pools here, the big 20-by-25-meter main pool, and the round teen splash pool, deep in the center and shallow on the outside. A toddler's pool is located near the North Wing, and swimming is permitted in the roped-off area of Bay Lake beside the beach. The bottom is delightfully sandy. (For hours, see *Sports*.)

Volleyball: Nets are set up on the beach.

Children's playground: Located near the North Garden Wing.

Jogging: The Fort Wilderness Exercise Trail is only a short run away. Inquire at the desk for directions, and pay careful attention so that you don't miss the turnoff—it's the first road to the left after you pass under the Water Bridge.

Fiesta Fun Center: On the first floor of the hotel, this is one of the World's great indoor recreational facilities, the biggest and most varied of all the Disney hotels' mechanical game rooms, boasting everything from skee ball to air hockey, not to mention Asteroids and Space Invaders and all the other favorites of the pinball-and-electronic-games-playing set—worth at least a look.

Movies: Two different Disney movies are shown each evening in the theater at the Fiesta Fun Center. A good place to get off your feet.

Shopping: The fourth-floor Grand Canyon Concourse is full of shops that are not only several cuts above those found in other Orlando-area hotels, but are also interesting enough to make browsing here a pleasant way to weather a late-afternoon thundershower. The Fantasia Shop sells kids' stuff and Walt Disney-themed merchandise (china figurines of Mickey Mouse, Minnie, the Cheshire Cat, the Mad Hatter, the White Rabbit, Pluto, and company; T-shirts and sweatshirts; and stuffed animals). Concourse Sundries and Spirits, next door, has a selection of newspapers, magazines, books, snack foods, and liquor—just what's needed for a cocktail party on your terrace. On the opposite side of the Concourse, the Contemporary Woman offers a range of good-quality women's clothing (and plenty of bathing suits) in all price ranges, and the adjoining Contemporary Man stocks casual and beachwear for men. Even tuxedo rentals are available.

The adjacent Kingdom Jewels, Ltd., displays men's and women's jewelry from around the globe. Bay View Gifts carries souvenirs, gifts, and fresh flowers.

TRANSPORTATION: The Contemporary Resort is connected to the Transportation and Ticket Center (TTC) by the monorail trains, which glide into the hotel every 10 or 15 minutes from 7:30 A.M. until 2 hours after the official park closing time. Board just above the Grand Canyon Concourse, inside the atrium area of the Tower. The monorails stop at the Polynesian Village (from which point you can board a bus to The Disney Inn), the Magic Kingdom, the Grand Floridian Beach Resort, and the TTC. From the TTC, Epcot Center can be reached by bus or by monorail, and the Disney-MGM Studios Theme Park can be reached by bus.

Watercraft also travel regularly from the marina to Fort Wilderness and Discovery Island.

POLYNESIAN VILLAGE RESORT

The Polynesian Village is as close an approximation to the real thing as Walt Disney World's designers could conceive. The vegetation is as lush as anywhere in the World; the architecture reeks of the tropics; and the atmosphere is more subdued than that of even the relatively placid Disney Inn. *Aitea-Peatea,* promises the hotel's motto: "There will be another day tomorrow just like today." Here, that's a pleasant thought.

The mood is set by a 3-story high garden that occupies most of the lobby. To call the construction at the center a fountain is to do it a grave injustice; it's more like a waterfall. The water cascades over craggy volcanic rocks. Coconut palms tower over 250 square feet of some 75 different species of tropical and subtropical plants—1,500 anthuriums, banana trees, ferns, gardenias, orchids, and other greens. The climatic conditions are nearly perfect, so that everything is verdant year round.

The structure that contains this mass of greenery, the so-called Great Ceremonial House, is the central building in the Polynesian Village complex. The front desk, the shops, and most of the restaurants are located here. Flanking the Great Ceremonial House on either side are eleven 2- and 3-story "longhouses" named for various Pacific islands. These structures house the resort's 855 rooms. On the east side, there is the Tangaroa Terrace restaurant, the resident snack bar, and the guest laundry, in a building that also houses the gameroom; on the west, there is Luau Cove, where the Polynesian Revue and Mickey's Tropical Revue (described in *Good Meals, Great Times*) is presented nightly. A marina is located just west of the Great Ceremonial House, and a powdery white-sand beach borders the resort property on the north. The fact that the monorail stops at this resort makes it a very convenient place to stay; in fact, it's just a couple of minutes' ride to the Magic Kingdom. But because the accommodations are so scattered, and because the hotel is not quite as large as the Contemporary

Resort, things seldom feel as hectic, and the Polynesian Village has a loyal following among returning Walt Disney World visitors. That, coupled with the appeal of the tropical theme, makes the Polynesian Village rooms sell out quickly, and it's the most difficult of the Disney-owned hotels in which to get a reservation.

The Polynesian Village Resort is also offering a special concierge service called King Kamehameha. The amenities are similar to those on the "suite" floor at the Contemporary Resort: free valet parking, special check-out service, complimentary juice and coffee in the morning, soft drinks and snacks in the afternoon, and a special concierge on duty from 8 A.M. to 9 P.M. The special Polynesian Village Resort rooms are located in the Tonga, Samoa, and Moorea longhouses, and are the most expensive rooms in the hotel.

The telephone number of the Polynesian Village Resort is 824-2000.

ROOMS: These are located in the longhouses. Many have a balcony or a patio, and most have a view of either the Seven Seas Lagoon or one of the swimming pools; those in the Oahu, Moorea, and Pago Pago longhouses are the largest. Most have 2 queen-size beds, and all rooms can accommodate 5 (plus a sixth under age 3). Adjoining rooms may be requested, though they cannot be guaranteed. (The Oahu and Pago Pago longhouses have some bathrooms specially equipped for handicapped visitors.) There are also non-smoking rooms available.

Suites are all located in the Bali Hai longhouse, and accommodate from 4 to 6. Most have a king-size bed in the bedroom and 2 queen-size Sico beds (similar to Murphy beds) in the parlor.

WHERE TO EAT: Some of the more interesting Walt Disney World eating spots are located at the Polynesian Village Resort. (See *Good Meals, Great Times* for more details.)

Papeete Bay Verandah: On the second floor of the Great Ceremonial House, Papeete Bay serves sit-down dinners daily, breakfast buffets Mondays through Saturdays, and a massive brunch buffet on

Sundays. All breakfasts and brunches offer a chance to meet the characters. The room is large and open, and offers fine views across the Seven Seas Lagoon all the way to Cinderella Castle. Minnie's Menehune Breakfast with the characters is served here. After dark, Polynesian dancers and a small combo entertain quietly. Reservations are requested for breakfast, dinner, and Sunday brunch; phone 824-1391.

Coral Isle Cafe: On the second floor of the Great Ceremonial House, around the corner from Papeete Bay. This standard coffee shop (with South Seas decor) serves the usual assortment of breakfast items each morning, and does a booming business at lunch and dinner. A good bet when you want a no-fuss meal.

Tangaroa Terrace: This sprawling establishment is on the eastern edge of the property near the Oahu longhouse. At breakfast there is banana-stuffed French toast (a specialty) plus other more traditional selections. The dinner menu is quite varied. Reservations are requested at dinner; phone 824-1361.

Captain Cook's Snack and Ice Cream Company: Located on the lobby level of the Great Ceremonial House, this is a good spot for continental breakfasts and for snacks and ice cream during the day.

Tangaroa Snack Isle: Most guests discover this snack bar on their way to Tangaroa Terrace, the game room, or the East Pool—to which it is extremely convenient.

WHERE TO DRINK: The resort's Polynesian theme has inspired a whole raft of deceptively potent potables like Seven Seas (fruit juice, grenadine, orange curaçao, and rum), Chi Chis (a standard piña colada made with vodka instead of rum), and WDW piña coladas (which include orange juice in addition to rum, pineapple, and coconut cream). There's even a special Polynesian Village non-alcoholic treat—the pink Lei-Lani, a delicious orange juice and strawberry mixture. These drinks are specialties at Polynesian Village lounges, listed below, but can also be ordered elsewhere in WDW. (Details about individual drink menus can be found in the *Good Meals, Great Times* chapter.)

Barefoot Bar: Adjoining the Swimming Pool Lagoon.

Tambu Lounge: Cozy and clublike, this lounge adjoins the Papeete Bay Verandah. A good spot for quiet conversation with entertainment nightly.

ROOM SERVICE: A variety of specialties is available, and the long waits for food of days gone by are no longer much of a problem. Still, for breakfast, it's

a good idea to fill out the order card and place it on the doorknob outside before going to sleep.

WHAT TO DO: A wide range of activities is available at the Polynesian Village, just as at the Contemporary Resort.

Boat rentals: Sailboats, speedy little Water Sprites, pedal boats, flote boats, and outrigger canoes (requiring 6 to paddle) are available for rent at the Polynesian Village marina. Waterskiing excursions are also available.

Swimming: There are 2 main pools here, the elliptical East Pool, in the shadow of the Oahu, Tonga, Hawaii, Bora Bora, and Maui longhouses, and the larger free-form Swimming Pool Lagoon, closer to the marina and the beach. This pool is framed by a large cluster of boulders that forms a water slide much beloved by youngsters; to get to the ladder that takes you to the top, you must duck underneath a waterfall. For swimming laps, the large pool at the Contemporary Resort is best. Toddlers have their own shallow areas in both Polynesian Village pools. Swimming is also permitted in the roped-off areas of the Seven Seas Lagoon (when there's a lifeguard on duty).

Children's playground: Located near the Great Ceremonial House, this assemblage of kid stuff features an assortment of apparatuses for climbing, swinging, and sliding. The Neverland Club is an evening activity program for children ages 3 to 12.

Jogging: The Fort Wilderness Exercise Trail and the roads around The Disney Inn are just a short jog away. Ask for directions at the Information Desk in the lobby.

Gameroom: Moana Mickey's Fun Hut, while not as large as the Contemporary Resort's Fiesta Fun Center, usually manages to keep youngsters occupied. Located alongside the Tangaroa Snack Isle.

Shopping: News from Civilization, on the first floor of the Great Ceremonial House, is the only place in Walt Disney World where you can buy a grass skirt, and for that reason alone it's worth a special trip, though most of the other merchandise there—with the exception of a few handsome shells—is of the utilitarian variety—daily newspapers, magazines, tobacco, film, and gifts. Crusoe and Son, right nearby, sells casual sportswear and swimwear for men and boys, while the Polynesian Princess stocks an appealing assortment of brightly colored resort fashions, bathing suits, and hotweather accessories. Kanaka Kids stocks children's resortwear and accessories. Outrigger's Cove features gifts and goods from the South Seas. Upstairs, Village Gifts & Sundries sells gift items, souvenirs, and miscellaneous items; Trader Jack's Grog Hut has food, liquor, wine, beer, and other fixings for an impromptu party.

TRANSPORTATION: The Polynesian Village is located right on the monorail line. The entrance is on the second floor of the Great Ceremonial House. Buses, which circulate between the Polynesian Village, The Disney Inn, and the Transportation and Ticket Center, stop at the traffic island in front of the hotel. From the TTC, Epcot Center is accessible by monorail or by bus, and the Disney-MGM Studios Theme Park by bus.

GRAND FLORIDIAN BEACH RESORT

At the turn of the century, Standard Oil magnate Henry M. Flagler saw the realization of his dream: The railroad he had built to "civilize" Florida had spawned along its right-of-way an empire of grand hotels, lavish estates, prominent families, and opulent lifestyles. High society blossomed in winter, as the likes of John D. Rockefeller and Teddy Roosevelt put up at the Royal Poinciana in Palm Beach, enjoying the sea breezes from oceanside suites.

The Royal Poinciana later burned to the ground, and Florida's golden era faded with the Depression. But nearly a century after Flagler first made Florida a fashionable resort destination, Walt Disney World has opened a grand hotel—a 900-room Victorian structure, with gabled roofs and carved moldings—on 40 acres of Seven Seas Lagoon shorefront, between the Magic Kingdom and the Polynesian Village Resort.

Like its late 19th-century predecessors, the Grand Floridian boasts abundant broad verandas, wicker rockers, ceiling fans, intricate latticework and balustrades, turrets, towers, and red-shingle roofs. White sand beaches hold the promise of clambakes. And yet, it has all the advantages of 21st-century living—air conditioning and monorail service. With 5 restaurants, 2 lounges, 2 snack bars, 4 shops, an arcade, a child-care facility, a swimming pool, a children's activity area, a health club, white

sand beaches, and a marina, the Grand Floridian is not only a grand hotel but a complete resort.

The main building houses a 14,800-square-foot Grand Lobby, a palatial space soaring five stories to a ceiling of stained glass domes, glittering chandeliers, and ornate metal scrolls. Potted palms, verdant ferns, and an aviary decorate the sitting area; an open-cage elevator carries guests to the second floor full of shops and restaurants. The turn-of-the-century theme is apparent everywhere, from the Edwardian costumes worn by the staff to the shop displays, from the restaurants to the room decor.

The telephone number of the Grand Floridian Resort is 824-3000.

ROOMS: The accommodations are WDW's most luxurious to date, with rooms decorated as they might have been a century ago: soft moss greens and salmon pinks, printed wall coverings, armoires and light-wood furnishings, marble-topped sinks, ceiling fans, and Victorian woodwork. The main building houses 61 concierge rooms and 34 suites; 5 lodge buildings, each 4 and 5 stories high, 624 standard rooms, and 176 slightly smaller "attic" chambers. Most rooms are about 400 square feet, and include 2 queen-size beds, plus a day bed, to accommodate up to 5 people. Many rooms have terraces. Suites include a parlor, plus 1, 2, or 3 bedrooms; each of the 6 honeymoon rooms, located in the third-, fourth-, and fifth-floor turrets, enjoy wonderful views from 5 windows. In the main building, access to the upper three concierge/suite levels is restricted to guests occupying rooms on those floors only, by private elevator. On the third floor, the concierge desks offer such personalized services as rapid check-in/check-out, reservations, and information. The fourth floor features a quiet seating area where continental breakfast and evening cocktails are served, and cocktails are also served on the fifth floor.

WHERE TO EAT: Most of the restaurants and lounges are on the first 2 floors of the main building.

Gasparilla Grill and Games: A snack bar on the Windsor Level (first floor), offers top-your-own burger fare and video games.

Grand Floridian Cafe: Its peaches-and-cream color scheme and veranda-like feel make this the best place to get a quick, sit-down breakfast. Located on the first floor.

1900 Park Fare: A buffet restaurant on the first floor, festively decorated with carousel horses, plenty of plants, and Big Bertha—the carnival organ.

Flagler's: The largest of the hotel's restaurants, seating 285, features seafood and pasta. Alcazar Level (second floor).

Victoria & Albert's: Also on the second floor, but much smaller than Flagler's, is the hotel's finest restaurant, named after the former queen and prince consort of England. Elegant meals are served by candlelight to no more than 56 guests; service is refined and diligent.

Narcoossee's: Octagon-shaped and open-beamed, this seafood restaurant and bar has a romantic shoreline location. Broiled, steamed, sautéed, and smoked fresh seafood characterize the menu, cooked in an open kitchen. There is live entertainment nightly.

WHERE TO DRINK: While guests staying on the concierge floors or in suites all have their own wet bars—as well as access to the fourth- and fifth-floor lounges—other guests will find lounges on the first and second floors of the main building.

The Garden View Lounge: Windsor Level, with a view of the hotel's lush, landscaped pool and garden area.

Mizner's Lounge: Named after the eccentric, wildly prolific architect who defined much of the flavor of Palm Beach County, this bar is on the Alcazar Level.

Summerhouse: The only bar serving the pool and beach.

WHAT TO DO: The Grand Floridian offers all the recreational facilities of a typical beachside resort—and much more.

Boat rentals: All manner of watercraft—sailboats and Water Sprites—are available for rent at The Captain's Shipyard marina.

Swimming: In addition to the 275,000-gallon swimming pool outside the main building, the hotel has its own white sand beach along the Seven Seas Lagoon.

Children's playground: An activity center and a child-care facility (The Mousekeeter Club) are in the main lodge, as part of the Gasparilla Grill and Games area.

Fitness: St. John's is the hotel's health club, offering an exercise room with state-of-the-art equipment, steamrooms, locker facilities, and a massage room.

Gameroom: The Gasparilla Grill and Games on the first floor of the main building features a video arcade.

Shopping: On the first floor (Windsor Level) of the main lodge is Summer Lace, a ladies' apparel shop, and Sandy Cove, where guests may purchase gifts and sundries. One floor up at the Alcazar Level is Commander Porter's, a men's shop; M. Mouse Mercantile is the character shop.

TRANSPORTATION: The Grand Floridian is connected to the Transportation and Ticket Center (TTC) by the monorail. Access to the monorail is located outside the hotel under an awning. From the TTC, Epcot Center is accessible by WDW's other monorail, or via a bus. The Disney-MGM Studios Theme Park is accessible by bus.

DISNEY INN

A recent remodeling has given The Disney Inn a new look and a Snow White theme. Guestrooms were redecorated, including dividers separating the sleeping area from the section with a sofa and table, to give each room more of a mini-suite feel. There is a quilt on each bed, the furniture is light oak, and the floral accents add to a basic countrified feeling. The Disney Inn also has a pleasantly relaxed atmosphere—more akin to that of the villas at the Disney Village Resort. But The Disney Inn is more convenient to the main activities of Walt Disney World since buses make the short trip between The Disney Inn, the Polynesian Village Resort, and the Transportation and Ticket Center every 15 minutes.

The Disney Inn's telephone number is 824-2200.

ROOMS: These are located in two 3-story wings behind the lobby area. All have patios or balconies and views of woods, the golf courses, the courtyard, or the pool; can accommodate up to 5 (plus a sixth under age 3); and have 2 queen-size beds and a sleep sofa. (No king-size beds are available here.) Adjoining or connecting rooms can be requested but are not guaranteed. (There are no special room provisions for handicapped guests here, but the hotel is accessible to all visitors.)

One suite, with 2 queen-size beds, a wet bar, a wide-screen television, and a Jacuzzi, is also available. It can accommodate up to 4 people. (For complete price information, see the chart "Rates at WDW-Owned Properties" later on in this chapter.)

MEETING AND CONVENTION SPACE: A small meeting can be accommodated in the 1,024-square-foot Summer Room.

WHERE TO EAT: The bright Garden Gallery is one of the most pleasant spots in the World for a meal. Many Disney executives frequent the Garden Gallery for lunch, because even when there are crowds at the other resort restaurants, tables here will tend to be fairly quiet. The menu focuses on "American cuisine." The seafood is fresh, as are the vegetables, and all dishes are prepared with very light sauces. At breakfast, there is an abundant, all-you-can-eat buffet; lunch features a varied salad bar, plus individual menu selections; the dinner menu features several fresh seafood selections, plus beef, veal, and fowl. There is a seafood bar with oysters, shrimp, and crab claws. There's also a children's menu.

The Diamond Mine: A snack spot offering sandwiches, burgers, chicken fajitas, salads, soft drinks, coffee, and beer.

Sand Trap: Poolside snack bar for drinks, sandwiches, hot dogs, and chips. Early-morning coffee, cereal, and Danish are also available.

WHERE TO DRINK: The Back Porch, adjoining the Garden Gallery, is a light and airy spot that's lovely for drinks, snacks, and sandwiches.

ROOM SERVICE: Selected items from the Garden Gallery are available through room service. Allow 30 to 45 minutes for delivery, and for the most prompt morning breakfast service, be sure to put the preorder card on the doorknob outside your room.

WHAT TO DO: The Disney Inn is landlocked, so when you decide to go boating, you've got to head for the Contemporary Resort or the Polynesian Village. But there are plenty of other activities.

Gameroom: The small Mine Arcade is located on the lobby level in the guestroom area. The Diamond Mine Arcade can be found at Happy's Hollow.

Golf: There are 2 par-72, Joe Lee-designed, championship courses—the tree-dotted Magnolia, to the north of the hotel, which plays from 5,414 (ladies) to 7,190 (championship) yards; and, south of the hotel, the Palm, ranked by *Golf Digest* magazine among the United States' top hundred courses—shorter and tighter, with more wooded fairways and 9 water hazards, playing from 5,398 to 6,957 yards. Each course has its own driving range. The Executive Course, a 6-hole, 1,525-yard experimental junior layout, occupies a 25-acre corner near the Magnolia. (See *Sports* for details.)

Shopping: The Pro Shop stocks men's and women's golf and tennis togs and gear, some emblazoned with Mickey and Minnie emblems. Gifts and Sundries sells souvenirs, books and magazines, daily newspapers, liquor, tobacco, film, toiletries, and a little bit of a lot of other things.

Swimming: The Disney Inn has 2 swimming pools. For beach action, head for the Polynesian Village.

Tennis: There are 2 courts tucked away behind the hotel. These are open from 8 A.M. to 10 P.M. daily, and are lighted for night play. (For more information, and for details about court reservations, see *Sports.*)

TRANSPORTATION: Buses make regular trips from The Disney Inn to the Polynesian Village and then on to the Transportation and Ticket Center (TTC). To get to the Magic Kingdom or the Contemporary Resort, it's quickest to take the monorail from the second-floor lobby at the Polynesian Village; to get to the Disney Village Marketplace, Epcot Center, or the Disney-MGM Studios Theme Park, stay on the bus until you get to the TTC, and then change for the bus marked for those areas. To get to Fort Wilderness, change to a bus marked Fort Wilderness.

CARIBBEAN BEACH RESORT

This colorful Disney-owned hotel, set on 200 acres southeast of Epcot Center and near the new Disney-MGM Studios Theme Park, fills the need for moderately priced accommodations on the Disney property (see "Rates at WDW-Owned Properties" later in this chapter). The hotel is composed of five brightly colored villages surrounding a 42-acre lake. Each village is themed to a different Caribbean island—Martinique, Barbados, Trinidad, Aruba, and Jamaica—and features cool pastel walls, whitewood railings, and vividly colored metal roofs. The total number of rooms is 2,112, making the Caribbean Beach Resort the sixth largest hotel complex in the United States.

The villages consist of a cluster of two-story buildings, a swimming pool, a guest laundry, and a lakefront stretch of white sandy beach. Guests check in at the Custom House, a reception building that immediately gives guests the feeling of a tropical resort. Decor, furnishings, and staff costumes all reflect the Caribbean theme. Old Port Royale, a complex located near the center of the property, evokes thoughts of a Spanish fortress. Stone walls, pirates' cannons, and tropical birds and flowers add to the atmosphere. The area houses the resort's six counter-service restaurants, a shop, a gameroom, and a lounge. The port opens onto a lakeside recreation area which includes a specially themed pool with waterfalls and slides; the main beach; the Barefoot Bay Marina, where watercraft and bicycles can be rented; a 1.4-mile promenade around the lake that's perfect for biking, walking, or jogging; and Parrot Cay, an island with a playground, a treasure hunt, and a wildlife walk.

The telephone number at the Caribbean Beach Resort is 934-3400.

ROOMS: Rooms are located in two-story buildings in each island village. A typical 400-square-foot room has two double beds and can sleep up to four. The rooms here are a bit smaller than the standard rooms at the other Disney-owned hotels, but the bathrooms are comfortable and fine for a family. The rooms are decorated in softer tones than the colors found on the exterior. The furniture is white oak, and bedspreads are pink and blue pastels.

WHERE TO EAT: The six counter-service restaurants are located in Old Port Royale. A 500-seat common dining area serves all diners.

Cinnamon Bay Bakery: Freshly baked rolls, croissants, pastries, and other treats are available.

Port Royale Hamburger Shop: Hot sandwiches, burgers, and soft drinks are on the menu.

Oriental Cargo: A variety of Chinese items, including egg rolls, spareribs, and soups are available.

SPECIAL ROOM REQUESTS

The Central Reservations Office (W-DISNEY—934-7639) can accept *requests* for a particular view or location, but although they will try to accommodate guest requests, they cannot guarantee that they will be able to fulfill every wish.

Montego's Market: Soups, salads, and cold sandwiches round out the offerings at this stand.

Bridgetown Broiler: Chicken fajitas, taco salads, and grilled chicken are among the offerings.

Royale Pizza & Pasta Shop: Pizza by the slice or the pie and a variety of hot and cold pasta dishes are available.

WHERE TO DRINK: The tropical, Caribbean theme is carried out in a variety of specialty drinking spots.

Captain's Hideaway: Tropical drinks, wine, beer, and traditional cocktails are served at this 200-seat lounge at Old Port Royale.

Banana Cabana: Drinks and snacks are available at this poolside spot.

WHAT TO DO: Recreational opportunities are many.

Boat rentals: Sailboats, toobies (oversize tires with zippy motors), and pedalboats are available for rent at the Barefoot Bay Marina for use on the resort's 42-acre lake.

Swimming: Each village has its own pool and the main pool features waterfalls and slides in a Caribbean themed setting.

Children's playground: A lovely playground is on Parrot Cay, across the footbridge from the Barefoot Bay Marina.

Jogging: The 1.4-mile promenade around the lake is perfect for a morning jog.

Gameroom: Goombay Games features a selection of electronic games at the Old Port Royale.

Shopping: Calypso Trading Post, at Old Port Royale, stocks a large selection of character merchandise and sundries.

Bicycling: Bikes can be rented at the Barefoot Bay Marina.

Nature walks: Walks are conducted at Parrot Cay.

TRANSPORTATION: The Caribbean Beach Resort is served by the Walt Disney World bus system. Buses go directly to Epcot Center and the Disney-MGM Studios Theme Park. Other routes lead to the Disney Village Marketplace, Pleasure Island, Typhoon Lagoon, and the Transportation and Ticket Center where guests can transfer for other buses.

DISNEY'S YACHT AND BEACH CLUB RESORT

The New England seaside is coming to Walt Disney World in the form of Disney's new Yacht Club & Beach Club resorts. Situated just west of Epcot Center, the two new hotels, designed by noted architect Robert A. M. Stern, are set around a 25-acre lake and are scheduled to open during this spring and summer. A total of 1,214 guestrooms and 51,000 square feet of meeting space will be available when the hotels are complete, making these properties attractive for medium-size conventions and meetings.

The two hotels complement each other, but have distinctive architectural styles. Each has its own entrance, main lobby, restaurants, and retail shops. The two properties share a common public area, highlighted by Fantasy Lagoon, a 2½-acre recreation area that boasts water slides leading from a shipwreck, plus a unique snorkeling experience in a sand-bottom lagoon stocked with bass, crappie, and other fish indigenous to Florida freshwater springs. A health club, game arcade, and a child care facility are also part of the common area.

The **Yacht Club Resort**'s design evokes images of New England seashore cottages of the 1880s. Guests enter the five-story, oyster-gray clapboard hotel via a wooden-planked bridge. Hardwood floors, millwork, and brass enhance the nautical motif, and a replica of a 1902 yacht, trimmed in mahogany, will be moored at the Yacht Club marina and will be available to guests for evening cocktail cruises. There's even a lighthouse on the pier.

At the **Beach Club Resort**, hosts and hostesses dressed in colorful "jams" and T-shirts greet guests as they make their way along the palm-lined entranceway. A colorfully patterned walkway leads to a croquet lawn and beachside cabanas along the white-sand shore. The 580-room, blue and white hotel is reminiscent of seaside resorts found on coastal New England during the 1870s.

Rooms at each of these resorts will be top-of-the-line, featuring tile balconies, mini-bars, two telephones (one in the bathroom), plush bathrobes, large bathrooms, special toiletries, hair dryers, and ceiling fans.

There will be six restaurants among the two hotels, including a steak and seafood house at the Yacht Club and an indoor clambake at the Beach Club. Themed lounges and shops are also planned.

Both hotels will provide boat service to the new World Showcase entrance at Epcot Center, or guests may walk or take a tram. Tram service also will be provided to the nearby Disney-MGM Studios Theme Park. The Magic Kingdom, Pleasure Island, the Disney Village Marketplace, River Country, Fort Wilderness, and Typhoon Lagoon will all be accessible by bus.

DISNEY VILLAGE RESORT VILLAS

The area near Disney Village Marketplace is dotted with exceptionally attractive villa-type accommodations, many fitted out with fully equipped kitchens and many other extras and amenities. Some may cost more than individual guestrooms at the 5 resort hotels, but they accommodate more people as well. For families of more than 5 (who might otherwise need to rent an extra hotel room), this is the most economical way to stay hereabouts. Smaller families can generally come out at least even by cooking some of their own meals (especially breakfast) in their villa.

Aside from the delights of having lots more space, the villas are exceptionally quiet and secluded; the pace is definitely more relaxed and the atmosphere very low-key. They are conveniently located with respect to Epcot Center, the Disney-MGM Studios Theme Park, Disney Village Marketplace, Pleasure Island, and Typhoon Lagoon.

The telephone number at the villas is 827-1100.

TYPES OF VILLAS: There are 5 major types of villas, each one available in several sizes. All have either full kitchens or wet bars with small refrigerators.

Check in and check out for all guests except convention-goers, takes place at the new Reception Center near the Vacation Villas. All WDW convention guests should check in at the WDW Conference Center.

One- and Two-Bedroom Villas: Formerly known as the Vacation Villas, these accommodations are located about 5 minutes' walk from the Village Clubhouse. They are pleasantly straightforward in feeling and decor, and have cathedral-height living room ceilings. One-bedroom units can accommodate 4, plus an additional child under 3; there's a king-size bed in the bedroom and a queen-size convertible sleep sofa in the living room. Two-bedroom units, which can accommodate up to 6, plus a 7th guest under age 3, have a king-size bed in each bedroom, and a Sico bed in the living room.

The Villa Center near these villas is the main recreation area. In addition to the 50-by-30-foot swimming pool, there are bicycle and electric-cart rentals, a laundry, snack bar, electronic games, and pinball machines. Another swimming pool, this one measuring 65 by 30 feet, is located closer to the Disney Village Marketplace.

Club Suites: Formerly known as the Club Lake Villas, these are located slightly northeast of the one- and two-bedroom villas. There are 316 regular villas and 8 full suites handsomely decorated in reds and blues. The smallest 1-bedroom units are roughly L-shaped, with a special sitting area (equipped with a wet bar) that is just far enough removed from the sleeping area (with its 2 queen-size beds) that business travelers who invite their colleagues in for a nightcap don't feel as if they're entertaining in the bedroom. While the layout was drawn up with special attention to the needs of those attending conferences at the Walt Disney World Conference Center, it works equally well in providing families with a bit more space and privacy than they get in the standard rooms at the WDW resort hotels. (The single disadvantage for families is the size of the bathrooms—small.) Note that these units, which cost about the same as rooms at the resort hotels, do not have kitchens—only a small refrigerator and a sink.

For the largest accommodations here, ask for a deluxe suite, which sleeps 5 and includes a Jacuzzi. These units have 2 queen-size beds upstairs and a sleep sofa downstairs.

There are 2 pools on opposite sides of the lake, and the Club Suite Villa Center offers amenities similar to those mentioned above.

Two-bedroom Villas: Until recently these units were known as the Fairway Villas. These cedar-sided, slant-roofed units, located near the 10th,

11th, 17th, and 18th fairways of the Lake Buena Vista Golf Course, are among the World's most spacious and attractive accommodations, with cathedral ceilings, rough-hewn walls, large windows, contemporary-styled furniture, and an overall feeling that there's lots of elbow room. They can sleep 6, plus 2 children under 12. Some units designed for the handicapped are available.

Joggers can loop through the shady Treehouse area or venture forth along Fairway Drive, alongside the golf course, and into the Club Suites area; the nearest swimming pool is the 65-by-30-footer at the Village Clubhouse, within walking distance of some units, a short drive from others.

Three-bedroom "Treehouse" Villas: Guests who lodge in one of these octagonal houses-on-stilts, scattered along a barbell-shaped roadway at the western edge of the villa area, go to sleep to a cacophony of crickets and wake up to a chorus of

birds. You're literally in the woods, alongside some of the winding WDW canals, and you feel a million miles from the rest of the WDW property and all its hubbub. Upstairs is the small (but modern) kitchen, with a breakfast bar; the living room (where the televison set and a sleep sofa are located); 2 bedrooms (each with a queen-size bed) and 2 bathrooms; the whole floor is surrounded by a deck where you can eat or just sit and look out into the trees. Downstairs, there's another bedroom with a double bed and a utility room equipped with a washer and dryer. The canals offer some of the World's best fishing, mainly for bass, and the roadways—shady, flat, and untrafficked as they are—are terrific for jogging. The nearest swimming pool is the new one at the treehouse area.

Grand Vista Suites: This quartet of ultraluxurious homes—originally designed as model homes for a development project that has been abandoned for the moment—are available for rent. Bed turndown service and daily newspaper deliveries are provided, refrigerators are stocked with staples when you arrive, and the furnishings are all first class. A golf cart and bicycles are included in the price of the suites. (For complete price information, see the chart "Rates at WDW-owned Properties" later on in this chapter.)

WHERE TO EAT: The villa complex does not have its own restaurant, but the Pompano Grill caters to guests staying in these accommodations. For breakfast, the options include the Pompano Grill or (for continental breakfasts only) the snack bar downstairs; at Pleasure Island, the *Empress Lilly* (where there's a character breakfast) and D-Zertz; at the Disney Village Marketplace, the pastry window at the Gourmet Pantry (which opens at 9:30 A.M.); or Chef Mickey's Village Restaurant. There are also abundant breakfast facilities at the nearby hotels in Disney Village Hotel Plaza. For lunch and dinner, the selections are even broader. (See *Good Meals, Great Times* for more details.)

Groceries: The Gourmet Pantry stocks staples of all sorts, as well as delicacies from around the globe, and good meat, poultry, and fresh green vegetables. Purchases can be delivered to your villa at no charge; if you can't be home to receive them, arrangements can be made for the delivery person to be let in so that perishables can be stashed in the refrigerator. It's also possible to order by phone. Touch "31" on your room telephone (before 1 P.M.), or dial 827-1100 when calling from someplace other than your villa. There is also a Gooding's supermarket located at the Crossroads of Lake Buena Vista shopping center, across the road from the Disney Village Hotel Plaza.

WHERE TO DRINK: For liquid refreshment, head for the Disney Village Marketplace—Cap'n Jack's Oyster Bar and the Village Lounge. At Pleasure Island is the lively Baton Rouge Lounge, aboard the *Empress Lilly* riverboat restaurant, or try Pleasure Island's newest clubs: Mannequins, the Neon Armadillo, XZFR Rockin' Rollerdrome, the Comedy Warehouse, or the Adventurers Club. (For details about these, see *Good Meals, Great Times* and *Everything Else in the World*.)

ROOM SERVICE: Room service is available at the villas of the Disney Village Resort. Touch "31" on your room telephone.

WHAT TO DO: In addition to boating, shopping, and fishing at the Disney Village Marketplace, and shopping and rollerskating at Pleasure Island (discussed in more detail in *Sports* and *Everything Else in the World*), you can also enjoy a variety of activities in and around the villas themselves.

Biking: The meandering, relatively untrafficked, and scenic roads around the Disney Village Resort, not to mention the 8 miles of bike paths there, can make for an enjoyable hour or 2 of pedaling. Two-wheelers are available for rent at the Villa Center. (See *Sports* for fees.)

Gameroom: Small arcades with electronic games and pinball machines are located at the two Villa Centers.

Golf: The par-72 Lake Buena Vista course plays from 5,315 to 6,763 yards, and is the shortest of the Disney courses; it's more like the Magnolia than the Palm, and doesn't have the latter's water hazards. There are practice tees and a driving range, and private lessons (with or without video replay) are available here as well; head pro Rina Ritson, the first woman golf pro ever to hold the top position at a major golf club, is a first class instructor. Good quality clubs and shoes can be rented at the Pro Shop. (For fees and starting information, see *Sports*.)

Swimming: There are 6 pools at the Disney Village Resort—2 near the one- and two-bedroom villas (one at the Villa Center, the other close to the shores of the Buena Vista Lagoon), the 3rd at the Village Clubhouse, the 4th and 5th on opposite sides of the lake at the mini suites, and the sixth at the Treehouses. Still, they're small; the best for swimming laps is at the Contemporary Resort.

Tennis: There are 3 courts, bordered by the woods and a section of the golf course, at the Village Clubhouse (open 8 A.M. to 10 P.M. daily; lit for play after dark). Racquets can be rented for a nominal fee; you must buy your own balls. (For fee information, see *Sports*.)

TRANSPORTATION: Buses go to Epcot Center, the Disney Village Marketplace, the Disney-MGM Studios Theme Park, and the Magic Kingdom. These circulate through the Villa areas, making pickups at bus stops located at regular intervals along the roadways; they arrive every 15 to 20 minutes.

Another option: A $30-a-day electric golf cart can get you from your villa to the Disney Village Marketplace or the Village Clubhouse. Or rent a bike. Either can be rented at the Villa Center.

WDW CONFERENCE CENTER

This sleek cedar creation is located on the banks of Club Lake at the Disney Village Resort. It was designed expressly with small- and medium-sized meetings and seminars in mind, and may be one of the most innovative structures of its type in existence. (Larger meetings are accommodated at the Contemporary Resort and the new Swan and Dolphin hotels. See individual hotel entries for details.) Four large rooms, each with its own light, sound, and projection systems, can be combined in a wide assortment of configurations, the largest comprising 6,500 square feet, to seat 505 theater-style.

Each of the rooms has big lakeview windows, sophisticated lighting (which, among other things, automatically turns up the room's lights when the sun goes behind a cloud), and rearview projection screens that can be supplemented by audiovisual equipment rented from Disney's own extensive equipment pool. In addition, technicians are available to record meetings, set up sound and lighting systems, and edit and splice film and tape. All rooms are extremely attractive; the chairs are comfortable enough for all-day sitting; and despite the fact that you're just a 15-minute ride from the Magic Kingdom, Epcot Center, and the Disney-MGM Studios Theme Park, the whole facility has a relaxed atmosphere.

ENTERTAINMENT: Meeting planners often choose one of several popular theme parties, each performed by an all-Disney cast. Anyone with a penchant for playing impresario (and the funds to pay the piper) can concoct a special affair with the aid of the vast WDW talent pool. Arrangements can be made for meeting guests to take advantage of just about everything in the WDW vacation inventory. Account managers can even set up tennis and golf tournaments. For information about WDW meetings and conventions, contact Walt Disney World Sales; Box 10000; Lake Buena Vista, FL 32830; 407-828-3200.

FORT WILDERNESS CAMPGROUND RESORT

The very existence of this 780-acre, canal-crossed expanse of cypress and pine, laced by pleasant blacktop roadways, always surprises visitors who come to WDW expecting to find the Magic Kingdom and nothing more. If they've heard about Fort Wilderness at all, they often confuse it with the park's Frontierland section.

But the Fort Wilderness atmosphere is relaxed and not at all frenetic. In one corner, a group of kids may be battling it out at tetherball, and on the playing fields there are often a couple of energetic touch football games in progress. In the mornings, the campground smells sweetly of dew-dampened pines, then of frying bacon. In the evening, the warmth and stillness of the afternoon give way to dinnertime bustle, and fish and steaks are thrown onto grills as next-door neighbors organize get-togethers. Later on, little clumps of teens and pre-teens gather alongside the trading posts or at Pioneer Hall, where the Fort Wilderness electronic-games-and-pinball arcade is located. Fort Wilderness also has a marina and a beach, a nature trail, and a number of waterways where fishing, canoeing, and paddleboating are popular; these and other recreational possibilities make Fort Wilderness one of the livelier places to be in WDW. A new expansion project has also added the Meadow Recreation Complex, located in the area behind the Meadow Trading Post. It features 2 lit tennis courts, a swimming pool, an arcade, and a snack bar.

You can enjoy the Fort Wilderness experience even if you don't have your own camping gear. Among the total of 1,190 campsites, there are 363 air conditioned Fleetwood Trailer Homes available for rent, complete with kitchen utensils, dishes, linens, color television wired for cable, daily maid service, and enough other amenities that the woods all around are the only reminders of the fact that you're camping out. The cost is comparable to that of some of the least expensive of the rooms at the resort hotels. (But those don't have kitchens and so don't offer the money-saving option of cooking some of your vacation meals "at home.")

The telephone number for the Fort Wilderness resort is 824-2900.

CAMPSITES: Fort Wilderness has 827 campsites, ranging in length from 25 to 65 feet, spaced throughout 21 camping loops. Some of them are set up for tent campers, and most of the rest are rented to trailer campers. Each site has a 110/220-volt electric outlet, barbecue grill, and picnic table. Most offer a sanitary-disposal hookup; all loops have at least one comfort station equipped with rest rooms, private showers, an ice machine, telephones, and a laundry room. The per-site fee allows for occupancy by up to 10 people.

The various campground areas are designated by numbers. The 100, 200, 300, 400, and 500 loops are the closest to the beach, the Settlement Trading Post, and Pioneer Hall. The 1500, 1600, 1700, 1800, 1900, 2000, and 2100 loops are farthest away from the beach and many other Fort Wilderness activities, but they are quieter and more private.

RENTAL TRAILER HOMES: It used to be that the 363 Fleetwood Trailers at Fort Wilderness were taken only by people who wanted hotel rooms and couldn't get a reservation. Now—mainly as a result of good word-of-mouth—almost every booking is specifically requested. Lodging here provides all the advantages of villa accommodations—with woodsy surroundings to boot.

There are 2 types of trailers. One model sleeps 4 adults and 2 children, with a bedroom at one end with a double bed and a bunk bed, plus a separate vanity area. There's a spacious living room with a pull-down bed and a paddle fan. The other trailers sleep 4, with a double bed in the bedroom and a sofa bed in the living room. Both types come equipped with pots and pans, dishes, and all the basic kitchen equipment, plus a color TV and a complete bathroom. The bathroom is not the sort of makeshift setup you might expect, but instead compares favorably to, say, a bathroom in a villa at the Disney Village Resort.

Note: No extra camping equipment is allowed on the site; all guests must be accommodated in the rental trailer. (For complete price information, see the chart "Rates at WDW-Owned Properties" later on in this chapter.)

WHERE TO EAT: Most people cook their own; groceries and supplies are available at the Meadow and Settlement Trading Posts (open from 8 A.M. to 10 P.M. in winter, to 11 P.M. in summer). Sandwiches, fruit, ice cream, and chips are available there for carry-out; you can eat them at your own site, on the beach, or at tables just outside River Country. A Gooding's supermarket is located at the Crossroads of Lake Buena Vista shopping center across from the Disney Village Hotel Plaza.

When you want to go out, there's the Trails End Buffet, an informal, log-walled, beam-ceilinged cafeteria inside Pioneer Hall, where home-style fare is served. Beer and sangría are also available. Crockett's Tavern, also inside Pioneer Hall, serves cocktails, unique appetizers, steaks, ribs, and chicken. A children's menu is available.

Snacks: Down on the shores of Bay Lake, the Beach Shack offers snacks and sodas.

Pizza: Served nightly at the Trails End Buffet inside Pioneer Hall from 9:30 P.M. to midnight, along with soft drinks, and beer.

WHERE TO DRINK: Full meals, beer, wine, and cocktails are served at Crockett's Tavern in Pioneer Hall. Snacks are also offered and there is nightly entertainment. If you have a car, make the short drive to the *Empress Lilly* riverboat restaurants or the many clubs at Pleasure Island or stop in at Cap'n Jack's or the Village Lounge at the Disney Village Marketplace.

FAMILY ENTERTAINMENT AFTER DARK: The Hoop-Dee-Doo Musical Revue is presented 3 times nightly at 5 P.M., 7:30 P.M., and 10 P.M.; reservations are required and are so hard to come by that they need to be made well in advance through the WDW Central Reservations Office (W-DISNEY—934-7639). Cancellations do occur, however. Fort Wilderness guests who can't get a reservation can have their names added to a waiting list by presenting themselves at the Pioneer Hall Ticket Window before the show.

There's also a nightly campfire program held at the center of the campground, near the Meadow Trading Post. A sing-along (featuring Chip 'n' Dale) and Disney movies and cartoons are the main goings-on (free). The Marshmallow Marsh Excursion (scheduled during the summer months), which begins at the campfire, includes more singing, a marshmallow roast, and a canoe excursion to a lakeside spot. From there, at 9:45 P.M., you can see the Electrical Water Pageant—a procession of waterborne floats, during which an assortment of sea creatures is outlined in a galaxy of tiny colored lights. This can also be viewed from the Fort Wilderness Beach; don't miss it. (For more details, see *Everything Else in the World* and *Good Meals, Great Times*.)

WHAT TO DO: There are more on-site activities at Fort Wilderness than at almost any other area in the World. There are 2 tennis courts in the area, but for golf it's necessary to travel to The Disney Inn or the Village Clubhouse.

There are 2 swimming pools and a 315-foot-long, 175-foot-wide beach for swimming in Bay Lake. You can rent tandems, Sting Rays, and other 2-wheelers at the Bike Barn for afternoon bicycle excursions or as reliable transportation around the campground. Visits to the Petting Farm and the horse barn near Fort Wilderness are amusing. Boating is popular; rentals are available at the marina. Canoes can be hired at the Bike Barn. Basketball, checkers, electric-cart rentals, fishing (on your own in the canals or on organized morning or afternoon angling excursions), horseback riding (on guided trail rides), horseshoes, jogging on the 2.3-mile exercise course, tetherball, volleyball, and waterskiing are also available. Or you can just go out for a stroll along the 1½-mile-long Wilderness Swamp Trail, near Marshmallow Marsh. All of these activities are described in detail in *Everything Else in the World* and *Sports*. There are two gamerooms: Davy Crockett's Arcade in Pioneer Hall and Daniel Boone's Arcade at the Meadow Trading Post.

River Country, a major attraction in its own right, with a separate admission charge, is also located at Fort Wilderness. The features of this watery playground—a WDW must, right along with the Magic Kingdom, Epcot Center, and the Disney-MGM Studios Theme Park—are discussed in detail in *Everything Else in the World*.

TRANSPORTATION: Trams and buses circulating at 7-minute intervals provide transportation within the campground, while buses and watercraft connect Fort Wilderness to the rest of the World. To get to the Contemporary Resort or the Magic Kingdom, watercraft (which have regular departures from the Fort Wilderness marina) provide the most efficient transportation during their operating hours. At other times, and to get to Disney Village Marketplace, take a bus from the Fort Wilderness bus stop, near the Settlement Trading Post and Pioneer Hall, to the Transportation and Ticket Center. This bus operates at regular intervals. Change to another bus for the Disney Village Marketplace, the Disney-MGM Studios Theme Park, and Epcot Center; the Monorail from the TTC to the Contemporary Resort or the Grand Floridian Resort; or a bus for the Polynesian Village and The Disney Inn.

PRACTICAL MATTERS

The Walt Disney World-owned hotels and villas have some important operating procedures that first-time guests don't always take seriously—much to their later dismay.

Deposit Requirements: Deposits equal to one night's lodging (or campsite rental) are required within 21 days of the time that a reservation is made. Personal checks, traveler's checks, cashier's checks, and money orders are acceptable forms of payment. To have deposit charges billed to an American Express, Visa, or MasterCard account, send your card number, its expiration date, the bank number (for Visa and MasterCard), and your signature. Deposits will be fully refunded if you cancel your reservation at least 48 hours before your scheduled arrival. Reservations are automatically cancelled if deposits are not received by the 21-day deadline. (Reservations booked less than 30 days prior to arrival will receive special instructions for deposits.)

Check-in and check-out times: While not unique in the Orlando area, the early check-out time (11 A.M. at all WDW lodging places) is almost invariably too early for most WDW guests, while the late check-in times (1 P.M. at the campsites, 3 P.M. in the resort hotels, 4 P.M. in the villas) are often painfully late. Even more frustrating is the fact that (except in slow seasons, when the Disney-owned hotels may not be entirely sold out from night to night), these are rules to which all the reservations clerks rigidly adhere. Desk clerks do try to accommodate a guest when possible, but it seldom is.

There is only limited storage space at the hotels, so when you try to check in and your room is not ready, store luggage in the trunk of your car, get your resort ID cards, and then head off to the Magic Kingdom, Epcot Center, or the Disney-MGM Studios Theme Park for the day.

Payment methods: Hotel bills may be paid with American Express, Visa, and MasterCard credit cards, with traveler's checks or cash, and with personal checks. Checks must bear the guest's name and address, be drawn on a U.S. bank, and be accompanied by proper identification—that is, a valid driver's license or a government-issued passport, and a major credit card such as American Express, Carte Blanche, Diners Club, MasterCard, or Visa.

ALL ABOUT WDW RESORT ID CARDS

Issued on arrival at WDW-owned resorts, these unprepossessing little squares of cardboard are among resort guests' most valuable possessions while in WDW. They entitle you to:

- Unlimited transportation by bus, monorail, and watercraft.
- Use of many of the roadways within Walt Disney World.
- Charge privileges: the cards may be used to cover purchases (up to certain account limits) in shops, lounge and restaurant charges, and recreational fees incurred anywhere in WDW—except the Magic Kingdom. At Epcot Center and the Disney-MGM Studios Theme Park, guests may use their IDs to charge meals at full-service restaurants.

Note: ID cards are valid for use of the transportation facilities through the end of the last day of your stay, but are not valid for charging past check-out time.

RATES AT WDW–OWNED PROPERTIES

CALL W-DISNEY (934-7639) FOR RESERVATIONS

	Charge for single or double occupancy		Room capacity	Types of beds	Check-out/ check-in times
	Season*	Off-season			
Contemporary Resort					
Rooms	$180 to	$160 to	5, plus 1 additional	2 queen beds. Some king	11 A.M./3 P.M.
Garden Wings	$205	$185	occupant under age 3	beds available	
Tower	$230	$210			
Suites	$230 to	$205 to	7 to 12	Most have 2 queen beds and	11 A.M./3 P.M.
	$710	$660		2 sleep sofas	

	Charge for single or double occupancy		Room capacity	Types of beds	Check-out/ check-in times
	Season*	Off-season			
Polynesian Village Resort					
Rooms	$190 to $245	$170 to $225	5, plus 1 additional occupant under age 3	2 queen beds, no cots available	11 A.M./3 P.M.
Suites	$550 to $590, all in Bali Hai longhouse	$510 to $550	4 to 6	King beds in bedroom and usually 2 queen sico beds in parlor	11 A.M./3 P.M.
Caribbean Beach Resort					
Rooms	$74 to $99	$69 to $95	4	2 double beds	11 A.M./3 P.M.
Grand Floridian Beach Resort					
Rooms Standard Concierge	$215 to $285 $330 to $335	$195 to $265 $310 to $335	4 to 5, plus 1 additional occupant under age 3	2 queen beds and 1 day bed	11 A.M./3 P.M.
Suites	$330 to $950	$310 to $950	4 to 8	King beds in bedroom and 1 or 2 day beds	11 A.M./3 P.M.
Disney Inn					
Rooms	$175 to $185	$155 to $165	5, plus 1 additional occupant under age 3	2 queen beds and a sleep sofa in all rooms; no king beds available	11 A.M./3 P.M.
Suites	$465	$420	Up to 7	2 queen beds and 2 sleep sofas; not cots available	11 A.M./3 P.M.
Disney Village Resort					
Club suite	$175	$150	5, plus 1 additional occupant under age 3	2 queen beds and a double sleep sofa	11 A.M./4 P.M.
Deluxe suite	$255	$230	6	2 queen beds upstairs; 1 sleep sofa downstairs	11 A.M./4 P.M.
One-bedroom villas	$225	$200	4, plus 1 additional occupant under age 3	1 king bed in bedroom; queen sleep sofa in living room	11 A.M./4 P.M.
with study	$245	$220	5 plus 1 additional occupant under age 3	1 king bed in bedroom, queen sleep sofa in living room, queen sleep sofa in study	11 A.M./4 P.M.
Two-bedroom Villas	$275 to $305	$250 to $280	6 to 8, plus 1 additional occupant under age 12	1 queen bed in 1 bedroom; 2 double beds (or another queen) in the other, 1 double sleep sofa in living room; or king bed (or 2 twins) in each bedroom, queen sleep sofa in living room	11 A.M./4 P.M.
with study	$295	$270	6	1 queen bed in each bedroom, plus sleep sofa in living room	11 A.M./4 P.M.
Grand Vista Suites	$775 to $850	$725 to $800	8	3 kings; 2 queens and 2 twins; or 1 king and 2 queens	11 A.M./4 P.M.
Fort Wilderness Mobile Homes	$165	$155	6	1 double bed in bedroom; and bunk beds in bedroom	11 A.M./3 P.M.

Campsites: Preferred loops 100, 200, 300, 400, and 500 with full hookups ($46 per night; $41 off-season); all other loops with full hookups ($40 per night; $35 off-season). Sites without hookups are $34; $29 off-season. Check-out is at 11 A.M., check-in at 1 P.M.

* Season refers to: December 20, 1989 through January 1, 1990; February 11, 1990 through April 28, 1990; and June 9, 1990 through August 18, 1990. All other dates are considered off-season, however, this designation in no way reflects park attendance.

The prices listed here were correct at presstime, but the rates have changed as many as three times in a single year, so be sure to double-check with the hotels before finally setting your vacation budget.

DISNEY VILLAGE

The 7 hotels here—Grosvenor Resort, Travelodge, Royal Plaza, Howard Johnson, Buena Vista Palace, Pickett Suite Resort, and the Hilton—occupy a unique position among non-Disney-owned Orlando-area accommodations. They are designated as "official" hotels and are actually located inside the boundaries of Walt Disney World, which makes them more convenient than hostelries located quite a distance away. Their guests enjoy certain privileges similar to those of guests at WDW-owned properties such as bus transportation directly to the TTC, to Epcot Center, and to the Disney-MGM Studios Theme Park, and the opportunity to make reservations for dinner shows before bookings are accepted from the general public. Guests can also use the tennis and golf facilities at the Village Clubhouse. WDW Central Reservations (W-DISNEY—934-7639) can take your bookings for Disney Village Hotel Plaza hotels (they're also included in several Walt Disney Travel Co. and Delta Air Lines packages), and most of these hotels have toll-free numbers that can be called at no charge.

GROSVENOR RESORT: The former Americana Dutch Resort has undergone an $8 million facelift, and changed its name. The renovation project has added 20 rooms (for a total of 629) and seen the refurbishing of all guestrooms, restaurants, public areas, and shops. Rooms are located in a white 19-story tower and 2 wings. The decor has been changed from the Dutch to British Colonial, with pale greens, peaches, and pinks evoking a Caribbean feel. Each room has a VCR and a refrigerator-bar. Current movies are available for rent at the guest services desk. Restaurants include Baskerville's, highlighted by a Sherlock Holmes museum, which serves breakfast, lunch, and dinner, with buffets available at breakfast and dinner. There's entertainment at Moriarity's Pub, and in the lobby, at Crumpets and Crickets, continental breakfasts, snacks, and lighter fare are available all day. Two lit tennis courts, raquetball and shuffleboard courts, a basketball court, 2 heated pools, a playground, and a gameroom are also available. The 13,000 square feet of meeting space here can accommodate up to

HOTEL PLAZA

1,200 people for meetings or banquets. Additional conference rooms of varying sizes, a reception center, and a board room are ideal for break-out sessions and seminars. The hotel's sales and convention staff can arrange for all necessary audiovisual equipment as well as for food and entertainment. Rates range from $95 to $155 for 2, year-round ($10 for cots). There are currently no rooms specially equipped for handicapped travelers. Details: Grosvenor Resort; 1850 Hotel Plaza Blvd.; Lake Buena Vista, FL 32830; 828-4444 (800-624-4109).

TRAVELODGE: This tri-arc hotel-tower has 325 spacious rooms and suites. All rooms were recently redecorated and have either one king or 2 queen-size beds, color TV, AM/FM radio, and private balconies offering very pretty views of Walt Disney World Village. The gameroom, pool, and playground are appreciated by youngsters. The Palm Grill serves a hearty buffet breakfast, lunch, and dinner. Calypso's Palm Terrace serves breakfast, lunch, and afternoon tea, and Chez Doughnut offers fresh donuts, pizza, croissant sandwiches, and other light snacks for breakfast, lunch, and dinner. The Club Calypso nightclub on the 18th floor offers a panoramic view of Walt Disney World. Small meetings can be accommodated in the 2,044 square feet of meeting space. Poolside receptions can be arranged for up to 150 people, and all audiovisual equipment and themed parties can be handled by the Travelodge sales staff. Rates are $119 low season (the months of January and September), $149 the rest of the year (no additional charge for children under 17 sharing parents' room; $10 for

rollaways). There are 6 rooms for handicapped travelers. Details: Travelodge; 2000 Hotel Plaza Blvd.; Box 22205; Lake Buena Vista, FL 32830; 828-2424 (800-348-3765).

ROYAL PLAZA: Offers 396 rooms in a 17-story high rise and 2-story garden-style wings. Each room has its own balcony or patio and safe deposit box. There are also 10 suites available, including two celebrity suites, the Burt Reynolds and the Barbara Mandrell. For on-site recreation, there's a heated pool, a children's pool, a spa, a gameroom, shuffleboard courts, putting green, 4 tennis courts, a tanning salon, and men's and women's saunas.

Dining includes El Cid Steak and Seafood House, specializing in continental cuisine, and the Knight's Table Coffee Shop. There are two lounges—La Cantina, serving pizza and chicken wings along with cocktails; and the Giraffe, a popular spot that features top-40 live entertainment and attracts an energetic young local crowd (many of them Disney employees). A barbershop, beauty salon, a 1-day film-developing service, and a video camera rental kiosk are also available on the premises. The Royal Plaza specializes in smaller meetings of fewer than 300 people. There's 12,000 square feet of space in 12 flexible meeting rooms, plus additional hospitality suites. Special events at the Magic Kingdom, Epcot Center, and the Disney-MGM Studios Theme Park can be arranged, and other Disney-related entertainment is available. "Superior" rooms on the hotel's lower floors run $115 per night; "premium" rooms with preferred views cost $127; "deluxe" poolside and tower rooms are $170. Room rates

Rates range from $85 to $165 year-round (no additional charge for children under 18; $8 for cots). Details: Howard Johnson; Box 22204; 1805 Hotel Plaza Blvd.; Lake Buena Vista, FL 32830; 828-8888 (800-654-2000).

BUENA VISTA PALACE: This is the largest of the Disney Village Hotel Plaza properties. It's actually a cluster of towers (one of them is 27 stories) boasting mirrored, multi-faceted facades, and a contemporary interior. Every one of the 841 rooms (including suites) has its own private patio or balcony, ceiling fan, air conditioning, and remote-control color TV. There are 78 Crown Level concierge rooms which include special services and amenities. Most rooms and suites provide a glimpse of Epcot Center's Spaceship Earth. Each has at least 2 telephones— 1 in the bathroom and a push-button Mickey Mouse telephone at bedside. Three guest rooms have hot tubs. There are 2 swimming pools, a kiddie pool, a health spa, 4 tennis courts, and a huge gameroom. Kid Stuff is an organized recreational program for children ages 5 to 17. The hotel also features 24-hour room service, Disney-run gift and sundry shops, and a self-service laundry. Aida Grey of

apply for up to 4 in a room using existing beds. There are 10 rooms specially equipped for handicapped travelers. Details: Royal Plaza; 1905 Hotel Plaza Blvd.; Lake Buena Vista, FL 32830; 828-2828 (800-248-7890).

HOWARD JOHNSON: Newly renovated, this 14-story establishment features 323 redecorated guestrooms located in a 14-story tower and a 6-story annex building. Tower rooms surround a plant-filled atrium and are reached by glass-walled elevators. There are 2 heated pools, one designed for toddlers; a playground, and a gameroom. The Howard Johnson restaurant on the premises was enlarged and renovated and is open around the clock. The newly refurbished conference center with 2,304 square feet of meeting space can accommodate up to 250 people. Meeting rooms overlook an indoor waterfall and breakout rooms and exhibit space are available. A deluxe board room is geared for meetings of 10 to 20 people. The sales staff will customize a menu, provide audiovisual equipment, arrange exclusive "Behind the Scenes" seminars, and set up entertainment and appearances by the Disney characters. Five special rooms are equipped with wider doors and grab rails for handicapped guests. Non-smoking rooms are also available.

Beverly Hills operates a fine beauty salon for men and women.

Eating spots include the Watercress Cafe and Bake Shop, the hotel's water's-edge restaurant (open 24 hours); Arthur's 27, an elegant rooftop dining room, recently won its third consecutive Golden Spoon award as one of Florida's 12 best, offers an ambitious menu; Arthur's Wine Cellar in the Sky stocks 800 bottles and features a private dining room (reservations essential); and The Outback Restaurant, which is accessible via a glass-enclosed private elevator. The adjacent Laughing Kookaburra Goodtime Bar offers live entertainment and 99 brands of beer from around the world. Unfortunately, noise from these restaurants tends to flow through the atriums and penetrate the solid oak doors, so if serenity and silence matter to you, choose accommodations in either the 5-story tower or the 27-story tower, neither of which has an atrium. This large convention facility has more than 83,000 square feet of meeting space, including a recent 23,000-square-foot expansion. There are 33 meeting rooms, 45 suites, 13 hospitality suites, and 9 breakout rooms. The Conference/Exhibition Hall offers 23,000 square feet of exhibit space; the Empire Ballroom, 18,125 square feet; and the Great Hall, 16,530 square feet. A special entrance and check-in facilities are available for convention guests, and a staff of professional meeting coordinators, banquet managers, and caterers is on hand to help plan any function. Disney-theme entertainment can also be arranged. Rooms range from $119 to $210 per night (no charge for additional persons using existing beds). Six rooms are equipped for handicapped guests. Details: Buena Vista Palace; 1900 Buena Vista Dr.; Lake Buena Vista, FL 32830; 827-2727 (800-327-2990; from Florida, 800-432-2920).

HILTON: Located directly across the street from the Disney Village Marketplace, this hotel features a state-of-the-art digital telephone system that adjusts air conditioning, controls the television set, and contacts the valet, room service, and operators with just the touch of a key. The 813 rooms are tastefully decorated in mauve, peach, and earth-tone color schemes. The hotel is set on 23 acres and features 4 restaurants and 2 lounges. The American Vineyards offers American regional cuisine; County Fair serves breakfast, lunch, and dinner; and the Rum Largo Pool Bar and Cafe offers hamburgers, salads, sandwiches, and tropical drinks. A branch of the Benihana Japanese Steakhouses opened recently. Recreational activities include 2 lit tennis courts and 2 swimming pools. Guests traveling with children will appreciate the Youth Hotel, a hotel-within-a-hotel that has been designed to accommodate children from 4 to 12 years of age. There is a video room and play area, as well as scheduled recreational activities supervised by a trained staff. The Hilton also provides a separate entrance for convention and meeting guests. A total of 51,000 square feet of space is available. The facilities are

very flexible and can accommodate up to 2,100 people. There are 21 meeting rooms, and the two ballrooms measure 11,850 square feet. Special Disney-related functions can be arranged. Rates range from $130 to $225, with the higher prices prevailing for rooms on the higher floors. There are 49 rooms designed for handicapped travelers. Details: Hilton at Walt Disney World Village; Box 22781; 1751 Hotel Plaza Blvd.; Lake Buena Vista, FL 32830; 827-4000 or 800-728-4414.

PICKETT SUITE: The newest Hotel Plaza establishment is WDW's only all-suite hotel. The 7-story structure contains 229 suites (including 12 designed for handicapped travelers), each of which measures 600 square feet and has a living room and a separate bedroom. Each suite can sleep up to 6 people, and a complimentary full breakfast is included in the price of the suite. Other amenities include 2 remote-control color television sets, plus a small TV in the bathroom, a wet bar, a stocked refrigerator, a coffeemaker, and an optional microwave oven. Recreational facilities include a heated pool with a whirlpool, a pool bar, a gameroom, a children's play area, and an exercise room. There's one restaurant, the Parrot Patch, where diners can enjoy meals indoors or outdoors on a terrace. A 2-story tropical bird aviary adds to the atmosphere. There's also an ice cream parlor and a snack bar by the pool. There is one meeting room here which can accommodate from 10 to 60 people, and is ideal for small business get-togethers, board meetings, or seminars. Though the facility is small, all services, from audio-visual equipment to themed entertainment, can be arranged. Rates run from $145 to $225. Details: Pickett Suite: 2305 Hotel Plaza Blvd.; Lake Buena Vista, FL 32830; 934-1000 (800-742-5388).

Two new waterfront hotels, the Walt Disney World Swan, operated by Westin, and the Walt Disney World Dolphin, operated by Sheraton, will comprise the Southeast's largest convention-resort complex when complete. (The Swan opened late in the fall 1989 and the Dolphin is slated to open during the summer of 1990.) Situated between Epcot Center and the Disney-MGM Studios Theme Park, these properties were both designed by architect Michael Graves in a style that is being described as "entertainment architecture."

Convenient Disney-operated transportation connects the hotels to Epcot Center via a new entrance at the France pavilion in World Showcase. Guests can walk in, take a boat across Crescent Lake, or ride a tram. The Disney-MGM Studios Theme Park is within walking distance, or can be reached by a tram or launch from either the Swan or the Dolphin. Buses make the trip to the Magic Kingdom, River Country, Pleasure Island, the Disney Village Marketplace, and Typhoon Lagoon. The two hotels are connected by a landscaped, covered causeway.

WALT DISNEY WORLD SWAN

The exterior of this 758-room hotel is painted a sun-washed coral beneath rolling waves of turquoise. The 758 guestrooms are encased in a striking 12-story main building and two 7-story wings. And just in case the shape and color of the buildings weren't distinctive enough, two 45-foot swan statues sit atop the resort at either end of the main building. By the way, the statues each weigh about 28,000 pounds, and it took a 400-ton crane to set them in their new home.

Guestrooms feature in-room safes, clock radios, multi-channel cable television, voice mail telemessaging, mini-bars, separate dressing areas, hair dryers, bathrobes, daily newspaper delivery, and 24-hour room service. There are 64 suites and 45 concierge rooms on the 11th and 12th floors.

The Swan has a large pool and a white sandy beach. A health club, gameroom, and 8 lit tennis courts round out the on-site recreational activities. Camp Swan, a hotel for children ages 4 to 12, offers supervised activities including food and entertainment. There is a beauty salon and several shops.

Dining opportunities include Palio, a Mediterranean-themed establishment open for breakfast and dinner; Garden Grove Cafe, set in a two-story, circular greenhouse, serves lunch and dinner; and Splash Grill, a poolside cafe, offers breakfast, lunch, and dinner. Kimonos and the Lobby Court Lounge are the hotel's cocktail spots.

There are 54,300 square feet of meeting space, including the 23,064-square-foot Swan Ballroom. A total of 31 meeting and breakout rooms are also available, as are seven hospitality suites and a spacious and elegant boardroom. The hotel can provide all necessary audiovisual equipment, and convention planners have access to all the areas and attractions at Walt Disney World. Special parties and recreational outings can be arranged. Details: Walt Disney World Swan; 1200 Epcot Resort Blvd.; Lake Buena Vista, FL 32830; 934-3000. Reservations can also be made through the Central Reservations Office: W-DISNEY (934-7639).

WALT DISNEY WORLD DOLPHIN

A 27-story triangular tower rises from a 14-story main building, a part of the hotel's design that was recently honored by *Progressive Architecture* magazine. There are also four guestroom wings, nine stories each, that stretch out to the shores of Crescent Lake. Not to be outdone by its Swan neighbor, two 55-foot-tall dolphin statues sit atop the main

A lush, tropical setting is being created with landscaping, fountains, and small lakes. A dramatic waterfall cascades down the face of the triangle into a series of seashells and on into a large shell-shaped pool supported by smaller Dolphin statues. The hotel's seven restaurants are located around the pool overlooking Crescent Lake. Restaurants include Coral Cafe, featuring all-day international menus; Ristorante Carnivale, a trattoria; the Safari Grille, a steak and seafood spot; the Dolphin Fountain, featuring specialty ice cream; and an oriental restaurant and a 1950s-style cafeteria. There are also two lounges and a nightclub.

There are 1,509 rooms in all, including 140 suites. The 12th through 18th floors of the tower are designated as concierge floors. There are two pools and a themed swimming grotto, a white sand beach, eight tennis courts, a health club, a gameroom, shops, Camp Dolphin (a full-service facility for younger guests), and a beauty salon. Delta Air Lines and National Car Rental will maintain reservation desks in the Dolphin lobby.

The enormous conference center has its own entrance and is also accessible from the hotel lobby. There is a total of 202,295 square feet of meeting space. The 55,903-square-foot Hemisphere Ballroom is the largest hotel ballroom in Florida. There are also 28 meeting rooms, a boardroom, a 51,275-square-foot exhibit hall, and other, smaller conference spaces available. The Dolphin's convention staff can provide all necessary audiovisual equipment and access to the entire Walt Disney World attraction inventory. Special parties, receptions, recreational outings, and golf and tennis tournaments can be arranged. Details: Walt Disney World Dolphin; 1500 Epcot Resort Blvd.; Lake Buena Vista, FL 32830; 934-4000. Reservations can also be made through the Central Reservations Office: W-DISNEY (934-7639).

U.S.-192 ACCOMMODATIONS

The motels along this 4-lane divided highway (this stretch of 192 was recently renamed Irlo Bronson Memorial Highway), which intersects I-4 in the community of Kissimmee, are closer to the WDW main gate than those along Orlando's International Drive, but the area itself is far less attractive and lacks International Drive's abundance of eating places. Still, the accommodations here can't be faulted for convenience, and on stays of short duration, that may be a consideration.

HOLIDAY INN–MAIN GATE EAST: Situated 3 miles from the WDW main gate, this 670-room property is not the most attractive of the local inns, yet it can easily be counted among the best-looking in its price range—about $63 to $84, depending on the season—and there are "king leisure" rooms featuring king-size beds and sleep sofas. The facilities are somewhat broader than those you usually get for that kind of money. For instance, there are 2 lit tennis courts, and in a somewhat perfunctorily landscaped courtyard at the center of each of the squares where the rooms are located, there are 2 Olympic-size swimming pools, a kiddie pool, and 2 Jacuzzis. There's a children's program, "Only for Kids," that includes a theater (open to youngsters 4'10" and under); grown-ups can park kids there and eat elsewhere in the hotel in peace. The children's clubhouse offers movies and other activities. Specialty drinks in the Mason Jar Restaurant and at the pool bar are served in Mason jars that you can keep. Three rooms are equipped for handicapped travelers. Details: Holiday Inn–Main Gate East; 5678 Irlo Bronson Memorial Highway; Kissimmee, FL 32741; 396-4488 (800-HOLIDAY).

HYATT ORLANDO: The closest non-Disney-owned resort to the WDW main gate is this large hotel, with some 924 rooms grouped in 4 clusters of buildings so complexly arranged that it takes some people a couple of days to find their way around. Each guestroom has a color TV, AM/FM radio, and in-room movie capacity. And there are 3 tennis courts and a 1.3-mile jogging-and-exercise trail right on the property. The gameroom here stands out, even in a town full of terrific competitors. Each of the 4 clusters has its own medium-sized heated swimming pool and spa and an innovative playground. There are also several restaurants—Limey Jim's offers a continental-style menu; the Palm Terrace is a kosher restaurant that is operated by the local Orthodox Union; The Summerhouse is a full service coffee shop open from 6:30 A.M. to 11 P.M.; the Market Place bills itself as a "gourmet deli"; and the Trellis Lounge serves snacks, and features entertainment every night but Sundays. Shuttle service to

WDW is available for a small fee. Room rates are high: $115 for standard rooms, $125 for superior rooms, and $139 for deluxe rooms; suites range from $180 to $470. Facilities for handicapped travelers are available. Details: Hyatt Orlando; 6375 West Irlo Bronson Memorial Highway; Kissimmee, FL 32741; 396-1234 (800-228-9000).

KING'S MOTEL: There are a handful of nonchain establishments on U.S. 192 as you head toward downtown Kissimmee and away from Walt Disney World. This 104-room establishment is among the better ones. Its small rectangular pool sits on the shore of a lake, and boats can be rented at the motel office (or you can fish from the dock). In addition to standard motel rooms, efficiencies accommodating 4 and 6 also are available. Many units have lake views. Rates are reasonable: $40 to $50. Two rooms are designed for handicapped travelers. Details: King's Motel; 4836 West Irlo Bronson Memorial Highway; Kissimmee, FL 32741; 396-4762 (800-327-9071; 800-432-9928 from Florida; 800-874-6715 from Canada).

KNIGHT'S INN: The royal purple, crushed-velvet bedspreads of this establishment (down the road from the Holiday Inn–Main Gate East) may take

are 4 tennis courts and a good miniature golf course as well. Restaurants include The Greenhouse, for buffet breakfast and dinner; the Sunset Grill, which serves dinner only; the Corner Market, a deli open from 7 A.M. to midnight; The Lamplighter, a quiet, candlelit dining spot; and Hurrican Sam's Lounge. The cost, about $63 to $89 per couple (no charge for children under 10), is lower than at the Hyatt Orlando and the WDW hotels, and there are enough amenities to make this a fairly good deal. Wide doors and ramps make most of the hotel accessible to wheelchair-bound travelers. Details: Sheraton-Lakeside Inn; 7711 West Irlo Bronson Memorial Highway; Kissimmee, FL 32741; 828-8250 (800-325-3535).

some getting used to, but this small hostelry offers an excellent choice of rooms—standard 2 double-bed ones; efficiency apartments (fitted out with a bed, a sofa bed, and a completely furnished kitchen); and 2 royal rooms (equipped with just one bed and a sofa). Both smoking and nonsmoking units are available in double rooms. The pool is small, but everything is on one story, and you can park right outside your door. Rates are about $50 for 2 (no charge for children under 18 sharing their parents' room). Details: Knight's Inn; 2880 Poinciana Blvd.; Kissimmee, FL 32741; 396-8186.

RAMADA RESORT MAIN GATE: Attractive landscaping makes this 400-room establishment, just west of I-4, another very pleasant spot. There are 2 medium-size, heated swimming pools—rectangular to make for good lap swimming; plus a pair of lit tennis courts; a gameroom; and a restaurant—the Cafe Terrace, where family-style breakfasts and dinners are served daily. The Mayan Lounge serves cocktails and specialty drinks. Rates are about $55 to $90, depending on the season; rates for the hotel's 10 suites are $220 to $360. The hotel has 2 rooms for the handicapped. Details: Ramada Resort Main Gate; 2950 Reedy Creek Blvd.; 5820 Irlo Bronson Memorial Highway; Kissimmee, FL 32741; 396-4466.

SHERATON–LAKESIDE INN: One of a pair of fancy resorts on U.S. 192, the Sheraton-Lakeside, located west of I-4 (not far from the Ramada Resort Hotel), has 651 rooms arranged in several buildings around 2 good-size trapezoidal swimming pools and along the shores of Black Lake, where guests go paddle boating (though swimming is not permitted). Playgrounds are located poolside, and there

CAMPING OUTSIDE WALT DISNEY WORLD

The lush, cypress-hung woods of WDW's Fort Wilderness are not duplicated at any other Orlando-area campground. But not everyone can get a reservation at Fort Wilderness, and in any case, not everyone wants to spend the money. If you fall into one of these groups, consider some of the other local campgrounds. Most offer planned activities, swimming pools, hot showers, and other amenities.

PORT O' CALL RV RESORT: This campground is big, with some 488 sites, and it has an expansive list of activities and facilities: fishing, shuffleboard, a playground, a gameroom, a laundry, evening entertainment, and a large heated swimming pool, very much like the one at WDW's own Polynesian Village. And you can't beat the location, just 4 miles east of the main gates. But there's not much shade. Rates are about $21 for 2 adults and children under 12 the year round, $2 per additional adult per night, including all hookups. Tenters are welcome. Details: Port O' Call; 5195 Irlo Bronson Memorial Highway; Kissimmee, FL 32741; 396-0110 (800-327-9120, or 800-432-0766 from Florida).

YOGI BEAR'S JELLYSTONE PARK CAMPGROUNDS: There are 3 Yogi Bear campground locations in the WDW area: 8555 West Irlo Bronson Memorial Highway; Kissimmee, FL 32741 (396-1311; 800-327-7115); 9200 Turkey Lake Rd.; Orlando, FL 32819 (351-4394; 800-327-7115); and 3000 South Clarcona Rd.; Apopka, FL 32703 (889-3048; 800-634-1694). The 3 sites offer similar facilities including a swimming pool and a mini golf course. Rates are $15 for tents without hookups; $19 for electric; and $20 for full hookups.

FLORIDA CENTER ACCOMMODATIONS

This area, 10 miles north of the WDW main gates—a 30-minute drive—is the best developed of the several areas where guests not staying in WDW-owned properties usually lodge. It comprises Sand Lake Road (S.R. 528A), which intersects I-4 and runs eastward to the airport; International Drive, the sidewalk-bordered boulevard that runs roughly northward off Sand Lake Road; and Kirkman Road (S.R. 435), which also heads north off Sand Lake Road.

The densest concentration of lodging and eating places is on International Drive. Most of the best-known motel chains are represented here, and many restaurant chains also have branches: Arby's, Baskin Robbins, Burger King, Cork and Cleaver, Denny's, Dino's Pizza, International House of Pancakes, Long John Silver's, McDonald's, Perkins Cake and Steak, Pizza Inn, Pizza Hut, Steak and Ale, Wendy's, and Western Sizzlin' among them. Bennigan's, a somewhat tonier chain, also has a restaurant here.

Most of the facilities on Sand Lake and Kirkman roads are clustered close to their intersections with International Drive. The city's more interesting restaurants are too far away to reach on foot, however, and the cost of shuttle transportation for a family of 4 is so close to that of renting a car that it seems pointless not to do so.

It's also worth noting that the distance to the WDW main gates from here (you have to figure an hour from Main Street to your hotel swimming pool) is such that leaving the Magic Kingdom for a rest at your hotel—a good idea, especially in the heat of summer—is not always practical unless the park is open late and you can muster the energy to go early, stay for a few hours, and then return after dinner to savor the nighttime delights of the park for a few hours more. This takes stamina; young children may not always have it. The traffic along International Drive tends to be very heavy all day, so be sure to add an extra 15 minutes to any schedule.

The area is, however, one of the livelier places to lodge outside WDW. Florida Center is also relatively accessible to downtown Orlando (10 to 15 minutes' drive away), and Winter Park (about 20 minutes from parking space to parking space), where there are more than a dozen interesting little shops and nearly as many intriguing restaurants, including one of the most pleasant ice cream parlors around.

A selection of some of the more attractive properties (in a variety of price ranges) follows.

DELTA COURT OF FLAGS: This lively, 800-room establishment in the Kirkman Road area of Florida Center has facilities for meetings of up to a thousand people, but the family trade wasn't forgotten either, and the place is as bright and cheery and appealing as any in the area, especially considering the price. Rooms are arranged in four 4-story buildings. There are 3 swimming pools—2 small round ones and another that is shamrock-shaped (but large enough for swimming laps); and they all have plenty of palm trees and chairs. There are 2 tennis courts nearby that are lit for night play. A recent renovation has added 2 kiddie pools, 3 hot tubs, 2 saunas, a new lobby, a full-service restaurant, the Center Court Cafe, and Mango's, which serves breakfast and dinner. Hollywood Nites, a dance club, and Wally's Kid's Club, a children's center round out the offerings. The somewhat secluded location, inside a complex of hotels where the roads are little used, off busy Kirkman Road, makes for good (if unshaded) jogging. The children's playground is nothing out of the ordinary. Doubles cost $64 to $82, depending on the location (no additional

charge for children under 18; $10 per cot). This is a little more than the neighboring Caravan Resort Inn and considerably less than the Sheraton-Twin Towers complex nearby (which does a big convention business)—but a better choice than either. (The Howard Johnson, the fourth in the Kirkman Road quartet, has some rooms that are less expensive than any offered at the Court of Flags, and if price is a prime consideration, it is your best bet.) Pet owners can bring small animals inside. Details: Delta Court of Flags Hotel; 5715 Major Blvd.; Orlando, FL 32819; 351-3340 (800-268-1133).

DAYS INN-LAKESIDE: In all, there are 21 Days Inns in the Orlando area, and they have played host to more WDW guests than any other chain because they provide especially good value for a traveler's lodging dollar. Facilities include swimming pools and, sometimes, gamerooms; other economical attractions are a "kids eat free" plan where youngsters 12 and under dine free when accompanied by a registered adult guest. The 691-room complex on Sand Lake Road, one of the largest of the chain, is located on the shores of Spring Lake, and the view from many of the rooms is particularly attractive. There are 3 swimming pools here, plus laundry facilities, 3 playgrounds, and a restaurant-and-cafeteria. Room rates are currently $70 during peak seasons and drop to $40 during the off-season ($6 extra per additional occupant over 18). Single rates, which cost $6 less, are even more economical. There are no special facilities for the handicapped. Details: Days Inn; 7335 Sand Lake Rd.; Orlando, FL 32819; 351-1900 (800-325-2525).

PEABODY ORLANDO: The only sister property to the famed Peabody hotel in Memphis, this imposing 27-story, 891-room hostelry is International Drive's most luxurious establishment. Facilities include an Olympic-size pool, 4 lit tennis courts, a health club, a fitness trail, a gameroom, and aerobics classes. There's also a children's hotel on the pool level where adult supervision is provided for the pool, gameroom, and reading room. Then there are the famous Peabody ducks, which every morning at 11 A.M. waddle from a private elevator into the enormous lobby, down the red carpet, then settle into a marble fountain—a spectacle that continues to attract hotel guests and locals. Dux (where no duck is served) is the hotel's signature restaurant. There's also Capriccio, an Italian trattoria and pizzeria; and the B-Line Diner, a casual dining room done in stainless steel and glass. The meeting facilities are vast. The property has 54,000 square feet of meeting space. The main ballroom is 26,680 square feet and can seat 3,200 auditorium style or 2,850 banquet style. There are also 2 junior ballrooms of 8,687 square feet and 8,378 square feet respectively, and there are 32 meeting rooms in all. Meetings for small groups can also be accommodated. Audiovisual equipment and stenographic, carpentry, and security services are also available. Rates run $145 to $185; $325 to $1,200 for suites. There are 27 rooms designed for handicapped travelers. Details: Peabody Orlando; 9801 International Drive; Orlando, Fl 32819; 352-4000 (800-732-2639).

QUALITY INN INTERNATIONAL: Next to Morrison's Cafeteria, this 728-room property is extremely pleasant, if not fancy. Quite well-kept rooms are in 2-story structures flanking the reception building, with the newest rooms located in two 6-story additions. Two Y-shaped pools are perfect for a few laps. And there's also a gameroom. There's good value here: rates are about $40 to $49 for 2 during the summer and over the Christmas holidays, $29 to $49 from September until mid-December. Some facilities for the handicapped are available. Details: Quality Inn International; 7600 International Dr.; Orlando, FL 32819; 351-1600 (800-228-5151).

SHERATON WORLD: Particularly attractive and situated off by itself, well south of Sand Lake Road and just a stroll from Sea World, this 800-room establishment has 3 good-size swimming pools, 2 children's pools, a gameroom, 5 lit tennis courts, a fitness center, and a miniature golf course. The surrounding area is ideal for early-morning jogging. There are 42 rooms suitable for the handicapped. Rates are reasonable: $85 to $120 (no charge for youngsters under 18 when accompanied by an adult). Details: Sheraton World; 10100 International Dr.; Orlando, FL 32821; 352-1100 (800-325-3535).

ORLANDO MARRIOTT HOTEL: Located at the corner of Sand Lake Road and International Drive, near the exit to I-4, this is one of the choicest of the lodging spots outside the World. It's not cheap—the appeal is primarily to businessmen and vacationers willing to pay for WDW-level accommodations but unable to get a reservation—though there is value here. The Marriott has 3 outdoor pools—one quite large and dogleg-shaped, another barbell-shaped and relatively small, and the third, Olympic-size—near the 4 lit tennis courts. The 1,078 smartly decorated guestrooms are arranged in some 16 two-story, cream-colored, stucco-walled "villas" scattered around grounds that are handsomely landscaped with ferns, palms, and other kinds of tropical vegetation. (You'll even find some lagoons, canals, and waterfalls.) Rooms can be opened up to form spacious quarters with 1 or 2 bedrooms, living room (or third bedroom), 2 or 3 baths, and a kitchenette. Rates are $102 to $110 for doubles. Suites are $200 to $450. Two rooms for the handicapped are available. Details: Orlando Marriott Hotel; 8001 International Dr.; Orlando, FL 32819; 351-2420 (800-228-9290).

HILTON INN FLORIDA CENTER: Comparable to the Marriott (described above), this 398-room establishment has a restaurant and a deli, 2 large swimming pools (one of them Olympic-size and under an open-air pavilion), a well-kept (but hardly huge) gameroom with about a dozen machines, and a large convention center. This means a certain amount of hubbub that may not appeal to all family vacationers, but the hotel itself is quite pleasant. Rates are $54 to $104. No charge for up to 3 children, regardless of age, sharing accommodations with parents. Cribs and rollaway beds are free, and there are a few rooms designed for handicapped travelers. Details: Hilton Inn Florida Center; 7400 International Dr.; Orlando, FL 32819; 351-4600 (800-327-1363; from Florida, 800-332-4600).

HOLIDAY INN-INTERNATIONAL DRIVE: This 654-room property's 13 tropically landscaped acres are occupied by 6 buildings—a 14-story tower, a 5-story annex, and 4 other buildings 2 stories high. There is a free-form pool (with a landscaped island in the center), a playground, an excellent gameroom that looks appropriately Space Age, and shuffleboard and volleyball courts. There are 2 restaurants—Gomba Joe's, which serves Italian and American specialties every evening, and the Terrace Cafe, one of the handsomest of area coffee shops, with its blond-wood Windsor chairs and glassed-in alcove overlooking the swimming pool. Twelve special rooms for the handicapped are available. Every room has a smoke detector, and a color television set wired for cable. Some rooms have clock radios. Rates for doubles in the hotel are about $75 to $90 (no charge for children 18 and under; rollaways $6). Details: Holiday Inn-International Drive; 6515 International Dr.; Orlando, FL 32819; 351-3500 (800-465-4329).

COMFORT INN: The rates—about $38 to $68 for doubles, depending on the season (with no charge for children under 16 sharing their parents' quarters)—are low enough that you wouldn't expect fancy accommodations, but the establishment is quite pleasant and well-kept. The 161 rooms are arranged in three 2-story wings that wrap around a small (but tidy) pool. Entrances to the rooms are in hallways inside; there's no at-door parking. A Denny's Restaurant which is open around the clock, is right next door to the hotel. Details: Comfort Inn; 5825 International Dr.; Orlando, FL 32819; 351-4100 (800-327-1366).

MISCELLANEOUS

The following establishments are located outside the U.S. 192 and Florida Center/International Drive areas. Each of the 12 has appealing features that make it stand out among Orlando-area hostelries.

HARLEY HOTEL OF ORLANDO: Lodging in downtown Orlando puts vacationers close to some of the more interesting local restaurants, and the Harley—one of the best among the Greater Orlando-area hotels—is the establishment of choice. You're only a few minutes' drive from Winter Park—a fact best appreciated when, at the end of a long day of sightseeing, you can have a late meal there. And you're only a couple of minutes from Rosie O'Grady's, a lively Orlando night spot. On the other hand, you are not quite as close to Walt Disney World. But driving the 17 miles or so to the WDW main gate early in the day is not difficult. Adults traveling without children will especially enjoy the atmosphere at this hotel, which is one of the few in the Orlando area that doesn't cater primarily to a family crowd. The Cafe on the Park, the hotel's restaurant, is lovely, with its rosy salmon-pink color scheme and its fine

view out over Lake Eola and the municipal fountain at its center. The hotel's swimming pool, which shares the view, is also an especially relaxing place to be. And the guestrooms' handsome decor warrants special mention. Rates are $85 to $105. Some rooms are equipped for handicapped travelers. Details: Harley Hotel of Orlando; 151 East Washington St.; Orlando, FL 32801; 841-3220 (800-321-2323).

OMNI INTERNATIONAL: A striking, mirrored glass structure, seemingly gift wrapped with a red stripe around its upper floors (the same mirrored glass, but in red), this is a 15-story, 290-room hotel in downtown Orlando. Facilities include a large pool with sundeck and whirlpool, a fitness center, and privileges at a nearby golf course and a tennis and racquetball club. All guestrooms have color television sets with cable hook up, AM/FM clock radios, desks, and at least 2 phones. Restaurants include the American Festival, specializing in fine American cuisine and Livingston Street Cafe, which resembles a Scottish teahouse and serves breakfast, lunch, and dinner. Ozone, one of Orlando's most popular nightspots, is located here. Rates range from $125 to $500. There are 68 rooms equipped for handicapped travelers. Details: Omni International; 400 West Livingston St.; Orlando, FL 32801; 843-6664.

GRENELEFE RESORT AND CONFERENCE CENTER: Located some 22 miles from the WDW main gate, this 950-acre resort is a fine destination in its own right with its three 18-hole golf courses, its 20 tennis courts, golf and tennis instruction programs, its lakefront marina, beach, pools, saunas, Jacuzzis, and 1.6-mile-long fitness course. Grenelefe is primarily of interest to those who want to add a visit to Walt Disney World to the beginning or end of a vacation in a country club–like atmosphere that is less oriented to the family trade than WDW's own resorts—not to mention lots less frenetic. The 950-odd rooms here are located in clusters of buildings scattered along winding drives next to the fairways of the golf courses; some are like standard hotel rooms, with 1 or 2 double beds, while 1- and 2-bedroom parlor suites with fully equipped kitchens are also available. The program of golf instruction is particularly interesting: private, semi-private, group, and playing lessons that use videotape analysis, as well as private lessons without video, are offered. There are 3 restaurants and 2 lounges. Rates range from $55 to $245 for hotel rooms and suites, depending on the season. Details: Grenelefe Resort and Conference Center; 3200 S.R. 546; Grenelefe, FL 33844-9732; 813-422-7511 (800-237-9549; from Florida, 800-282-7875).

PARK PLAZA: Orlando's closest approximation of a cozy country inn occupies a prominent location on Park Avenue in Winter Park. The guestrooms don't quite measure up to the lobby, but with their thick

ORLANDO RESERVATIONS

The Orlando Central Reservations Center can make finding accommodations in the area easier for travelers. Orlando Central represents about 40 hotels in various price ranges. For information and reservations, call 800-322-2220.

ACCOMMODATIONS

carpet, subdued color scheme, and polished wooden moldings, they're attractive enough—particularly the 2-room suites ($125 nightly), with a sitting area and balcony. Smaller rooms, more suitable for 1, could be cramped for 2; they're available with parkside views and balcony at $100 nightly. Continental breakfast in your room is included in the rates. No children under 5 are permitted—but this is not basically set up for families because of the size of the rooms and bathrooms. (Nor is the hotel set up for handicapped travelers.) The distance from Walt Disney World, a 45-minute drive or so, makes it a good choice only for those who don't plan to spend a great deal of time in the World. Details: Park Plaza; 307 Park Ave. South; Winter Park, FL 32789; 647-1072.

LANGFORD RESORT: This esteemed 218-room hotel is set on its own tree-shaded grounds, just off the beaten path in the ritzy community of Winter Park. The Park Avenue shopping district is a block away, but the hubbub of commerce (what little hubbub is allowed in the exclusive shops there) never reaches the guests at Langford—even those lounging by the side of the Olympic-size pool. A recent addition here is the health spa. It has a dining room, the Bamboo Room, which features live entertainment opportunities for ballroom dancing. Rates are $50 to $55 a night for a single; $60 to $80 for a double. Details: Langford Resort; 300 East New England Ave.; Winter Park, FL 32789; 644-3400.

STOUFFER ORLANDO RESORT: This $86-million hotel located directly across the street from Sea World offers 778 guest rooms and has been designed as a convention facility with a 17,325-square-feet main ballroom, 2 smaller ballrooms, and 23 other convention and meeting rooms. Each guestroom has individual climate controls, color TV, radio, telephone, and either 2 double beds or 1 king-size bed. One-bedroom suites have a parlor, wet bar and conference table. The rooms are built around a 65,000-square-foot atrium and are reached by 6 glass-enclosed elevators. There are 5 restaurants: Trade Winds, a 24-hour dining room; Atlantis, an elegant restaurant serving innovative dishes; Haifeng, specializing in authentic Chinese cuisine; L'Orangerie, a buffet dining room; and Winston's English Pub. Palms is a poolside snack bar, and Dolphins is the bar in the lobby. Recreational facilities include a swimming pool, a Jacuzzi, 6 lit tennis courts, a health club, and a professionally staffed children's activity center. Rates are $160 to $220; $320 to $480 for suites. Details: Stouffer Orlando Resort; 6677 Sea Harbor Dr.; Orlando, FL 32821; 351-5555 (800-327-6677).

EMBASSY SUITES: The city's first all-suite hotel is located near the Convention Center and features an 8-story atrium with a waterfall and piano lounge below, where complimentary cocktails are served to hotel guests between 5 P.M. and 7 P.M. Each of the 246 suites includes a bedroom, living room, dressing area, bathroom, and wet bar. Guests receive a complimentary deluxe buffet breakfast. Recreational facilities include an indoor/outdoor pool, whirlpool, steamroom, sauna, and an exercise center. Rates are $110 to $150. Details: Embassy Suites; 8250 Jamaican Court; Orlando, FL 32819; 345-8250 (800-362-2779).

MARRIOTT'S ORLANDO WORLD CENTER: This is one of Florida's largest hotels, with 1,503 guestrooms located in a 27-story, Y-shaped tower. The hotel is situated on nearly 200 landscaped acres and is surrounded by an 18-hole, Joe Lee-designed golf course. The atrium lobby offers a sampling of exotic plants, including Sabal palms, banana trees, and jade plants. Waterfalls, museum-quality 16th- and 17th-century Chinese artifacts, and a couple of lounges make the lobby a very pleasant place to linger. The guestrooms are decorated in peach and mauve tones, and the wicker furniture reinforces the tropical theme. Two floors (the 11th and 12th) have been set aside as special concierge-served levels. There are 3 heated swimming pools (1 indoor), 12 lit tennis courts, a health club, a beauty parlor and barbershop, a gameroom, and several retail shops. The enormous hotel also includes 6 full-service restaurants, including Mikados, a Japanese steakhouse, and 5 lounges. The convention facilities are appropriately vast with 92,000 square feet of meeting space, all located on one level. The Grand Ballroom is 38,000 square feet and may be divided into 14 sections. The Crystal Ballroom offers slightly more than 40,000 square feet. There are 46 potential meeting rooms in all. Complete food and banquet services are available, as are sophisticated

---

SHORT-TERM RENTALS

Apartment, condominium, and bed-and-breakfast accommodations can be arranged locally. For a list of availabilities, write Tourism Development; Greater Orlando Chamber of Commerce; Box 1234; Orlando, FL 32802; 425-1234.

audiovisual equipment and other meeting services. Rates range from $150 to $190. Details: Marriott's Orlando World Center; World Center Drive; Orlando, FL 32821; 239-4200.

DAYS INN-LAKE BUENA VISTA: Perhaps the most conveniently located Days Inn; very close to Disney Village Marketplace and Epcot Center, with a pool, gameroom, restaurant, and 203 guestrooms. Rates range from $51 to $86, plus $6 for each additional person over 18 sharing a room. There is a laundry and free transportation to Walt Disney World. Details: Days Inn-Lake Buena Vista; 12799 Apopka-Vineland Rd.; Lake Buena Vista, FL 32830; 239-4441.

GRAND CYPRESS RESORT: The Hyatt Regency, a $110-million hotel, is the centerpiece of a 1,500-acre resort. Directly adjacent to the Disney Village Hotel Plaza area and just 3 miles from Epcot Center, the 18-story building is T-shaped with 3 wings of guestrooms off the 200-foot atrium lobby. There are 750 rooms (72 are suites), and each has air conditioning, a ceiling fan, color television, and 1 king-size or 2 double beds. The 11th and 17th floors have been designated the Regency Club, and guests receive a complimentary breakfast buffet and the convenience of a concierge. (There are also 3 concierges in the lobby for other hotel guests.) There's a half-acre, free-form swimming pool with 12 waterfalls and a 45-foot water slide. The 21-acre lake is a perfect place to try out one of the sailboats, sailboards, canoes, or paddleboats available for rent. The tennis complex features 12 courts, and

there are racquetball and volleyball courts as well. There are also a children's playground, walking and jogging trails, and a health club. The 45-hole, Jack Nicklaus-designed golf course stands out among the facilities. The superb course features 2 Scottish-style shared greens, grassy dunes, and elevated tees. The course is currently open to hotel guests only, and the greens fee will set you back $90. The Jack Nicklaus Academy of Golf offers 3- and 5-day programs, which allow golfers to practice situations encountered during a regular round.

This hotel offers space for meetings ranging from small executive sessions to large conventions of up to 2,500 people. There is 57,000 square feet of meeting space, including the 25,000-square-foot Grand Cypress Ballroom and the 20,826-square-foot Regency Hall exhibition area. There are potentially 27 meeting rooms in all.

The hotel has 5 restaurants and 3 lounges, plus a poolside bar. The Palm Cafe, a cafeteria-style restaurant, offers breakfast, lunch, and dinner. Cascade serves lunch, and dinner. Hemingway's offers a touch of Key West, specializing in seafood; La Coquina is the more formal dining spot; and the White Horse Saloon is an 1840s-style western restaurant specializing in prime ribs dinners. Sixteen guestrooms are designed for handicapped travelers. Rates range from $130 to $330; suites begin at $305.

There are also 48 luxury villas situated around the fairways. There are luxury hotel rooms called club suites and 1-, 2-, 3-, and four-bedroom villas. Each villa includes a full kitchen, master suites with private bath and dressing rooms, cathedral ceilings, tile floors, and large picture windows. Some feature a bi-level floor plan with fireplaces, balconies, and patios. The Grand Cypress Village Executive Conference Center offers meeting space for up to 200 participants. Located near the Grand Cypress Village Villas and the Jack Nicklaus-designed golf course, the center features 3 rooms: the Muirfield, the Gleneagles, and the St. Andrews. These can be arranged into 7 separate meeting areas. Decks and terraces offer a dramatic lakeside view and fine spots for evening gatherings. Full catering services are also available. Rates range from $150 to $225 for club suites and $225 to $900 for villas. Details: Hyatt Regency Grand Cypress; One Grand Cypress Blvd.; Orlando, FL 32819; 239-1234; 239-4700 for the villas (800-228-9000).

SONESTA VILLAGE: Something a little different in the Orlando area, this complex features 383 1- and 2-bedroom villas. Each beautifully decorated villa features a living room, dining room, 1 or 2 bathrooms, and a fully equipped kitchenette. The complex is set on 93 acres facing 300-acre Sand Lake. The hotel currently offers 2 tennis courts, 10 Jacuzzis, a swimming pool, health club, and golf privileges at nearby courses (Cypress Creek, International Golf Club, and Orange Tree). There is one restaurant, a lounge, a gift shop, and meeting space. There's full maid service daily. Rates for a 1-bedroom villa are $125 to $170; 2-bedroom units are $180 to $270 depending on the season. Details: Sonesta Village; 10000 Turkey Lake Rd.; Orlando, FL 32819; 352-8051 (800-343-7170).

THE MAGIC KINGDOM

Though occupying only 98 acres of Walt Disney World's 27,400 total acreage, the Magic Kingdom is the most special part of the World. Few who have visited it are disappointed, and even the most blasé travelers manage a smile. Every day is like a great festival and fair. The sight of the soaring spires of Cinderella Castle, the gleaming woodwork of the Main Street shops, the tiny white lights that edge their rooflines after dark, and the crescendo of music that follows the parades never fail to have their effect. Even when the crowds are large and the weather is at its warmest, a visitor who has toured this wonderland dozens of times still can look around and think how satisfying this place is for the spirit.

But the delight that most guests experience upon their first sight of the Magic Kingdom can quickly disappear when disorientation sets in. There are so many nooks and crannies, so many bends to every pathway, and so many sights and sounds clamoring for attention—not to mention over 45 attractions and adventures and dozens of shops and restaurants—that it's too easy to wander aimlessly and miss the best that the Magic Kingdom has to offer. So we earnestly suggest that you peruse this chapter carefully before you make your own visit.

At the same time, it's also interesting to learn a little about how the Magic Kingdom works. This wonderland started out as little more than vintage Florida swampland. When the Seven Seas Lagoon was dredged, the leftover soil was used to build up the level of the Magic Kingdom site, to provide proper drainage, to supply dry land on which to plant trees and flowers, and to accommodate a vast subterranean system of dressing rooms, computer banks, and connecting hallways where the magic of the Magic Kingdom is manufactured. One vast room of the underground warren is given over solely to computers, used in everything from food planning to the timing of the presidents' nods in Liberty Square's Hall of Presidents. Another area houses a photo library and darkrooms. Yet another whole network of rooms houses the world's largest working wardrobe, where the thousands of costumes worn by the Magic Kingdom hosts and hostesses hang on row upon row of racks. The place looks like the world's gaudiest department store. Another room is given over solely to the wig department. And that's only the beginning.

Every land has a theme, which is carried through from the hosts' and hostesses' costumes to the food served in the restaurants, the merchandise in the shops, and even the design of the trash bins. Thousands of details contribute to the overall effect; paying attention to these small touches makes any visit more enjoyable.

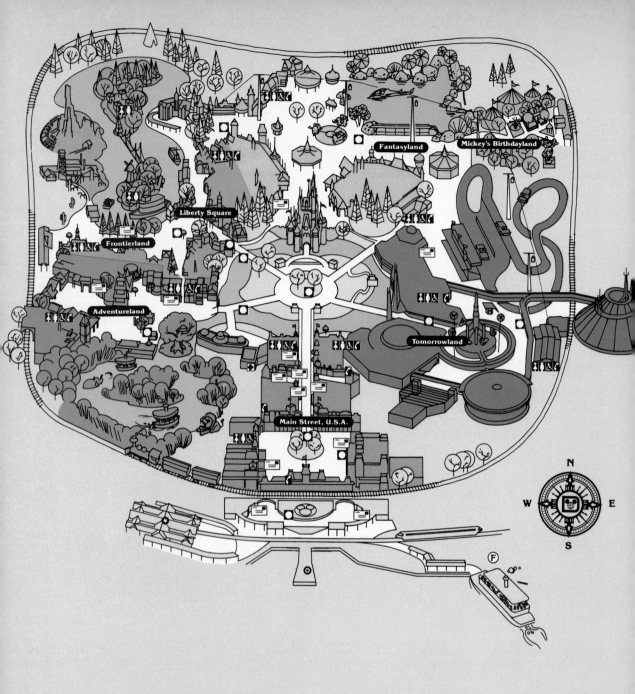

Fantasyland

Mickey's Birthdayland

Liberty Square

Frontierland

Adventureland

Tomorrowland

Main Street, U.S.A.

N
W E
S

F

MAGIC KINGDOM MAP

- ✚ FIRST AID
- 🚻 RESTROOMS
- ♿ WHEELCHAIR RESTROOMS
- ☎ TELEPHONES
- 📷 KODAK PHOTO SPOT
- ✉ MAIL DROP LOCATIONS

- ✪ MONORAIL STATION
  - • Express service to car and bus parking
  - • Local service to resorts
- ⊙ LAUNCH TO DISCOVERY ISLAND AND FORT WILDERNESS
- Ⓕ FERRYBOAT TO CAR/BUS PARKING

HOW TO GET TO THE MAGIC KINGDOM

From the Contemporary Resort, the Polynesian Village Resort, and the Grand Floridian Resort: The monorail is the easiest way to go.

From The Disney Inn: Take the bus in front of the hotel to the Polynesian Village, walk through the lobby to the second floor, then to the monorail boarding area.

From Epcot Center: Take the monorail or the bus to the Transportation and Ticket Center (TTC), then transfer to the other monorail or ride a ferry.

From Disney Village Resort: Board a bus at one of the bus stops located at frequent intervals throughout the villa area, ride to the TTC, then take the monorail or ferry. Guests coming from the Disney Village Marketplace take the bus to the TTC, then the monorail or ferry.

From the Disney-MGM Studios Theme Park: Take the bus to the TTC, then the monorail or ferry.

From Fort Wilderness: Buses make the trip from the campground to the TTC; depending on the location of your campsite, it may be more convenient to take one of the boats that call at the dock.

From the hotels at Disney Village Hotel Plaza: Take the bus that stops at the front door of your hotel. Because WDW's private roads are off-limits to all but guests at WDW-owned establishments, guests who are staying at one of the 7 Hotel Plaza properties and who want to drive must go out onto I-4, drive 4½ miles west, then enter the park via the Auto Plaza along with other day visitors; this can mean grappling with traffic (see "When to Arrive," below), so in most cases it's more efficient to take the bus—even though it may mean a wait at both ends.

From Orlando or Kissimmee: Follow the signs for Walt Disney World on I-4, take the Magic Kingdom turnoff, and proceed to the Auto Plaza. Go straight ahead and then turn left into the parking lots. Gray Line and Rabbit shuttle buses serve most hotels, but the per person charges are so high relative to the low local car rental rates that it usually makes economic sense to drive. Some hotels offer free shuttle service to WDW.

across the manmade Seven Seas Lagoon, or a slightly shorter trip by monorail around its shore. Each section of the trip—the drive from the I-4 exit to the Auto Plaza and then to the parking lot, then the lake crossing—serves to heighten the suspense, and by removing guests from the workaday world, to prepare them for the visual delights to come.

TRANSPORTATION COSTS: Parking in the Magic Kingdom lots costs $3 (free to guests at WDW-owned resorts, upon presentation of their ID cards). To ride the bus between Disney Village Hotel Plaza and the Transportation and Ticket Center, and to board the bus between Disney Village Marketplace and the Transportation and Ticket Center, it is necessary to show an ID card from a Hotel Plaza establishment or a WDW-owned property; all multi-day All Three Parks Passports also provide free use of the buses.

WHEN TO ARRIVE: Especially during the busy summer and holiday seasons—when the highways leading to the Auto Plaza can look like a Los Angeles freeway during rush hour, and when there are long queues at WDW monorails and ferries—it's advisable to plan on reaching the park by 7:30 A.M. or 8 A.M. Eat breakfast at your hotel, if you will—or wait and eat inside the park. Or if this just seems too early, wait until later—about 1 P.M.—or even later than that during the seasons when the park is open late. During less congested periods, when the park closes at 7 P.M., plan to arrive around 10 A.M.

PARKING: After passing through the Auto Plaza, drive straight ahead and bear left for the parking lots. Parking attendants will direct you to a spot in one of a dozen areas. Each lot is named for a

GETTING IN: One of Walt Disney's greatest personal disappointments was the fact that the citrus groves that originally rimmed the Disneyland site in Anaheim, California, soon gave way to unsightly commercial development. Finally, only the berm rimming the park protected it from surrounding eyesores. When planning Walt Disney World, he pledged to prevent a repeat of that situation and set the Magic Kingdom some 4 miles from the nearest public highway.

From the Walt Disney World exit off highway I-4, it's 4 miles to the Auto Plaza, from there it's under a mile to the main entrance complex known as the Transportation and Ticket Center (TTC). Even then, Magic Kingdom visitors have not completed their journey: There remains a 5-minute ride by ferry

Disney character—Daisy, Donald, Sneezy, Bashful, Grumpy, Happy, Goofy, Pluto, Chip & Dale, Minnie, Sleepy, and Dopey. Minnie, Sleepy, and Dopey are within walking distance of the Transportation and Ticket Center (TTC); other lots are served continuously by tractor-drawn trams that make periodic stops to pick up and discharge passengers.

Before leaving your car, check the name of your section and your aisle number; there is a spot for noting this information on the back of your parking ticket. Roll up all windows and lock all doors. Also, do not leave any pets in the car! The Pet Care Kennel, presented by Gaines Foods, Inc.—it's air conditioned, far more comfortable for the animal, and far safer for him—is conveniently located right at the TTC.

Guests who leave the park at midday for their hotels should keep their parking tickets; the tickets are good for reentry to the parking area throughout the day. Also remember that to reenter the parks on the same day, you must have your valid ticket or All Three Parks Passport *and* a hand stamp.

FERRY VS. MONORAIL: Once you've bought your admission ticket or All Three Parks Passport and made your way through the TTC turnstiles, it's necessary to decide whether to travel to the Magic Kingdom by ferry or by monorail.

The monorails make the trip in a bit less than the 5 minutes required by the ferries—but the latter often will get you there more quickly during the busier seasons, because long lines can form at the monorails; most people just simply don't make the short extra walk to the ferry landing. When there's no line for the monorail, it's your best choice.

Wheelchair vacationers should note that while the monorails are accessible, the ramp leading to the boarding area is a bit steep.

Guests staying at The Disney Inn may take a bus to the Polynesian Village, where they can join guests from that resort, the Grand Floridian Resort, and from the Contemporary Resort on the monorail, which links the 3 hotels directly to the Magic Kingdom.

ADMISSION MEDIA: A one-day ticket provides admission to the Magic Kingdom, plus unlimited access to all its rides, shows, and attractions. (All admission tickets and passports can be upgraded for longer stays; do it at City Hall in the Magic Kingdom, at Earth Station in Epcot Center, or at Guest Services at the Disney-MGM Studios Theme Park. You will not have to pay a full 1-day price, just the difference between the original cost and the new ticket.)

Four- and 5-day All Three Parks Passports are also available. These allow not only admission to the Magic Kingdom and unlimited use of all the rides, shows, and attractions there, but also admission to Epcot Center, unlimited use of the attractions there, admission to the Disney-MGM Studios Theme Park, unlimited enjoyment of all the attractions there, and unlimited use of the transportation system inside Walt Disney World. Multi-day All Three Parks Passports do not have to be used on consecutive days. Note that old multi-day World Passports are not accepted for admission to the Disney-MGM Studios Theme Park.

Those who last visited WDW when the system of coupons and general admission tickets (now completely phased out) was in effect may redeem unused ride coupons at the ticket booths at the Transportation and Ticket Center (TTC); the value of those coupons can be applied to the cost of a new ticket or All Three Parks Passport. Check at City Hall on Main Street for further information.

All Three Parks Passports may be purchased at the TTC and at many local resorts and hotels, including WDW-owned establishments. (Note that day guests may purchase tickets only at the TTC.)

All Three Parks Passports by mail: Send a check or money order payable to Walt Disney World Company in the exact amount plus $2 for handling to:

Walt Disney World;
Box 10030; Lake Buena Vista, FL 32830-0030
Attention: Ticket Mail Order

Remember to include your return address. Allow at least 4 to 6 weeks for ticket requests to be processed.

Buying All Three Parks Passports at the airport: Admission media may also be purchased at the guest services counter of "Walt Disney World on Parade" at Orlando International Airport.

Guided tours: Three- to four-hour guided walking tours of the Magic Kingdom are available (except during some peak seasons). These include the services of a guide and admission to attractions during your tour of all lands in the Magic Kingdom. These tours are terrific for first-time visitors, especially those without a great sense of direction, and the cost is quite reasonable ($5 for adults and $3.50 for children, in addition to the applicable price of admission media). For details call Guest Relations (824-4633) or inquire at the Transportation and Ticket Center.

MONEY MATTERS: WDW resort guests who buy their All Three Parks Passports at WDW resorts may charge them to their rooms by using their resort ID cards. At the TTC, cash, traveler's checks, personal checks, MasterCard, Visa, or American Express cards are accepted as payment for all admission media; personal checks must be imprinted with your name and address and must be accompanied by a driver's license and a major credit card (that is, American Express, Visa, MasterCard, Diners Club, or Carte Blanche).

At sit-down restaurants and for merchandise: American Express, Visa, and MasterCard are accepted, as are cash and traveler's checks. WDW resort identification cards are not accepted as payment for food and merchandise purchases inside the Magic Kingdom.

At fast-food restaurants: No credit cards are accepted at fast-food eating spots. You must pay cash; traveler's checks are also accepted.

Guests may also want to purchase Disney Dollars, available in one- and five-dollar denominations. Disney Dollars are accepted at all Magic Kingdom, Epcot Center, and Disney-MGM Studios Theme Park restaurants, shops, and food stands, and at all WDW resorts. They can be redeemed for greenbacks at any time. Many visitors, however, take at least one home as a souvenir. When purchasing tickets or passports at Walt Disney World ticket locations, guests can request Disney Dollars as change.

ADMISSION PRICES*

ONE-DAY TICKET

Adult	$29
Child**	$23

FOUR-DAY PASSPORT

Adult	$97
Child**	$77

FIVE-DAY PASSPORT

Adult	$112
Child**	$90

The cost of a **ONE-YEAR ALL THREE PARKS PASSPORT** is $180 for adults and $155 for children; renewals are $160 for adults and $135 for children.

*The prices quoted here do not include a 6% sales tax.

**3 through 9 years of age

Note: Multi-day All Three Parks Passports need not be used on consecutive days.

These prices were correct at press time, but may change during 1990.

THE LAY OF THE LANDS

Not long ago, one Magic Kingdom visitor spent an entire day in Tomorrowland—thinking it was the full extent of the place. To avoid having a similar experience, it's essential to understand the lay of all the lands *before* you arrive on Main Street.

There are 7 sections, or "lands," in the Magic Kingdom—Main Street, U.S.A.; Adventureland; Frontierland; Liberty Square; Fantasyland; Mickey's Birthdayland; and Tomorrowland. The monorail stations and ferry docks at which all guests arrive are just outside the Magic Kingdom gates; just inside them is Town Square, at the head of Main Street, which runs straight to Cinderella Castle. The area in front of the Castle is known as the Central Plaza, or, more aptly, the Hub. It is surrounded by small canals, the Hub Waterways, which are crossed by bridges to enter each of the lands. The first bridge to your left goes to Adventureland; the next, to Liberty Square and Frontierland. On your right, the first bridge heads to Tomorrowland, the second to Fantasyland and Mickey's Birthdayland. The end points

of the avenues leading to the lands are linked by a roadway that is roughly circular, so that the layout of the Magic Kingdom resembles a wheel. All of the attractions, restaurants, and shops are arranged along the rim of the wheel and along its spokes.

In theory, it couldn't be simpler; in practice, it's only too easy to get confused because of the many bends and curves in the pathways, the many entrances to each shop and restaurant, and the somewhat angular placement and architecture of many of the buildings. But if you keep mental notes of your own route, losing your bearings becomes fairly difficult. If you still manage to get confused, however, any park employee can help set you straight.

A note on north, south, east, and west: When you stand at the Magic Kingdom entrance and face Cinderella Castle, you're looking north. Main Street is straight ahead, with Fantasyland and Mickey's Birthdayland beyond the Castle. Adventureland, Liberty Square, and Frontierland are to the west. Tomorrowland flanks the Hub on the east.

MAIN STREET, U.S.A.

This is the Disney version of turn-of-the-century small-town Main Streets all over the country—freshly painted, full of curlicued gingerbread moldings and pretty details, and with its baskets of hanging plants and genuine-looking gaslights, a showplace both in the bright light of high noon and after nightfall, when the tiny lights edging all of Main Street's rooflines are flicked on.

What's particularly amazing is that all the variety of furbelows and frills that a real, growing Main Street would have enjoyed have been assimilated into the Disney version. Most of the structures along the thoroughfare are given over to shops, and each one is different, from the wallpaper and layout of displays to the flooring materials, the style of chandeliers, and even the lighting level. Some emporiums are big and bustling, others are relatively quiet and orderly; some are spacious and airy, others are cozy and dark. Floors are made of black-and-white tile or of wide oak planks set in with wooden pegs; some are covered with Victorian-patterned carpets. Where wallpaper is used, it is striped, or gaudily flowered; in contrast, some walls are paneled in subdued mahogany or oak. The effect is far more sophisticated than first-time visitors probably would have imagined, and it doesn't really matter that some of the "wood" is fiberglass.

Inside and outside, maintenance and housekeeping are superb. White-suited sanitation men patrol the street to pick up litter and quickly shovel up any droppings from the horses who pull the trolley cars from Town Square to the Hub. The pavement, like all in the Magic Kingdom, is washed down every night with fire hoses. There's one crew of maintenance men whose sole job is to change the little white lights around the roofs; another crew devotes itself to keeping the woodwork painted. As soon as these men have worked their way as far as the Hub, they start all over again at Town Square. Epoxy, acrylic, and more ordinary varieties of paints are used, depending on the area to be painted. The greenish, horse-shaped cast-iron hitching posts are repainted 20 times a year on the average—and totally scraped down each time. It's no wonder the professional painters who visit here marvel at the quality of work they see.

Visitors from outside the United States find all these details so fascinating that it takes them a good deal longer than the 40 minutes spent by the average guest to get from one end of Main Street to the other. There are only 4 real "attractions" along Main Street, and they are relatively minor compared to the really big deals such as Tomorrowland's Space Mountain and Frontierland's Big Thunder Mountain Railroad. But each and every shop has its own quota of merchandise that is meant as much for fun and show as for sale—the monster masks at the House of Magic, for instance, or the large Hummel figurines at Uptown Jewelers. It's also entertaining to stand and watch the host or hostess demonstrating tricks at the House of Magic and the cooks stirring up batches of peanut brittle at the Confectionery. The windows at the Emporium and the House of Magic are also worth a look.

While walking along the street, note the names on the second-story windows. Above Crystal Arts are the names of Roy Disney, Walt's brother, and Patty Disney; above the Shadow Box, that of Dick Nunis, who heads Outdoor Recreation (the company's theme parks division). Above the House of Magic are the names of Ted Crowell, WDW's vice president of facilities support, who, among other things, is responsible for maintenance and for the World's own electric generating plants, and John de Cuir, the Disney artist in charge of the production of the paintings filmed for The Hall of Presidents show. Card Walker, the "practitioner of Psychiatry and Justice of the Peace" mentioned nearby, is the company's former Chairman of the Executive Committee. Other names, as well as those on signs elsewhere in the Magic Kingdom, are also those of real people connected with the company.

Finally, some advice. Before heading toward the Castle, stop at City Hall and inquire about the times and places where live entertainments are scheduled to take place all around the park that day and night. Also, do your shopping in the early afternoon, rather than at day's end when the shops are normally jammed; purchases can be stored in lockers under the Walt Disney World Railroad's depot or, in the case of very large items, behind the desk at City Hall.

PENNY ARCADE: Scarcely a motel in Orlando lacks its blipping, bleeping, squeaking room full of electronic games; the one at the Contemporary Resort ranks among the largest in the country. The Magic Kingdom also has its games room—but here on Victorian Main Street, in addition to the modern machines, there are authentic old-time games—a Kiss-O-Meter, tests of strength, and an antique football game.

In addition, in the center of the front section of the arcade, there are a number of machines that show very early "moving pictures"—that is, stacks of cards on a roller that can be turned to flip the cards and thereby "animate" the images they contain. There are 2 types of viewing devices—Mute-o-scopes, first introduced around 1900, whose rollers must be turned by hand, and Cail-o-scopes, developed about a decade later, which are turned automatically. Both of these are worth your while. Most stories here are comedies; the humor is broad and slapstick—good for at least a smile (if not a roar) and as an amusing comment on the changing ideas about what tickles a funny bone. On the Cail-o-scopes, there are such stories as *Yes, We Have No Bananas,* in which a suitor slips on a banana peel and is ridiculed; *Tough Competition,* in which sailors come to blows over a pretty girl; *Texas Rangers,* where the good guy lassoes the robber; and *Run Out of Town*, in which one unfortunate man has paint dumped on him, falls into a manhole, is knocked over by a car, sits on a freshly painted bench, and knocks over a paint bucket—all in a single day. During *A Raid On A Watermelon Patch,* two fellows do and are discovered. *Oh Teacher* concerns the antics of a teacher's pest. *Brigitte On A Bike* shows a real sourpuss taking a tumble; it might be subtitled, "Or The Trials of Riding in a Long Skirt." Particularly interesting is *Captain*

Kidd's Treasure, in which a pirate lass shows knees, bare arms, and ankles. The display of skin—which would rate a solid *G* today—must have looked very risqué three-quarters of a century ago.

Among the Cail-o-scopes, the best is probably *Expecting,* which is a funny cartoon about people waiting. Some of the others are also worth a peek—and the cost is only a penny.

While you're looking, you can be pumping the big coin-operated antique PianOrchestra against the Arcade's south wall; its ringing tones almost block out the clatter and clacks of the pinball and electronic games machines (at least when it's not out of order; it's as temperamental as a prima donna, and even the ministrations of the resident musical-instrument caretaker can't always keep it singing). Before leaving, also note the paintings that hang on the walls. They depict a roadster race, the Wright Brothers and an early flying machine, a Victorian-era amusement arcade, and a rural Illinois river valley scene. All of these were created for the film that precedes the chief executives' roll call in Liberty Square's Hall of Presidents.

MAIN STREET CINEMA: The beauty of this prominent attraction on Main Street is that most vacationers bypass it in their rush to get to 20,000 Leagues Under The Sea in Fantasyland, or Pirates of the Caribbean in Adventureland, or other thrill-a-minute attractions. Yet on a steamy summer afternoon—when everyone else is standing in line for these blockbusters—this air conditioned theater is a fine place to relax. Vintage Disney cartoons are shown simultaneously. *Steamboat Willie* is featured. It is the first sound cartoon, in which a little mouse named Mickey, making his film debut, meets Minnie and then makes beautiful music on (among other instruments) a cow's udder, a feat that drew one of the film's biggest laughs at the time of its November 1928 release. (By the way, Mickey was originally scheduled to be named Mortimer, but Mrs. Disney convinced Walt to make the change.)

WALT DISNEY WORLD RAILROAD: The best introduction to the layout of the Magic Kingdom, the 1½-mile, 15-minute journey on this rail line is as much a must for the first-time visitor as it is for railroad buffs. For the former, it offers an excellent orientation, as it passes through Adventureland and Frontierland and skirts Fantasyland and Tomorrowland. A special station has been added for Mickeyland. The 1928 steam engine happens to be exactly the same age as Mickey Mouse. En route, viewers see alligators and other Audio-Animatronics animals, and pass an Indian village, as well as the flooded mining town glimpsed on the fly from the cars at the runaway Big Thunder Mountain Railroad. Aficionados of railroadiana may remember that Disney himself was among their number and perhaps, during the early years of television, saw films of him circling his own backyard in a one-eighth-scale train, the *Lilly Belle,* named for his wife. The Walt Disney World Railroad also has a *Lilly Belle* among its quartet of locomotives. All of these were built in the United States around the turn of the last century and later were taken down to Mexico to haul freight and passengers in the Yucatan, where Disney scouts found them in 1969. The United Railways of Yucatan was using them to carry sugarcane.

Brought north once again, they were completely overhauled, and even the smallest parts were reworked or replaced. New boilers and fiberglass cabs were built, along with new tenders and tanks. (The cast-iron wheels, side rods, frames, and parts of the hardware, however, are original.) Originally designed to burn coal or wood, then converted by the Mexicans to use oil, they now consume diesel fuel—considerably less dirty than either of the former fuels.

The *Lilly Belle* is a Mogul-type engine, with 2 small front wheels and 6 drive wheels, while the *Roy O. Disney* is an American Standard 8-wheeler (with 4 small wheels forward and 4 drive wheels), and the *Walter E. Disney* and the *Roger Broggie* (named for a Disney imagineer who shared Walt Disney's enthusiasm for antique trains) are both 2-wheelers, with 4 small forward wheels and 6 large drive wheels.

THE WALT DISNEY STORY: Housed in the yellow building on the east side of Town Square, this film tells the story of the boy from Marceline, Missouri, who built a Kingdom around a mouse. Walt himself narrates part of the presentation, which includes some rare film footage. Well worth your while.

In the waiting area outside the screening room there are a number of exhibits dealing with Walt Disney, the honors he earned, and his life: letters from Harry Truman, Dwight Eisenhower, Richard Nixon, U Thant, Winston Churchill, Dag Hammarskjold, and Leopold Stokowski; posters from old Disney movies; photos of the Mouseketeers (and a real Mouseketeer hat); Zorro's cape; and—among the other medals and honors—the Oscar presented for *Snow White and the Seven Dwarfs,* the familiar tall golden figure with seven miniature versions arranged alongside. Note the photo of Walt Disney with Stan Laurel and Oliver Hardy against the wall to your right as you pass through the turnstiles.

OLD-FASHIONED VEHICLES: A number of these can be seen traveling up and down Main Street—horseless carriages and jitneys patterned after turn-of-the-century vehicles (but fitted out with Jeep transmissions and special mufflers that make the putt-putt-putting sound); a spiffy scarlet fire engine, which can be seen in the Firehouse adjoining City Hall when not in operation; and a troop of trolleys drawn by Belgians and Percherons, 2 strong breeds of horses that once pulled plows in Europe. These animals—aged between 6 and 10, weighing in at about a ton each, and shod with plastic (easier on their feet)—pull the trolley the length of Main Street about 2 dozen times during each of their 3 to 4 working days; afterward, they're sent back to their homes at the barn at the Fort Wilderness Campground.

CINDERELLA CASTLE

Just as the courtly little mouse named Mickey stands for all the joy and merriment in the whole of Walt Disney World, the many-spired Cinderella Castle, childhood's storybook castle made real, represents the hopes and dreams of those youthful years when anything seems possible.

This Castle is different from Disneyland's Sleeping Beauty Castle: Measuring some 180 feet in height, the Florida castle is more than 100 feet taller; and with its slender towers and lacy filigree work, it's also more graceful, taking its inspiration not only from the architecture of 12th- and 13th-century France, the country where Charles Perrault's classic fairy tale originated, but also from the mad Bavarian King Ludwig's castle at Neuschwanstein, and from the designs prepared some 3 decades ago for the motion picture version of Perrault's story—and the imaginations of a whole troupe of creative Disney imagineers who have collectively spent several lifetimes turning fantasies into reality.

Unlike real European castles, this one is not made of granite, but of steel beams, fiberglass, and some 500 gallons of paint. There are no dungeons underneath it, but rather service tunnels for the Magic Kingdom's day-to-day operations. In the Castle's upper reaches there are broadcast facilities, security rooms, and the like; toward the top, there's the apartment originally meant for members of the Disney family (but never occupied).

When mounting the curving staircase to King Stefan's Banquet Hall, the parapet-level restaurant, or when passing through the Castle's main gateway—or as seen by night from the Contemporary Resort's observation deck, with fireworks exploding all around those slender towers—the Castle looks as if it had come straight out of some never-never land of make-believe.

The mosaic murals: The elaborate murals in the 5 panels beneath the Castle's archway-entrance rank as one of the true wonders of the World. Measuring some 15 feet high and 10 feet wide, these creations of the Disney artist Dorothea Redmond, crafted by the mosaicist Hanns-Joachim Scharff, tell the familiar story of a little cinder girl, a hard-hearted stepmother, 2 ugly stepsisters, a fairy godmother, a pumpkin transformed, a handsome prince, a certain glass slipper, and one of childhood's happiest happily-ever-afters, using

a million bits of Italian glass in some 500 different colors, plus real silver and 14-karat gold. The renderings of the stepsisters and of the many small woodland animals are particularly faithful to images from the Disney film; but every passerby has favorite sections. Don't fail to stop and look.

Coats of arms: The one above the Castle on the north wall belongs to the Disneys. Others belonging to assorted Disney executives hang in the waiting hall just inside the door to King Stefan's; the hostess keeps a book behind the desk that details which belong to whom, for any interested party to see. Some of the same names show up as on the second-story windows of the Main Street shops.

ADVENTURELAND

Adventureland seems to have even more atmosphere than the other lands. That may be a result of its neat separation from the rest of the Magic Kingdom, by the bridge over Main Street on the one end, and by a gallery like structure where it merges with Frontierland on the other; or possibly it's because of the abundance of landscaping. There are Canary Island date palms, the small Cape Sable palms, as well as pygmy date species, and more. On the Adventureland Bridge alone, visitors will see Cape honeysuckle from South Africa, flame vines from Mexico, bougainvillea from Brazil, Chinese hibiscus, hanging sword ferns, spider plants, and Australian tree ferns, to name just a few. It's hard to imagine that 15 years ago, the landscape of this little piece of real estate was as bare and flat as that flanking the WDW entrance road.

As for the architecture, even though it derives from such diverse areas as the Caribbean, Polynesia, and Southeast Asia, there's a strong sense of being in a single place, a nowhere-in-particular that is both exotic and distinctly foreign, smacking of island idylls and tropical splendor. Shops offer imports from India, Thailand, Hong Kong, Africa, and the Caribbean islands. The Adventureland Veranda serves food cooked in the Magic Kingdom's most exotic style (never mind that it's simple Chinese fare).

Strolling away from Main Street, there is the sound of the beating of drums, the squawk of a couple of parrots, the regular boom of a cannon. Paces quicken. And the wonders soon to be encountered do not disappoint.

THE ENCHANTED TIKI BIRDS: The first of the Audio-Animatronics attractions, the one that laid the foundation for attractions such as *Great Moments With Mr. Lincoln* at the 1964-65 New York World's Fair, this one, introduced at Disneyland in 1963, features 4 emcees—José, Michael, Pierre, and Fritz—plus some 225 birds, flowers, and Tiki god statues singing and whistling up a tropical storm with such animation that even the most blasé folks can't help but smile.

PIRATES OF THE CARIBBEAN: One of the very best of the Magic Kingdom's adventures, this cruise through a series of sets depicting a pirate raid on a Caribbean island town is a Disneyland original added to WDW's Magic Kingdom, in revised form, because of popular demand. Here there are flowerpots that explode and mend themselves, drunken pigs whose legs actually twitch in the porkers' soporific contentment, chickens that look for all the world like the real thing (even when seen at close range);

the observant will note that the leg of one swashbuckler, dangled over the edge of a bridge, is actually hairy. Each pirate's face has remarkable personality, and the rendition of "Yo-Ho-Yo-Ho"—the attraction's theme song—makes what is actually a rather brutal scenario into something that comes across as good fun.

Before entering the plaza queue area, be sure to stop and give a nod to the parrot, dressed in the pirate costume, near the Pirates of the Caribbean sign.

JUNGLE CRUISE: Inspired in part by the 1955 documentary *The African Lion,* this 10-minute cruise adventure is one of the crowning achievements of Magic Kingdom landscape artists for the way it takes guests through landscapes as diverse as a Southeast Asian jungle, the Nile valley, the African veldt, and an Amazon rain forest. Along the way, passengers encounter zebras and giraffes, impalas, lions, vultures, and headhunters; they see elephants bathing and tour a Cambodian temple—and listen to the amusing spiel delivered by the skipper. For most passengers, this is all just in fun. Gardeners, however, are especially impressed by the variety of species coexisting in such a small area. To keep some of the more sensitive of subtropical specimens alive, 100 gas-fired heaters and electric fans concealed in the rocks pump hot air into the jungle at the rate of 25 million BTUs per hour when temperatures fall to 36° F. This adventure, which is best enjoyed by daylight, is one of the

Magic Kingdom's most popular attractions, and it does tend to be crowded from late morning until late afternoon, so plan accordingly.

SWISS FAMILY TREEHOUSE: "Everything we need right at our fingertips" was how John Mills, playing the father in Disney's 1960 remake of the classic novel *Swiss Family Robinson*, described the treehouse that he and two of his three sons constructed to house the family after the ship transporting them to America was wrecked in a storm. When given a chance—several adventures later—to leave the island, all but one son decided to stay on. That decision is not hard to understand after a tour of the Magic Kingdom's version of the Robinsons' banyan-tree home. This is everybody's idea of the perfect treehouse, with its many levels and many comforts—patchwork quilts, lovely mahogany furniture, candles stuck in abalone shells, even running water in every room. (The system is ingenious.)

The Spanish moss draping the branches is real; the tree itself—unofficially christened *Disneyodendron eximus*, which translates roughly as "out-of-the-ordinary Disney tree"—was constructed by the props department. Some statistics: The roots, which are concrete, poke 42 feet into the ground; and some 800,000 leaves and flowers (vinyl) grow on 600-odd branches, which stretch some 90 feet in diameter. "Boy, Dad sure went out on a limb for that one," quipped a Disney prop worker's son on hearing of his father's task.

With the Rivers of America lapping up at its borders and Big Thunder Mountain rising toward the rear, this re-creation of the American Frontier encompasses the area from New England to the Southwest, from the 1770s to the 1880s. Hosts and hostesses wear denim, calf-length cutoffs, long skirts, or similar garb. Additionally, the shops, restaurants, and attractions have unpainted barn siding or stone or clapboard walls, and outside there are a few of the kind of wooden sidewalks down which Marshal Matt Dillon used to stride.

Near Pecos Bill Cafe, the landscape seems desertlike (even on humid summer days), with mesquite providing shade and Peruvian pepper trees nearby; the latter's twisted branches boast clusters of bright red berries in fall and winter. Jerusalem thorns blossom with sweet-smelling yellow flowers in the spring. Century plants and Spanish bayonets also can be seen. Farther down the Frontierland avenue, slash pines provide some shade, along with other evergreens of a variety known as cajeput, which can be recognized by its spongy, light-colored bark and white flowers.

DIAMOND HORSESHOE: The half-hour-long show, the Diamond Horseshoe Jamboree, presented in this re-creation of a western dance hall saloon is the kind of thing that makes sophisticated folk laugh in spite of themselves. The jokes range from corny to absolutely preposterous, yet seldom fall flat, thanks to the enthusiastic, energetic efforts of the talented crew of singers and dancers who perform here several times each day. Reservations are necessary and must be made in person at the Hospitality House on Main Street on the morning of the day of the performance. Since they are dispensed on a first-come, first-served basis, it's essential to show up within an hour of park opening.

FRONTIERLAND SHOOTIN' ARCADE: Silver bullets have given way to infrared beams at the completely electronic shooting arcade. Genuine Hawkins 54-caliber buffalo rifles have been refitted, and when an infrared beam strikes any of the 97 reactive targets, a humorous result is triggered. The arcade is set in an 1850s town in the Southwest Territory. Gun positions overlook Boothill, a town complete with bank, jail, hotel, and cemetery. Struck tombstones rise, sink, spin, or change their epitaphs; hit the cloud and a ghost rider gallops across the sky; a bull's-eye on a gravedigger's shovel causes a skull to pop out of the grave. Sound effects—howling coyotes, creaking bridges, and the

shooting guns—are created by a digital audio system. Note that All Three Parks Passports do *not* include use of the arcade, and there is an additional charge here.

COUNTRY BEAR VACATION HOEDOWN: An occasional determined sophisticate will remain impervious to the charms of this country-and-western hoedown (aka, informally, the Country Bear Jamboree) in Frontierland's big stone-walled Grizzly Hall. But most guests call it one of the Magic Kingdom's best attractions. Ostensibly concocted by one Ursus H. Bear after an especially inspiring hibernation season, it is performed mainly by a cast of close to 20 life-size Audio-Animatronics bruins, with results more believable than almost anywhere else in the park, outside the Hall of Presidents. Henry, the debonair, seven-foot-tall master of ceremonies, introduces the Five Bear Rugs (a C&W plinking group made up of Zeke, Zeb, Ted, Fred, and Tennessee); a big-bodied, tiny-headed pianist named Gomer; the girthy Trixie, the Tampa Temptation, who laments her lost love after being jilted at an ant-plagued picnic; dressed in a yellow slicker, rain bonnet, and galoshes, Teddi Barra floats down from the ceiling crooning "Singing in the Rain"; Bubbles, Bunny, and Beulah, in sweet harmony, sing "Wish

They All Could Be California Bears"; and assorted other bruins, including Terrence, the shank shaker; Wendell, the overbearing baritone; Liver Lips McGrowl; and Big Al, one of the few Audio-Animatronics figures with a following great enough to create a demand for his image on postcards and stuffed animals.

Since the Country Bear Vacation Hoedown is a top attraction, lines can get quite long during busy periods. They usually seem longer than they are, however, and it's worth noting that huge bunches of people are admitted all at once so, that once a line starts moving, it dwindles fast. Seats in the rear of the house are just as good as seats toward the front, if not a little better.

TOM SAWYER ISLAND: This small landfall in the middle of the Rivers of America has hills to scramble up, a working windmill, Harper's Mill, with an owl in the rafters and a perpetually creaky waterwheel, and a pitch-black (and scary) cave.

There are oaks, pines, and sycamores here, red maples and elms, and a number of small plants—dwarf azaleas; firethorn, an evergreen shrub that sprouts bright red berries in December; Brazilian pepper trees, which also grow berries at the end of the year; and American holly plants, which acquire their masses of berries in fall. Dirt paths wind this way and that, and it's easy to get disoriented, especially the first time around. There also are two bridges—an old-fashioned swing bridge and a so-called barrel bridge, which floats atop some lashed-together steel drums. When one person bounces, everybody lurches—and all but the most chicken-hearted laugh. Both bridges can easily be missed, so keep your eyes peeled and ask for directions if the path eludes you.

Across the bridge is Fort Sam Clemens, where there is a guardhouse in which the figure of a ratty-looking drunk is Audio-Animatronically snoring off his last bender, accompanied by a mangy-looking dog, chickens, and a pair of horses. On the second floor of the fort, there are close to a dozen air guns for youngsters to trigger into ceaseless cacophony. This area offers a fine view across the Rivers of America to Big Thunder Mountain Railroad. Keep poking around and you'll find the twisting, dark, and occasionally scary escape tunnel out of the fort. Walk along the pathway on the banks of the Rivers of America, and you're back at the bridges.

The whole island seems as rugged as backwoods Missouri, and probably as a result, it actually feels a lot more remote than it is, enough to be able to provide some welcome respite from the bustle of the Magic Kingdom. One particularly pleasant way to pass an hour here is over lemonade and a sandwich on the porch at Aunt Polly's Landing. While adults in the party are giving their feet some rest, watching the stern-wheelers plying the Rivers of America, kids can go out and burn up some more energy. Rest rooms are located at the main raft landing. Note that this attraction closes at dusk.

WALT DISNEY WORLD RAILROAD: The old-fashioned steam trains also pick up and discharge passengers at the depot in Frontierland. There's seldom a waiting line, and the breezy, open-sided passenger cars are good places to cool off from the heat of summer afternoons, for putting up your feet, and for getting from Frontierland to Main Street without expending too much energy. The vegetable-like plants in front of the depot, flowering cabbage, are edible but not tasty—and are mainly ornamental; the trees flanking this Victorian station are laurel oaks, and, behind it, towering slash pines, long-leaf pines, and evergreen elms.

BIG THUNDER MOUNTAIN RAILROAD: This attraction, located partly inside the 197-foot-high redstone mountain that pokes into the sky behind the Tom Sawyer Island rafts landing, is something of a cross between Tomorrowland's Space Mountain (an honest-to-goodness roller coaster) and Adventureland's Pirates of the Caribbean (a tame but very exciting and scenic boat tour). As any true coaster buff could tell you, this 3-minute ride is a relatively mild one, despite the posted warnings; the thrills are there, but the experience is not so extreme that you'll be left with a determination never to subject yourself to it again. The pleasant rush of adrenaline that comes with some of the swoops and curves, as well as the attractive scenery along the 2,780 feet of track, gives most visitors the opposite reaction. There are the bats, the phosphorescent pools and waterfalls, and best of all, Tumbleweed, the flooded mining town (best seen to your left during one of the uphill climbs). There are some 20 Audio-Animatronics figures here—including real-looking chickens, donkeys, possums, a goat, a longjohn-clad resident spinning through the flood in a bathtub, and a rainmaker whose name is Professor Cumulus Isobar. Careful observers will note a party still going on in a not-yet-sunken second-story room of a saloon, whose weathered look (like that of some other sections of the Magic Kingdom) derives from a judicious mixture of plant food and paint. The $300,000 worth of real antique mining equipment sprinkled around the attraction's 2.5 acres—an ore-hauling wagon, a double-stamp ore crusher, a wooden mining flume, and an old ball mill used to extract gold from ore—were picked up at auctions all over the Southwest, at something less than bargain prices, since the high price of gold and the resulting profitability of small-scale mining operations had boosted demand by genuine miners themselves. As with Pirates of the Caribbean, every trip

yields new sights, and even a second or third trip in a matter of days is as amusing as the first time.

The summit of the mountain, whose name refers to an old Indian legend about a certain sacred mountain in Wyoming that would thunder whenever white men took out its gold, is entirely Disney-made. It was in the planning for some 15 years and under construction for 2, and required some 650 tons of steel, 4,675 tons of cement, and 16,000 gallons of paint; hundreds of rock-makers contributed, applying multiple coats of cement and paint, throwing stones at the mountain, kicking dirt on it, and banging on it with sticks and picks to make the whole thing resemble the rocks of Monument Valley, Utah—that is, as if Mother Nature herself had created it. Design was largely by Tony Baxter, a Disney imagineer who started his career with the company with a job at a Disney ice cream parlor while in high school. (His name now can be seen on one of the doors in the unloading and boarding area.) The area inside the mountain that does not house the tunnels of the ride itself is occupied by the machinery that makes the ride go—pumps, electronic equipment, and part of the computer that runs the show. The total cost was about $17 million, which, give or take a few million, was as much as it cost to build all of California's Disneyland in 1955. Incidentally, that park's version of the attraction, which opened in 1979, is similar, but lacks the flash-flood scene and a few other details.

Note on timing: Certain aspects of the ride are more convincing after dark. Optimally, you should experience it first at night, then have a second go-round by the light of day. Since the trip is extremely popular, plan to take it in during the 9 P.M. running of the Main Street Electrical Parade (in season), or just before park closing, when the lines are generally shorter. By day, go during the early morning hours or just before dinnertime.

LIBERTY SQUARE

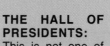

The transition between Frontierland on one side and Fantasyland on the other is so smooth that it's hard to say just when you arrive, yet ultimately there's no mistaking the location. The small buildings are clapboard or brick and topped with weather vanes; the decorative moldings are Federal or Georgian in style; the glass is sometimes wavy, and there are flower boxes in shop windows, brightly colored gardens, neatly trimmed borders of Japanese yew, and masses of azaleas in a number of varieties—George Tabor azaleas, which blossom white and pink in March and May; redwing-hybrid Kurume azaleas, which boast red blossoms in winter; southern charms, which from February to April turn rosy pink; and more. There are a number of good shops, most notably the Yankee Trader, and Olde World Antiques; plus 2 of the park's most popular attractions—The Haunted Mansion and The Hall of Presidents—and the Liberty Tree Tavern, one of the few Magic Kingdom restaurants to offer table service, and one of just two to take reservations. Liberty Square also is home of one of the most delightful nooks in all the Magic Kingdom—the small, secluded area just behind the Silversmith Shop. There are tables with umbrellas, plenty of benches, and big trees to provide shade—and the sound of the crowds seems a million miles away.

THE LIBERTY TREE: Not an attraction per se, this 130-year-old live oak (*Quercus virginiana*)—which recalls trees all over the colonies, on which the Sons of Liberty used to hang lanterns after the Boston Tea Party of 1773—was found on the southern edge of WDW's 27,400 acres, and then moved to its present site in one of the more complex of the Magic Kingdom's landscaping operations. Since the tree was so large (weighing an estimated 35 tons, with a root ball that measured some 18 by 16 by 4 feet around), lifting it by cable was out of the question—the cable would have sliced through the bark and into the trunk's tender cambium layer, injuring the tree. Instead, 2 holes were drilled horizontally through the sturdiest section of the trunk; the holes were fitted with dowels, and a 100-ton crane lifted the tree by these rods, which were subsequently removed and replaced with the original wood plugs. Unfortunately, the wood plugs had become contaminated, and a serious infection set in and rotted out a portion of the inside of the trunk. To save the tree, the plugs again were removed, the holes were filled with cement, the diseased areas were cleaned out, and a young *Quercus virginiana* was grafted onto the tree at its base, where it grows even today. Careful observers will be able to spot the plugs and the portions of the trunk that were damaged. The 13 lanterns hanging on the branches represent the 13 original states.

THE HALL OF PRESIDENTS: This is not one of those laugh-a-minute attractions, like Pirates of the Caribbean or the Country Bear Vacation Hoedown; it's long on patriotism and short on humor. But the detail certainly is fascinating. After a film (presented on a sweeping 70-mm screen) discusses the importance of the Constitution from the time of its framing through the dawn of the Space Age, the curtain goes up on what some guests have mistakenly called the "Hall of Haunted Presidents." A portion of today's Hall of Presidents presentation derives from the Disney-designed Illinois Pavilion's presentation *Great Moments with Mr. Lincoln* from New York's 1964–65 World's Fair.

At the Magic Kingdom show, Lincoln's remarks are prefaced by a roll call of all 41 American presidents, including George Bush. Each chief executive responds with a nod; careful observers will note the others swaying and nodding, fidgeting, and even whispering to each other during the proceedings.

Costumes were created by 2 famous film tailors who were coaxed out of retirement. Not only are the styles those of the period in which each president lived, but so are the tailoring techniques and the fabrics. Some had to be specially woven for the purpose. Each figure has at least 1 change of clothes, and jewelry, shoes, hair texture, and even George Washington's chair are all re-created exactly as indicated by the results of careful research using paintings, diaries, newspapers, and government archives. The observant should be able to see the brace on Franklin Delano Roosevelt's leg. The effect is so lifelike that the figures look almost real, even at close range.

The paintings in the waiting area outside the hall are just a few of the 85 created for the pre-roll call film—in the style of the period during which the event depicted took place—by a dozen artists working under the direction of the Academy Award-winning artist John De Cuir. Other paintings can be seen in Main Street's City Hall and Penny Arcade, and Liberty Square's Liberty Tree Tavern and Columbia Harbour House.

LIBERTY SQUARE RIVERBOAT: The *Richard F. Irvine*, built in drydock at WDW and named for a key Disney designer, is a real steamboat. Its boiler turns water into steam, which is then piped to the engine, which drives the paddle wheel that propels the boat. It is not the real article in one respect, however: It moves through the half-mile-long, 7-foot-deep Rivers of America on an underwater rail. The ride is more pleasant than thrilling, but it's good for beating the heat on steamy afternoons. En route, a variety of props create a sort of Wild West effect: moose, deer, cabins on fire, and the like. (Many of these are also visible from the Walt Disney World Railroad.) Best seats are in front or rear and center, so that you can see both riverbanks equally well.

The trees framing the entrance to Riverboat Landing, which bear crinkly blossoms of bright red throughout much of the year, are crepe myrtles; these can also be seen in other areas of the park.

MIKE FINK KEEL BOATS: Named for a riverboat captain who lived from 1770 to 1823 and once met up with Davy Crockett, the pair of squat, oddly shaped Mike Fink Keel Boats—*Bertha Mae* and the *Gullywhumper*—also traverse the Rivers of America. Since they take in the same scenery as the Liberty Square Riverboats (from a different angle), you wouldn't want to do both in the same day. Closes at dusk.

THE HAUNTED MANSION: Those who expect to get the daylights scared out of them inside this big old house, modeled on those built by the Dutch in the Hudson River Valley in the 18th century, will be a tad disappointed. In deference to the number of small children and other easily frightened souls who tour the Magic Kingdom every day, the most terrifying parts were expunged and a pleasant voice-over keeps things from getting too serious. Even then, the experience that's left is among the Magic Kingdom's best. Special effect is piled upon special effect, and just when you think you've seen it all, there's something new: the raven who appears over and over again; the bats' eyes on the wallpaper; the plaque that reads "Tomb, Sweet Tomb"; the suit of armor that comes alive; the horrible transparent specter in the attic; the terrified cemetery watchman and his mangy mutt; the ghostly teapot pouring ghostly tea; the difficult-to-identify flying objects above the image in the crystal ball (which is actually of a woman who works in the wardrobe department).

In the portrait hall (which you enter after passing through the mansion's front doors), it's amusing to speculate: Is the ceiling moving up—or is the floor descending? It's one way here, and the other way at the Haunted Mansion in California's Disneyland.

At both places, one of the biggest jobs of the maintenance crews is not cleaning up, but keeping things nice and dirty. Since each mansion's attic is littered with some 200 trunks, chairs, dress forms, shovels, harps, rugs, and assorted other knick-knacks, it requires a good deal of dust. This is purchased from a West Coast firm by the five-pound bagful and distributed by a device that looks as if it were meant to spread grass seed. Local legend has it that enough has been used since the park's 1971 opening to bury the mansion. Cobwebs are bought in liquid form and strung up by a secret process.

When waiting to enter, note the amusing inscriptions on the tombstones in the overgrown cemetery.

MICKEY'S BIRTHDAYLAND

It may be hard to believe that the world's most famous mouse is 61 years old, but on November 18, 1989 (the same day in 1928 that "Steamboat Willie" premiered), Mickey celebrated 61 years in show business. In October 1988, to celebrate Mickey's 60th, Walt Disney World created "Mickey's Birthdayland," a special addition to the Magic Kingdom that covered a 3-acre site adjacent to Fantasyland. The area was of special interest to younger WDW visitors, but parents also enjoyed watching their offspring join in the celebration of Mickey's birthday with Minnie, Pluto, Goofy, Chip and Dale, and Donald Duck. Audience participation was the major component of the birthday bash, and youngsters truly had the time of their lives. So successful was the original year-long birthday party, that it was decided to celebrate Mickey's special day every year.

The best way to get to Mickey's Birthdayland is aboard the Walt Disney World Railroad. Observant visitors will notice a variety of characters and props along the way, including the Mad Hatter's Tea Party and Goofy trying to fix a flat tire on his car.

Upon arrival in Duckburg, where the welcome sign reads "The Home of Mickey Mouse," a 65-foot-tall, red-white-and-blue Mickey balloon greets guests. The two enormous oak trees at the entrance each weigh 20 tons and were moved here from the Walt Disney World tree farm.

The main street of Duckburg, where guests visit Mickey Mouse's house, is also lined with such establishments as Scrooge McDuck's Bank and Daisy Duck's Millinery. Outside Mickey's house is his balloon-tired car and Pluto's doghouse; a swing sways on the front porch. Once inside, visitors see Mickey's bedroom, where his pants are laying on the chair; a radio plays some old Disney song favorites in the den; the television set shows "The Magical World of Disney"; in the memorabilia room, photos of Mickey with Walt and other celebrities cover the walls; a phone is off the hook in the kitchen, and Minnie's voice can be heard calling "Mickey where are you?"; the teapot is boiling and all evidence indicates that Mickey's around, but no one can find him.

From Mickey's house, birthday party guests head for a tent for an 8-minute cartoon shown on 10 television monitors. Then it's on to the live show, where Minnie, Pluto, Goofy Chip, Dale, and Donald Duck join with a seven-piece band as they prepare for Mickey's big party. The characters bake a cake for Mickey, throwing everything they can get their hands on into a 10-gallon mixing bowl. Once the cake is in the oven, Goofy is left in charge. The oven turns a bright red, shakes, rumbles, and then an explosion reveals a magnificent birthday cake.

In another room four 6-foot-by-4-foot screens show DTV (the Disney version of MTV), as children dance on a floor shaped like Mickey's face. One screen is set up so children passing before a camera will see themselves on TV. There is also a miniature cut-out storybook that's just the right size for curious youngsters, and 3-dimensional cut-outs of Mickey, Donald, the Gummi Bears, and others.

In the outdoor area of Mickey's Birthdayland, after guests leave the party tent, Mickey's dressing room offers the chance to shake the mouse's hand and have someone take a picture. Mickey's Treehouse and Minnie's Doll House offer opportunities for climbing, exploring, and having an all-around good time. There's also Grandma Duck's Farm, where children can get up close to some extremely cuddly baby animals; a maze, called the Mouskamaze, where topiary shrubs and trees create a not-too-confusing path for children; Disney cartoonists who draw caricature portraits of guests and place them in special souvenir birthday cards; and a balloon man who creates a whole menagerie of colorful animals right on the spot. Drink, cookie, and ice cream carts are located all around the outdoor area.

Special entertainment is featured throughout the year, ranging from jugglers and puppeteers to guest musical groups. And plans are in the works to originate portions of a new television series from Mickey's Birthdayland for the Disney Channel. Guests may be chosen to attend shows during production on the sound stages at the new Disney-MGM Studios Theme Park.

Guests leave Mickey's Birthdayland along a path guarded by topiary trees and shrubs that have been pruned into many shapes, including Disney characters. The path leads directly to Fantasyland, so the transition is a smooth and pleasant one.

FANTASYLAND

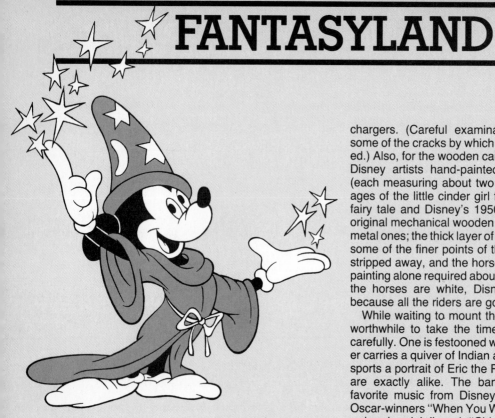

Walt Disney called this a "timeless land of enchantment," and his successors term it "the happiest land of all"—and it is, for some. Although it's not precisely a kiddieland, it is the home of a number of rides that are particularly well liked by younger children. The nursery-song cadences of "It's a Small World" appeal to them, as do the bright colors of the trash baskets, the flowers, and the tentlike rooftops; and they delight in the fairy-tale architecture and ambience, reminiscent of a king's castle courtyard during a particularly lively fair. Fantasyland is also one of the most heavily trafficked areas of the park.

CINDERELLA'S GOLDEN CARROUSEL: Not everything in the Magic Kingdom is a Disney version of the real article. This carousel, discovered at the now-defunct Maplewood, New Jersey, Olympic Park, was built for the Detroit Palace Garden Park (also long gone) by Italian-born wood-carvers of the Philadelphia Toboggan Company back in 1917. That was the end of the golden century of carousel-building that began around 1825 (when the Common Council of Manhattan Island, New York, granted one John Sears a permit to "establish a covered circus for a Flying Horse Establishment"). "Liberty"—as the Philadelphia Toboggan Company's red, white, and blue creation was called during that patriotic era—originally featured 72 horses on an oversize moving platform measuring 60 feet in diameter, plus several stationary chariots. During the Disney refurbishing these were removed, and many were replaced with additional horses made of fiberglass. Also, the original horses' legs, which were arranged in a rather decorous pose, were ingeniously rearranged to make the steeds look like real

chargers. (Careful examination seems to reveal some of the cracks by which this change was effected.) Also, for the wooden canopy above the horses, Disney artists hand-painted 18 separate scenes (each measuring about two by three feet) with images of the little cinder girl from Charles Perrault's fairy tale and Disney's 1950 film. Additionally, the original mechanical wooden parts were replaced by metal ones; the thick layer of paint that had obscured some of the finer points of the original carving was stripped away, and the horses were repainted. The painting alone required about 48 hours per horse. All the horses are white, Disney spokespeople say, because all the riders are good guys!

While waiting to mount the carousel's steeds it's worthwhile to take the time to study the animals carefully. One is festooned with yellow roses, another carries a quiver of Indian arrows, and yet another sports a portrait of Eric the Red on its back. No two are exactly alike. The band organ, which plays favorite music from Disney Studios (such as the Oscar-winners "When You Wish Upon A Star," "Zip-a-dee-doo-dah," and "Chim-Chim-Cheree"), was made in one of Italy's most famous factories.

MAD TEA PARTY: The theme of this ride—in a group of oversize pastel-colored teacups that whirl and spin as wildly as many carnivals' Tubs of Fun—derives from a scene in the Disney studio's 1951 production of Lewis Carroll's novel *Alice in Wonderland*. During the sequence in question, the Mad Hatter hosts a tea party for his un-birthday. Unlike many of the other rides in Fantasyland, this attraction is not strictly for the younger children; the 9-to-20 crowd seems to like it best. Be sure to note the soused mouse that pops out of the teapot at the center of the platform full of teacups.

DUMBO, THE FLYING ELEPHANT: This is purely and simply a kiddie ride—though personages as varied as Romanian gymnast Nadia Comaneci and Muhammad Ali have loved it. The character of the flying elephant was developed for the 1941 film release of *Dumbo*, one of the shortest of Disney's animated features and one of the best, starring a baby elephant born with inordinately large ears and an ability to fly that is discovered after he accidentally drinks a bucket of champagne. The mouse that sits atop the mirrored ball in the middle of the circle of the ride's flying elephants is the faithful Timothy Mouse, who in the film becomes Dumbo's manager after the circus folk who had once laughed at the flying elephant hire him to be a star.

MAGIC JOURNEYS: Back by popular demand. This spectacular 70mm 3-D motion picture (it used to play at Journey into Imagination in Epcot Center), which is viewed while wearing purple-rimmed polarized eyeglasses, is one of the largest-format films of this type. It is also remarkably realistic: when the screen fills with apple blossoms or a kite heads right at the audience, nearly everyone in the theater reaches out; when lightning strikes, people jump back in fright.

To get dramatic results like these, Disney cameramen developed a new system of 3-D photography, which some observers have called the most precise and versatile in existence today. Two synchronized cameras are used, one for each of the images that each visitor's eyes see. The amount of depth that the viewer perceives is determined by the distance between the cameras and the direction in which they are aimed. The new Disney system offers greater-than-ever control over both of these variables. The 18-minute film was directed by Murray Lerner, who won an Academy Award in 1981 for his documentary *From Mao to Mozart: Isaac Stern in China*. Presented by Kodak.

PETER PAN'S FLIGHT: The inspiration for this attraction was the Scottish writer Sir James M. Barrie's play about the boy who wouldn't grow up, which appeared as a Disney movie in 1953. Riding in flying versions of Captain Hook's ornate ship—which are suspended from an overhead rail once they leave the boarding area—visitors swoop and soar through a series of scenes that tell the story of how Wendy, Michael, and John get sprinkled with pixie dust and, heading for "the second star to the right and straight on till morning," fly off to Never-Never-Land with Tinkerbell; and meet Princess Tiger Lilly, the evil Captain Hook, his jolly-looking sidekick Mr. Smee, and the crocodile—who has already made off with one of Hook's hands and is on the verge of getting the rest of him as you sail out into daylight. As in the movie, one of the most beautiful scenes—one that makes this attraction a treat for adults as well as for littler folk—is the sight of nighttime London, dark blue and speckled with twinkling yellow lights, complete with the Thames, Big Ben, London Bridge, and vehicles that really move on the streets. The song that accompanies the trip is "You Can Fly, You Can Fly, You Can Fly" by Sammy Cahn and Sammy Fain.

SKYWAY TO TOMORROWLAND: Entered from near Peter Pan's Flight, this aerial tram transports guests one-way to Tomorrowland. En route it's possible to see the clear aquamarine pool traversed by Captain Nemo's ship, the striped tent tops of Cinderella's Golden Carrousel, Tomorrowland's Grand Prix raceway, and the not-so-wonderful rooftops of the buildings where many Magic Kingdom adventures actually take place. This attraction is best boarded at its Tomorrowland terminus, where the lines are usually slightly shorter.

IT'S A SMALL WORLD: Originally created for New York's 1964–1965 World's Fair, with a tunefully singsong melody written by Richard M. and Robert B. Sherman (the Academy Award-winning composers of the music for *Mary Poppins,* among other Disney scores), this favorite of young children and senior citizens involves a boat trip through several large rooms where stylized Audio-Animatronics dolls—wooden soldiers, cancan dancers, balloonists, chess pieces, Tower of London guards in scarlet beefeater uniforms, bagpipers and leprechauns, gooseherds, little Dutch kids in wooden shoes, Don Quixote and a goatherd, yodelers and gondoliers, houri dancers, dancers from Greece and Thailand, snake charmers, Japanese kite flyers, hippos and giraffes and frogs, hyenas, monkeys, and elephants, hip-twitching Polynesians, surfers, and even dolphins—sing and dance to a melody that will run through your head for hours after you float out of their wonderland. Of the 2 queues that are usually found here, the one to the left is almost always shorter.

SNOW WHITE'S ADVENTURES: This attraction near the carousel retells the scary part of the Grimm Brothers' fairy tale, which Walt Disney made into the world's first full-length animated feature in 1937 and 1938. Though basically a ride for kids, Snow White's Adventures features two skeletons and plenty of spooky darkness; also, the wicked witch—evil, long-nosed, and practically toothless—appears more than once with such suddenness and menace that some youngsters can be really frightened. At the end, the hag dumps a rock on the passengers; the stars you see are among the attraction's best special effects.

MR. TOAD'S WILD RIDE: Wild in name only, this attraction is based on the October 1949 Disney release *The Adventures of Ichabod and Mr. Toad,* which itself derives from Kenneth Grahame's classic novel *The Wind in the Willows.* It seems that a gang of weasels has tricked that memorable man-about-town Mr. J. Thaddeus Toad into trading the deed to his ancestral mansion for a stolen motorcar. In the attraction, flivvers modeled on this very car take guests zigging and zagging along the road to Nowhere in Particular, through dark rooms painted in neon colors and illuminated by black lights where the redoubtable Mr. Toad is trying to get out of the scrape. In the process, you crash through a fireplace, narrowly miss being struck by a falling suit of armor, go hurtling through haystacks and barn doors and into a coop full of squawking chickens, then ride down a railroad track on a collision course with a huge locomotive. Some of this is scary enough that some children end up momentarily frightened. By and large, though, this is for kids.

20,000 LEAGUES UNDER THE SEA: Jules Verne, on whose novel Disney based the 1954 release that provides the theme for this attraction, described the Machiavellian Captain Nemo's ship as an undersea monster, with headlights that appeared as eyes in the dark water. The 61-foot-long, 58-ton, 38-passenger crafts that ply the beautiful, blue Fantasyland lagoon are far too handsome to fit the description, but—at least on the outside—they bear a remarkable resemblance to the craft piloted by the nefarious Nemo toward Vulcania. In the course of the trip, visitors tour an 11½-million-gallon pool filled with sea grass, kelp, giant fishes, clams, seahorses, coral, icebergs, and rock formations fashioned of fiberglass, plastic, steel, stucco, and epoxy paint. The ship's course passes by the lost city of Atlantis and under a rather attractive "polar ice cap"; as in the film, passengers listen to Nemo playing the organ, and endure an attack by a giant squid. The special effects aren't the Magic Kingdom's best, and the queues outside move rather slowly—so don't line up unless it's not too busy.

Incidentally, the nautical flags above the entrance—which now spell out the word "Leagues" in the attraction's name—read S-E-U-G-A-E-L when the park first opened. A Navy visitor pointed out the mistake. The queue area is done up with Disney-made rocks, which are meant to resemble the volcanic boulders that would have been found on Nemo's Vulcania. The area is also graced with a large Senegal date palm and a Southern magnolia, which were so heavy that the ceiling of the Magic Kingdom basement down below had to be specially reinforced to support them. The cliffs into which the submarines disappear, on the far side of the lagoon, conceal the backstage area where much of the scenery is set up; a better view of the layout is available from the Skyway above.

TOMORROWLAND

With its vast expanse of concrete, Tomorrowland offers a picture of the future that is a little less than wonderful, since the architecture looks a bit too much like yesterday's version of Tomorrow: As Disney planners have discovered, it isn't easy to portray a future that persists in becoming the present. Flight to the Moon, for instance, became Mission to Mars in 1975, when the earth's lunar neighbor began to seem almost as close-to-home as the neighborhood McDonald's. But the extreme forms into which many of the trees and bushes have been pruned do look vaguely futuristic. Note the ligustrums between the Grand Prix Raceway and the Tomorrowland Terrace—shrubs that have been shaped into single-trunked trees topped with spheres; the oleanders, another type of shrub pruned like a tree, located in raised planters near the Carousel of Progress; and many others. One of the most interesting of the plantings, the ligustrum near Tomorrowland Terrace—which looks a bit like an octopus balancing many green trays—was found by a Disney landscape artist in the 1960s on the front lawn of a Sarasota home whose owner was persuaded to give up her pet for a check and a promise to repair any damages incurred in the transplanting operation. (Eventually, that meant not only fixing the lawn, but also repaving the lady's driveway.)

Also, Space Mountain—which anchors this land at its eastern edge (with the bulky contours of the Contemporary Resort rising just beyond)—has a shape that seems almost timeless. Though this attraction is usually very crowded in the afternoon during peak seasons, most others—high-capacity adventures that they are—may require no waits then, so Tomorrowland is a good area to visit during a busy time on one of the Magic Kingdom's busier days.

SPACE MOUNTAIN: Rising to a height of over 180 feet and extending some 300 feet in diameter, this gleaming white steel and concrete cone (shaped vaguely like Japan's Mount Fuji) houses an attraction that most people call a roller coaster. Actually, it bears the same sort of resemblance to the traditional thrill ride as the Magic Kingdom does to the garden variety of theme park. It's the Disney version—a roller coaster and then some. While the 2-minute-and-38-second ride does not exactly duplicate a trip into outer space, there are some truly phenomenal and quite lovely special effects—

shooting stars and strobelike flashing lights among them; and the whole ride takes place in an outer space-like darkness that gets progressively inkier—and scarier—as the journey progresses. The 6-passenger rockets that roar through this blackness attain a maximum speed of just over 28 miles per hour. Just how terrifying this actually is to any given passenger depends on his or her level of tolerance. In general, the Space Mountain trip seems to inspire in lovers of thrill rides an immediate desire to go again; it's just wild enough to send eyeglasses, purses, wallets, and even an occasional set of false teeth plummeting to the bottom of the track, so be sure to find a safe place for your possessions before the ride starts. It's also turbulent enough to upset the stomachs of those so unwise as to ride it immediately after eating—but not so harrowing that passengers shake and weakened knees persist for more than a minute or two after "touch-down." Those in a quandary about whether or not to line up can get a preview from the WEDway PeopleMover described below; and those who decide to pass after hearing the shrieks and the clatter of the cars from the queue area have their own special exit.

After experiencing the space journey, it's interesting to note some statistics: The mountain itself—which occupies a 10-acre site and contains 4,508,500 cubic feet, enough to accommodate a small skyscraper—is composed of 72 pre-stressed concrete beams cast nearby, then hoisted into place by mammoth cranes. Each rib weighs 74 tons, and measures 117 feet in length and, in width, 4 feet at the top and 13 feet at the bottom. With the work lights on, the interior of Space Mountain looks humdrum and almost commercially common, with its tangled array of track and supporting scaffolding. Some of the shooting stars are produced quite simply, by aiming a beam of light at a mirrored globe; and legend has it that the meteors visible to guests in the queue area are actually projections of chocolate chip cookies! The whole ride is controlled by a computer and is monitored on a board full of

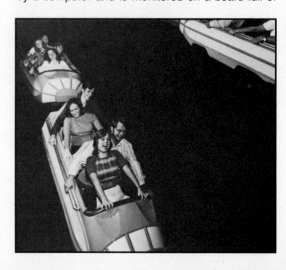

dials and a battery of closed-circuit television screens by Disney hosts and hostesses sitting in a control room (whose eerie blue glow is another striking feature of the queue area). As a result, any guest caught acting in an unsafe manner can be warned, and the ride stopped, if necessary. Children under seven years old or less than 44 inches tall must be accompanied by an adult; no children under three are permitted; and as the many signs at the attraction warn, "You must be in Good Health, and Free from Heart Conditions, Motion Sickness, Back or Neck Problems, or Other Physical Limitations" to ride. It is also suggested that expectant mothers pass up the trip. Presented by Thomson Consumer Electronics.

RYCA/DREAM OF A NEW WORLD: The moving sidewalk that takes guests out of Space Mountain also carries them past scenes in which some of the Magic Kingdom's less sophisticated Audio-Animatronics figures demonstrate the uses of the electronic media in the future, in business and in the home. Far more interesting are the RCA Broadcast Systems ($70,000 to $80,000 each) that allow guests to see themselves on television—in living color.

SKYWAY TO FANTASYLAND: This aerial cable car takes guests from Tomorrowland to a point near Peter Pan's Flight in Fantasyland. The trip takes 5 minutes, and the cable car—built by Von Roll, Ltd., of Bern, Switzerland, then shipped to Miami and on to Orlando—is notable for being the nation's first conveyance of its type able to make a 90-degree turn. If you're going to ride the Skyway, this is the place to get on: The lines at the Fantasyland end are usually slightly longer.

STARJETS: Towering high over Tomorrowland, this is purely and simply a thrill ride and ought to delight anyone who loves Space Mountain, but doesn't necessarily want to get in line all over again.

WEDWAY PEOPLEMOVER: Boarded near the StarJets, these small, 5-car trains move at a speed of about 10 miles per hour along close to a mile of track, alongside or through most of the major attractions in Tomorrowland. If you have any doubts about riding Space Mountain, a trip on the People-Mover—which travels through the queue area inside and offers a view of the rockets as they hurtle through the darkness—will probably help you make your decision. Just as important, from an intellectual standpoint, is the fact that the WEDway People-Mover shows off an innovative means of transportation: It is operated by a linear induction motor that has no moving parts, uses little power, and emits no pollution.

MISSION TO MARS: After a preflight briefing in a room styled to look like Mission Control, and a narration by an Audio-Animatronics flight engineer who looks just like the father in the Carousel of Progress family, guests enter a round cabin for a simulated trip to Mars that was developed in cooperation with NASA. Seats tilt and shake, sub-audible sound waves are sent out, and oversize speakers let out great roars and hisses that sound like a washing machine during the spin cycle; corny though the idea is, the realization is okay. The attraction is located opposite CircleVision 360 (described below). Films screened during the flight, some developed from photos taken during the Mariner Nine space program, show a section of Mars's surface called Mariner Valley and its 40-mile-wide Olympus Mons, the universe's largest known volcano. The best viewing for this show is from the third and fourth rows.

CAROUSEL OF PROGRESS: First seen at New York's 1964–1965 World's Fair and moved here in 1975, this 22-minute show features a number of tableaux starring an Audio-Animatronics family, and

will spend as many hours driving the Mark VII-model gasoline-powered cars as they can; one 87-year-old grandmother comes here just to watch. Like true sports cars, the vehicles—which cost about $6,000 each—have rack-and-pinion steering and disc brakes; unlike most sports cars, these run on a track. Nonetheless, even expert drivers have a hard time keeping them going in a straight line until the technique is mastered: Just steer all the way to the right, or all the way to the left, and you've got it made. One lap around the track takes about 4 minutes, and the cars (which are manufactured by a Disney company called MAPO, short for Mary Poppins) can travel at a maximum speed of about 7 mph. You must be at least 4'4" to drive the cars.

Presented by Goodyear.

demonstrates the great improvements in American life that have come about as the result of increased use of electricity.

CIRCLEVISION 360 "AMERICAN JOURNEYS": This 21-minute film, the first attraction on the far right just over the Tomorrowland Bridge, is a travel film like few others. Instead of showing only what's in front, it also lets viewers see what's behind and to either side. American Journeys was in the planning and production stages for four years. The crews trekked across the country from the Statue of Liberty to the ice floes of Glacier Bay, Alaska, with a 700-pound rig consisting of 9 cameras mounted so that they point up into a circle of mirrors. For one scene the crew placed the cumbersome camera rig atop a steam locomotive in the Colorado Rockies; in another the rig was attached to the bottom of a helicopter for a fly through Monument Valley, Arizona; and the first-ever underwater CircleVision scenes were done off the Florida coast using a custom-designed enclosure. This footage is shown in the big theater by an equally innovative arrangement of 9 projectors, nine 20-by-30-foot screens, and 12 channels of sound reproduced through 9 different speakers, plus 6 others, affixed to the ceiling, which carry the narration. Consequently, the experience is really impressive (and a few of the flight scenes are realistic enough to make some guests airsick). The journey includes stops at Mount St. Helens, just 2 days after it erupted in 1980; a ship-carver's workshop in Mystic, Connecticut; a bluegrass musical performance in Norris, Tennessee; Dodger Stadium in Los Angeles; and Cape Canaveral, Florida, for the launching of Space Shuttle Columbia. The grand finale is a spectacular fireworks display at the Statue of Liberty. The attraction can accommodate up to 3,100 people an hour, so don't be discouraged if you see a crowd outside; it disappears every 20 minutes or so. This is generally one of a handful of spots where the queues on a busy afternoon are the least discouraging. Note that there are no seats in the theater.

GRAND PRIX RACEWAY: The little cars that *vroom* down the four 2,260-foot-long tracks at this attraction opposite the Tomorrowland Terrace provide most of the background noise in Tomorrowland—and that's another grim thought about the future. Older kids and teenagers love the ride and

DREAMFLIGHT: A whimsical look at the adventure and romance of flight—as seen through the eyes of a child—awaits guests at this newest Tomorrowland attraction. A mixture of 2- and 3-dimensional media combine with special effects and digitally produced stereo music to take visitors on an entirely delightful journey. The attraction opens with a scene from a giant pop-up book, in which man's first attempts at flight are humorously depicted. Three-dimensional aircraft are used in a variety of scenes from the early days of flight. A barnstorming flying circus segment features a man and woman, each standing on a wing and keeping up a tennis match. The next segment highlights a 70mm live-action film, produced in the Northwest exclusively for this attraction, in which stunts are performed to the oohs and ahs of the audience. A wing walker does acrobatic feats, another stuntman out on a wing comes within 5 feet of the ground to pick up a ribbon, and a plane comes out of a barrel roll and sets down on a lake, all to the thrilled delight of onlookers.

From the world of barnstorming, guests make the transition to the age of commercial aviation. A full-size segment of an M-130 Flying Boat, a popular plane during the late 1930s, is on view. An elegant dining room (particularly by today's standards) is displayed as monitors allow glimpses of the faraway places the M-130 made accessible. In one scene, two dancers perform outside a Japanese temple garden; in another, the sun sets over Paris as a flower merchant packs up his blossoms on the steps of Montmartre. Next stop on the 4½-minute journey is the jet age, in its most pure form. Guests actually ride through a real engine. Digitally prepared graphics and special effects recreate the rotation of the turbine in a very realistic fashion.

In another 70mm film segment, visitors get that "you are there" feeling as they speed down a runway and fly off towards space. The moon, backlit by the sun, provides the lighting for some spectacular views over canyons, valleys, and flat terrain, where the suggestion of cities of the future are depicted. The finale features another pop-up book measuring 16 feet tall and 11 feet wide showing contemporary London and New York.

If this journey fuels the desire to travel, Delta is prepared to fulfill it. Brochures, ticket information, and flight schedules are available at the Delta counter at the Contemporary Resort.

Presented by Delta Air Lines.

SHOPS IN THE MAGIC KINGDOM

No one travels all the way to the Magic Kingdom just to go shopping. But as many a first-time visitor has learned with some surprise, shopping is one of the most enjoyable pastimes there. Donald Duck key chains and Mickey Mouse lapel pins, Alice in Wonderland dresses for little girls, Walt Disney World sweatshirts, and other Disney souvenir items make up a large portion of the merchandise you see on display.

But the Magic Kingdom's boutiques and stores stock much more than just Disneyana, and it's possible to buy antiques and silver-plated tea services, escargot holders and cookbooks, mock pirate hats and toy frontier rifles, 14-karat gold charms and filigreed costume jewelry in Main Street shops that also sell magic tricks and film, peanut brittle and Droste chocolate apples. In Adventureland, you can buy imported items from around the world—hand-carved elephant statues from Africa, inlaid marble boxes from India, batik dresses from Indonesia, and much more. Shops stock items that complement the themes of the various lands (and so, in Tomorrow-land, one finds contemporary wall hangings and futuristic-looking table lamps). Every store offers a selection of items from the inexpensive to the costly: In Tinkerbell Toy Shop in Fantasyland, for instance, kids can beg for a $5 windup toy after requests for the larger-than-life-size $350 stuffed animals are denied. At Uptown Jewelers on Main Street, a 3-foot-high Hummel figurine costs thousands of dollars. And in many shops, you can watch craftsmen at work—peanut brittle being poured in the Main Street Confectionery, a glass blower in Main Street's Crystal Arts and Adventureland's La Princesa de Cristal, and the like.

Consequently, there's no need to spend a fortune to have a good time. Budget-watchers should note, though, that the temptation to nickel-and-dime yourself into penury is very strong, and you need to be careful. It's a good idea to set a spending limit for each member of your party in advance—and try to stick to it.

MAIN STREET

EAST SIDE

STROLLER SHOP: Just after the turnstiles into the Magic Kingdom, to the right as you face Cinderella Castle. A limited number of strollers and wheelchairs can be rented here on a first come, first served basis, and assorted souvenirs purchased.

THE CHAPEAU: This Town Square shop is the place to buy Mouseketeer ears and have them monogrammed, and to shop for visors, straw hats, derbies, top hats, and other headgear. The shop sells decorated ladies' hats—fun to try on, if not necessarily worth the investment.

KODAK CAMERA CENTER: Gleaming glass-fronted mahogany cases show off the Canon, Minolta, Pentax, Nikon, and other 35mm, instant-load, quick-developing cameras for sale at this high-ceilinged shop near Town Square. Flashcubes, film, and other photo supplies are also available, and very minor repairs can be made. Cameras, including RCA Video Camcorders, are available for rent (a deposit is required).

You can also have an 8-by-10 Kodak portrait taken in old-fashioned costumes that look for all the world like something a favorite grandmother would have worn—except that the backs of the costumes are treated like hospital gowns; sitters pose on the rear end of a caboose. Even if you decide not to spend the money, it's amusing just to stand and watch other guests lining up to say "cheese."

MAIN STREET CONFECTIONERY: Delicious chocolates are available in this old-fashioned pink-and-white paradise. A delight at any time of day, but especially when the cooks in the shop's glass-walled kitchen are pouring peanut brittle onto a huge tabletop to cool, and the candy is sending up clouds of scent that you could swear were being fanned right out into the street. Some 18 to 20 batches are made each day. The sweet product is for sale in small bags, along with pastilles, jelly beans, marshmallow peanuts and nougats, mints and kisses, and dozens of other nemeses for a sweet tooth. When your stomach is growling, this is a good place to grab a snack.

UPTOWN JEWELERS: Fine china and other gift items—china birds and figurines, swans, china flowers, Dresden and Lladro figurines, and all manner of pretty teacups, Disney character figurines——priced from $1 to $16,500—are the stock-in-trade of this airy establishment. The most expensive item, at last look, was a giant Hummel statue, depicting ruddy-cheeked peasant children in an apple tree; at least peek at it, even if it is a bit rich for most pocketbooks. There's also a selection of good-quality and costume jewelry. One counter stocks wonderful souvenir charms in 14-karat gold and sterling silver: Tinkerbell, Cinderella Castle, and the Walt Disney World logo (a globe with mouse ears). Clocks and watches in all shapes and sizes, not to mention Mickey Mouse watches in a variety of configurations, are available here. There are clocks for the kitchen and clocks for the living room, clocks with chimes and clocks without them, alarm clocks for bedside tables and others for travel, digital watches and watches with hands, and even some pocket watches and a Mickey Mouse telephone—with Touch Tone. Purchases can be shipped on request. Presented by Lorus.

DISNEY & COMPANY: The wallpaper at this shop on Center Street (the cul-de-sac just off Main) is Victorian and the woodwork elaborate; and old-fashioned ceiling fans twirl slowly overhead. This character shop offers sweatshirts and T-shirts, hats and bags, pens and pencils, stuffed animals, and other items. The selection is not as vast as the Emporium, but neither is Disney & Company quite so overwhelming.

MARKET HOUSE: An old-fashioned spot, with pretzels, pickles, honey, and all kinds of tea and snack items arranged in oak cases. The floors are oak and pegged, the lighting comes in part from brass lanterns, and in one corner there's a real old-fashioned hand-crank telephone. Tobacco products are also available, and very attractive souvenir matchbooks are handed out with each purchase.

THE SHADOW BOX: Watching Rubio Artist Co. silhouette cutters snip black paper into the likenesses of children is one of Main Street's more fascinating diversions, and there's always a crowd on hand—some folks waiting their turn, some just inspecting the progress and the results. Framed silhouettes cost $4.

CRYSTAL ARTS: Cut-glass bowls and vases, urns and glasses, plates and shelves glitter in the mirror-backed glass cases of this high-ceilinged, brass-chandeliered emporium. An engraver or a glass-blower is always at work by the bright light flooding through the big windows. The wares available at La Princesa de Cristal are similar. Presented by the Arribas Brothers.

WEST SIDE

NEWSSTAND: No newspapers are sold in the Magic Kingdom—even at its Newsstand, which is opposite the Stroller Shop, to your left as you face

window displays, which usually feature Audio-Animatronics displays ranging from themes of the season to the most recent Disney movie.

HARMONY BARBER SHOP: The setting is quaint and old-fashioned, worth a peek even if you've no need for a trim. Nostalgic shaving items and moustache cups are for sale.

DISNEY CLOTHIERS: Disney-character merchandise has always been popular, as evidenced by the number of T-shirts, Mickey Mouse ears, wristwatches, and sweatshirts sold each year. This shop caters to fashion-conscious shoppers with a love for Disney gear. There is a vast array of men's, women's, and children's clothing and accessories, all of which incorporate Disney characters in some way. There are men's golf shirts with a small Mickey Mouse embroidered on the pocket, and satin-look jackets with Mickey (as the sorcerer's apprentice in *Fantasia*) embossed on the back. Hats, ties, exercise clothing, and dress shirts round out the adult selections. Children's items include socks, suspenders, tops, pants, and bathing suits.

Cinderella Castle, just after you've passed through the turnstiles at the entrance to the Magic Kingdom. Character merchandise and souvenirs are for sale. The selection is fairly limited, but you can usually pick up items you've forgotten during your travels through the rest of the park.

THE EMPORIUM: Framed by a two-story-high portico, this Town Square landmark, the Magic Kingdom's largest gift shop, stocks a little bit of everything—stuffed animals and toys; an array of dolls; sundries, film, Florida souvenirs, and more. Everyone seems to have an armload of Walt Disney World T-shirts and sweatshirts, towels and handbags, Mouseketeer ears and other hats, and various items emblazoned with Mickey, Minnie, or Walt Disney World logos. The cash registers almost always seem to be busy, especially toward the end of the afternoon and before park closing. It's a good place to souvenir-shop, though, since it's only a few steps from lockers (under the train station) where purchases can be stowed. Don't forget to note the

HOUSE OF MAGIC: Magicians can make ordinary playing cards simply disappear, balls pass through cups, water pour out of a jug that looks empty, coins pass through solid sheets of rubber, and a wand turn into two silken handkerchiefs. Some believers can produce coins from thin air, or pour the milk from a whole pitcher into a thimble. This Main Street shop sells the kind of magician's tools that can turn everyday travelers into magicians, along with party-joke items such as phony arm casts, slimy reptiles, and similar stuff.

MAIN STREET STATIONER: Greeting cards are featured in this boutique, along with wrapping paper and pretty party items, including paper plates, napkins, and tablecloths.

ADVENTURELAND

TRADERS OF TIMBUKTU: This shop is in a marketlike complex in the plaza opposite the Enchanted Tiki Birds, and displays a fine selection of the sort of handsome (but inexpensive) trinkets that travelers find while visiting the erstwhile Dark Continent—carved wooden giraffes and antelopes, ethnic jewelry (including carved bangles, malachite, and elephant-hair jewelry), dashikis, and khaki shirts.

BWANA BOB'S: A whimsical and colorful hut full of the critters you may have just seen on the Jungle Cruise or at the Tropical Serenade.

TIKI TROPIC SHOP: Hawaiian and tropical clothing, short sets, shoes, and jewelry, plus a fine assortment of bathing suits are featured at this establishment located near Traders of Timbuktu, opposite the exit of Sunshine Tree Terrace.

ELEPHANT TALES: A variety of women's and men's clothing with a safari theme are featured at this shop. Women's accessories and safari plush toys are also available.

COLONEL HATHI'S SAFARI CLUB: This emporium near the entrance to the Swiss Family Treehouse, named after the elephant in the 1967 film *The Jungle Book*, smells sweetly of the rattan and straw goods that give it its tropical character. Merchandise here is all summer stuff: sunglasses and wind chimes, thongs and cotton sportswear, straw handbags and shells, coral bangles, palmetto fans, and sharks' teeth necklaces.

PIRATES OF THE CARIBBEAN PLAZA

LAFFITE'S PORTRAIT DECK: Hidden away near the Plaza del Sol Caribe, this is the Adventureland counterpart of the photography studio in Main Street's Camera Center. Here, though, instead of posing in the most genteel of Gay Nineties garb, you dress up as swashbucklers and pirate maids amid what look to be pieces of eight and chests brimful of pearls and precious jewels.

HOUSE OF TREASURE: The only spot in the Magic Kingdom that sells pirates' hats, this swashbuckler's delight adjoins Pirates of the Caribbean on the west and stocks piratical merchandise—toy rifles and brass dolphins, a Pirate's Creed of Ethics printed on parchment, Jolly Roger flags, rings, old-looking maps, pirate dolls, sailing ship models, ships in a bottle, and eye patches. There's as much for adults as for youngsters.

THE GOLDEN GALLEON: A real antique diver's helmet is the centerpiece of this neighbor of La Princesa de Cristal, a low-ceilinged, tile-floored shop full of golden treasures—handsome nautical items, globes, brass cannons, ships' wheels, and a spyglass—not to mention nautical and resort ready-to-wear fashions for men and women as well as comfortable, casual shoes.

LA PRINCESA DE CRISTAL: The cut-glass items, custom-engraved goblets and bowls, and blown-glass baubles sold at this emporium tucked away behind the snack stand called El Pirata y El Perico, opposite Pirates of the Caribbean, are about the same as those in Crystal Arts on Main Street—but the ceilings here are lower and beamed, and the floors are red tile instead of linoleum—so the feeling is totally different.

Warning to the squeamish: The sound made by the engravers is for all the world like fingers scraping on a chalkboard. Eek! Presented by the Arribas Brothers.

PLAZA DEL SOL CARIBE: This market next to the Pirates of the Caribbean sells candy and snacks, a variety of straw hats (including colorful oversized sombreros), piñatas, pottery, straw bags, ready-to-wear, and artificial flowers.

FRONTIERLAND

FRONTIER TRADING POST: This is the place to stock your chuck wagon with venison chili, wild boar meat, buffalo, cornbread mix, and buttermilk biscuit mix. Or you can outfit a youngster like a true child of the Great Frontier: Cowboy hats or feathered headdresses and moccasins, hefty brass belt buckles, sleeve garters, sheriff's badges, gold nugget and turquoise jewelry, and reproduction pistols and rifles should do the trick. Also available are western items like tom-toms, peace pipes, plastic toy horses, and forts. Film and sundries are in stock, too.

TRICORNERED HAT SHOPPE: This emporium offers hats of all descriptions (though the specialties of the house are western styles), plus feathered hatbands and leather goods. It's tucked away near the arcade leading to Adventureland, between the ornamental Frontierland stockade, alongside the Diamond Horseshoe Saloon.

BEARLY COUNTRY: At the exit from the Country Bear Vacation Hoedown. Features hand-crafted goods plus Big Al stuffed bears. Country skirts with matching blouses are also available.

WOOD CARVERS: A good spot for personalized, wood-carved gifts. Presented by Rubio Artist Co.

FRONTIER WOOD CARVERS: Located along the river, this shop features hand-carved decorative items. A craftsman is usually on hand to demonstrate his talent. Presented by Rubio Artist Co.

BRIER PATCH: Also along the river, woodsy gifts, woven baskets, and stuffed forest animals are available at this shop.

LIBERTY SQUARE

OLDE WORLD ANTIQUES: One of the first of the Liberty Square shops that visitors pass after crossing the bridge from the Hub area in front of Cinderella Castle, this little, lace-curtained emporium stocks real antiques—hutches, drop-leaf tables, and assorted decorative items in brass, pewter, copper, mahogany, oak, and pine—as well as some reproductions. Other unique treasures from the past include jewelry and clothing. Prices run into thousands of dollars, and bargains are nowhere to be found, but every item is in tip-top condition and tagged with a description of its origin, so the browsing is good.

HERITAGE HOUSE: Among the Early American reproductions that predominate in the stock of this store next to The Hall of Presidents, youngsters may go for the parchment copies of famous American documents, while homeowners might snap up pewter plates and candlesticks, creweled items, wooden candlesticks and pepper mills, busts of the presidents, souvenir spoons, mugs in Early American motifs, wrought-iron knickknacks, or lovely enameled paintings of clipper ships. Both perfumes created to order and name-brand fragrances are available here.

YANKEE TRADER: No first-time visitor to the Magic Kingdom would expect to be able to buy stoneware soufflé dishes and espresso makers, cast-iron muffin tins and escargot holders. But this wonderfully fragrant shop, immediately to the right after you turn into the lane leading to the Haunted Mansion, is crammed like a too-small kitchen cabinet with just these kitchen knickknacks, and more: cookie cutters and choppers, graters and spatulas, french-fry slicers, wooden-handled whisks, egg timers, and wall plaques made of dough, to name just a few of the sorts of items available here. There are also displays of Smucker's jams and jellies in more varieties than any supermarket shopper would have imagined existed. Cookbooks are also for sale—not

only the old favorites like *Joy of Cooking*, but also unusual volumes of historic recipes. The store is located near the archway-entrance to Fantasyland.

ICHABOD'S LANDING: This small shop, situated next to Mike Fink's Keel Boats, gives guests on their way to the Haunted Mansion a taste of things to come with a stock of horrific monster masks and assorted ghoulish goodies (in a more limited selection than at Main Street's House of Magic).

SILVERSMITH: The sign above the entrance to this tiny shop adjoining Olde World Antiques (just next to the Liberty Square bridge to the Hub) reads "J. Tremain, Prop." That refers to the main character in the 1957 Disney film of the Esther Forbes novel about a silversmith's apprentice who joins the Boston Tea Party and helps hang the lights on the Liberty Tree during America's colonial days. At this low-ceilinged, plank-floored establishment, antique-looking cabinets display tongs and teaspoons, Revere-style bowls, tea sets, silver-coated roses, candelabra, and more—all in sterling or silver plate.

FANTASYLAND

THE KING'S GALLERY: Situated inside Cinderella Castle, near the entrance to King Stefan's Banquet Hall, this shop is one of the Magic Kingdom's best. The walls are dark and the ceilings beamed, and the stock includes large tapestries, suits of armor, unicorns of all sizes, decorative boxes, cuckoo clocks, Spanish-made swords, German beer mugs with lids, chess sets, and more—very little of it at rock-bottom prices. Also here, practiced artisans demonstrate the art of damascening, a form of metalworking originated by the inhabitants of Damascus in the sixth century A.D.; it is mastered today by only a handful of specialized craftsmen around the world. Painstakingly, these skilled workers dip steel pendants into acid to create tiny pores, then use a combination of sterling silver and 24-karat gold wire to outline butterflies and other designs onto the acid-blackened steel.

MICKEY'S CHRISTMAS CAROL: A wide selection of Christmas items, including tree-top dolls and souvenir ornaments, is available here.

DISNEYANA SHOP: This shop near Cinderella Castle, opposite Cinderella's Golden Carrousel, specializes in Disney collectibles such as limited edition Disney plates, cels from Disney movies, and other one-of-a-kind Disney items.

THE MAD HATTER: Another place to buy Mouseketeer ears and other souvenir hats and have your name embroidered on them on the spot. This shop was named for the Mad Hatter, who held the tea party for his un-birthday in Disney's 1951 film version of Lewis Carroll's classic *Alice in Wonderland*.

TINKERBELL TOY SHOP: One of the more wonderful boutiques in the Magic Kingdom, and a fine toy store by any standards. For sale are stuffed animals, miniature model cars and trucks, character patches, windup toys and wooden toys, bar soap emblazoned with Disney scenes, Mickey and Minnie toys and clothing, Alice in Wonderland dresses, Snow White dresses (with Dopey on the skirt), and a positively marvelous array of Madame Alexander dolls. A must.

THE ARISTOCATS: Most of the lands have one store that specializes in Disney souvenirs; this stone-walled, vaguely Gothic shop slightly to the northeast of Cinderella Castle is Fantasyland's spot for Donald and Mickey key chains, sweatshirts and T-shirts, china Disney figurines, salt and pepper shakers, Minnie tote bags, tennis balls with a Mickey logo, and more.

THE ROYAL CANDY SHOPPE: This souvenir stand next to Gurgi's Munchies & Crunchies sells assorted Disneyana, including Mickey Mouse back scratchers, key chains, and stuffed animals, plus a selection of jelly beans and peppermint sticks, Tootsie Rolls, lollipops, and other hard candy.

KODAK KIOSK: A convenient location to buy film and other photo supplies.

NEMO'S NICHE: Features whimsical, colorful, plush stuffed characters and toys.

TOMORROWLAND

MICKEY'S MART: One of the best places in the Magic Kingdom for Disney-themed items.

SKYWAY STATION SHOP: A small spot tucked away near the Tomorrowland terminus of the Skyway to Fantasyland; great for Disney souvenirs.

SPACE PORT: Sells the kind of contemporary decorative gifts that teens and preteens seem to love: futuristic toys, games, jewelry, watches, clothing, and other such items. This is one of the Magic Kingdom's most popular shops.

SPACE PLACE: This small shop features Florida T-shirts, candy, film, and cameras.

WHERE TO BUY RAIN PONCHOS: The show doesn't stop just because of a storm. Instead, shops all over the Magic Kingdom stock ponchos to outfit guests who have left their own back home, at their hotel, or in the car. Among them are:

    Main Street: The Emporium
    Adventureland: Tropic Toppers
    Frontierland: Frontier Trading Post
    Fantasyland: Tinkerbell Toy Shop,
        Nemo's Niche,
        Mad Hatter, AristoCats,
        (also umbrellas)
    Tomorrowland: Mickey's Mart,
        Skyway Station Shop,
        Space Place

MAIL-ORDER MICKEY: T-shirts, Mouseketeer ears, stuffed animals, and any other souvenir items for sale in Walt Disney World shops can be ordered by mail. For details, write: Mail Order Department; Walt Disney World; Box 10070; Lake Buena Vista, FL 32830. Or call 407-824-4718.

WHERE TO EAT IN THE MAGIC KINGDOM

A complete listing of all Magic Kingdom eateries—full-service restaurants, fast food emporiums, snack shops, and food vendors—will be found together with all other WDW eating spots in the *Good Meals, Great Times* chapter.

HAPPENINGS AND LIVE ENTERTAINMENT

Walt Disney World is constantly adding new live shows to its repertoire, so before heading down Main Street, check at City Hall to get times for special Magic Kingdom happenings, as well as a schedule of entertainment at the resorts, the Disney Village Marketplace, Epcot Center, the Disney-MGM Studios Theme Park, and Pleasure Island. Others may be encountered serendipitously in the course of the day, and occasionally shows scheduled for a given place or time may be changed or canceled at the last minute—but more often than not, the shows proceed as planned.

DAPPER DANS: Are likely to be encountered while you're strolling down Main Street. This barbershop quartet, its members clad in straw hats and striped vests, tap dance and let one-liners fly during their short 4-part harmonic performances. Occasionally, they bring out their set of bamboo organ chimes.

WALT DISNEY WORLD MARCHING BAND: This concert band performs during the morning every day in Town Square, and on occasion at the Fantasy Faire stage in Fantasyland.

REFRESHMENT CORNER PIANIST: Tickles the ivories of a snow-white upright daily at this centrally located hamburgers-and-hot dogs restaurant.

ALL-AMERICAN COLLEGE MARCHING BAND: Featuring college students from around the country. Performs throughout the Magic Kingdom weekdays in the afternoon and early evening. Part of a 12-week summer program.

KIDS OF THE KINGDOM: During the summer and Easter seasons, this group performs every day in the Castle Forecourt, in a show featuring lively singing and dancing to classic Disney tunes—plus appearances by Disney characters such as the portly Winnie the Pooh and Mickey Mouse himself.

FLAG RETREAT: Usually around 5:10 P.M., a small band and color guard march into Town Square, take down the American flag that flies from the flagpole there, then release a flock of snowy homing pigeons symbolic of the dove of peace. Watch carefully lest you miss them: As one wag quipped, these are union pigeons; they flap away toward their lofthome (behind the Castle) practically before you can say "Cinderella." The whole flight takes just 20 seconds. Some trivia: The carts in which the birds are transported are fashioned from authentic peddlers' carts bought in England for the 1971 Disney film *Bedknobs and Broomsticks*.

J. P. AND THE SILVER STARS: Play familiar tunes on the instruments so well known in the Caribbean islands, steel drums—oil barrels whose sides have been cut to a foot or less from the bottom (which itself has been pounded hollow). On a stage near Adventureland's Pirates of the Caribbean.

THE DIAMOND HORSESHOE JAMBOREE: A dance hall such as might have been found in 19th-century Missouri. Five times a day, there's a lively old-time show with cancan dancers. Reservations are required; to get them, appear in person at the Hospitality House on Main Street in the morning shortly after park opening.

FANTASY IN THE SKY: Even those rare recalcitrant souls who resist fireworks displays as though they were other people's home movies have little quarrel with this spectacular show, which is presented nightly when the park is open until midnight. The 150-odd shells that were mortarized over a 15-minute period when the program was first introduced are now ignited in a period of just 4 minutes—a rate of 1 shell every 2 seconds. They're detonated electrically, so that firings coincide perfectly with the announcer's voice on the P.A. system. The big symmetrical starburst shells are generally Japanese-made, while the ones whose explosions look as if they had been poured from a pitcher (with a concentrated area of particularly vivid color at the center) are manufactured in England.

BANJO KINGS: Play specialty songs and comic ditties from the Roaring Twenties on washboards and banjos, mostly on Main Street.

FANTASY FAIRE: This lively musical revue features the Disney characters in zany performing roles backed up by 2 vocalists and a trio of musicians. Presented 5 times daily, 5 days a week at the Fantasy Faire stage.

THE MAIN STREET ELECTRICAL PARADE

Since it premiered on June 9, 1977, this dazzler has been WDW's biggest hit. Featuring a million twinkling lights, some 100 performers, and nearly 30 floats, it is presented in busy seasons—usually during Easter, summer vacations, and when the park is open until midnight, usually at 9 P.M. and 11 P.M. each evening—and it's a little like all the world's best Christmas trees rolled into one, so undeniably, incredibly, supercalifragilisticexpialidociously spectacular that it's well worth enduring the Magic Kingdom's busiest periods to see. Part of the fascination is the presentation: One minute the lights are twinkling along the edges of the Main Street roofs; the next, as soon as the announcer heralds its arrival, everything is black. The crowds, already impatient, strain anxiously for a sight of the procession. And then it comes, aglitter with tiny colored lights, accompanied by some of the most tuneful music that ever graced a parade, the "Baroque Hoedown," written by Gershon Kingsley and Jean-Jacques Perrey. Heads nod and feet tap. Windows and eyeglasses reflect the sparkle of the lights. One by one the floats cruise by: Alice, atop her mushroom; Cinderella and Prince Charming; Pete, atop his dragon; and more. While the parade theme is piped over the park's P.A. system, each float carries radios that receive their own variations from a transmitter atop Cinderella Castle, and the floats' speakers broadcast these tunes. The combination creates a complex tapestry almost as grin-inspiring as the spectacle of the lights. Presented by Energizer.

Where to catch the parade: Of all the spots along the route outlined in the first paragraph of this section, the single best vantage point for watching this stupendous procession is the very center of the platform of the Walt Disney World Railroad's depot. From there, it's possible to see the floats circling Town Square, and then you can get the effect of the whole stream of lights as the parade continues down Main Street and around the Hub. You're close enough to catch the glitter, but far enough away so that you don't see the framework that holds it all together. Unfortunately, only a couple of seats here have views that are not obstructed by trees.

The next-best viewing point is from the curbs on either side of Main Street. It's very crowded here, and you must claim your foot of curb as much as an hour before the parade (particularly for the busier 9 P.M. running). But there's something about seeing the show at its beginnings, on the edge of one of the quaintest avenues on earth, that enhances the experience enormously.

If you hate crowds, head for Pecos Bill's; park yourself on one of the restaurant's stools right next to the parade route.

Note that the 9 P.M. parade is always more crowded than the one at 11 P.M.

How to photograph the parade: Using an adjustable camera with a normal or wide-angle lens, open the aperture as wide as possible to f/1.4 or f/2.8, and shoot around 1/15 or 1/30 second, using fast films such as Kodacolor 400 (for prints), Ektachrome 160 Tungsten, or Ektachrome 400 Daylight (faster, though it yellows color slightly). To get an artistic blur, slowly pan with the camera as the float moves past. No tripod is necessary, though a steady hand assures best results.

HOLIDAY DOINGS

EASTER SUNDAY: A holiday promenade helps make this holiday extra special.

FOURTH OF JULY CELEBRATION: The busiest day of the summer—and with reason: There's a double-size fireworks display, whose explosions light up the skies not only above Cinderella Castle, but also over the Seven Seas Lagoon.

CHRISTMAS: A Christmas tree—a real Douglas fir that is as perfect among trees as Main Street is among small-town thoroughfares—goes up in Town Square, and the entire Magic Kingdom is decked out as only Disney can do it. There are also special Christmas parades, shows, and carolers. The crowds, of course, are thick. But the scenery is beautiful, and the weather is fine (if chilly)—so it's no wonder that some veteran Magic Kingdom lovers call this the very best time of year.

NEW YEAR'S EVE CELEBRATION: With nearly 93,000 people streaming through the gates of the theme park, New Year's Eve Day of 1980 hosted the biggest crowd in Magic Kingdom history. And though the visitation rate was a little higher than in years past, it has always been true that on December 31, the throngs are practically body to body. For a celebration, that's fun. (On an introductory visit, it could be less delightful; first-timers take note.) There is a double-size fireworks display, and the Main Street holiday decorations (including that almost surrealistically perfect Christmas tree presiding over Town Square) are still up. There's plenty of nip in the air as the evening wears on, so dress accordingly.

WHERE TO FIND THE CHARACTERS

The characters now appear next to City Hall throughout the day. A queue has been set up to allow each guest a turn to meet the characters and perhaps have a photo taken. There are also character shows in Fantasyland; Check at City Hall for the exact times. Be sure to visit Mickey's Birthdayland where Mickey, Minnie, Pluto, Donald, Goofy, and Chip and Dale are on hand for a spectacular show.

TIPS FROM WDW VETERANS

• Study up before you arrive in the Magic Kingdom so that you're familiar with the layout and the things to see and do in the park. Special services are occasionally available to guests during slack seasons, so be sure to peruse any printed information you find in your room.

• Allow plenty of time so that you can sample the Magic Kingdom in small bites. Trying to see it all in a day (or even just two) is like eating a rich ice cream sundae too quickly.

• Try to visit the park on a weekend in summer—and any day but Mondays, Tuesdays, or Wednesdays (the busiest days) year-round.

• Start out early. Most people arrive between 9:30 A.M. and 11:30 A.M., when the roads approaching the Auto Plaza and the parking lots are jammed. If you're coming at Easter, Christmas, or in summer, plan to arrive before 8:30 A.M., or wait until nightfall, when things are less crowded. Arrive very early, so as to be at the gates to the Magic Kingdom when they open, have breakfast at Tony's Town Square Cafe or the Crystal Palace, and then be at the end of Main Street when the rest of the park opens.

• Organize your visit so that you don't hop around from area to area, for that wastes time. Plan to eat early or late; before 11 A.M. or after 2 P.M., and before 5 P.M. or after 8 P.M.

• Break up your day. Buy a River Country/Discovery Island ticket at the entrance to the Magic Kingdom and plan on heading for its beach when the crowds get thickest. Or take in Discovery Island. Or head back to your hotel, if it's not too far, for some swimming or other activities available there. Guests not staying at WDW's own resorts should be sure to have their hands stamped and hold on to their parking-ticket stubs, to avoid paying additional fees when returning.

• At busy times on busy days, take in the following not-so-packed attractions:

Main Street: Walt Disney World Railroad,
        Main Street Cinema
Adventureland: Pirates of the Caribbean
Liberty Square: Liberty Square Riverboats
Tomorrowland: Mission to Mars,
        WEDway PeopleMover, Carousel
        of Progress, Dreamflight
        CircleVision
        360 "American Journeys"
Fantasyland: It's A Small World (after 5 P.M.)

• Shop on Main Street in the early afternoon, not at day's end, when everybody else goes. Besides, the stores are good places to escape the afternoon heat.

• Many attractions have two lines. Before getting into the one on the right-hand side, look at the one to your left. Most of the time it will be less crowded, since most Magic Kingdom visitors automatically head for the one on the right.

• Wear your most comfortable shoes: You'll be spending a lot of time on your feet. (Note that no bare feet are permitted in the Magic Kingdom.)

• Don't take food into the Magic Kingdom. (There are, however, picnic facilities and lockers at the TTC.)

• If your party decides to split up, set a fixed meeting place and time that can't be confused. Avoid meeting in front of Cinderella Castle, since this area can become congested during showtimes and parades.

• If you have arranged to meet members of your group somewhere, don't get into a queue as the meeting time approaches.

• If you have a limited amount of time remaining before meeting the rest of your group, don't hesitate to ask a Disney employee for suggestions about things to do.

USEFUL STOPS

Cash: The Sun Bank, located in Town Square next to City Hall. Open 7 days a week, from 9 A.M. to 4 P.M.

Tobacco: The prime outlet is the Market House on the east side of Main Street.

Baby care needs: The Magic Kingdom Baby Services, at the Hub end of Main Street, next to the Crystal Palace, is the best source. This is a good area for nursing mothers. Check at City Hall for operating hours. Sponsored by Gerber. Disposable diapers and other infant paraphernalia are also available on request at other shops.

Strollers: For rent at the Stroller Shop, located to the right in the souvenir area near the turnstiles at the entrance to the Magic Kingdom.

Haircuts and shaves: At the Harmony Barber Shop on Center Street, the flower-filled cul-de-sac off the west side of Main Street. The barber chairs are heavy, curlicued metal, like the cash register—the real McCoy.

Postcards and stamps: The Emporium on the west side of Main Street is the prime source for postcards; stamps are sold at City Hall.

Mailboxes: Located up and down Main Street, they're olive-drab. An elaborate polished brass one can be found near the entrance to Disney Clothiers, Ltd. Postmarks read Lake Buena Vista, *not* Walt Disney World.

EPCOT CENTER

Imagine a typical world's fair, with the requisite number of pavilions devoted to nations from all around the world, and others depicting the most advanced state of modern technology. Then add the inevitable fast-food facilities and the obligatory souvenir stands. Got all that?

Now imagine that same world's fair as the creators of the Magic Kingdoms in Disneyland and Walt Disney World might have created it, using every creative skill and resource at their considerable command, not to mention the investment of about one billion dollars. You now have some small inkling of what Epcot Center is all about.

Walt Disney suggested the idea back in October 1966. "Epcot will be an experimental prototype community of tomorrow that will take its cue from the new ideas and new technologies that are now emerging from the creative centers of American industry." It would never be completed, he said, but would always be introducing and testing and demonstrating new materials and systems." And it would be "a showcase to the world for the ingenuity and imagination of American free enterprise."

Walt Disney's dream has become a wonderful reality as his successors have used the ideas that inspired him to create a marvel of entertainment, a unique combination of pure imagination and innovative technological virtuosity.

There are two "entertainment worlds" that comprise Epcot Center— Future World and World Showcase. The former examines complex and often controversial concepts, such as energy and transportation, in ways that suddenly make them seem not only comprehensible but also downright irresistible. In the latter, the nations of the Earth are portrayed in all their dazzling variety, with the same extraordinary devotion to detail that makes the Magic Kingdom so enchanting. Appropriate entertainment and menus full of ethnic

specialties enhance the experience: the food has been chosen for its intrinsic appeal to American taste, though in only a few instances have native cuisines been modified in any substantive way to make them more palatable. And the shops in each pavilion are stocked with merchandise that was actually made in the featured nation.

This chapter first describes Future World and then World Showcase. Both of these are huge and complicated complexes, and to get the most-out of your visit, read the following pages in their entirety before arriving. It's also wise to study our specific hints and insider's tips on page 152.

WORLD SHOWCASE

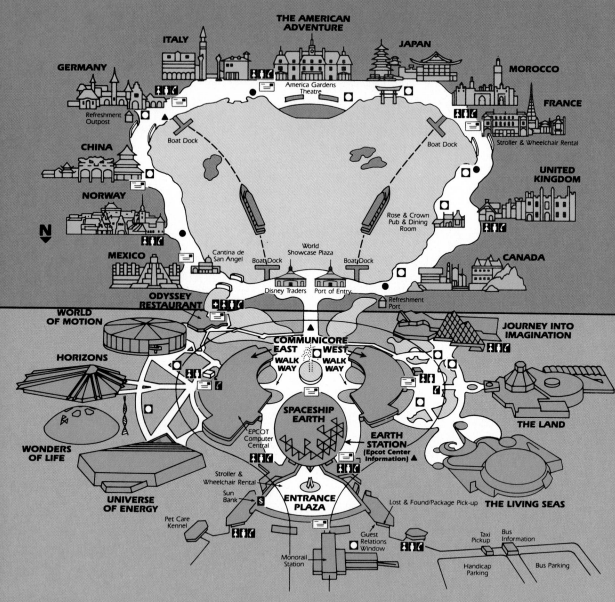

THE AMERICAN ADVENTURE

ITALY

JAPAN

GERMANY

MOROCCO

Refreshment Outpost

FRANCE

America Gardens Theatre

Boat Dock

Boat Dock

Stroller & Wheelchair Rental

CHINA

UNITED KINGDOM

NORWAY

Rose & Crown Pub & Dining Room

N

World Showcase Plaza

MEXICO

Cantina de San Angel

Boat Dock

Boat Dock

CANADA

ODYSSEY RESTAURANT

Disney Traders

Port of Entry

Refreshment Port

WORLD OF MOTION

COMMUNICORE
EAST   WEST
WALK   WALK
WAY   WAY

JOURNEY INTO IMAGINATION

HORIZONS

SPACESHIP EARTH

THE LAND

WONDERS OF LIFE

EPCOT Computer Central

EARTH STATION (Epcot Center Information) ▲

Stroller & Wheelchair Rental

THE LIVING SEAS

UNIVERSE OF ENERGY

Sun Bank

ENTRANCE PLAZA

Lost & Found/Package Pick-up

Pet Care Kennel

Guest Relations Window

Taxi Pickup

Bus Information

Monorail Station

Handicap Parking

Bus Parking

LEGEND
▲ WorldKey Information Satellites

✚ First Aid

✆ Telephone

✉ Mail Drop Locations

● Bus Stops

🚻 Restrooms

◻ Kodak "Photo Spot" – Symbols indicate prime photo-taking locations

FUTURE WORLD

PRINTED IN U.S.A.

GETTING IN AND AROUND

TRANSPORTATION TO EPCOT CENTER: These WDW entertainment worlds are every bit as easy to get to as the Magic Kingdom.

By car: An interchange (the third) was constructed on I-4 especially for Epcot Center visitors, about halfway between the exits for Route 535 and U.S. 192. Take this exit and follow the signs along Epcot Center Drive through Epcot Center's main gate. Epcot Center has its own 9,000-space parking lot; daily parking costs $3. Parking is free for Walt Disney World resort guests with proper identification. Trams carry visitors from their parking space right to the ticket booths.

By WDW monorail and bus: In general, allow about 30 minutes to get from one point to another, whether you go by bus or by monorail. Contact WDW Information (824-4321) before leaving your room to confirm the following routes and for the latest operating schedules. (Monorail and bus schedules coordinate with Epcot Center operating hours, so there's little chance of being stranded.)

- From the Contemporary Resort, Grand Floridian Resort, or Polynesian Village Resort, take the local hotel monorail to the TTC, walk down the ramp and across the platform, and board the TTC-Epcot Center monorail.
- From the Magic Kingdom, take the express monorail to the TTC, then walk down the ramp and up the adjacent ramp to board the TTC-Epcot Center monorail.
- From the Disney-MGM Studios Theme Park, take the bus directly to Epcot Center.
- From The Disney Inn, take the bus to the TTC, then change to the TTC-Epcot Center monorail.
- From Fort Wilderness, take the bus to the TTC, then change to the TTC-Epcot Center monorail.
- From the Disney Village Resort villas, take the bus directly to Epcot Center.
- From the Disney Village Marketplace, take the bus directly to Epcot Center.
- From Disney Village Hotel Plaza, take the bus directly to Epcot Center.
- From the Caribbean Beach Resort, take the bus directly to Epcot Center.

HOURS: Epcot Center is usually open from 9 A.M. to 8 P.M.; hours are extended during Washington's Birthday week, spring school breaks, summer months, and certain holidays. Occasionally, during busy periods, the park may open earlier or close later. Call 824-4321 for up-to-the-minute schedules.

GETTING ORIENTED: Epcot Center is shaped something like a giant hourglass. Future World fills the northern bulb, while World Showcase occupies the southern half. In Future World, which is anchored on the north by the imposing "geosphere" known as Spaceship Earth, most pavilions are arranged around the bulb's perimeter. The exceptions are the two CommuniCore buildings (East and West), which occupy the area at the center of the bulb. In World Showcase, pavilions are arranged around the edge of World Showcase Lagoon, with the American Adventure directly south of Spaceship Earth on the southernmost shore of the lake.

BABY CARE: Changing tables and facilities for nursing mothers can be found at Baby Services, near the Odyssey Restaurant between World of Motion (in Future World) and Mexico (in World Showcase). Check at Earth Station for operating hours. Disposable diapers also are kept behind the counter at many merchandise locations in both worlds; just ask.

CAMERA NEEDS: A large Camera Center is located on the west side of the Entrance Plaza. A good variety of film is available, and several different types of cameras can be rented or purchased. There is a satellite camera shop in Journey into Imagination. Film is available at many World Showcase locations.

ENTERTAINMENT: There is a much wider range of entertainment in both Future World and World Showcase now that the Disney characters are finally on the scene. You'll encounter them dressed in costumes appropriate to the pavilion they are visiting.

IllumiNations, a spectacular after-dark laser, light, and music show, is the highlight. (Details are on page 134.) The America Gardens Theatre is the main stage for scheduled daily shows that are performed frequently. Check at the stage for exact times; the WorldKey Information Services, at Earth Station and throughout the park, also have details on shows and times; schedules are available at the Guest Relations kiosks in Earth Station and at all merchandise locations.

FIRST AID: Minor medical problems can be handled at First Aid, which is near the Odyssey Restaurant, between the World of Motion (in Future World) and Mexico (in World Showcase).

GETTING AROUND: Five 66-foot water taxis, the *FriendShip* launches, shuttle guests back and forth across World Showcase Lagoon. Docks are located at both sides of World Showcase Plaza, in front of Germany, and near Morocco. Several double-decker buses, in styles once found all over New York City, London, and Berlin, can be boarded for a ride around the World Showcase Promenade, stopping at several points along the way.

HANDICAPPED VISITORS: Nearly all the attractions, shops, and restaurants in Epcot Center are completely barrier-free. Parking for handicapped guests is available; inquire at the Auto Plaza. The monorail platform is accessible via elevator. Wheelchairs can be rented at the Stroller and Wheelchair Rentals shop on the east side of the Entrance Plaza, at the Gift Stop on the west side, and at the France pavilion. A guidebook for handicapped visitors is available at Earth Station. Personal Translator Units (PTU), which amplify the audio in selected attractions, are available at Earth Station. Written descriptions of most Epcot Center attractions are also available for hearing-impaired guests at Earth Station. Special complimentary tour cassettes are available at Earth Station for sight-impaired guests. A refundable $5 deposit is required for the cassette player.

INFORMATION: Once inside Future World, visit Earth Station, beside Spaceship Earth, to use the intriguing computer terminals of the WorldKey Information Service there. Hosts and hostesses also are on hand. Visit the WorldKey satellite in World Showcase outside Germany.

LOCKERS: These can be found at the Bus Information Center in the bus parking lot, just outside the Entrance Plaza, and in a small area on the west side of the plaza, underneath Spaceship Earth.

LOST AND FOUND: Located on the west side of the Entrance Plaza.

MEMORABILIA: Gateway Gifts, located alongside Spaceship Earth in the Entrance Plaza, Centorium in Future World's CommuniCore, and Disney Traders in World Showcase Plaza are the three main sources for Epcot Center souvenirs. The Gift Stop and the Stroller and Wheelchair Rentals shop near the Entrance Plaza are good shopping spots too. Souvenirs of the participating nations are found in each World Showcase pavilion and at Disney Traders in World Showcase Plaza.

MONEY MATTERS: Currency exchange and other banking services are available at the Sun Bank on the east side of the Entrance Plaza, just beyond the ticket booths. Both credit cards (American Express, Visa, and MasterCard) and traveler's checks are accepted in shops and (with the exception of fast-food locations, where you must pay with cash or traveler's checks only) in restaurants as well.

PACKAGE PICKUP: Cumbersome or heavy purchases can be transported free of charge (by Disney hosts or hostesses) to this small office on the west side of the Entrance Plaza for later pickup. Ask your salesperson to arrange this service.

THE GIFT STOP: Rental wheelchairs and strollers are available, and film, gift items, sundries, and tobacco are sold. Located near the handicapped parking lot at the entrance to the park.

PETS: No pets are permitted in Epcot Center, but there is the Pet Care Kennel, presented by Gaines Foods, Inc., just east of the Entrance Plaza. *Do not leave pets in the car.* The cost for boarding pets is $4 per day; pets may not be boarded overnight at the Epcot Center kennel.

STROLLER AND WHEELCHAIR RENTALS: Available in the shop of that name on the east side of the Entrance Plaza, and at the France pavilion. Wheelchairs are also available at the Gift Stop. Replacement strollers and wheelchairs are available in Germany, France, and the United Kingdom. Remember to keep your rental receipt; it can be used on the same day in the Magic Kingdom, at the Disney-MGM Studios Theme Park, or again in Epcot Center should you leave and return at a later hour.

ADMISSION PRICES*

ONE-DAY TICKET

Adult	$29
Child**	$23

FOUR-DAY PASSPORT

Adult	$97
Child**	$77

FIVE-DAY PASSPORT

Adult	$112
Child**	$90

The cost of a **ONE-YEAR ALL THREE PARKS PASSPORT** is $180 for adults and $155 for children; renewals are $160 for adults and $135 for children.

*The prices quoted here do not include a 6% sales tax.

**3 through 9 years of age

Note: Multi-day All Three Parks Passports need not be used on consecutive days.

These prices were correct at press time, but may change during 1990.

ADMISSION: Tickets and All Three Parks Passports are available for 1, 4, and 5 days. The Disney organization defines a ticket as admission for 1 day only; other forms of admission media (for longer periods) are called All Three Parks Passports. One-day tickets may be used at Epcot Center, in the Magic Kingdom, or at the Disney-MGM Studios Theme Park, but not at more than one site on the same day. Four- and five-day All Three Parks Passports can be used at Epcot Center, the Magic Kingdom, and the Disney-MGM Studios Theme Park on the same day; unlike 1-day tickets, they also include unlimited use of the transportation system inside Walt Disney World. There are no admission media for 2-day or 3-day visits; a 2- or 3-day guest must buy two or three 1-day tickets. Cash, traveler's checks, personal checks (with proper ID), American Express, Visa, and MasterCard can be used to pay for all admission media. Note that multi-day All Three Parks Passports do not have to be used on consecutive days.

FUTURE WORLD

A mere listing of the basic themes covered by the Future World pavilions—agriculture, communications, the ocean, energy, health, imagination, and transportation—tends to sound a tad academic, and perhaps even a little forbidding. But when these serious topics are presented with that special Disney flair, they become part of an experience that ranks among Walt Disney World's most exciting. Some of these subjects are explored in the course of lively and unusual Disney "adventures," involving a whole arsenal of remarkable motion pictures, special effects, and Audio-Animatronics figures so lifelike that it is hard to remain unmoved. Other themes come into play at hands-on exhibits full of touch-sensitive video screens, 2-way television sets, computers that play special games, and other high-tech equipment that few people ever actually get a chance to experience in everyday life. Far from depicting the kind of sci-fi future seen in the Magic Kingdom's Tomorrowland, this look into the future seems far more practical and realistic. In addition, the basic elements of Future World are warm, attractive, and appealing in their own right, from the palm-dotted Entrance Plaza and the massive (but airy) glass-walled buildings of CommuniCore East and West to the stupendous fountain just past Spaceship Earth and that many-faceted "geosphere" that has rapidly become the universal symbol of Epcot Center.

There is so much to see and enjoy that it's hard to know just what to do first. Many guests simply stop at Spaceship Earth on their way into Epcot Center and proceed to wander at random from one pavilion to the next through the morning. As a result, many of the pavilions are frustratingly crowded in the morning—especially Spaceship Earth, which has its largest crowds before lunch.

A wise alternative is to choose one pavilion from those described below—or perhaps two, if you've arrived early enough to be there when the gates to Epcot Center open—and then to head for World Showcase, moving clockwise around the lagoon on one day of your visit and counterclockwise on the next. Then in the afternoon, when the majority of guests are lining up at World Showcase pavilions, return to Future World. World of Motion, Horizons,

Universe of Energy, and The Living Seas have relatively few visitors during the late afternoon hours; CommuniCore East and World of Motion's TransCenter are not only fascinating spots to pass the exceptionally busy hours after lunch, but also very cool refuges when high temperatures prevail outdoors. And although queues can be found during peak seasons at Journey into Imagination and at The Land throughout most of the late morning and afternoon—not only for the several attractions that each one houses, but also at the pavilion entrances—the period from late afternoon through closing is usually less hectic.

GETTING ORIENTED

As a guest crosses the enormous Entrance Plaza, the gleaming silver ball straight ahead (and facing south) is Spaceship Earth (not to be confused with Earth Station, which is at its base). CommuniCore East (at left) and West (to the right) are the two large crescent-shaped buildings that flank the large fountain just past Spaceship Earth. Universe of Energy, Wonders of Life, Horizons, and World of Motion lie to the left (east) of CommuniCore East; Journey into Imagination, The Land, and The Living Seas are located to the right (west) of CommuniCore West. The World Showcase section of Epcot Center surrounds the shoreline of the large World Showcase Lagoon.

Future World pavilions are described here as a visitor encounters them while moving counterclockwise (from right around to the left, that's west to east around the area).

1. Spaceship Earth
2. CommuniCore West
3. The Living Seas
4. The Land
5. Journey into Imagination
6. World of Motion
7. Horizons
8. Wonders of Life
9. Universe of Energy
10. CommuniCore East

SPACESHIP EARTH

As it looms impressively just above the earth, this great faceted silver geosphere—visible on a clear day from an airplane flying along either Florida coast—looks a little bit like it's ready to blast off like the gigantic spaceship in *Close Encounters of the Third Kind*. It looks large from a distance, and seems even more immense when viewed from directly underneath. It's no surprise that most visitors simply stop beneath it and gawk. The show inside, which explores man's continuing search for ever more efficient means of communication, remains one of Epcot Center's most visually compelling.

Weighing 1 million pounds, measuring 164 feet in diameter and 180 feet in height, and encompassing 2,200,000 cubic feet of space, this geosphere is held aloft by 6 legs supported by pylons sunk 100 feet into the ground. The distinctive sheen of its covering derives from a sort of quarter-inch-thick sandwich made of 2 anodized aluminum faces and a polyethylene core. This sheath is made up of 954 triangular panels, not all of equal size or shape.

A common misconception about Spaceship Earth is that it is a geodesic dome. Not so. The designers had to make up the word *geosphere* because the structure is unlike any other pre-existing building. A geodesic dome is composed of only half a sphere, while Spaceship Earth is completely round. Nor can it be compared to the similarly faceted creation that housed the U.S. pavilion at Montreal's Expo 67, which actually was only three-quarters of a sphere.

In fact, this extraordinarily large Disney creation is not even a perfect sphere; the steelworkers' requirements dictated its slightly uneven dimensions. Presented by AT&T.

SPACESHIP EARTH SHOW: The noted science fiction writer Ray Bradbury, together with a number of consultants and advisers from the Smithsonian Institution, the Los Angeles area's prestigious Huntington Library, USC, and the University of Chicago (among others), collaborated with Disney designers in developing this memorable journey. It begins in an inky black time tunnel complete with a musty smell that suggests the ages, and continues through history from the days of Cro-Magnon man (30 or 40 thousand years ago) to the present.

En route, an Egyptian temple shows off the pictorial representations of words and sounds known as hieroglyphics, which were first used around 3000 B.C., and hieratic writing, a form of script used to write on papyrus. A Phoenician scene set in the 9th century B.C. acknowledges civilization's debt to those tireless traders who introduced a 22-character alphabet (based on sounds) that put written communication, once the province of the intelligentsia alone, within the grasp of the masses. The Roman systems of roads, the Islamic empire, the efforts of 11th- and 12th-century Benedictine monks to handcopy religious and classical manuscripts, the Gutenberg press, the Renaissance in Italy, and a number of the 20th century's inventions are all represented, and in most cases it's not necessary to

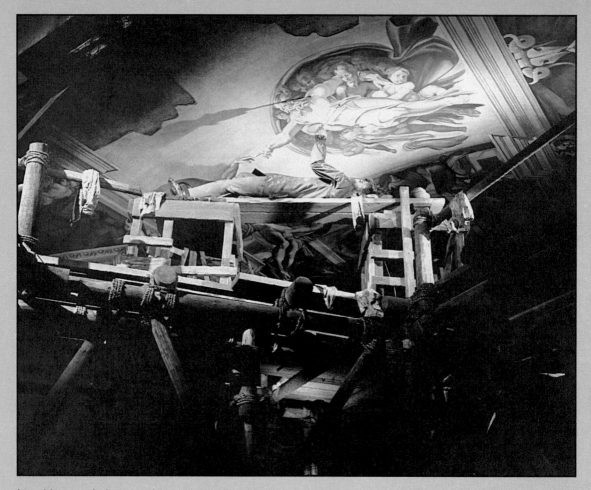

be a history scholar to understand why. The Greek theater scene, whose meaning here may not be as widely understood as it should be, reminds viewers that it was the Greeks who refined the alphabet (by the addition of vowels) and then went on to use the language so expressively. Then, as now, theater was an important means of examining and transmitting the moral and social questions of the time.

The attraction features some remarkable special effects: the flickering candles in the scene where a monk (himself crafted with such precision and authenticity as to appear to be breathing) has nodded off; the smell of smoke coming from the fall of Rome, to name only a couple.

And every scene is executed in remarkable detail. The symbols on the wall of that Egyptian temple really are hieroglyphics, and the content of the letter being dictated by the pharoah was excerpted from a missive actually received by an agent of a ruler of the period. The actor in the Greek theater scene is delivering lines from Sophocles' Oedipus Rex. In the scene depicting the fall of Rome, the graffiti reproduces markings from the walls of Pompeii. In the Islamic scene, the quadrant—an instrument used in astronomy and navigation—is a copy of one from the 10th century. The type on Johann Gutenberg's press actually moves, and the page that the celebrated 15th-century printer is examining is a replica of one from a Bible in the collection of the above-mentioned Hungtington Library. In the Renaissance scene, the book being read is Virgil's

Aeneid; the musical instruments in that scene are a lute and a lyra da braccio, both replicas of real period pieces. During the 20th-century scenes, the steam-powered press is a reproduction of one that had been developed by William Bullock around 1863, notable because it used paper in continuous rolls rather than individual sheets.

Some visitors wonder as to the identity of the excerpts from the radio and television shows broadcast in this area. Take note: The former include The Lone Ranger, The Shadow, a commentary by Walter Winchell, and the Joe Louis–Max Schmeling 1938 rematch. It's the first round, and Schmeling, who had inflicted Joe Louis' first loss in a 1936 12th-round K.O., is on the mat. The referee is counting—and the crowds are going wild. Among the television programs·are Walter Cronkite's reports from the March 10, 1964, New Hampshire Republican primary, Walt Disney introducing The Wonderful World of Color, Ed Sullivan and the Harlem Globetrotters, the Colts versus Browns NFL championship game (1964), and Ozzie and Harriet, featuring David and Ricky Nelson. Film buffs may recognize clips from the movies Girl Shy with Harold Lloyd (1924), Top Hat with Fred Astaire and Ginger Rogers (1935), and 20,000 Leagues Under the Sea (1954).

All these sights are enough to keep necks craning and heads turning as the "time machines" wend their way upward. But the most dazzling scene is the ride's finale, when the vehicles arrive at the topmost point in the geosphere, and visitors gaze in awe into a vast inky dome full of what seem like thousands of tiny stars. These are projected by the "star ball," created by the Disney special effects department when it was discovered that the inside ceiling of the geosphere was too large for conventional planetarium equipment.

Note: The lines for this attraction are usually at their longest during the morning hours, and at their shortest just before park closing time.

GATEWAY GIFTS AND CAMERA CENTER: These 2 shops are located quite near the entrance to Spaceship Earth. The former sells Epcot Center souvenirs—T-shirts, mugs, toys, etc.—as well as suntan lotion, tissues, and the like. Film and various other Kodak products are sold at the Camera Center. Cameras, including RCA Video Camcorders, are sold or rented here and same-day film processing is available.

EARTH STATION: The similarity of names between this area (just south of Spaceship Earth) and that of the attraction itself can be confusing to first-time visitors, and that's unfortunate because this area is one of the most vital parts of Epcot Center.

Not only is it the principal source of Epcot Center information, but it is also the spot to make dinner reservations via the easy-to-use touch-sensitive TV screens found in abundance at Epcot Center. For more specific details on making these reservations, see page 209. When the terminals are not being utilized to arrange tables for dinner, they can be used to get an overall picture of Epcot Center, to learn about each pavilion in considerable detail, and to discover nearly everything else that a guest could conceivably want to know about Epcot Center. If the system's electronic A-to-Z index to shops, restaurants, attractions, and services does not answer a question, it's possible to communicate with a specially trained human host or hostess, who will be able to hear and see the querying guest with the aid of a microphone and video camera unobtrusively placed adjacent to the screen. These hosts and hostesses also manage the message service for Epcot Center guests. (Many WorldKey Information Service hosts and hostesses speak Spanish; some speak other languages.)

Meanwhile, overhead, huge multifaceted screens provide an overview (albeit a somewhat cubistic one) of everything Epcot Center offers, while hosts and hostesses are on duty in person at the counter. They also keep records of any lost children who may be at Baby Services at any given time.

COMMUNICORE WEST
This pavilion, the large crescent-shaped building located just west of the 3-tiered fountain south of Earth Station (to your right while facing World Showcase Plaza), is the setting not only for one of Future World's most attractive fast-food eateries, but also for an exhibit known as FutureCom that is similar to the lively Epcot Computer Central in CommuniCore East.

Don't miss the gardenias on the fountain plaza side of the CommuniCore West breezeway. These fragrant bushes usually bloom about 3 times a year, from spring into summer.

FUTURECOM: How people gather information—via signs and satellites, newspapers and traffic lights, ticker tape and telephones—is the topic here. Dominating the area is a sculpture known as the Fountain of Information, made up of just about all the forms of communication with which 20th-century denizens are bombarded: books and records, magazines, maps, TV screens, laser discs, signs, labels, seed catalogues, stock certificates, movie film, neon lights, and more.

Equally compelling are a couple of hands-on exhibits that show new technology. At one bank of touch-sensitive TV screens, a visitor merely touches the machine to find out what's happening in his or her home state. Another exhibit demonstrates video teleconferencing; increasingly, businesses are using this device in lieu of flying their employees all over the country for meetings. At Epcot Center it gives guests the chance to see themselves on TV.

Don't miss the Phraser. It actually speaks, in a curious monotone, the words that guests peck out on a typewriter keyboard, and it does so with remarkable accuracy—so long as the words follow standard rules of pronunciation.

Also amusing is an adjacent Network Control game, which, by giving visitors a chance to try it for themselves, demonstrates how network controllers at the telephone companies manage the flow of long-distance telephone calls. The idea of the nearby Chip Cruiser game is to use "laser beams" to blast computer-control-room contaminants before they affect the service.

Presented by AT&T.

Note: The Mickey Mouse clock in the Age of Information animated mural on FutureCom's east wall was once one of the few reminders in Epcot Center of the pint-size character that built the World. Now look for your favorite characters strolling all around Epcot Center. In World Showcase, they'll be dressed in international costumes and available for photographs at World Showcase Plaza.

EPCOT OUTREACH: No single Epcot Center pavilion pretends to tell the whole story of the subject it covers, but with this information and resource center (to the northern half of CommuniCore West, the section closest to Spaceship Earth), no visitor can complain about the lack of fact-finding sources at Epcot Center. That's because Epcot Outreach provides access to information from encyclopedias, periodicals, and wire services via a computerized data service. A research librarian and a group of assistants can extract appropriate printed materials from the files at hand to answer any lingering questions that might remain. The topics covered? Anything and everything that's presented in either Future World or World Showcase.

Teacher's Center: This is a lounge where educators can preview films, videos, filmstrips, multimedia kits, and computer software. Special bonuses are the complimentary lesson plans on Future World themes, geared to students from elementary through high school levels. The Epcot Teacher's Center is open from 10 A.M. to 6 P.M.

THE LIVING SEAS

A trip 4 fathoms deep into the Caribbean Sea awaits visitors here. The Living Seas is the largest facility ever dedicated to man's relationship with the ocean and was designed by the Disney Imagineers, the company's creative design organization, in cooperation with a board of some of the world's most distinguished oceanographic experts and scientists.

At the entrance to The Living Seas is a stylized rockwork marquee that suggests a natural coastline with waves cascading into tidal pools. Upon entering, there's a 125-foot-long sea mural that leads to a display depicting the technological advances in undersea exploration, from Leonardo da Vinci's sketches of underwater breathing devices and submersibles to photos of John Lethbridge's diving barrel and Frederic de Drieberg's 1809 breathing device. Also featured is the diving suit from Walt Disney's classic film *Twenty Thousand Leagues Under the Sea*, and the actual 11-foot-long model

Nautilus used in the movie. Next, as part of the introduction to The Living Seas, is a 2½-minute multimedia presentation that salutes the pioneers of ocean research, beginning with early ships, diving bells, submarines, and aqualungs. The show also features a 7-minute special effects film that attempts to demonstrate the critical role of the ocean as a source of energy, minerals, and protein. Some scenes were filmed in very remote parts of the world.

There's a ride through a Caribbean coral reef, housed in a huge tank 200 feet in diameter and 27 feet deep, plus Sea Base Alpha, where hands-on activities, underwater movies, video monitors, and the opportunity to communicate with the divers in the tank are sure to prolong visitors' stays. The Coral Reef Restaurant offers fresh seafood in a setting where diners can look out at the coral reef through acrylic windows 18 feet high and 8 inches thick. Tables are arranged on tiers so that all patrons have an unobstructed view.

Presented by United Technologies.

CARIBBEAN CORAL REEF RIDE: To reach the 2-passenger sea cabs that make the trip to the coral reef, visitors enter "hydrolators," elevator-like capsules that actually descend only 2 inches while creating the illusion of diving deep under the sea. The manmade reef exists in a 5.7 million gallon tank where more than 200 varieties of sealife, ranging from tiny crustaceans to large predators, live in a simulated environment that accurately recreates the chemistry and life-support ecosystems of the Caribbean Sea. Among the 5,000 inhabitants are sea bass, parrot fish, puffers, barracuda, butterfly fish, angelfish, sharks, croakers, hog snappers, dolphins, sea lions, and diamond rays.

In addition to the vast array of sealife and vegetation, guests also get to see scuba divers testing and demonstrating the newest diving gear and underwater monitoring equipment, as they carry on training experiments with dolphins. New wireless radios allow the divers to talk to onlookers and explain their work. Other undersea attractions include a diver in a "JIM" suit, the latest in atmospheric diving-wear technology (at Sea Base Alpha, guests have the chance to try one on personally), 2 one-manned submarines, and 2 mini-robotic submersibles.

Scientists had to develop foods to simulate the taste, chemistry, and nutritional value of natural coral. The resulting meal for parrot fish, for example, consists of dry dog food, chicken's-laying pellets, a complete amino-acid solution, and a vitamin B complex solution, all held together by dental plaster. Yum! Following the ride, guests are conveniently deposited at the Visitors Center of Sea Base Alpha.

SEA BASE ALPHA: This prototype undersea research facility, set up on 2 levels connected by escalators, includes a visitors center and 6 modules, each dedicated to a specific subject. One module focuses on ocean ecosystems and shows various forms of adaptation, including camouflage, symbiosis, and bioluminescence. A 6,000-gallon tank displays another coral reef where Bermuda morays, barracuda, and bonnethead sharks swim

about. Another module is dedicated to the study of dolphins, porpoises, and sea lions. A large holding tank features a step-in port, where guests can see the mammals up close. At another Sea Base Alpha station, a delightful show stars an Audio-Animatronics submersible named Jason who describes the history of robotics and their use in underwater exploration to visitors. In the same area, guests can try on a cut-away "JIM" suit, and test its maneuverability by doing a series of tasks as part of a game. There are also video screens around the Sea Base where visitors can test and expand their knowledge of oceanography.

SEA BASE CONCOURSE: Adjacent to the 6 modules, the concourse features 3 displays. The floor-to-ceiling diver lock-out chamber is where the crew enters and exits the ocean environment. Visitors can see the divers enter the chamber, ascend, and disappear through the ceiling of the concourse. A 24-foot-long glass tank features a wave machine that provides a dramatic visualization of the dynamics of wave motion. A full-size mock-up of the latest one-man submersible vehicle, the Deep Rover, is suspended from the mezzanine of the concourse. The Deep Rover is capable of descending more than 3,000 feet below the ocean's surface.

WHERE TO EAT IN EPCOT CENTER

For all the details on all the restaurants in Epcot Center—including both those in Future World and World Showcase—plus information about how to obtain restaurant reservations, see the *Good Meals, Great Times* chapter that begins on page 203.

THE LAND

Occupying 6 acres, this enormous skylighted pavilion examines the nature of one of everybody's favorite topics—food. A film, *Symbiosis*, dramatically explores the creative partnerships between mankind and the land we inhabit. A boat ride takes a look at farming in the past and future. Guided tours give interested visitors the chance to learn more about the experimental agricultural techniques actually being practiced in the pavilion and nearby greenhouses, and to get ideas about applications in the garden. In addition, the subject of nutrition is touched upon in one of Future World's wackiest attractions, an Audio-Animatronics musical revue (called the Kitchen Kabaret) which was inspired by the Country Bear Vacation Hoedown in the Magic Kingdom.

Since this is also the home of 2 of Epcot Center's most interesting eating spots, The Land is understandably popular. During peak seasons, lengthy queues do build up, not only for the boat ride but also for entry to the pavilion itself, especially around 11 A.M. (Those with reservations for the guided tour or for a meal in The Land Grille Room restaurant are permitted to bypass the queue within 15 minutes of the time of their appointment.) The best plan is to visit the pavilion first thing in the morning, have a quick breakfast here, and perhaps make reservations for lunch in The Land Grille Room. Or wait until afternoon, when—though there may be a wait for the boat ride—it probably won't be necessary to line up just to get inside. Count on spending a total of 2 hours at The Land, longer if plans include eating here.

Presented by Kraft.

LISTEN TO THE LAND: This 13½-minute boat ride ventures into 3 ecological communities (rain forest, desert, and prairie) that covered much of the world before man arrived on the scene. It then cruises through a turn-of-the-century American farm and, finally, moves among growing areas full of live plants for a mind-expanding sample of innovative agricultural techniques. In an Aqua Cell area, fish and shrimp are raised in a controlled environment, and in the Desert Farm area, plants receive nutrients through a drip irrigation system that delivers just the right amount of water, and no more—important in an arid climate.

As fantastic and unreal as they appear, the plants on view in the experimental greenhouses are all living. In contrast, those in the biomes (ecological communities) were manufactured in Disney studios out of flexible, lightweight plastic that simulates the cellulose found in real trees. The trunks and branches were molded from live specimens; the majestic sycamore in the farmhouse's front yard, for example, duplicates one that stands outside a Burbank, California, car wash. Hundreds of thousands of polyethylene leaves, made in Hong Kong, were then snapped on. These are fire retardant, as are the blades of grass, which are made of glass fibers implanted into rubber mats. In the South American rain forest scene, the water on the leaves and trunks is supplied by a special drip system that provides a constant flow of moisture.

KITCHEN KABARET: Bonnie Appetit is the star of this zany show about good nutrition. Each of the 4 acts focuses on one of the main food groups—dairy products, fruits and vegetables, meats and proteins, and grains and cereals. But that is almost peripheral to the entertainment, presented by the Kitchen Krackpots Band, Mr. Dairy Goods and the Stars of the Milky Way, the Boogie Woogie Bak'ry Boy, the Cereal Sisters (Mairzy Oats, Rennie Rice, and Connie Corn), the Colander Combo, the Fiesta Fruit, and Mr. Hamm and that incurable punster Mr. Eggz, who joke up a corny storm. ("Cheese! I cheddar to think about it," says one. And: "Why was Chicken Little so upset when his mom fell asleep in a hot tub? His brother was born hard-boiled.") The characters are endearing, especially Mr. Broccoli, with his punk-rocker hairdo and pink-rimmed glasses.

HARVEST TOUR: Guided tours take place daily every half hour between 9:30 A.M. and 4:30 P.M. They cover basically the same topics as the boat ride, but because they last at least 45 minutes, they can go into far more detail. And participants do have an opportunity to ask questions—and listen to what the home gardeners and farmers who commonly make up at least part of the tour groups have to say. Guides are all members of the agricultural operations staff, and all have degrees in some area of agriculture. Reservations, which are required, must be made in person early on the day of the tour near the Broccoli & Co. shop at the entrance to the Kitchen Kabaret on the pavilion's lower level. The "Listen to the Land" boat ride is a suggested prerequisite.

SYMBIOSIS: Presented in the Harvest Theater (near The Land's entrance) on a 23-by-60-foot screen, this 19-minute 70mm motion picture examines the delicate balance between technology's progress and environmental integrity, reinforcing the sound ideas behind some of the techniques seen in The Land's growing areas. There are some horror stories about the misuse of land, including tales of the pollution of lakes and streams throughout the

world. But there also are some tremendously reassuring tales—the timely rescue of the Thames, Europe's Lake Constance, and Oregon's Willamette River from death-by-pollution, and sound forest management practices in Sweden, in Germany's Black Forest, and in the United States' Pacific Northwest. Filming took place in about 30 nations, and there is some terrific scenery. The breathtaking opening scene shows the magnificent rice terraces located near Banaue in the Philippines. Don't let the ominous-sounding name of the film put you off: this is a highlight of any Epcot Center visit.

BROCCOLI & CO.: This little shop between the Farmer's Market and the Kitchen Kabaret stocks merchandise such as hydroponic plants, seeds, books, topiaries, and kitchen accessories, including magnetized plastic stick-ons to embellish the front of a refrigerator, place mats, and more.

JOURNEY INTO IMAGINATION

The oddly shaped glass pyramids that house Journey into Imagination (as you face World Showcase Lagoon and then straight ahead to your right) are striking, but they pale by comparison with the experiences inside—which may be the most exciting of all at Epcot Center. Dreamfinder, a jolly, red-headed, professorial figure, who sports a carrot-colored beard and is accompanied by a purple baby dragon called Figment, is only one of the pavilion's delights. He appears in person outside and again when he escorts guests through the imagination world during a 14-minute ride inside.

There's also a dazzling 3-D movie, starring Michael Jackson, called *Captain EO*. Not to mention the electronic fun house known as the Image Works. Or the quirky fountains outside—the Jellyfish Fountains that spurt streams of water that spread out at the top, look like their namesake sea creature for an instant, and then fall back to earth; or the Serpentine Fountains, which send out smooth streams of water that arc from one garden plot to another in the most astonishing fashion.

Plant lovers will recognize the sculpted trees in this garden as podocarpus—the same type that are planted in many other locations (but pruned to many different shapes) throughout Epcot Center.

Count on spending an hour and 15 minutes at the very least at this pavilion—2 hours wouldn't be too long at all. During peak seasons, the queue outside seems to be longest between around 10 A.M. and noon and remains fairly lengthy throughout most of the day. Early mornings and late evenings are the least congested times to visit.

Presented by Kodak.

JOURNEY INTO IMAGINATION RIDE: It is here that Dreamfinder creates Figment out of a lizard's body, a crocodile's nose, a steer's horns, 2 big yellow eyes, 2 small wings, and a pinch of childish delight—and commences the visitor's journey into the world of imagination.

First-timers may not realize that the 14-minute ride doesn't present a random assortment of scenes that are handsome and scary by turns, but rather an

organized exploration of how imagination works and the areas of life in which it functions.

First there is a visit to the Dreamport, the area of the mind to which the senses are constantly sending data to be stored for later use by the imagination. Subsequent scenes depict the way imagination suffuses the worlds of the visual arts, of literature, of the performing arts, and of science and technology. In the course of all this, laser beams dance, lightning crackles, and letters pour out of a giant typewriter like notes from an organ. The images are as fanciful as imagination itself.

It's interesting to note that the iridescent painting-in-progress on the wall in the visual arts scene—a so-called "polage" produced by refracting light through polarized filters—is the largest of its kind anywhere. The artist who executed the mural had previously done paintings no larger than 4 feet in height. Also, when you see flashing lights (about three-quarters of the way through the ride), be sure to sit up straight and smile—your picture is being taken. You'll see your photo at the end of the ride.

THE IMAGE WORKS: It's a rare Image Works visitor who doesn't experience at least some of the emotion experienced by one 4-year-old girl who cried every time her parents tried to take her home. That's not surprising, because the Image Works is literally crammed with activities that give every visitor the chance to use his or her imagination.

For instance, at Dreamfinder's School of Drama, near the entrance to the Image Works, visitors have the opportunity to be in a TV film. Five guests at a time step onto a small stage and, thanks to a new Chroma-Key video effects technique that involves foreground and background matting, perform in short video stories—"Daring Deputies and the Return of Sagebrush Sam," a Western; "Acrobatic Astronauts in Galactic Getaway," in a sci-fi setting; or "Enchanted Travelers—Wily Wizard and the Cranky King," a sort of fairy tale. Spectators and performers alike see the results as they happen via strategically placed video screens. It's *always* fun to watch the groups of senior citizens, teenagers, or families jumping crazily around on stage following on-screen instructions from Dreamfinder (and, in fact, having the time to spend more than just a few

seconds watching these goings-on is sufficient reason to allot more time to your overall Epcot Center visit).

Not far from Dreamfinder's School of Drama is another especially lively area known as The Sensor, a sort of electronic maze whose various elements react to a visitor's presence by producing lights and sounds. Upon entering the Rainbow Corridor, you'll find a tunnel full of neon tubes in all the hues of the rainbow. Image Warp's pneumatically powered Mylar mirrors produce moving versions of old-style funhouse reflections in a room wackily illuminated by strobe lights. Then there's the Lumia—a plastic ball 7 feet in diameter, inside which swirling patterns of light and color appear in response to the sounds of voices of different frequencies and intensities. At Stepping Tones, hexagonal splotches of colored light on the floor correspond to sounds—a drumroll, a flourish on the harp, a couple of chords sung by a men's chorus, a snippet of hoedown fiddling, and such—that are emitted when the area is trodden upon; the last red hexagon in the room, located in the farthest corner from the entrance, sends out the sound of a beautiful chord played on a harp. In fact, the first tones recreate the music heard in *Close Encounters of the Third Kind*. The floor was "orchestrated" by an avant-garde San Francisco Bay Area composer so that all possible combinations sound interesting at the very least— and the more the merrier.

Outside The Sensor maze, the Image Works offers the Lightwriter, which involves drawing geometric patterns with laser beams, and the Magic Palette, where a special stylus and a touch-sensitive control surface can be used to create all kinds of images, mostly in Day-Glo colors. People often queue up to try these, while huge kaleidoscopes nearby and the very unusual pin screens are practically overlooked. Manufacturing the latter involved putting thousands of straight pins through a screen illuminated with colored lights from below (visitors run their hands across the bottom, thereby creating sweeping patterns of color). Producing the pin screens, however, was not an easy task: Every straight pin had to be identical, and since production-line straight pins simply aren't made quite so precisely, the artist who worked on the project spent a month at the Dayville, Connecticut, pin factory to monitor pin production and thereby assure total uniformity.

The Electronic Philharmonic, one of the most amusing sections of the Image Works, allows guests to take turns conducting an orchestra. Here's how this works: Each patch of light on the console represents a group of instruments (strings, woodwinds, brass, percussion). Raising and lowering one's hand above that patch of light increases and decreases the volume of the sound produced by that section of the "orchestra"; by covering 3 out of 4 patches of light, it is theoretically possible to bring up only the strings or only the brass. This is very difficult to do alone, however, so it's wise to enlist a partner.

CAPTAIN EO: This dazzling, 3-D musical fantasy stars Michael Jackson as the captain of a spaceship. The band of characters includes Hooter, Fuzzball, and Geex. Their mission: to transform the

dismal planet ruled by the evil Supreme Leader (played by Academy Award winner Angelica Huston) into a happy place through the magic of music and dance. Jackson wrote and performs 2 songs: "We Are Here to Change the World" and "Another Part of Me." The theater has been redesigned and outfitted with state-of-the-art audio and video equipment, as well as devices that help create the spectacular series of special 3-dimensional effects.

CAMERAS AND FILM: A good selection of film is for sale here, along with a small selection of cameras, filters, cable releases, and other necessities of life for the traveling photographer. Some souvenir items are also available.

WORLD OF MOTION

This wheel-shaped, stainless-steel-clad structure, 318 feet in diameter and about 60 feet high, presents the story of transportation past, present, and future through a whimsical show full of Audio-Animatronics figures (the most colorful since the hairy-legged Pirates of the Caribbean, in the Magic Kingdom) and exhibits that look far into the future of transportation.

The tall trees on the plaza in front of the pavilion are eucalyptus: They were grown from seeds planted a dozen years ago. The tops are being pruned flat and the branches trimmed so that in a few years passengers on the monorail will look across a flat plane of treetops, while guests on the ground will be shaded by a spreading canopy of green.

Presented by General Motors.

WORLD OF MOTION SHOW: Chronicling man's passion for always getting somewhere just a little bit faster, this appealing, if rather unsophisticated, show reflects the eccentric humor of one of its chief designers—longtime Disney art director Ward Kimball, who also shares the credit for creating Jiminy Cricket. The 14½-minute ride-through attraction begins with a look back to the sometimes painful days when foot power was the only means of transportation. It then moves wackily forward through time as man tries out ostriches and zebras, dreams of magic carpets, invents the wheel, rides in chariots, and tinkers with flying machines, balloons, steam carriages, riverboats, stagecoaches, buckboards, airplanes, automobiles, and assorted other vehicles.

In the show's 22 scenes, about 150 Audio-Animatronics figures make their debut. (Actually, some of the faces of the "people" in the group are used several times, but since they wear different expressions, only the exceptionally keen of eye recognize the duplication.)

In order to lend verisimilitude to each scene, bicycles, streetlights, cars, carts, wagons, and trains were added as props—some of them genuine antiques and some of them line-by-line reproductions. The Wells Fargo Stagecoach in the Western wagons scene is a 150-year-old item imported from Phoenix, Arizona, and then restored, along with several others unearthed in northern California. In the city scene, the telephone wire is the real thing (made around 1920), and all of the early automobiles are authentic. Especially amusing is the final

scene, which shows Americans enjoying the good life on the road in a trio of spiffy vintage cars that looked modern not too long ago.

The journey through the history of transportation is followed by trips through special "speedrooms" that provide a dizzying you-are-there feeling. The film was shot in 70mm, and includes a visit to a breathtaking city of the future, where trainlike vehicles shoot through the air from skyscraper to skyscraper.

It's worth noting that this attraction is almost empty during the first half-hour after park opening; it usually is at its busiest from midmorning until around 5 P.M.

TRANSCENTER: Far from being just a showroom for the latest model GM cars, this area situated at the ride's exit contains entertaining exhibits about the 20th century's most important means of transportation. One section, called The Bird and the Robot, stars a cigar-puffing, Groucho Marx-like toucan bird originally built for Tokyo Disneyland's Enchanted Tiki Room, and a General Motors assembly-line robot whose dexterity and flexibility make it easy to understand how similar devices can be used for painting and welding a new car on an assembly line.

Then there's *The Water Engine*, an amusing animated film that explores possible alternatives to the internal combustion engine (including "Equus Cheapus"), and the "Dreamer's Workshop," an exhibit that shows off sleek prototype cars of the future like the Aero 2000, an experimental 4-seat subcompact designed specifically for display at Epcot Center. Other areas demonstrate the torture test that

GM vehicles must pass—locks flicking up and down, windows and visor mirrors and door handles opening and closing, keys turning, and more so as to make the TransCenter a fine place to spend time when you don't feel like queueing up at another attraction.

HORIZONS

For generations, visionaries have been making predictions about life in the future. Jules Verne forecast rockets that would fly like bullets. The 19th-century French artist Albert Robida envisioned subways and dirigible taxis and sketched what life in Paris would be like in 1950. And in the 1930s, pulp

science-fiction magazines circulated ideas about automatic barber chairs that would give their owners shoeshines and haircuts, about air conditioners that would pipe in alpine chills, about robots that would do housework, and about suntan lamps and televisions.

The 3-acre Horizons show, which draws on the wisdom of countless scientists, adds its own predictions in a pavilion located between Universe of Energy and World of Motion, just beyond CommuniCore East. After a nod to the visions of earlier centuries in a Looking Back at Tomorrow sequence, the pavilion's continuously moving, suspended, 4-passenger vehicles convey guests into an OmniSphere. Here, on a pair of spectacular hemispherical screens (80 feet in diameter), projectors with special lenses show filmed scenes of a Space Shuttle launch and of growing crystals, together with animated sequences of life in a space colony, a DNA chain, computer chips, etc. All this is a prelude to a voyage through a series of sets demonstrating aspects of life in the future. In Nova Cite, the first destination, advanced transportation and communication systems, such as holographic telephones and trains that work by magnetic levitation, keep members of far-flung families in touch with one another. In the Mesa Verde sequence, voice-controlled robot harvesters and genetically engineered fruits and vegetables populate a once-arid desert. Overhead, "hoverlifts" with spinning blades function as automatic shade controls, and "helium lifters" drop their hooks, collect baskets of the harvest from the robots, and fly the produce off to market. In the future farmer's home, shown nearby, there's an electronic pantry that delivers food to the inhabitants at the push of a button and a home communications center where youngsters can study math (or other subjects) by computer. In the Sea Castle sequence, depicting a movable—but otherwise islandlike—floating city in the Pacific, schoolchildren take underwater field trips to nearby mining and kelp-farming operations manned by robot devices. And in Brava Centauri, a free-floating colony in space, crystals are grown for use by computers back on Earth and colony inhabitants keep in shape in a health-and-recreation center that features games like zero-gravity basketball (seen in shadow along the rear wall), and rowing and bicycling in simulators that allow space folk the opportunity to pursue their favorite sport in any environment they choose. Boaters, for instance, may shoot the Colorado River's rapids in the Grand Canyon, or paddle a Louisiana bayou, or float through the canals of Venice. Home life is just like that on Earth, but with a couple of twists: When a boy newly arrived at the colony doesn't put on his shoes in the morning, he floats away. (They're magnetic shoes, designed for this zero-gravity environment.) And when the family gets together to celebrate a birthday, those who can't attend in person put in an appearance via a holographic telephone.

There's another fine experience at the ride's conclusion: Visitors pick the journey's ending. Just push a button, and a special audience-polling device inside your vehicle delivers the 30-second experience that the majority of your fellow riders have requested. The car tilts back and vibrates, and the sound effects enhance the sensation of great speed created by fast-moving, close-up filmed visuals of travel on land, in the sea, and in space, not unlike those found in the speed rooms in the nearby World of Motion.

Trivia buffs will be curious about the sources of the science-fiction clips presented in the Looking Back at Tomorrow sequence. These include the films *Metropolis* (1926) and *Woman in the Moon* (1928) by the director Fritz Lang; *Mars and Beyond* and *Magic Highways U.S.A.*, shown on the *Disneyland* programs of the 1950s; and Woody Allen's *Sleeper*.

Presented by GE.

WONDERS OF LIFE

The 72-foot-tall steel DNA molecule at the entrance to Epcot Center's newest pavilion beckons guests to a humorous, informative, and healthful experience. Housed in a 100,000-square-foot geodesic dome and two attached buildings, this $100 million attraction allows guests to enjoy both a serious and amusing look at health, fitness, and modern lifestyles. Wonders also boasts Epcot Center's first authentic thrill ride called "Body Wars"—a fast and furious ride through the human body.

From outside the gold-topped dome, the Wonders of Life sign seems to rest on the flumes of water shot up by two fountains. Once inside the building, guests find themselves at the Fitness Fairgrounds. A mobile measuring 50 feet in diameter is suspended from the 65-foot ceiling and it swings gently in the air currents of the building.

At the Fairgrounds, a variety of shows and activities for both children and adults are offered. "Goofy

About Health," is an 8-minute film cartoon presentation that sees Goofy go from a sloppy-living guy to a health conscious fellow. Using old Goofy cartoons that haven't been seen for many years, the show traces Goofy's ups and downs, and winds up with new footage of Goofy at his doctor's office. The film is shown in a 100-seat open theater where visitors can come and go as they wish.

At the Anacomical Players Theater, a corny (but nonetheless informative) show is presented by an improvisational theater group. Audience members are asked to participate, and it's all a lot of fun. This theater also seats 100 people. The third theater at the Fitness Fairgrounds is enclosed. The film shown here, *The Making of Me*, is a 10-minute story about a man who wonders how he came into existence. To find out, he travels back in time to the birth of his parents, their first few years together, and their decision to have a child—him. Footage from an actual delivery is part of the film, and it is sensitively done, and provides a very tangible and touching view of childbirth. Parents should be aware, however, that the film is quite graphic and so may not be suitable for some children.

There are plenty of hands-on activities in areas surrounding the theaters. Guests can ride Wonder-cycles, computerized stationary bicycles that enable guests to pedal through a variety of locales including Disneyland and the Rose Parade. At Coaches Corner, golf, tennis, or baseball swings are analyzed, and a professional knowledgeable in each sport offers free, albeit taped, advice to help you on your way to being the next Nancy Lopez, Chris Evert, or Gary Carter. The Sensory Funhouse offers hands-on activities for kids. It's the Disney version of a children's museum, where education and entertainment go hand in hand.

At the Met Lifestyle Review, guests punch in such information as age, weight, height, exercise habits, whether they smoke, and perceived stress levels at an interactive computer terminal. The computer then processes the information and offers some advice on how to lead a healthier and less stressful existence.

Frontiers of Medicine, located toward the rear of the Fitness Fairgrounds, features the only completely serious segment of Wonders of Life. Here guests can see some scientific and educational exhibits of leading-edge developments in medicine and health sciences. The exhibits change regularly.

Desserts & Things, offers a variety of healthy snacks including oat bran waffles and smoothies (made with frozen yogurt). There is a pleasant seating area, and nearby Well & Goods, Ltd. features men's, women's, and children's athletic wear, most of which features Disney characters participating in a variety of sports, and some educational materials.

Presented by Metropolitan Life.

BODY WARS: The state-of-the-art technology that has been sending guests on a rollicking ride through space at the Star Tours attraction at Disneyland has come to Wonders of Life in the form of the thrill ride called Body Wars. After boarding the vehicles, which are actually the same type of flight simulators employed by military and commercial airlines in pilot training, guests are whisked away on a bumpy, rocky, and exciting ride through the human body. (Note that when instructed to fasten your seatbelt, do so. This is a rough ride.) Movie buffs immediately will think of the film *Fantastic Voyage* and the more recent *Inner Space*. The queue area features exhibits from a fictional company specializing in the latest technology in the miniaturization of people. Guests pass through two special effects portals and are declared ready to do a routine medical probe of the human body—from the inside.

Signs posted outside Body Wars warn that in order to ride passengers must be free of back problems, heart conditions, motion sickness, and other such physical limitations. Pregnant women and children under 3 are not permitted to board. Children under 7 must be accompanied by an adult.

CRANIUM COMMAND: The third major area of Wonders of Life welcomes guests into the mind of a 12-year-old boy. Inside a 200-seat theater, the enormously exaggerated head of our 12-year-old subject is piloted by Buzzy, a delightfully corny Audio-Animatronic figure. The two large eyes are actually rear-projection video screens, and it is through them that the audience gets an idea of how a 12-year-old thinks and reacts. The other animated participant, General Knowledge, helps Buzzy learn which portion of the mind is required for a particular situation. The right and left brain, the stomach, the heart, and the adrenal gland are all represented by endearing characters. It's an altogether whimsical and entertaining show.

UNIVERSE OF ENERGY

When strolling through Future World toward World Showcase Plaza, it's easy to spot this pavilion's mirrored, asymmetrical pyramid off to the left. But the facade doesn't provide any clue at all to the 38 minutes of surprises in store for those who venture inside. One of the most technologically complex experiences at Epcot Center, the Energy show consists of 3 motion pictures and a ride-through attraction. Not one of these is exactly what you might expect.

The first film, seen when you enter the pavilion, examines types of energy used today. Its vivid images of falling water, leaping fire, burning coal, enormous piles of logs, jet engines, and beautiful yellow flowers are the makings of a fine photo essay—but there's a twist: the 14-by-90-foot projection surface is not at all a conventional flat motion picture screen, but is made up of 100 solid triangular elements. These actually rotate on cue from a computer, in synchronization with the changing images, to produce what its creator (Czech filmmaker Emil Radok) described as a "kinetic mosaic."

The second film, shown in an adjoining area, is a 4½-minute animated feature depicting the eras in which today's fossil fuels were created. This film was photographed with the multiplane camera developed by the Disney organization over 40 years ago, and the feeling of depth it gave to the forest scenes in famous films like *Bambi* and *Snow White* also enhances the cinemascape here.

But contrary to the expectations of some visitors, there's not an adorably Disneyesque creature in the show. The animals lumbering across the giant screen (which measures 32 feet by 155 feet, over half the length of a football field) are gigantic prehistoric beasts, and the landscape is an eerie one, full of volcanoes, exotic plants, and bizarre insects. Even more astonishing is the moment at the conclusion of the movie when the whole seating area suddenly begins to rotate, and then breaks up into 6 smaller sections that slowly move forward—usually to the accompaniment of a chorus of oohs and aahs from startled members of the audience.

Before very many people have even begun to grasp the transformation, the vehicles have embarked upon an odyssey through a 3-dimensional re-creation of the primeval world suggested in the film, an otherworldly region of sulfur-scented air, eerie blue moonlight, unearthly fogs, and lava so ominously authentic that few visitors dare reach out and touch it—even when told that one of its main ingredients is a type of commercial styling gel.

Huge trees crowd the forest. Millipedes duel on a log to the left of the vehicles. Brontosauruses wallow in the lagoon out front. A lofty allosaurus battles dramatically with an armored stegosaurus a bit farther along, and an elasmosaurus bursts out of a tidal pool with frightening suddenness—all under the vulturelike gaze of winged creatures known as pteranodons. All of these were created only after months of research, including interviews with countless well-known paleobotanists and paleontologists. The Audio-Animatronics animals are the largest of their type ever to be fabricated, and the 250 prehistoric trees are the first ever to come off any production line. There are so many sounds, smells, and sights here that the time passes in a flash, and before you know it the vehicles have entered another theater.

Here a 12½-minute motion picture, shown on a 220° screen whose breadth intensifies the impact of every image, dramatizes sources of energy for the future. During the filming of the North Sea segment, temperatures dropped so low that the three 65mm cameras used in the filming—specially mounted to generate the almost seamless image projected on the curved screen—had to be taken indoors and

defrosted before work could continue. Footage depicting the Space Shuttle's thunderous blast-off, so unusual that even NASA wanted a copy, serves as the film's grand finale and provides images that stay with you as you travel into another Energy adventure, a splendid computer-animated light show of what looks like dancing laser beams.

Fully as intriguing as the whole Energy experience is the advanced technology behind it. The traveling vehicles measure 29 feet long and 18 feet wide, and weigh about 30,000 pounds when fully loaded with their complement of 96 passengers. Yet they are guided along the concrete floor by a guide wire only ⅛-*inch thick*. And some of the pavilion's required energy is generated by 2 acres of photovoltaic cells mounted on the roof. These cells generate enough energy to run 6 average homes.

In leaving the pavilion, home gardeners should note that the southern live oaks immediately to the east of the Universe of Energy (to your right as you face the entrance) are pruned to follow the slanted roofline of the pavilion. These trees were among a handful started from acorns for Hotel Plaza Boulevard (the broad street that runs down the center of Hotel Plaza) for Walt Disney World's opening over 15 years ago; a quartet of their siblings, in an unpruned state, can still be seen in front of The American Adventure, in World Showcase.

Presented by Exxon.

COMMUNICORE EAST

Officially, CommuniCore—short for Community Core—is the central area of Future World, just beyond (south of) Earth Station. It comprises the 2 large crescent-shaped buildings to the left and right (east and west) and the fountain in the center. The entire complex, which explores the subject of present-day technology, ranks as one of the most interesting areas at Epcot Center.

EPCOT COMPUTER CENTRAL: Computers that talk and play games are the focus of this area located to the left of the fountain plaza entrance to the building. Within the area, there are several activity islands (described below).

Presented by UNISYS.

SMRT-1: He looks like a little purple space man; he talks in a sweet little-boy voice; he has a great time playing simple guessing games with guests, of whom he asks questions like "Is Lincoln buried in Grant's Tomb?" and "Guess Your Birthday." He also chortles with considerable glee when someone flubs an answer.

None of this would be very remarkable if not for the fact that the questioner, SMRT-1, is a computer. To judge from the rapt faces that surround him throughout most of Epcot Center's operating hours, guests enjoy the games as much as he does. It's amusing just to watch, even if the time spent waiting for a turn to talk back isn't in the day's program.

Note that the instructions relating to SMRT-1 aren't as crystal clear as they could be: Remember to push the button on the telephone set as soon as you arrive on the scene so that SMRT-1 will know you're there.

Compute-A-Coaster: Via a bank of touch-sensitive video screens, this area makes the point that designing rollercoaster-type thrill rides is the job of a computer. Players get the chance to build their own coaster using the parts that the computerized program provides—long and short rises, a loop-the-loop, a semi-spiral, and a big drop. The reward for a job well done: a simulated (and rather remarkably scary) ride on the finished product.

Backstage Magic: Accessible via a ramp along the north wall of Epcot Computer Central, this short show is designed to explain the evolution of computers, how they work, and how they are used at Walt Disney World, and to provide a glimpse of the role computers will be playing in the 21st century. It features an array of special effects that help bring computers to life, plus I/O (for input/output), a mime who adds a little life to computers.

Great America Census Quiz: It's difficult to say which aspect of this attraction is more compelling: the chance to use those amazing touch-sensitive TV screens, or the facts that are revealed about this nation in the course of the computers' guessing games. A list of topics appears on the screen at the start of the quiz, and guests choose the ones on which they'd most like to be questioned—The Fifty States, School Days, On the Farm, Communication Line, Home Sweet Home, Population Clock, etc. The answers reveal—among other interesting facts—that there are approximately 12,000 centenarians alive in the United States today, that women in the 1800s had an average of 7 children, that the citizens of Alaska have a higher average income than those of any other state, that Florida will be the fastest growing state during the rest of the century, and that more motorbikes are registered in Michigan than in any other state. Every time someone answers a question incorrectly, a bleep is heard, provoking an embarrassed titter from the erring player—and a good deal of warmhearted sympathy from lookers-on.

Get Set Jet Game: The idea of this game, which aims to demonstrate the use of computers in some passenger-related sections of the aviation business, is to load the greatest possible number of passengers and luggage and to complete a required checklist of safety and maintenance precautions within 60 seconds. To accomplish this successfully requires considerable hand-eye coordination, but the game is amusing even for members of the all-thumbs crowd. The touch-sensitive video screens on which the game is played are located practically alongside those of the Great America Census Quiz.

Flag Game: Designed to illustrate the role of computers in manufacturing, this bank of touch-sensitive video screens (not too far from the ones described just above) gives players a chance to try to build an American flag. Most people with good hand-eye coordination can complete the assignment with flying colors—and the whole area is usually filled with the patriotic music that celebrates their success so enthusiastically that it's hard to resist another go-round.

AMERICAN EXPRESS TRAVELPORT: In this area (opposite Epcot Computer Central), touch-sensitive video screens, located in each of a handful of booths dubbed "vacation stations," provide a would-be traveler with the opportunity to preview a vacation anywhere in the world, from Singapore to Mexico to France to the California coastline. Guests choose the region that interests them—or ask the machines to make suggestions—and then are shown short slide presentations about the destination they've selected. Further prompting elicits lodging, dining, and sightseeing suggestions. The near-by American Express Travel Service office can sell traveler's checks, travel insurance, airplane tickets, tours and cruises, etc., and can arrange for car rentals and individual trips as well. Various services for American Express cardholders are also provided here.

Incidentally, the mysterious-looking 14-foot sphere near the entrance to the TravelPort was designed by the same artist who created the massive lucite sculpture at the entrance to Future World.

Presented by American Express.

ENERGY EXCHANGE: Biomass, synthetic fuels, and solar, wind, nuclear, and mechanical energy are among the subjects explored here. But although the overall subject matter is serious, the exhibits are so diverting that it's entirely possible to spend an hour or more in the area without being aware of the passage of time. One display gives guests the opportunity to compare the amount of energy that they personally can generate by pedaling a stationary bicycle with the power contained in a gallon of gasoline. (Even pedaling at top speed, human beings come in a poor second.) In a related exhibit nearby, turning a crank lights a bulb, and a monitor tells how long it would take to produce $1 worth of electricity.

Elsewhere, there are buttons to push to activate taped programs discussing hydropower, geothermal power, and wind power (and the new-style windmills). One bank of touch-sensitive video screens provides information about conserving energy in the home—about radiators and registers, the proper use of a fireplace and a wood-burning stove, air conditioning, and other such stuff. Another set of screens answers queries on energy sources, energy conservation, and the energy outlook; it also solicits guest opinions about thought-provoking and sometimes controversial energy-related issues. A coal-mining display informs guests about different kinds of coal and shows samples; it also compares reserves of U.S. coal with the nation's other recoverable energy resources and with oil from the Middle East. There is a model of an offshore drilling platform and an exhibit that explains what a "guyed" platform is about. How wells are drilled—from hole-making to processing drilling fluid and oil-shale rock—is one of the many other topics.

Presented by Exxon.

ELECTRONIC FORUM: Located in CommuniCore East (close to the lagoon), this attraction contains Future Choice Theater, Epcot Center's ongoing poll of guest opinions. It works this way: Visitors enter a small theater whose seats are equipped with a number of push buttons. A moderator at the front of

Disney news, sports news, and weather. While one channel broadcasts live from the House of Representatives, others bring the news from French Canada, news from the Caribbean and South and Central America (in Spanish), and from Japan (in Japanese). As a backdrop, there's an exhibit that explains how the satellites responsible for these stations work.

CENTORIUM: This large, sleek shop, the most spacious in all of Epcot Center, stocks a vast selection of Epcot Center and Disney character memorabilia and souvenirs—bumper stickers, watches, books, key chains, pennants, T-shirts, license plates, pencils, hats, visors, memo pads, and much more. In addition, there are all kinds of items related to other areas of Future World, such as dolls that look like the little dragon Figment (one of the Disney creations found exclusively at Epcot Center).

Upstairs there are toy cars and elaborate models of all kinds of vehicles, plus unique games, electronic watches, and tape players—all state-of-the-art items that are amusing to look at even when you've no intention of buying. Youngsters will particularly enjoy the glassed-in elevator.

ILLUMINATIONS: A spectacular display of lasers, fireworks, and dancing fountains to the accompaniment of symphonic music is one of the highlights of any Epcot Center visit. The extravaganza is scheduled nightly at closing time throughout the year. Check for exact times upon arriving at the park.

the room gives a brief account of an issue (often accompanied by videotapes or film clips that feature people who are authorities on the subject). The moderator then solicits individual opinions, and participants push the right button for the answer that is appropriate. The feelings of the audience are immediately flashed on a screen at the front of the room; often the responses are broken down by age group or sex.

Most people really enjoy themselves here, and better still, few ever have to wait more than the 20 minutes that each session takes to gain admission. (The theater is open from 11 A.M. to 7 P.M.) In any event, that time speeds by thanks to the exhibits outside the theater—a veritable armada of television sets showing regional news, national news,

WORLD SHOWCASE

Noble sentiments about the brotherhood of man and the fellowship of nations, which have motivated so many world's fairs in the past, also inhabit World Showcase. But make no mistake about it: This half of Epcot Center, located to the south of Future World, is unlike any previous international exposition.

It is instead a group of pavilions that encircle World Showcase Lagoon (a body of water that, incidentally, is the size of 85 football fields) to demonstrate Disney conceptions about participating countries in remarkably realistic, consistently entertaining styles. You won't find the real Germany here; rather, the country's essence, much as a traveler returning from a visit might remember what he or she saw. Shops, restaurants, and an occasional special attraction are all housed in a group of structures that are an artful pastiche of all the elements that give that nation's countryside and towns their distinctive flavor. Although occasional liberties have been taken when scale and proportion required, careful research governed the design of every nook and cranny.

In the shops, all wares on display represent the country in whose pavilion they are offered for sale. The food focuses on native cuisine, and the entertainment is as authentic as the Disney casting directors can make it, with native performers consistently featured. And craftspeople are occasionally on hand to demonstrate their art in the appropriate shops. Thanks to special Epcot Center cultural exchange programs and the personnel department's energetic efforts to recruit nationals from around Central Florida, nearly all the World Showcase staff members in restaurants, shops, and attractions were born in the countries the pavilions represent

(or at least spent many years living there), and that contributes still more atmosphere. The ongoing efforts of the entertainment department mean that festivities are always in the works, and that new performers are continually making Epcot Center debuts.

Home gardeners should be sure to note the World Showcase landscaping: Each pavilion's plantings closely approximate what would be found in the featured nation. The 1.3-mile World Showcase Promenade, which links pavilions on the shores of the World Showcase Lagoon, has its own interesting vegetation, beginning in World Showcase Plaza with 75-foot Washingtonia fan palms, Arizona-California natives that were imported to Central Florida. Underneath them is a garden full of rosebushes, numbering among the more than 10,000 tree roses, teas, grandifloras, and miniatures planted throughout World Showcase. The Y-shaped trees nearby are callery pears, which can be seen in several other spots in World Showcase. Those encircling the lagoon on the Promenade are camphor trees, which should eventually grow to a height of 60 or 80 feet and about the same dimensions in breadth, to provide the walkway with abundant and welcome shade.

Note that World Showcase pavilions are at their least crowded from the time the park opens until about 11 A.M., and then again from 6 P.M. or 7 P.M. until park closing. So while most of the crowds are standing in line at Future World attractions, shows at World Showcase often are almost empty.

Pavilions are described here in the order that they would be encountered while moving counterclockwise (west to east) around the lagoon after crossing the bridge from Future World.

CANADA

Celebrating the beauties of America's neighbor to the north, the area devoted to the Western Hemisphere's largest nation is complete with its own mountain, waterfall, rushing stream, rocky canyon, mine, and splendid garden massed with colorful flowers. There's even a totem pole, a trading post, and an elaborate, mansard-roofed hotel similar to ones built by the Canadian railroads as they pushed west around the turn of the century. All this is imaginatively arranged somewhat like a split-level house, with the section representing French Canada on top, and another devoted to the mountains alongside it and below. From a distance, the Hôtel du Canada, the main building here, looks like little more than a bump on the landscape—as does Epcot Center's single Canadian Rocky Mountain. But up close they both seem to tower as high as the real thing, thanks to a motion picture designers' technique known as forced perspective, which involves exaggerating the relative smallness of distant parts of a structure to make the totality appear taller than it really is.

The gardens were inspired by the Butchart Gardens in Victoria, British Columbia, a famous park created on the site of a limestone quarry. The hotel is modeled after Ottawa's Victorian-style *Château Laurier*.

Entertainment is provided by the Caledonia Bagpipe Band, featuring 2 pipers and a drummer.

Willow, birch, sweet gum, plum, and maple trees can all be found in the Victoria Gardens; Canada's hemlocks are represented here by deodar cedars, a Himalaya native that can withstand torrid Florida summers with aplomb.

O CANADA!: This motion picture, presented in CircleVision 360 inside Canada's mountain, portrays the Canadian confederation in all its coast-to-coast splendor—the prairies and the plains, the sparkling shorelines and rivers, and the untouched snowfields and rocky mountainsides. The Royal Canadian Mounted Police also put in an appearance. The maritime provinces are all pictured, with their covered bridges and sailing ships, as is Montreal, with its Old World cafés and imposing churches; the scene in the Cathédral de Notre Dame, with its organ booming and choirboys in attendance, is particularly stirring. The great outdoors gets equal play. In one scene, Canada geese take off all around the screen, and the beating of their wings is positively thunderous. Eagles, possums, mallards, bobcats, wolves, bears, deer, bison, and herds of reindeer were all filmed, along with steers being roped at a rodeo and the chuck wagon race that takes place every year at that great provincial fair known as the Calgary Stampede. Skiers in the vast and empty Bugaboos, dogsledders, and ice skaters are featured in the winter scenes; in a hockey game, the sound system almost perfectly conveys the scratch of skates on ice and the sharp whack of sticks against puck. And throughout, the motion picture conveys a sense of the vast size of Canada, providing a you-are-there feeling that makes all of this spectacular scenery still more memorable.

This is partly due to the filming technique, Circle-Vision 360. Also used in the Magic Kingdom's *American Journeys*, it involves a special 5-foot-tall, 600-pound camera rig composed of 9 individual 35mm cameras evenly arranged around a tubular shaft containing the motor that drives the mechanisms for all the cameras. In some scenes the rig was suspended from a helicopter; when depicting the precision-flying Canadian Snowbirds, Canada's answer to the U.S. Air Force's Thunderbirds, it was mounted on a B-25 bomber; in the Calgary sequence, it was placed in one of the racing buckboards; and in the reindeer roundup scene, which took place on the edge of the Arctic Ocean, it was concealed by burlap and hidden.

NORTHWEST MERCANTILE: The first shop to the left upon entering the pavilion's plaza on the way to the Hôtel du Canada, this emporium does a booming business in Canadian sheepskins, which are piled high just inside the entrance. Heavy lumberjack shirts, maple syrup, and other wares that trappers might have purchased back in pioneering days round out the stock. Skeins of rope, tin scoops, lanterns, and a pair of antique ice skates hanging from the long beams overhead set the mood, together with the structure itself. That, like the adjacent Trading Post, is built of adze-hewn logs and ornamented by stone statues, masks, and paintings done in the style of the Ojibway Indians. Located to the rear of the shop are Indian artifacts and assorted souvenirs—items like toy tomahawks, fur vests and moccasins, and sleek-lined sculptures (some made of imitation marble and some carved in soapstone by the Inuit). The small teepees are made from the bark of deciduous trees, which can be gathered up only once a year when the tree goes dormant. These are among several handcrafted Canadian items that are seldom seen elsewhere in the American market.

LA BOUTIQUE DES PROVINCES: This shop offers Canadian merchandise with a French flavor.

UNITED KINGDOM

In the space of only a few hundred feet, visitors to this pavilion stroll from an elegant London square to the edge of a canal in the rural countryside—via a bustling urban English street framed by buildings that constitute a veritable rhapsody of historic architectural styles. But one scene leads to the next so smoothly that nothing ever seems amiss. Here again, note the attention to detail: the half-timbered High Street structure that actually leans a bit, the hand-painted "smoke" stains that make the chimneys look as if they had been there for centuries. When a thatched roof is required, it's right where it should be—though the roof may be made of plastic broom bristles because fire regulations prohibit the real thing. London plane trees, so common in British cities, are represented, and a sundial punctuates the Promenade. Off to the side is a pair of scarlet phone booths identical to those that used to be found all around the U.K. And there are 8 different architectural styles characteristic of the streetscapes, from English Tudor and Georgian to English Victorian.

There is no single major special attraction in this pavilion; instead, it features a half-dozen fine shops and a pub that serves a selection of British-brewed beers and ales that would be the toast of any first class "local" in London itself. There's also plenty of good entertainment including a group of comedians called the Renaissance Street Players, who, when not engaged in general clowning on the World Showcase Promenade, coax audience members into participating in their farcical and altogether entertaining (if unsophisticated) playlets.

Sharp-eyed visitors with an interest in horticultural matters will have a field day examining the landscaping here. The geometrically trimmed bush in

137

front of The Toy Soldier shop is not an Irish yew, so common to the British Isles, but instead a podocarpus; Irish yews don't grow well in Florida. A podocarpus, left in its natural shape, also flanks the shop door just to the rear. A similar substitution had to be made for the London plane tree, also not suited to the Epcot Center climate; its replacement, crowding the half-timbered walls of The Magic of Wales, is a western sycamore, which looks nearly identical and belongs to the same genus. Don't miss the perennial-and-herb garden next to Anne Hathaway's cottage (to the left of the entrance to The Tea Caddy as you face it), and the small path that leads to the garden courtyard to the rear of the shops.

THE TOY SOLDIER: All the necessities are here for such beloved youthful pastimes as sailing (wooden boats), creating works of art ("colouring" books), and just having a good time (Corgi toys).

No toy shop is complete without temptations for adults, and this one is no exception: There are elegant dolls designed expressly for collectors.

Be sure to notice the display at the shop's Promenade entrance—a miniature, glitter-strewn medieval banquet hall peopled by royalty and nobles, musicians, jesters, and a host of other court figures. On the windows downstairs are the heraldic crests for 8 of the U.K.'s principal cities, plus those for the 3 nations that make up the U.K. (Scotland, England, and Northern Ireland—but not Wales, which is a principality). In addition, there are the 3 crosses that, combined, make up the Union Jack—the crosses of St. Andrew, St. George, and St. Patrick.

Outside, the shop resembles a stone manor built during the last half of the 16th century; the Scottish stepped gable parapet and the round turrets are inspired by Scotland's Abbotsford Manor, where the novelist Sir Walter Scott lived for a period, wrote his most famous romances, and died in 1832.

LORDS & LADIES: This shop looks like a backdrop for a child's fantasy of the days of King Arthur, with its high rafters decked out with bright banners, its vast fireplace (and crossed swords above), and its immense wrought-iron chandelier. Pottery replicas of British cottages, dart boards, fragrance products, "pub mugs," limited-edition chess sets, coin and stamp sets, and tapes and records are the stock in trade at this emporium adjoining The Toy Soldier.

PRINGLE OF SCOTLAND: On a sweltering summer day in Central Florida, trying on lamb's wool and cashmere may not hold terrific appeal. But the huge selection of styles and colors in men's and women's sweaters, knitted by Scotland's most famous maker, may well prove enticing despite the temperature outside. Tam o' shanters, socks, hats, ties, scarves, mittens, and kilts are only some of the items offered. Don't fail to look at the fascinating tartan map on the wall across from Lords & Ladies; this identifies plaids from Glen Burn and Gordon to Langtree and St. Lawrence.

THE QUEEN'S TABLE: Sponsored by the Royal Doulton china makers, this shop (opposite Pringle of Scotland) may be one of the loveliest in Epcot Center. That's particularly true of the elegant Adams Room, embellished with elaborate moldings, hung with a chandelier made of crystal, and painted in cream and robin's egg blue in a geometric pattern designed to match the carpet. The setting is a perfect background for the selection of superbly crafted collector's statuettes. The detail is almost photographically perfect, and the prices range from $5 to $12,500.

Among the Royal Doulton shop's more affordable delights are the company's famous Bunnykins cup-and-bowl sets for youngsters. Also intriguing are the small and large Toby mugs—cups that are shaped and painted to represent the visages of famous historical figures. A small selection of attractive Royal Doulton china dinnerware is also available.

Don't fail to inspect small, serene Britannia Square just outside the shop entrance furthest from World Showcase Promenade. But for its somewhat reduced scale and the distinctively Floridian climate, it almost feels like London itself. The statue in the center of this Georgian oasis is of William Shakespeare, and the crests on the shop's upstairs windows are those of four major U.K. schools—Oxford, Cambridge, Eton, and Edinburgh.

THE MAGIC OF WALES: This small emporium offers pottery, slate, jewelry, souvenirs, and handcrafted gifts from Wales. Despite its modest size, it does the highest volume of business (per square foot of size) among the Great Britain shops.

THE TEA CADDY: Fitted out with heavy wooden beams and a broad fireplace to resemble the Stratford-upon-Avon cottage of Shakespeare's Anne Hathaway, this shop, sponsored by Twinings Tea, stocks various types of English teas, both loose and in bags in a variety of flavors. Other items include teapots, biscuits, and candies.

FRANCE

The buildings here have mansard roofs and casement windows so Gallic in appearance that you expect to see some sad, bohemian poet looking down from above. A canal-like offshoot of the World Showcase Lagoon seems like the Seine itself; the footbridge that spans it recalls the old Pont des Arts. There's a kiosk nearby like those that punctuate the streets of Paris, a sidewalk café at which to sip a glass of wine and watch the crowds go by, an elegant bookstore, and a bakery whose absolutely heavenly rich aromas announce its presence long before it's visible. Shops sell perfumes, fine leather wares, jewelry, crystal, and other luxury items. Their roofs are real copper or slate, and the cabinetry is crafted finely enough to dazzle even the most skilled woodworker. Galerie des Halles—the iron-and-glass-ceilinged market that Paris counted as one of its most beloved institutions (until its demolition several years ago)—lives again (near the Palais du Cinéma exit).

But perhaps most special of all are the people. On the Promenade in front of the pavilion, a strolling trio is on hand to entertain. The music is evocative, the repertoire familiar—"Frère Jacques" and "Sur le

Pont d'Avignon" are standards. Similarly, hostesses who hail from Paris and the French provinces answer questions in lyrically French-accented English.

Some interesting background notes: The dusty rose-colored, lace-trimmed costumes that the hostesses wear were inspired by the dresses in the Impressionist painter Edouard Manet's *Le Bar aux Folies-Bergère*, and the park to the west of the pavilion, with its tall Lombardy poplars, was inspired by Neo-Impressionist Georges Seurat's painting *A Sunday Afternoon on the Island of La Grande Jatte*. The main entrance to the pavilion recalls the architecture of Paris, most of which was built during the Belle Epoque ("beautiful age") years of the last half

of the 19th century when, following the designs of city planner Baron Georges Eugène Haussman (he's also responsible for the master plan of Washington, D.C.), thoroughfares were widened and 7 stories became the standard height for city buildings. The lane known as La Petite Rue ("the little street") is inspired by small provincial byways. The sinuously curved, Art Nouveau–style facade of the entrance to the arcade between La Signature and Plume et Palette ("pen and palette") recalls the entrances to Paris's great underground transportation system, the Métro. Don't miss the quiet garden on the opposite side of this arcade—one of the most peaceful spots in World Showcase.

Horticulturally, France offers still other delights, beginning on the World Showcase Promenade. Here a row of Western sycamores that normally grow to 60 or 80 feet—planted in lieu of London plane trees—is being pruned French-style to a height of about 18 feet to develop knots on the end of each branch. These make a distinctive abstract pattern in winter, and in spring send out spiky leaf-bearing shoots that provide bountiful shade in summer. To the west, on the opposite side of the Promenade, a small square edged with miniature rose bushes has been planted to outline the shape of a *fleur de lis*.

PALAIS DU CINEMA: This intimate, elegant little "palace of cinema," a theater not unlike the one at Fontainebleau, is the setting for showings of *Impressions de France*, a lyrical and enchanting 18-minute-long travel film that takes viewers from one end of France to the other. The film shows off a beautiful tree-dotted estate; fertile fields and vineyards at harvest time; a village flower market and a luscious pastry shop; the ribbed tongue of a glacier and a harbor full of squawking gulls; black-clad Breton ladies with headdresses made of starched lace shaped into unique styles that reveal the wearer's origin; Paris on Bastille Day—in all some 4 dozen locations (out of 140 originally shot). Several scenes take place in world-famous landmarks like the Eiffel Tower; Versailles and its gilt Hall of Mirrors (just outside Paris); Mont St. Michel, close to the Brittany-Normandy border in the northwest corner of the country; the French Alps near Mont Blanc, in the southeast; and Cannes, the star-studded resort city on the Mediterranean coast. The automobile competition is Cannes's Bugatti Race; the chateau—which Francophiles will immediately recognize as one of those in the Loire River valley—is fabulous Chambord. (This scene, incidentally, was shot from a helicopter which could fly within 3 feet of any object being photographed.)

All this is even more appealing thanks to a superbly melodic sound track almost entirely made up of the music of French classical composers such as Jacques Offenbach (1819-1880), known for his operettas; Charles Camille Saint-Saëns (1835-1921), a conductor, pianist, organist, and composer celebrated for his lush melodies; Claude Debussy (1862-1918), who did with sound what the Impressionist painters did with light; and Erik Satie (1866-1925), known for his piano works. Selections include Debussy's *Syrinx*, the haunting piece for solo flute, and his *Afternoon of a Faun*, which accompany an aerial shot of fertile fields. Listen for Offenbach's *Gaieté Parisienne* in the biking sequence and Satie's *Trois Gymnopédies* in the Alps scene. The Aquarium section from Saint-Saën's *Carnival of the Animals* accompanies the swamp scene, and the same composer's *Organ Symphony* is heard during the Eiffel Tower ascent. The whole is woven together with transitional segments written and arranged by long-time Disney musician Buddy Baker.

The exceptionally wide screen adds yet another dimension. This is not a Circle-Vision 360 film; it was not shot with the 9 cameras needed for the motion pictures at China and Canada. Instead, the France film used only 5 cameras, but it is shown on a screen made up of 5 projection surfaces, each measuring 21 feet in height and 27½ feet in width— 200 degrees around. It's one of Epcot Center's best films.

There is generally not a long wait here except during peak seasons, but it's still best to see the film first thing in the morning or in the early evening.

PLUME ET PALETTE: One of the loveliest of the World Showcase shops, this one is devoted to art and crystal. The best of the Art Nouveau style is reflected in the sinuous curves embellishing the

in a delicate antique rose color and pale green embellish still others. The curtains are a beautiful dusty pink with white lace.

All this makes a fine backdrop for an array of merchandise that includes collectible miniatures, small china boxes, and tapestries. On the mezzanine level, a handful of fine oil paintings (by well-known French landscape artists) are for sale from $300 to $3,000 each, along with attractive prints of French countryside scenes.

LA SIGNATURE: Another beautiful spot, with wallpaper that resembles watered silk, a fine chandelier, brass-and-crystal sconces, and velvet curtains, this shop stocks lovely French fragrances and bath products, as well as French apparel.

GALERIE DES HALLES: French cookies and chocolate bars—plus souvenirs—are the stock in trade at this area located at the exit from the Palais du Cinéma. The area is modeled on France's now-demolished Les Halles, originally designed by the architect Victor Baltard (1805-1874).

TOUR POUR LE GOURMET: This shop presents a selection of very sophisticated cooking equipment. There are madeleine pans, for making the kind of small, mild-flavored tea cookies that inspired the 19th-century French novelist Marcel Proust to one of the lengthiest reveries in the history of fiction. To round out the offerings, there is an array of exotic herbs, conserves, and fancy foods.

LA MAISON DU VIN: Selections in this lovely shop range from the inexpensive to the pricey, from a few dollars for *vin ordinaire* to upwards of $290 for a relatively rare vintage. Wine tastings are held here to sample the offerings (a small charge is levied, but you get to keep the glass). Those who don't want to carry their purchases all over World Showcase may have them dispatched to Package Pickup for retrieval at the end of the day.

wrought-iron balustrade edging the mezzanine and the moldings that decorate the shining cherry-wood cabinets and shelves. The woodworking is superb, and one case seems more beautiful than the next. Stained glass in purple, yellow, and lavender ornaments the top of one of them. Stylized tulips painted

MOROCCO

Nine tons of tile were handmade, handcut, and shipped to Epcot Center to create this World Showcase pavilion. To capture the unique quality of this North African country's architecture, 19 Moroccan artisans were brought to Epcot Center to practice the mosaic art that has been a part of their homeland for thousands of years. Koutoubia Minaret, a detailed replica of the famous prayer tower in Marrakech, stands guard at the entrance. A courtyard with a fountain in the center—and flowers everywhere—leads to the Medina (Old City). Between the traditional alleyways and the more modern sections are the pointed arches and swirling blue patterns of the Bab Boujouloud gate, a replica of the one that stands in the city of Fez. An ancient working waterwheel irrigates the gardens of the pavilion and the motifs repeated throughout the buildings include carved plaster and wood, ceramic tile, and brass.

GALLERY OF ARTS AND HISTORY: This museum houses ever-changing exhibits of Moroccan art, artifacts, and costumes.

MOROCCAN NATIONAL TOURIST OFFICE: This informative center offers literature useful in planning a visit to Morocco, and the Royal Air Maroc desk makes it easy to book a trip if the mood strikes. There is a 3-screen projection area where a continuous slide show depicts the lifestyles and landscapes of the country.

CASABLANCA CARPETS: Hand-knotted Berber carpets, Rabat carpets with brightly colored geometric designs, prayer rugs, wall hangings of lifelike scenes, and handloomed bedspreads and throw pillows are among the offerings here.

JEWELS OF THE SAHARA: Silver and gold Berber jewelry and beaded pieces with glass, onyx, amber, and other natural stones are the big sellers.

TANGIER TRADERS: Here's the perfect place to buy a fez, plus woven belts, leather sandals, leather purses, and other traditional Moroccan clothing.

MARKETPLACE IN THE MEDINA: Handwoven baskets, sheepskin wallets and handbags, assorted straw hats, and split bamboo furniture and lampshades are available.

THE BRASS BAZAAR: Brass, brass, and more brass—and it's all shiny. Pitchers, planters, pots, and serving sets.

FASHIONS FROM FEZ: Features contemporary women's clothing and accessories from Morocco.

BERBER OASIS: A tent on the promenade spills over with a craftsman's brasswork. Baskets and leathergoods abound.

MEDINA ARTS: A representative selection of crafts from all parts of Morocco makes this an interesting and colorful stop.

JAPAN

Occasionally, when the group known as the "Kanto Abare Daiko" is performing in this pavilion, the surrounding area resounds with the most amazing drumming that most visitors will ever hear. The staccato rhythm is as rapid as the fire of a machine gun, and the booms are deeply resonant and loud.

But for the most part, serenity rules in Japan. The principal entertainment, aside from Kanto Abare Daiko, is a young man known as Nasaji Teresawa, who pursues the 2,400-year-old art of snipping and swirling blobs of brown rice toffee into the shapes of swans, unicorns, crabs, and a score of other remarkable creatures.

The landscaping, designed in accordance with traditional symbolic and aesthetic values, also contributes to the peaceful mood. Rocks, which in Japan represent the enduring nature of the earth, were brought from North Carolina and Georgia (since boulders are scarce in the Sunshine State). Water, symbolizing the sea (which the Japanese consider a life source), is abundant; the Japan pavilion garden has a little stream and a couple of pools inhabited (in good weather) by colorful fish. A small bamboo device at the edge of one of these rivulets regularly fills up with water falling from above, and then, weighted by its contents, empties out and makes regular, but somehow soothing, clacking noises in the process. Evergreen trees, which in Japan are symbols of eternal life, are here in force.

Disney horticulturalists created this very Japanese landscape without using very many plants or trees native to that country, where the climate is so different from that in Florida. The evergreens near the brilliant vermilion *torii* gate are native Florida slash pines. The palm near the courtyard entrance to the Yakitori House is a sago palm, which is among the oldest living bits of flora on earth. The curly leaved trees alongside the stream are corkscrew willows. Among the few trees actually native to Japan are the two Japanese maple trees (identifiable by their small leaves) not far away (near the first stairway from the Promenade on the left side of the courtyard as you face it), and the prickly branched, prickly leaved monkey puzzle trees near the walkway to the Promenade, on The American Adventure side of the pagoda; needle-sharp thorns

make this the only species of tree that monkeys cannot climb.

Visitors who have actually been to Japan will be interested to observe that most of the structures inside the pavilion have their Japanese antecedents. The pagoda that occupies such a prominent place along World Showcase Promenade was modeled after an 8th-century structure located in the Horyuji Temple in Nara. The brilliant vermilion *torii* gate on the shores of World Showcase Lagoon derives from the design of the one at the Itsukushima shrine in Hiroshima Bay, one of the most beautiful sites on the inland sea.

BIJUTSU-KAN GALLERY: A changing cultural display, this small museum has offered, among other shows, "Echos Through Time," an exhibit of traditional and contemporary Japanese art forms.

MITSUKOSHI DEPARTMENT STORE: There are kimonos in silk, cotton, and polyester; attractive all-cotton T-shirts bearing Japanese characters; expensive, almost sculptural traditional headdresses that seem fabricated of lacquer-stiffened netting; and an excellent selection of bowls and vases meant for flower arranging. But on the whole, no one would ever apply the term "quaint" to this spacious store set up by Mitsukoshi—an immense, 3-century-old retail firm that was once dubbed "Japan's Sears." Some of the china dinnerware is too often seen elsewhere in the U.S. in department stores or inexpensive chain import stores to arouse

THE AMERICAN ADVENTURE

When it came to creating The American Adventure, the centerpiece of World Showcase, the Disney imagineers were given virtually a free hand. So the 110,000 bricks of the imposing colonial-style structure that houses the show, a counter-service restaurant, and a shop are real brick—made *by hand* from soft, pinkish-orange Georgia clay. The show inside stands out because of its wonderfully evocative

more than passing interest. It's unfortunate that this familiarity also makes it easy to dismiss some of the other merchandise that, though it appears to be of the same trinket quality, has considerable meaning in Japanese culture. One example is the dolls, of which there are literally rows and rows, priced from $3.50 to $3,000, and clad in elaborate kimonos sashed with wide, stiff *obis*. These are traditionally given to female children on Girls' Day, a popular Japanese national holiday. The blank-eyed, egg-shaped pâpier-maché scarlet masks, which come in a wide range of sizes from small to very large, are part of the traditional New Year celebration. The Japanese color in one eye when making a New Year's resolution, keep the one-eyed "face" in plain view throughout the next 365 days as a reminder of the holiday vow, and celebrate success when the year draws to its close by completing the face.

The structure housing the merchandise was inspired by a section of the Gosho Imperial Palace, which was constructed in Kyoto in the year A.D. 794, and is widely recognized as a fine example of early Japanese architecture.

settings, its innovatively detailed sets, and the 35 superb Audio-Animatronics players, some of the most lifelike ever created by the Disney organization: The American Adventure's Ben Franklin even walks up stairs. The digital sound system is also the most advanced that the Disney organization has ever used, and the show is the most technically complex, involving the world's largest rear-projection screen (72 feet in width) and a number of very sophisticated sets that rise up from below the stage to the delight and awe of the audience. A superb vocal group called The Voices of Liberty entertains inside the building.

Be sure to note the 4 luxuriant trees out front. They were originally planted in 1969 on Hotel Plaza Boulevard, the main thoroughfare of Disney Village Hotel Plaza, and along with a handful of their contemporaries (which can be seen in their pruned and unpruned states throughout Epcot Center, most notably trimmed diagonally alongside Future World's Universe of Energy) have been moved 4 times in the intervening years.

Presented by the Coca-Cola Co. and American Express.

THE AMERICAN ADVENTURE SHOW: One of the truly outstanding Epcot Center attractions, this 29-minute presentation celebrates the American spirit from our nation's earliest years right up to the present. Beginning with the arrival of the Pilgrims at Plymouth Rock and their hard first winter on the western shore of the Atlantic, the Audio-Animatronics narrators—Ben Franklin and a cigar-puffing Mark Twain—recall certain key people and events in American history—the Boston Tea Party, George Washington and the grueling winter at Valley Forge, the influential black abolitionist Frederick Douglass, the celebrated 19th-century Nez Percé Chief Joseph, and many more. The Philadelphia Centennial Exposition is remembered, along with women's rights campaigner Susan B. Anthony, telephone inventor Alexander Graham Bell, and the steel giant and philanthropist Andrew Carnegie. Naturalist John Muir converses on stage with Teddy Roosevelt. Charles Lindbergh, Rosie the Riveter, Jackie Robinson, Marilyn Monroe, and Walt Disney are all represented. So are John Wayne, Lucille Ball, Margaret Mead, John F. Kennedy, Martin Luther King, Muhammed Ali, and Billie Jean King. The idea is to recall episodes in history, both negative and positive, which most contributed to the growth of the spirit of America, either by engendering "a new burst of creativity" (in the designers' words) "or a better understanding of ourselves as partners in the American experience." The presentation is hardly comprehensive; instead, it's "a hundred-yard dash capturing the spirit of the country at specific moments in time."

Throughout the show, the attention to historical detail is meticulous. Every one of the rear-projected illustrations was executed in the painting style of the era being described. The Chief Joseph and Susan B. Anthony figures are speaking their originals' very own words. The exact dimensions of the cannonballs in another scene were carefully investigated—then reproduced. In the Philadelphia Centennial Exposition scene, Pittsburgh's name is spelled without the *h* that subsequent years have added.

For information about how each of the various historical figures actually spoke during their lifetimes, researchers contacted about half a dozen historians and cultural institutions—the Philadelphia Historical Commission, Harvard's Carpenter Center of Visual Arts, the State Historical Society of Missouri, the Department of the Navy's Ships Historical Branch, and others. When recordings were not available, educated guesses were made: Bell's voice was created on the basis of contemporary comments about his voice's clarity, expressiveness, and crisp articulation, coupled with the fact that his father taught elocution. To select Will Rogers's speeches for the Depression scene, whole pages of quotes were collected, reviewed, edited, and re-edited; the voice is the humorist's own, from an actual broadcast, as is that of FDR, here heard over the radio in the roadside gasoline stand scene. That particular scene was suggested by a *Life* magazine photograph; details were based upon research in architectural magazines from the 1930s. Even the type of radio and the style of microphone, and the price (18¢) and the color (red) of gasoline in the tanks were the result of researchers' long hours and close scrutiny.

One of the most interesting aspects of the show is its inner workings, however. Underneath the entire theater is a movable carriage device that designers have dubbed "the war wagon," measuring 65-by-

35-by-14 feet and weighing 175 tons. The base-ment that supports "the war wagon" is itself sup-ported by pilings driven approximately 300 feet into the ground; it carries 10 different sets and during the presentation rolls forward or backward to position the appropriate set underneath the stage at the appropriate time. Also, because the height of the space underneath the theater is relatively limited, the sets themselves were specially designed to allow certain sections to contract telescopically as proved necessary. These operations are computer controlled.

The 12 life-size statues on either side of the stage represent the "Spirits of America." These are, on the left, from front to rear, Individualism, Innovation, Tomorrow, Independence, Compassion, and Dis-covery; and, on the right, from front to back, Free-dom, Heritage, Pioneering, Knowledge, Self-Reli-ance, and Adventure. The 44 flags flanking the Hall of Flags corridor in the escalator area are those that have flown over the United States. Revolutionary War flags, Colonial flags, and even flags represent-ing the countries that had claims to American soil before Independence, can all be seen. A special highlight of the show is the majestic music played throughout by the Philadelphia Symphony Orches-tra. The "Golden Dream" finale, one of several memorable Epcot Center theme songs, is available on record or tape—so if you like it, be sure to ask at the Centorium. The pavilion's carillon plays the same music on the hour.

As one of the most compelling of all the World Showcase attractions, The American Adventure is occasionally quite busy. Perhaps the best time to schedule a visit to the show is first thing in the morning or in the early evening. Seats in the front of the house give the optimal view of the Audio-Animatronics characters (although all seats provide an acceptable view). While waiting for the show to begin, be sure to read the quotes on the walls—Wendell Wilkie, Jane Addams, Charles Lindbergh, Ayn Rand, Archibald Macleish, Herman Melville, Thomas Wolfe, and George Magar Mardikau are all represented.

HERITAGE MANOR GIFTS: Visit this shop for pre-1940s Americana. Decorative gifts include glass-ware, handmade wooden and cloth items, hand-painted porcelain, toys, and food products.

AMERICA GARDENS THEATRE: A variety of en-tertainment, including an exceptionally lively show of international folk dances and songs, is presented periodically in this lakeside amphitheater in front of The American Adventure pavilion. The folk show is particularly worth a detour; get performance times from the information desks at Earth Station (on your way into the park), or check at any WorldKey Infor-mation System kiosk. Showtimes are also posted on the promenade at the east and west entrances to the amphitheater.

Be sure to note the pruning of the Western syca-mores overhead; the old-fashioned pollarding meth-od used, which involves trimming the treetops flat and allowing the lower branches to fill out and interlock, will eventually produce a thick canopy. The flower beds outside are planted in red, white, and blue; the bushes are East Palatka holly.

145

ITALY

The arches and cut-out motifs that adorn the World Showcase reproduction of Venice's Doge's Palace are just the more obvious examples of the attention to detail lavished on the individual structures in this relatively small pavilion. The angel atop the scaled down Campanile was sculpted on the model of the original right down to the curls on the back of its head—then covered with real gold leaf, despite the fact that it was destined to be set almost 100 feet in the air. The other statues in the complex, including the sea god Neptune presiding over the fountain in the rear of the piazza, are similarly exact. Even the marble-like material used in the facade resembles that used in the real Doge's Palace. And the pavilion even has an island like Venice's own, its seawall appropriately stained with age, plus moorings that look like barber poles, with several distinctively Venetian gondolas tied to them. St. Mark the Evangelist is also remembered, together with the lion that is the saint's companion and Venice's guardian; these can be seen atop the 2 massive columns flanking the small arched footbridge that connects the landfall to the mainland. The only deviation from Venetian fact is the alteration of the site of the Doge's Palace in reference to the real St. Mark's Square.

The pavilion is equally interesting from a horticultural point of view. The island boasts a brace of kumquat trees, citrus plants typical of the Mediterranean, and a couple of olive trees that can be seen on both side walls of the Arcata d'Artigiani; originally located in a Sacramento, California, grove, they were moved to Anaheim and then were piled onto a flatbed truck, their branches spreading wide, for the trip to Florida. But they got only as far as the Arizona border. As Disney gardeners tell the story, that state's regulation prohibiting loads beyond a given width is so erratically enforced that no problems had been anticipated. So it came as quite a surprise when the inspector on duty decreed that the trees be trimmed to 10 feet. A chain saw soon materialized, and within minutes the ancient olives were shorn. Despite horticulturalists' fears, the trees survived, leaving only their scars to remind visitors of

the ordeal; the darker bark is what remains of the original, while the lighter areas are the new growth. The tall trees that stand like dark columns at various points in the pavilion are Italian cypress, which are very common in Italy; Florida slash pines replace that nation's abundant Italian stone pines, which would not grow here.

Entertainment is another highlight of the pavilion. A very lively group known as the Teatro di Bologna puts on 15-minute shows such as "The Great Impasta," in which selected members of the audience have the chance to play heroes, heroines, and the vilest of villains in a style reminiscent of the Renaissance *commedia dell' arte*. The Teatro di Bologna players are very funny (if very broad) and shouldn't be missed.

ARCATA D'ARTIGIANI: This open-air market on the western edge of the piazza is a good spot for a sweet snack with its selection of tasty Italian chocolates and other goodies for sale. The reasons for Italy's fame as a producer of fine leather goods are immediately obvious inside, where you'll find a nice selection of leather items and other Italian-made gifts and accessories, including purses, scarves, belts, perfumes, and sportswear.

LA GEMMA ELEGANTE: Located to the rear of the piazza on its eastern edge, this small shop focuses on jewelry. There are gold and silver chains galore, and some are expensive, but it's also possible to find handsome—and affordable—beads, earrings, and pendants made of Venetian glass; intricate glass-mosaic brooches and pillboxes bearing images of tiny bouquets; cameos; and coral necklaces.

IL BEL CRISTALLO: The production of fine glassware has been a tradition in Italy for centuries, and so a shop like this one just off the Promenade on the Germany side of the piazza was a must for the pavilion. Typical Venetian glass paperweights and other items, their bright colors trapped in smooth spheres or teardrops of clear or milky glass, small porcelain figurines and flower bouquets so finely crafted that they look almost real, pastel flowers made of beads, and lead crystal bowls and candlesticks are all on display. The name of the shop means "the beautiful crystal."

GERMANY

There are no villages in Germany quite like this one. Inspired in part by towns in the Rhine region and Bavaria, and in part by communities in the German north, it boasts structures reminiscent of those found in such diverse urban enclaves as Frankfurt, Freiburg, and Rothenburg. There are stair-stepped roof lines and towers, balconies and arcaded walkways, and so much overall charm that the scene seems to come straight out of a fairy tale. The beer hall to the rear is almost as lively as the one at Munich's famed Oktoberfest, especially during the later shows, and the shops, which offer a range of merchandise from wine and sweets to ceramics and cuckoo clocks, toys and books, and even art, are so tempting that it's hard to leave the area empty-

handed. The various elements that make up the Germany pavilion are described here as they would be encountered while walking from west to east (counterclockwise) around the cobblestone-paved central plaza, which is known as the St. Georgsplatz, after the statue at its center. St. George, the patron saint of soldiers, is depicted with the dragon that legend says he slew during a pilgrimage to the Middle East.

Try to time your World Showcase peregrinations to bring you to Germany on the hour, when the handsome, specially designed glockenspiel at the plaza's rear can be heard to chime in a melody composed specifically for the pavilion.

DER BÜCHERWURM: This 2-story structure, whose exterior is patterned after a merchants' hall known as the *Kaufhaus* (located in the southern German town of Freiburg in Breisgau), stocks prints and English books about Germany; handsome prints of German cities full of gabled old houses and gloriously spired cathedrals; and an assortment of souvenir items like ashtrays and vases and spoons bearing images of German cities. The building itself is worth noting. In order to correctly reproduce the statues of the German emperors on the facade, designers hired a photographer who, shooting from a "cherry picker," submitted close-ups from a number of angles. Observant travelers may remember that the Freiburg building has one additional statue—that of Emperor Maximillian—omitted here in the interests of maintaining the proper proportions. (Film and sundries are available here.)

VOLKSKUNST: This small, exceptionally appealing establishment is full of a burgher's bounty of German timekeepers, plus a smattering of other items made by hand in the rural corners of the nation. The latter include beer steins in all sizes, from the petite to the enormous and expensive ($2,800); wood carvings made in the southern German town of Oberammergau; bright, fringed Tyrolean scarves; nutcrackers; and a whole collection of "smokers," carved wooden dolls with a receptacle for incense and a hollow pipe for the smoke to escape. As for cuckoo clocks, some are small and unprepossessing, and some are so immense that they'd look appropriate only in some cathedral-ceilinged hunting lodge. The largest measures about 5 feet in height and is embellished not only with carvings of birds and rabbits and a hunting horn and crossed rifles, but also with a genuine pair of antlers. A must.

WEINKELLER: The Germany pavilion's wine shop, situated between the cookie shop and the Biergarten toward the rear of St. Georgsplatz, offers approximately 250 varieties of German wines produced and bottled by H. Schmitt Söhne, one of Germany's oldest and largest vintners. Wine tastings are held here daily. The selection includes not only those meant for everyday consumption, but also fine estate wines whose prices run into the hundreds of dollars per bottle. These are white (with a few exceptions), because white wine constitutes the bulk of Germany's vinicultural output. (In fact, only 20 percent of all German bottlings are red.) Long, tall beer mugs and glasses, wine glasses in traditional German colors of greens and ambers, fragile crystal goblets, decanters, and other accessories are also available. The setting itself is quite attractive—low-ceilinged and cozy and full of fir cabinets that have been embellished with carvings of vines and bunches of grapes. The original designs, which decreed that all those grapes be painted purple, were altered to include plenty of green fruit, the main ingredient in white wine.

DER TEDDYBÄR: Located alongside Volkskunst, this toy shop would be a delight if only for the lively mechanized displays high up on either side of the entrance and against the rear wall: Some of the stuffed lambs and the dolls in the full-skirted folk dresses (known as *dirndls*) have been animated so that tails wag and skirts swirl in time to German folk tunes. The shop is also home to one of WDW's very best selections of toys. There are wonderfully detailed LGB-brand miniature trains and the expected assortment of expensive stuffed keepsakes from Steiff. Colorful wooden toys are tempting as well, along with all kinds of building blocks. Last but not least, the collection of dolls is simply wonderful.

SÜSSIGKEITEN: It is a mistake to visit this tiny, tile-floored confectionery shop on an empty stomach: Chocolate cookies, butter cookies, and almond biscuits mix with caramels, nuts, and pretzels on the crowded shelves; and there are boxes upon boxes of *Lebkuchen*, the spicy crisp cookies traditionally baked in Germany at Christmas, not to mention Gummi Bears (which the packages announce as *Gummibaeren*). Children enjoy the special alphabet cookies and animal crackers, both of which are different from those made in U.S. bakeries. Don't miss the attractive display of old Bahlsen cookie tins by the door. Incidentally, Bahlsen, the shop's sponsor, was among the first companies in the world to pack baked goods in air-tight wrappers to preserve freshness; the firm's logo is an Egyptian hieroglyph that signifies *long life*.

PORZELLANHAUS: This is a shop that can set a visitor's mind to thoughts of Christmas—even in the dog days of summer. Christmas ornaments, decorations, and gifts manufactured by various German companies line the shelves of this store.

GLAS UND PORZELLAN: Featuring glass and porcelain items made by the German firm of Goebel, this is an attractive establishment with rope-turned columns, curved moldings, delicate scrollwork, and tiny carved rosettes. But no matter how attractive the backgrounds, the stars of the show are the M.I. Hummel figurines, which Goebel manufactures. Cherubic, rosy-cheeked children, shown carrying baskets, trays, umbrellas, and other items, as in the drawings of a young German nun named Berta Hummel, are favorites of collectors around the world. One group features redheads, while others have youngsters perched on the edges of ashtrays. There is always an elaborate showpiece at the center of the shop, and a Goebel artist is here to demonstrate the process by which Hummel creations are painted and finished. An excellent display (which includes figurines in all stages of completeness) tells the story.

CHINA

Dominated by a Disney equivalent of Beijing's Temple of Heaven, and announced by a pair of banners which offer good wishes to passersby (the Chinese characters translate *May good fortune follow you on your path through life* and *May virtue be your neighbor*), this pavilion offers a level of serenity that makes an appealing contrast to the hearty merriment of nearby Germany and the Latin gaiety of Mexico. Part of this quiet environment is the byproduct of the soothing traditional Chinese music that plays over the sound system. The attractive gardens also make a major contribution. They are full of rose bushes (because roses are native to China), and there is a century-old mulberry tree (to the left of the main walkway into the pavilion), with a pomegranate tree and a wiggly-looking Florida native known as a water oak nearby. In addition, a spacious emporium devoted to Chinese wares has opened, and 2 Chinese restaurants add to the overall atmosphere. However, all this is secondary to the fabulous motion picture shown inside the Temple of Heaven—a CircleVision 360 film that is one of the best World Showcase attractions.

WONDERS OF CHINA: LAND OF BEAUTY, LAND OF TIME: This 19-minute presentation shows the beauties of a land that few Epcot Center visitors will ever see first hand—and does it so vividly that it's possible to see the film over and over and still not fully absorb all the wonderful sights. The Disney crew was the first Western film group to film certain sites, and their remarkable effort includes such marvels as Beijing's Forbidden City; vast, wide-open Mongolia and its stern-faced tribesmen; the 2,400-year-old Great Wall; the Great Buddha of Leshan, 8 centuries old and dramatically imposing; the muddy Yangtze River and the 3,000-year-old city of Suzhou, whose location on the Grand Canal, which is generally believed to be the largest man-made waterway in the world, encouraged Marco Polo to call it the Venice of the East. There are shots of Shanghai, as well as Hangzhou, where a handful of Chinese are shown doing their morning exercises along the river's edge. Also shown are Huangshan Mountain, wreathed in fog; the Shilin Stone Forest of jagged rock outcroppings in Yunnan Province; Urumqi, whose distance from the sea in Xinjiang Province earned it the title of the most inland city on earth; Lahsa, in Tibet, and its Potala Palace, boasting a thousand rooms and ten times that many altars. Just as fantastic are the Reed Flute Cave and the bizarrely shaped hills of Kweilin above, to

say nothing of the very European-looking city of Shanghai. To complete the picture, there are fields of snow and of wheat, high meadows and beaches dotted with tropical palms, harbors and rice terraces, calligraphers, checkers and Ping-Pong players, lightning-fast acrobats, championship horseback riders, camels and a panda bear, glittering ice sculptures, and millions of bicycles.

Almost every step of the way, the film crews were besieged by curious Chinese, even in empty Mongolia. For the Huangshan Mountain sequence, which lasts only seconds, the crew and about three dozen hired laborers had to carry the 600-pound camera uphill for nearly a mile. The Chinese government would not permit Disney cameramen to shoot aerial footage in some areas, so Chinese crews were sent aloft to record the required scenes, first on videotape and later—after approval from the Disney director in charge of the project—on film. You can see for yourself just how well this collaboration worked.

Be sure to spend some time before viewing the film examining the details that embellish the building that houses the theater. The design is based on that of the Hall of Prayer for Good Harvest, the major section of Beijing's Temple of Heaven complex, which was built in the year 1420 (during the Ming Dynasty) and reconstructed after being damaged by lightning in 1896. The name of the World Showcase structure is represented by the characters above the entrance. The number of stones in the floor was chosen for auspicious associations; the center stone is surrounded by nine stones because nine is a lucky number in China. Around the edge of the room rise 12 columns—because 12 is both the number of months in the year and the number of years in a full cycle of the Chinese calendar. Closer to the room's center, there are 4 columns—1 for each of the seasons; the japonicus vines entwining each column symbolize long life, while the square beam that they all support alludes to earth, and the round beam above signifies heaven. The dragons on the beams allude to imperial strength, while the phoenixes are reminders of peace and prosperity. The measurements and proportions are all similarly symbolic. Be sure to stand on the round stone in the absolute center of the anteroom: Every whisper is amplified.

When exiting, pass by the House of the Whispering Willows, an exhibit of ancient Chinese art and artifacts. Changed about every 6 months, it invariably includes fine pieces from well-known collections. Note that the best time to see the film is during the first couple of hours that Epcot Center is open and again just before closing.

YANG FENG SHANG-DIAN: This vast Chinese emporium, located off the narrow, charming Street of Good Fortune at the exit to the film, offers a huge assortment of Chinese merchandise—silk robes, prints, paper umbrellas and fans, embroidered items, change purses and glasses cases, and more. Trinkets, medium-priced items, and expensive antiques are all available in an array that may be matched in few other places in the U.S. The calligraphy on the curtains wishes passersby *good fortune, long life, prosperity, health, and happiness.*

NORWAY

Set between the Mexico and China pavilions is Norway, Walt Disney World's 11th World Showcase attraction. Built in conjunction with many Norwegian companies, the pavilion celebrates the history, folklore, and culture of one of the world's oldest countries.

Most appropriately, visitors tour Norway by boat—16-passenger, dragon-headed longboats like those Eric the Red and his fellow Vikings used 1,000 years ago—to begin a voyage through time. The journey begins in a 10th-century Viking village where a ship is being readied to head out to sea. Seafarers then find themselves in a mythical Norwegian forest, populated by trolls who cause the boats to plummet backwards downriver, through a maelstrom to the majestic grandeur of the Geiranger fjord, where the vessel narrowly avoids spilling over a waterfall. Ultimately, after a harrowing plunge through a rocky passage, the boats wind up in the North Sea, caught in the fury of a full-blown storm. Lightning flashes reveal an enormous oil rig; as the boat passes the concrete platform legs, the storm calms and a friendly coastal village appears on the horizon.

Survivors disembark there and enter the village. Moments later, guests are invited to a theater where the journey continues on-screen, giving visitors a very tangible sense of the natural scenic spectacles and unique personalities that make up modern Norway. Outside the theater, visitors find they have returned to a cobblestone town square, an architectural showcase in the styles of such Norwegian towns as Bergen, Alesund, Oslo, and Setesdal.

There's also a Norwegian castle fashioned after Akershus, a 14th-century fortress still standing in Oslo's harbor. Shops in the castle stock authentic Norwegian handicrafts and folk items: hand-knit woolens, wood carvings, and glass and metal artworks.

Outside, on the Showcase Lagoon, don't miss the

50-foot *Norseman*, an exact replica of the Viking ship believed to have carried Bjarni Herjulfsson and his fellow explorers on their 10th-century voyage to the New World—some 14 years before Leif Eriksson got the credit. The Viking ship replica actually sailed the North Atlantic, beginning in Nova Scotia and continuing down to Boston and New York before being shipped to Walt Disney World in September 1987.

MEXICO

The tangle of tropical vegetation surrounding the great pyramid that encloses this pavilion and the Cantina, the Mexican restaurant at the lagoon's edge on the Promenade, provide only the barest suggestion of the charming area inside. Dominated by a reconstruction of a quaint plaza at dusk, this area is rimmed by balconied, tile-roofed, colonial-style structures. Crowding a pretty fountain area is a quartet of stands selling Mexican handicrafts, and off to the left is an attractive shop stocked with other handsome wares. Mariachi bands keep things lively. To the rear, the San Angel Inn, a corporate cousin of the famous Mexico City restaurant of the same name, serves authentic Mexican fare. Behind it, the pavilion's main show chronicles Mexican culture from earliest times right up to the present.

Queues for the boat ride often extend into the Promenade in the morning—but if you just want to visit the shops and see the cultural exhibit inside the pyramid entrance, it's perfectly fine to walk straight in, bypassing the line.

Note that the pyramid itself was inspired by Meso-American structures dating from the 3rd century A.D. The serpent heads on either side of the stairway evoke the Aztec god Quetzalcoatl.

EL RIO DEL TIEMPO: THE RIVER OF TIME: In the course of this 6-minute boat trip, sprinkled with vignettes of pre-Columbian, Spanish-Colonial, and modern Mexican life, visitors greet a Mayan high priest, watch stylized dances by performers in vivid costumes, and are assailed by vendors at a lively market. A band costumed to look like skeletons entertains at one juncture (in a reference to the Day of the Dead, a holiday celebrated in Mexico with candies and sweets shaped like skulls or skeletons). In addition, there are a handful of film clips depicting present-day Acapulco (with its cliff divers and flying dancers), Tulum, Manzanillo (and its speed boats), and Isla Mujeres (with its gorgeous sea life). The assemblage of film, Audio-Animatronics figures, and props is reminiscent of the Magic Kingdom's It's A Small World. During peak seasons, long lines, which prevail from mid-morning on, usually thin out in the afternoon as the crowds drift into the more distant parts of World Showcase. If you are in the area, skip the boat ride the first time around and return in the evening or late in the afternoon when the crowds are likely to be far smaller.

itself. The colorful pâpier-maché piñatas that figure so strongly in the scenery here are so popular that Epcot Center has to buy them from suppliers by the truckload. Irresistible.

ARTESANIAS MEXICANAS: This shop stocks more expensive versions of some of the merchandise sold in the Mercado—onyx ashtrays, bookends, plaques, chess sets, malachite, and unique Mexican decorative gifts.

LA FAMILIA FASHIONS: This shop features Mexican ready-to-wear and fashion accessories for women and children, plus examples of silver and turquoise jewelry.

EL RANCHITO DEL NORTE: Gift items and souvenirs from northern Mexico are the featured items here.

WORLD SHOWCASE PLAZA

PORT OF ENTRY: Features unique gifts, clothing, and accessories from around the world including countries not featured in World Showcase. Sunglasses, film, and cigarettes are available.

DISNEY TRADERS: Merchandise combining the charms of Disney characters and World Showcase themes are the stock in trade. Sunglasses, film, cigarettes, and sundries are also available.

PLAZA DE LOS AMIGOS: Brightly colored paper flowers, sombreros, wooden trays and bowls, peasant blouses, baskets, and pottery make this shopping area (*mercado* in Spanish) at the plaza's center as bright and almost as lively as one in Mexico

HOT TIPS

- Get precise, up-to-date information about the procedure for getting reservations in Epcot Center restaurants as soon as you arrive in Central Florida. Call 824-4321 for *information*, not reservations.
- Stop by Earth Station for an entertainment schedule in order to be sure you won't miss any of the special shows scheduled for the day or evening.
- During peak seasons, preferred reservation times at Epcot Center's full-service restaurants are usually fully booked by 10 A.M. So be sure to arrive at Epcot Center at least 30 minutes ahead of the official opening time to get a jump on the day and help assure that you get the restaurant and seating time of your choice. Study the special box on Epcot Center restaurant reservations in the *Good Meals, Great Times* chapter. Remember, too, that non-prime dining hours are often available to those making late reservations, so adjustment of your eating schedule may well help you to try the restaurant of your choice.
- Have dinner at one of the WDW resort

hotels or in the Disney Village Marketplace if you don't have a reservation and want something more elaborate than what the fast food eateries are offering. But if your time is limited, consider eating at one of the fast food outlets, since Epcot Center fast food is no worse than that served elsewhere.
- Save the shops, CommuniCore East and West, and the World of Motion's TransCenter for the most congested hours. Go to as many of the most popular attractions as possible during early morning and late afternoon hours.
- Visit World Showcase in the morning—it's normally uncongested until about 11 A.M. See Future World in the evening, avoiding the busy mid-morning hours. Remember that lines throughout Epcot Center are longest during midday, and shortest (sometimes nonexistent) during the early evening.
- Don't queue for the World Showcase Promenade buses. You'll get where you're going faster by walking, and spend a comparable amount of time on your feet.

DISNEY-MGM STUDIOS THEME PARK

Welcome to "the Hollywood that never was and always will be." So said Walt Disney Company Chairman Michael Eisner when he officially opened the Disney-MGM Studios Theme Park. A bit corny? Sure. But also true.

In the solid Disney tradition, a dream Hollywood set in some indeterminate time in the 1930s and 1940s has been lovingly created. A rose-colored view of the movie-making capital has been combined with a backstage tour that breaks new ground, a variety of entertaining attractions, and a delightful selection of eateries to create the newest Walt Disney World enclave. It marks the first time that a look at a fully functioning television and movie production facility has been combined with a chance for visitors to be part of the show.

The Studio is situated on a 110-acre site southwest of Epcot Center. The watertower, known to punsters (for obvious reasons) as the "Earffel Tower," is reminiscent of the types of towers looming over most Hollywood studios of the era. Here, however, it gets that special Disney touch and is capped by a mousketeer-style hat. The tower stands 13 stories tall and has become a landmark at Walt Disney World.

The Studio contains several components. There's Hollywood Boulevard, with its shops, restaurants, and art deco architecture; the Great Movie Ride, where guests visit some famous scenes from famous motion pictures; SuperStar Television, where lucky audience members actually appear with TV's greatest stars in a variety of television skits; the Monster Sound Show, which allows visitors to create the sound effects for a film with very funny results; the Epic Stunt Spectacular, in which the death-defying Indiana Jones stunts from "Raiders of the Lost Ark" are restaged; the Animation Building, where a hilarious movie is combined with a look at animators at work; and the Backstage Tour, during which guests see movie and TV production in progress and tour the backlots. There's also a wide assortment of restaurants where the settings are the entertainment (all of the restaurants are described in detail in *Good Meals, Great Times*.

What makes this area of Walt Disney World different from other Disney creations is the extent to

which guests can participate in the attractions. Our best advice is to volunteer, wherever and whenever possible. It's great fun, and it adds enormously to the experience.

The enormous popularity of the Disney-MGM Studios recently led to the decision to double the size of the theme park during the next few years. In the meantime, lines can get very long, so we urge visitors to arrive early and follow our suggested itineraries.

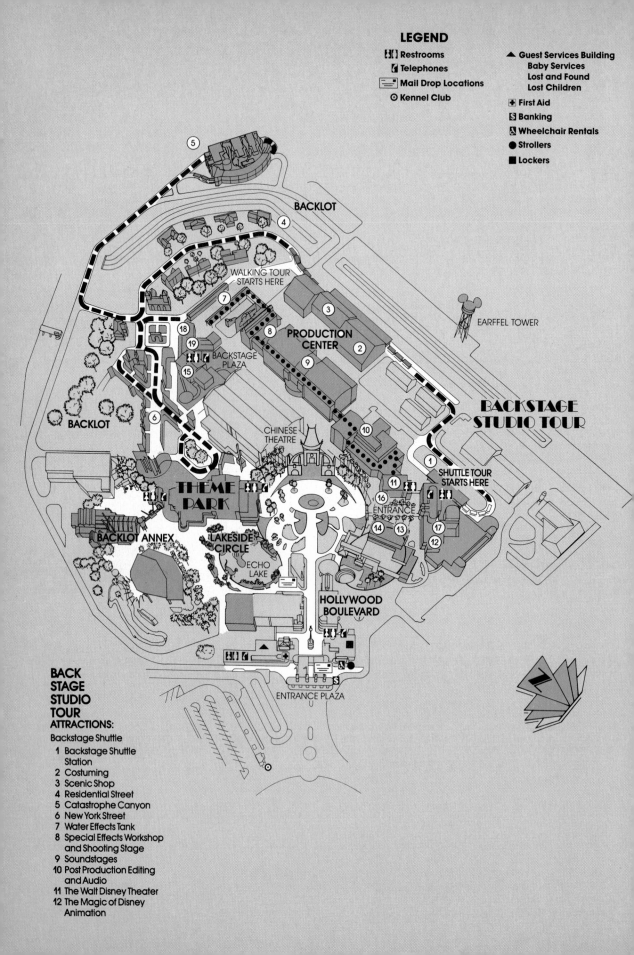

LEGEND

🚻 Restrooms
📞 Telephones
✉ Mail Drop Locations
☉ Kennel Club

▲ Guest Services Building
　Baby Services
　Lost and Found
　Lost Children
✚ First Aid
$ Banking
♿ Wheelchair Rentals
● Strollers
■ Lockers

BACKLOT

5

4

WALKING TOUR
STARTS HERE

7

18

19

15

BACKSTAGE
PLAZA

8

3

PRODUCTION
CENTER

2

9

EARFFEL TOWER

BACKLOT

6

CHINESE
THEATRE

10

BACKSTAGE
STUDIO TOUR

1

SHUTTLE TOUR
STARTS HERE

THEME
PARK

11

BACKLOT ANNEX

LAKESIDE
CIRCLE

ECHO
LAKE

16

ENTRANCE

14

13

17

12

HOLLYWOOD
BOULEVARD

ENTRANCE PLAZA

BACK STAGE STUDIO TOUR ATTRACTIONS:

Backstage Shuttle

1 Backstage Shuttle Station
2 Costuming
3 Scenic Shop
4 Residential Street
5 Catastrophe Canyon
6 New York Street
7 Water Effects Tank
8 Special Effects Workshop and Shooting Stage
9 Soundstages
10 Post Production Editing and Audio
11 The Walt Disney Theater
12 The Magic of Disney Animation

GETTING IN AND AROUND

TRANSPORTATION TO THE DISNEY-MGM STU-DIOS THEME PARK: It's very simple to get to the newest Disney theme park.

By car: Take the exit off I-4 marked for the Caribbean Beach Resort, Walt Disney World Village, and the Disney-MGM Studios Theme Park. The entrance to the Studio is about half a mile from I-4. Follow the signs to the 4,500-space parking lot. Parking is $3; free for Walt Disney World resort guests. Trams carry visitors from their parking space to the ticket booths.

By WDW bus: Buses make the trip to the studios from a variety of locations: from the Magic Kingdom and its surrounding resorts (Contemporary, Grand Floridian, Polynesian Village, and Disney Inn), from Disney Village Resort Villas, from the Disney Village Marketplace, from Disney Village Hotel Plaza, from the Caribbean Beach Resort, and from Epcot Center. Call 824-4321 to confirm all the available transportation options.

HOURS: The Disney-MGM Studios Theme Park is usually open from 9 A.M. to 9 P.M.; hours are extended during holiday weekends and the summer months. During busier periods, the park often opens earlier than the posted time. Call 824-4321 for up-to-the-minute schedules.

BABY CARE: Changing tables and facilities for nursing mothers can be found at the Guest Services building at the main entrance.

CAMERA NEEDS: The Darkroom is located to the right as you enter the park. Kodak Disc Cameras, camcorders, and 35mm cameras are available for rent or for purchase, and 2-hour film processing is offered. A wide assortment of film and accessories is sold, and the shop will also recharge certain batteries. Film is available in most of the shops around the theme park.

ENTERTAINMENT: The Star Today program features a prominent celebrity who will make several guest appearances around the premises at various locations. For information about the star of the day, stop by the Guest Services building. "Streetmosphere Characters" are the entertaining troupe of performers along Hollywood Boulevard. Watch for autograph hounds, budding starlets, gossip columnists, a flim flam man, and others who are out doing their thing all day and evening. The outdoor stage in the heart of Hollywood Boulevard presents a musical history of the silver screen, led by Mickey Mouse. Check at Guest Services for exact showtimes.

ADMISSION PRICES*

ONE-DAY TICKET
Adult	$29
Child**	$23

FOUR-DAY PASSPORT
Adult	$97
Child**	$77

FIVE-DAY PASSPORT
Adult	$112
Child**	$90

The cost of a **ONE-YEAR ALL THREE PARKS PASSPORT** is $180 for adults and $155 for children; renewals are $160 for adults and $135 for children.

*The prices quoted here do not include a 6% sales tax.

**3 through 9 years of age

Note: Multi-day All Three Parks Passports need not be used on consecutive days.

These prices were correct at press time, but may change during 1990.

FIRST AID: Minor medical problems can be handled at First Aid, in the Guest Services building at the main entrance.

HANDICAPPED VISITORS: Most of the attractions, shops, and restaurants are accessible to wheelchair-bound guests. Special parking for handicapped guests is available; inquire at the Auto Plaza. Wheelchairs can be rented at Oscar's Super Service Station, just inside the main entrance. Quantities are limited. A guidebook for handicapped guests is available at Guest Services. For hearing-impaired guests, a Telecommunications Device for the Deaf (TDD) is available at Guest Services. Complimentary tape cassettes and portable tape players are available at Guest Services for blind and sight-impaired guests.

LOCKERS: Public locker facilities, which cost 50¢, are located next to Oscar's Super Service Station at the main entrance.

LOST CHILDREN: Report lost children to the Guest Services building at the main entrance, call 560-4668, or tell an employee.

LOST AND FOUND: Claim or report lost articles at the Guest Services building on the day of your visit. To claim or report lost articles after your visit, call 824-4245.

MONEY MATTERS: An automated bank teller is located next to the Production Information Window at the main entrance. Credit cards (American Express, Visa, and MasterCard) and traveler's checks are accepted for merchandise and tickets and at full-service restaurants. Cash only is accepted at food carts and counter-service establishments. Disney Dollars, available in colorful $1 and $5 denominations, are good for dining and merchandise and can be exchanged at any time for U.S. currency, though many guests take a few home as inexpensive souvenirs.

STROLLER AND WHEELCHAIR RENTAL: Both are available for rent at Oscar's Super Service Station inside the main entrance, but quantities are limited. Remember to keep your rental receipt; it can be used on the same day in the Magic Kingdom, Epcot Center, or again at the Studio.

ADMISSION: Tickets and All Three Parks Passports are available for 1, 4, or 5 days. The Disney organization defines a ticket as admission for 1 day only; other forms of admission media (for longer periods) are called All Three Parks Passports. One-day tickets may be used at the Studio or the Magic Kingdom or Epcot Center, but not at more than one site on the same day. Four- and five-day All Three Parks Passports can be used at the Studio, the Magic Kingdom, and/or Epcot Center on the same day; unlike 1-day tickets, they also include unlimited free use of the transportation system inside Walt Disney World. Cash, traveler's checks, personal checks (with proper ID), American Express, Visa, and MasterCard can be used to purchase all admission media. Note that multi-day All Three Parks Passports do not have to be used on consecutive days.

HOLLYWOOD BOULEVARD

Enter the gates of the Disney-MGM Studios Theme Park and the mosaic of flashy neon, chromed art deco and streamlined moderne architecture, and star-gazing street characters immediately plunge guests into the Hollywood of the 1930s and 1940s. Palm-lined Hollywood Boulevard conveys the spirit of a city that never existed, but one we all wish had. Assorted characters ask guests for autographs, while would-be starlets search for their big break. There's a guy selling maps to the stars' Beverly Hills homes, roving television reporters, and even a flim flam man, all of whom populate this rosy image of Hollywood's heyday.

Great movie music is piped in when small strolling bands aren't entertaining; the streets are spotless; and as is the case in the Magic Kingdom and Epcot Center, guests are transported to another time and place.

The shops and attractions of Hollywood Boulevard are described here. For details about Studio restaurants, see the *Good Meals, Great Times* chapter.

EAST SIDE OF THE STREET

MOVIELAND MEMORABILIA: Located just to the left of the main entrance, this kiosk stocks stuffed toys, hats, books, sunglasses, film, key chains, and other souvenirs. It's a good place to pick up that one last item forgotten during your travels through other parts of WDW.

CROSSROADS OF THE WORLD: In the middle of the entrance plaza, Mickey Mouse keeps watch from atop this Hollywood Boulevard landmark. The circular shop offers souvenirs, sunglasses, film, raingear, sundries, and information.

SID CAHUENGA'S ONE-OF-A-KIND: Authentic antiques and curios are the stock in trade here. Autographed photos, old movie magazines and posters, and assorted Hollywood memorabilia are among the collectibles with which old Sid is willing to part—for a price.

MICKEY'S OF HOLLYWOOD, PLUTO'S TOY PALACE, DISNEY & CO.: These three shops are connected, similar to the set-up at the Magic Kingdom's Emporium and Epcot Center's Centorium. This is the place to find T-shirts, sweatshirts, hats, plush toys, watches, jackets, socks, wallets, tote bags, books, and sunglasses, all emblazoned with the Studio logo.

KEYSTONE CLOTHIERS: Jackets complete with flashing electric bulbs (selling for about $200), women's fashions, and jewelry are the specialties of this flashy shop. There's a wonderful pair of earrings—one Mickey and one Minnie—that will set you back $290. A favorite item sold here is a Mickey Mouse umbrella that sprouts two ears when opened.

LAKESIDE NEWS: A terrific selection of comic books is found here along with old *Life* and *Modern Screen* magazines. Souvenirs are also available.

SIGHTS & SOUNDS: Guests are invited to record their own music videos. A particular favorite with children and teens.

WEST SIDE OF THE STREET

OSCAR'S CLASSIC CAR SOUVENIRS & SUPER SERVICE STATION: The 1947 Buick parked out front gets plenty of attention. Automotive memorabilia, mugs, models, and key chains are for sale. The car, by the way, is not. The gas being pumped from the tanks out front is from the Mohave Oil Co., the same company whose oil tanks explode at Catastrophe Canyon on the Backstage Tour. Services offered here include stroller and wheelchair rental, lockers, and products for infants.

THE DARKROOM: The art deco facade of this shop allows guests to enter through an aperture-like doorway. Rental cameras are available: Kodak Disc cameras are free to use, but a $50 refundable deposit is required; Kodak Explorer 35mm cameras cost $5 per day to rent, with a $145 refundable deposit; and Kodak VHS video cameras rent for $40 per day, with a refundable deposit of $400 and a driver's license or $1,200 without a license. Deposits can be charged on American Express, MasterCard, or Visa. Film is not included in the rental price. Cameras are also available for purchase, as is a wide variety of film and accessories. Some batteries can also be recharged.

COVER STORY: Just through The Darkroom, this is where guests can have their images put on the front cover of a large choice of favorite popular magazines, including *Life*, *Sports Illustrated*, *Muscle*, *Time,* and—for the younger set—*Muppet*. Costumes and appropriate accessories are provided by the shop.

CELEBRITY 5 & 10: Modeled after a 1940s Woolworth's, this large shop carries trinkets, costume jewelry, picture frames, shirts, jackets, aprons, teddy bears, magnets, and memorabilia associated with old Hollywood. This is the place to pick up a director's clapboard and other non-Disney, film-related merchandise.

SWEET SUCCESS: Specialty candies and more mundane treats are available at this sweet smelling shop—plus plush M & M toys.

PACIFIC ELECTRIC PICTURES: Star in your own home video version of a Hollywood spectacular. Personalized merchandise is sold.

SHOPPING BEYOND THE BOULEVARD

GOLDEN AGE SOUVENIRS: Located between the Monster Sound Show and SuperStar Television, there are gifts from the early days of television and radio, plus Disney Channel merchandise.

ENDOR VENDORS: Just outside Star Tours (opening early in 1990), this shop offers intergalactic souvenirs associated with the Star Wars films and the Star Tours attraction.

THE DISNEY STUDIO STORE: Just outside the Walt Disney Theater, this is the place for clothing and accessories emblazoned with Touchstone and Walt Disney Studios logos.

THE LOONY BIN: A perfect stop between parts 1 and 2 of the Backstage Tour. Lots of Roger Rabbit merchandise and some gag gifts are on sale. There's a host of hands-on fun in the form of props from the movie "Who Framed Roger Rabbit?"

ANIMATION GALLERY: Located in the Animation Building, this is the place to find original Disney animation cels, exclusive limited edition reproductions, figurines, and other collectibles. It's a pleasant place to browse, even if buying isn't on your mind.

THE GREAT MOVIE RIDE

Housed in a full-scale reproduction of historic Grauman's Chinese Theater, this attraction captivates the imagination of guests from the start. The queue area winds through the precisely reproduced lobby and into the heart of filmmaking, where guests will see some famous movie scenes on a large screen. (Note that if the queue extends outside the building, you're in for a long wait. It takes about 25 minutes to reach the ride vehicles once you've entered the theater.)

Visitors board ride vehicles in an area where a giant cyclorama of Hollywood Hills hangs just below a soundstage lighting grid. Several tiers of sets picturing hillside homes, Griffith Park Observatory, and the original vintage "Hollywoodland" sign blend with a California sunset. The vehicles then pass under an old-fashioned theater marquee and on into a Hollywood set.

More than 60 Audio-Animatronics dancers atop a large-tiered revolving cake greet guests, in a replay of the "By a Waterfall" scene from the Busby Berkeley musical "Footlight Parade." These dancing girls are not among Disney's finest Audio-Animatronic creations. Gene Kelly's most memorable performance from "Singin' in the Rain" is the next scene on the tour. Rain seems to drench the soundstage, but doesn't dampen the spirits of the Audio-Animatronic Kelly, who sings his heart out. Then Mary Poppins and Bert the chimney-sweep entertain as Mary floats from above via her magical umbrella

and Bert dances on a rooftop to the tune of "Chim Chim Cher-ee."

From the world of musical entertainment, guests move on to adventure. James Cagney recreates his role from "Public Enemy" as the ride proceeds along Gangster Alley. A Prohibition-style mob shoot-out begins and guests find themselves in the midst of an ambush. An alternate route leads to a trip to a western town, where John Wayne can be seen on horseback eyeing some would-be bank robbers. The thieves blow the safe and flames pour from the building. The heat can be felt from the trams, so don't be too surprised.

The ride vehicles whisk guests past danger and into the spaceship "Nostromo" from the film "Alien." Officer Ripley guards the corridor while a convincing monster threatens riders with its slimy body from an overhead compartment. (Note that this scene and the gangster and western scenes are presented in a darkened setting and may be upsetting to younger children.) Next stop is the Well of Souls from "Raiders of the Lost Ark," where Harrison Ford and John Rhys-Davies struggle to remove the ancient ark from its sepulcher.

In the jungle, Tarzan's familiar cry fills the air as he swings in on a vine. Jane is there, too, atop an elephant, and Cheetah screeches and jumps around appropriately. As nightfall approaches, a legendary film scene is replayed. Rick and Ilsa say

their goodbyes as the plane's engines sputter in the timeless "Casablanca" finale. The plane, by the way, may actually be the same one used in the movie. When Disney Imagineers set out to find an Electra 12A (built by Lockheed during the 1930s), they found it on an airfield in Hondo, Texas. Number 1204, according to the oral history offered by its owner, not only appeared in "Casablanca," but in several other movies as well. It was most recently used in a made-for-television movie about the disappearance of Amelia Earhart.

Guests are taken from the airfield in "Casablanca" to the swirling winds of Munchkinland, where a house has just fallen upon the Wicked Witch of the East. Her sister, as portrayed by Margaret Hamilton, appears to keep the tension peaked. This Audio-Animatronic figure represents the third generation of this technology, and she is quite impressively lifelike. But happy endings prevail and guests follow Dorothy, the Tin Man, the Cowardly Lion, the Scarecrow, and Toto along the Yellow Brick Road to the Emerald City of Oz.

As the ride draws to a close, a film montage of memorable moments from Academy Award-winning films is shown.

The 59 Audio-Animatronic figures created for this ride were done by many of the same artists who created the characters in the Hall of Presidents in the Magic Kingdom. Attention to detail is very precise. John Wayne's horse and rifle, for example, match those he used in his westerns. The costumes worn by the Julie Andrews and Dick Van Dyke Audio-Animatronics figures are modeled after the originals used in "Mary Poppins." And Gene Kelly personally inspected his likeness before it was shipped from California to Florida.

BACKSTAGE STUDIO TOUR

On this combination walking and tram tour, guests go backstage to see work in progress on television shows and movies. The tour begins in the queue area with a presentation of the history of The Walt Disney Studios shown on overhead television monitors and narrated by Tom Selleck and Carol Burnett. There are some funny comments from such luminaries as Mel Brooks, Clint Eastwood, Richard Dreyfus, Robert Zemeckis, Francis Ford Coppola, and Eddie Murphy.

In typical Disney fashion, the line weaves up and back through a gallery of milestones and memories from the early days of the Disney studios. There is a sign as guests enter the gate for the backstage tour that announces a 45-minute wait from that point. It takes about 25 minutes to wind through the main queue area when full, so be prepared. The crowds seem to thin out during the late afternoon hours, so if the line is beyond the 45-minute mark, your time will be better spent at one of the other attractions.

The "Backstage Shuttles" are comfortable and roomy trams and tours are hosted by enthusiastic guides. (Note that when boarding the trams, those on the left side will get wet at Catastrophe Canyon, while those on the right will stay dry. Choose accordingly.) The trams pull out and guests have a view of bungalows housing production departments where actual work is being done on several television shows, such as the teen version "Win, Lose, or Draw" and the "All New Mickey Mouse Club." Guests pass through the "greens" department, where trees, plants, and shrubs are kept until they are needed on the set. The tram then winds through a tunnel where guests can see the wardrobe department at work on the left through large windows. Original costumes such as those worn by Bette Midler in "Big Business," Warren Beatty in "Dick Tracy," Julie Andrews in "Mary Poppins," Michael Jackson in "Captain EO," and the co-stars of "Who Framed Roger Rabbit" can be glimpsed through the windows. More than 100 artists produce the costumes for all of Disney's motion picture, television, and entertainment projects, and with two and a quarter million garments, Walt Disney World has the world's largest working wardrobe.

The tram then passes through the camera, props, and lighting departments, where equipment is stored until it is needed both on and off the studio's sets. Disney's camera equipment is so advanced that many visiting network television crews often borrow it when covering space shuttle launches at the Kennedy Space Center, about 70 miles to the east. A look into the scenic shop reveals carpenters at work on sets which are finished later on the soundstages.

The tram turns into the backlot residential street where empty, hollow facades give the outward appearance of a lovely neighborhood. Used mainly for exterior shots, the houses on the street include Vern's home from "Ernest Saves Christmas." That's where Herbie the Love Bug parks. There's also the facade of "The Golden Girls" home. Exteri-

or shots for the show have been filmed here. A backlot church can play two parts: one side looks like a small town church, while the front has the big city look.

With a bit of flourish, the tour guide explains how landscapes can be created by set designers to fill certain needs and then asks "where, in central Florida, can you find an active oil field in the middle of a dry, rocky, barren desert canyon prone to flash floods?" The answer is Catastrophe Canyon, which produces some of the best special effects most visitors will ever experience. As the story goes, the crews are filming a movie in which a backstage tram gets stuck in the canyon during a flash flood. But the guide will tell you that it's safe to go in because they're not filming today. Astute guests will notice that the oil company, Mohave, is the same one represented at Oscar's Super Service Station on Hollywood Boulevard.

In a spectacular series of special effects, a rain storm begins; then there's an explosion, complete with flames that are so hot even riders on the right side of the tram feel them; followed by a flash flood that is so convincing it forces everyone to lean the other way. The road along which the tram rides shifts and dips hydraulically, lending even more reality to the scary adventure. A later behind-the-scenes look reveals the tanks that release enough water to fill 10 Olympic-size swimming pools. Some

of the water is blown out by air cannons, which can shoot 25,000 gallons of water over 100 feet. To put that in better perspective, if a basketball was stuck into one of the cannons, it could be shot over the top of the Empire State Building.

From Catastrophe Canyon, the tram heads for New York City where meticulously reproduced facades line the urban streets. Though the brickwork looks authentic, these backless facades are constructed mostly of fiberglass and styrofoam. Production designers spent a year and a half designing and constructing the New York lot. The skyscrapers, including the Empire State Building and the Chrysler Building, are actually painted flats. Forced perspective (the same technique that makes Cinderella Castle appear much taller than it is) is employed here to make the 4-story Empire State Building appear as if it's the real 104-story structure. Tour groups often encounter film crews setting up for or taking down equipment from shoots done on the lot. Be sure to take careful note of the storefronts, as you'll encounter them again later during a short film starring Bette Midler. Though clearly a New York reproduction, the streets can be altered to fit the role for any city USA. Both the Empire State Building and the Chrysler Building can be removed and facades changed to serve any purpose.

On the way to part 2 of the tour, trams pass the trolley and "Dipmobile" used in "Who Framed Roger Rabbit?" The guide reminds any "Toons" on board to be careful when going by the Dipmobile.

Part two of the tour is on foot, and guests begin by following Roger Rabbit's big purple footprints to the Loony Bin shop and the Studio Catering Company where salads, burgers, sodas, and snacks are sold. The Loony Bin stocks Roger Rabbit souvenirs and offers a chance to play with some of the props used in the movie. Children especially love the boxes that emit animal sounds, street sounds, and laughter when opened. A hole in one wall is the shape of Roger Rabbit, and kids can climb through, something they tend to do over and over again. Following the footprints leads to another queue area, where a Goldie Hawn/Rick Moranis video is presented to entertain tourers while they're waiting. The wait for part 2 averages 20 minutes.

First stop on part 2 of the tour is an outdoor special effects area where a guest dresses up in yellow rain gear and is filmed at the helm of a ship set adrift in a storm at sea. More than 400 gallons of water are dumped on the unsuspecting guest, and the final result is quite humorous when seen on monitors overhead. Then it's on to the prop room where guests get to see a variety of familiar creatures, including members of the cast of "Captain EO." Be sure not to miss the sketches on the walls which show the genesis of several of the props displayed.

Three children are chosen from the crowd in the prop room to participate in the next portion of the tour. A giant bee, used in "Honey, I Shrunk the Kids," is suspended from the ceiling. One of the children is put atop the bee, one on the wing, and the third in the director's chair. In this part of the tour, guests are shown how film shot against a blue screen can then be superimposed onto any back-

ground chosen by the producers. The kids are filmed, and the footage is cut in with real scenes from the movie.

Then it's on to the soundstages where specially designed, soundproof catwalks allow visitors to gawk and talk all they want. The tour takes in three soundstages, where at any given time filming may be in progress for movies or television shows. It is also possible, however, that nothing will be happening on the set. In one of the soundstages there is sometimes a 65-foot portion of a Delta L-1011 fuselage from the nose to the wings. The section was actually removed from an airplane which was flown by Lockheed for many years. The mock-up was designed and built by Delta Air Lines and located at the Studio for use in filming commercials, motion pictures, promotional shots, and in-flight demonstration videos. The film set separates into three distinct sections for easy camera access. Overhead monitors show explanations of the use of soundstages and the art of filming a television series is explained by an assortment of stars, including the cast of "The Cosby Show" and Warren Beatty.

From this area, guests are led into a walkway where a Bette Midler short film is presented on overhead monitors. The film was shot entirely at the studio, exclusively for the Disney-MGM Studios Theme Park. Guests will recognize the sets from the New York City street set. It's a cute tale in which Midler discovers she's holding a winning lottery ticket, and it graphically records her trials and tribulations as she tries to retrieve it after it falls out of her window. At the film's conclusion, guests are escorted into a large warehouse in which the interior sets for the movie are stored. In the warehouse a hostess explains some of the special effects used to create certain highlights of the film.

In the area known as the Post Group, George Lucas, C3PO, and R2D2 narrate a presentation about film and editing techniques, and Mel Gibson and Pee Wee Herman explain sound effects.

Last stop on the tour is The Walt Disney Theater, where clips from recent and soon-to-be-released Disney and Touchstone films are shown. Narrated by Walt Disney Company Chairman Michael Eisner and Mickey Mouse, the stop in the theater is a welcome rest for tired tourists. Don't miss the watch Mickey Mouse is wearing in the film; it has Michael Eisner's face on it!

WHERE TO EAT AT THE DISNEY-MGM STUDIOS THEME PARK

A complete list of all Disney-MGM Studios Theme Park eateries—full-service restaurants, fast food emporiums, snack shops, and food vendors—can be found together with all other WDW eating spots in the *Good Meals, Great Times* chapter.

SUPERSTAR TELEVISION

Roles in famous television shows are up for grabs at this remarkable attraction. In the outdoor pre-show area, with scores of TV sets strung overhead, a host or hostess chooses members of the audience to star in a variety of famous television scenes. **NOTE:** Although a few guests are chosen from the rear of the area, most would-be stars are picked from nearer the front. While just being in the audience will provide a lot of laughs, if there's even a little ham in you, move up front and volunteer loudly.

After an entertaining introduction hosted by Alan Alda (viewed on those overhead television sets) audience members are led into a 1,000-seat theater reminiscent of the days of live television broadcasting. At the same time, would-be stars head backstage for costuming, make-up, and meetings with the directors.

The stage has several sets, and as the camera operators shoot the actors in action, the audience watches on one of eight 6-foot-wide projection screens suspended from the ceiling. But the pictures on the screens vary significantly from the live goings-on on-stage because the use of "bluescreen" electronic techniques allows backstage editors to merge the live action with historic clips from the classic shows.

The first scene features a gentleman guest in the news reporter's seat on the "Today" show on July 17, 1955, the day Disneyland opened. Applause signs flash when appropriate, and audience members respond enthusiastically for their fellow tourists. Next, a woman guest gets to play the Ethel Mertz part opposite Lucille Ball's Lucy Ricardo in what is perhaps the single most famous scene from "I Love Lucy". Complete with white smock and tall white hat, the guest star tries to wrap chocolates as they quickly come along a conveyor belt, and though seen dozens of times, the scene is still funny, even with an amateur in the role of Lucy's second banana.

Soap opera fans will get an especially big kick out of a scene from "General Hospital," in which chosen members of the audience play two of the three leading roles in a love triangle.

Several youngsters are chosen to star in the opening theme song from "Gilligan's Island," while three guests dress up as the "Vonzells" and sing "Da Doo Run Run" on the "Ed Sullivan Show." Other scenes include a classic from "Cheers," in which Woody the bartender, Norm, and Cliff star with four guests. One lucky youngster has the opportunity to hit a grand slam homerun at New York's Shea Stadium and then be interviewed by Howard Cosell. Scenes from "The Tonight Show," with Johnny Carson, "The Three Stooges," and "The Golden Girls" round out the fun.

There are no bad seats in the house since the eight monitors can be seen easily by the entire audience. This attraction tends to be less crowded during the morning hours, so try it then, and if time permits go again as each new cast brings a fresh flavor to the presentation. The entire attraction takes about 45 minutes, from the choosing of stars to the end.

Presented by Sony.

ANIMATION BUILDING

This is perhaps the finest, funniest, and most entertaining of all the attractions at the Studio. Located next to the entrance to the backstage tour, it has proven so popular that the only way to see it without

waiting more than 30 to 45 minutes is to go first thing in the morning—or make it your last stop in the evening. Morning visits are preferable, however, because the animators who work in the building normally quit for the day between 5 P.M. and 6 P.M.

In the lobby, the 15 Oscars won by the Disney Animation Team and a collection of drawings of characters from "Snow White," "Fantasia," and other Disney cartoon classics are on display. From the lobby, guests move into the Disney Animation Theater, where an uproariously funny film starring Robin Williams and Walter Cronkite offers a lesson in the basics of animation. It even allows guests a look at what it's like to be a cartoon character through the eyes of Williams.

The producers of this film will tell you that each scene was a struggle to complete, because Walter Cronkite had trouble keeping a straight face. Williams is at his best as one of the lost boys from "Peter Pan." His non-stop banter is so funny that a second trip may be necessary to take it all in. In one segment, he's turned into a variety of recognizable characters, including Mickey Mouse. "I can even be a corporate symbol," he proclaims in his best Mickey Mouse voice. All in all it's great fun, and Cronkite is an absolutely perfect straight man.

The eight-minute film is followed by a walk through the working animation studios, where the tour continues to be narrated by Williams and Cronkite, who appear on overhead monitors. First stop is

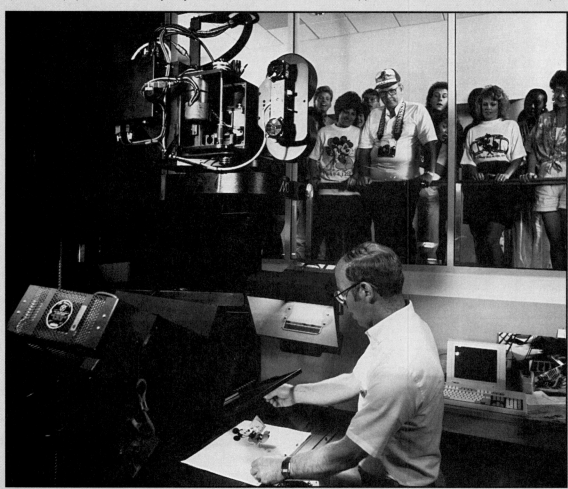

the story room, where animators develop story lines. Onward to the drawing boards where Mickey, Minnie, and other characters undergo the metamorphosis from pencil sketch to moving picture. Working at their desks in full view of visitors, animators are seen creating the drawings that will later appear in real films.

Guests also view the clean-up room, the special effects area, and the special camera that was designed to transfer drawings to cels. Then artists can be seen hand painting up to 25 different colors onto these transparent sheets.

The 71-member animation team at the Disney-MGM Studios Theme Park work in shifts, to cover seven days a week. To produce one 24-minute film, the team must complete 34,650 drawings, and add scenes from at least 300 background paintings before finishing the work with musical scores and special effects.

Last stop on this funny and fascinating trip is a presentation of magical moments from the world's best-loved animated films, shown in the Disney Classics Theater. Be sure to stop in at the Animation Gallery, where original Disney animation cels, exclusive limited edition reproductions, books, figurines, and other collectibles are for sale.

MONSTER SOUND SHOW

Parents, don't be fooled by the name. There is nothing scary about this attraction, where guests have the opportunity to create the sound effects for a short film, with predictably funny results.

The pre-show begins outside the theater where a short video presentation stars David Letterman in a very funny introduction to what's inside. His comments close with a very atypical (for a Disney amusement attraction) warning that, "If you break anything, security guards in mouse suits will beat you senseless."

Upon entering the 270-seat theater, the host chooses several "Foley" artists from the audience. (Foley is the Hollywood sound-effects system named for its creator, Jack Foley.) The audience is then treated to a cute Martin Short/Chevy Chase

comedy-mystery film that includes the sounds of thunder, rain, creaking doors, and falling chandeliers. The amateur sound crew watches the film a second time as they try to match the proper sound effects to the action on-screen. The third viewing of the film features the new soundtrack created by the studio's newest Foley artists. The thunder never seems to match the storm and the crash of the chandelier seems most often to take place as the creaking door opens, but that's the whole point and it's all a lot of fun.

The show features many original gadgets created by sound master Jimmy Macdonald. Macdonald, who became the voice of Mickey Mouse during the 1940s, was responsible for more than 20,000 sound gadgets during his 45 years with Walt Disney Studios in California. There are some special artifacts, including Tinkerbell's chimes, a door used in "Alice in Wonderland," and the coconut shells used to produce the hoofbeats in the "Legend of Sleepy Hollow." But most of the sounds are created by the ingenious use of barrels, nails, sandpaper, and other gadgets that go bonk, buzz, zip, or bump.

The post-show area, SoundWorks, offers some hands-on fun for the rest of the audience. Earie Encounters allows visitors to reproduce the flying-saucer sounds from the 1956 film "Forbidden Planet." At Movie Mimics, guests can dub in the voice of Roger Rabbit and other stars; and at Soundsations, our personal favorite, an adventure in "3-D audio" puts guests in an enclosed room filled with sound so realistic that the wind from a hair dryer can almost be felt.

Presented by Sony.

INDIANA JONES EPIC STUNT SPECTACULAR

Earthquakes, fiery explosions, and assorted other dramatic stunts give guests some insight into the science of movie stunts and special effects at this impressive 2,000-seat amphitheater. Stuntmen and women recreate scenes from hit films to demonstrate the skill required to keep audiences on the edge of their seats. Show director Glenn Randall, who served as stunt coordinator of such well-known adventure films as "Raiders of the Lost Ark," "Indiana Jones and the Temple of Doom," "Poltergeist," "Never Say Never Again," "E.T.," "Firestarter," and "Jewel of the Nile," calls the show "big, visual excitement."

But the 20-minute show isn't all flying leaps. Guests also see how the elaborate stunts are pulled off—safely—while the crew and an assistant director explain what goes on both in front of and behind the camera.

The show opens with the scene from "Raiders of the Lost Ark" in which a 12-foot tall rolling ball chases a Harrison Ford lookalike out of the temple. There is steam and flame so intense that the audience can feel the heat. The crew dismantles the set, revealing the remarkable lightness of movie props, as two assistants roll it uphill for the next show.

The next scene is a busy Cairo street market, where "extras" chosen from the audience again participate. The famous scene in which Indiana Jones pulls a gun while others are fighting with swords is played out. The death-defying action continues, and leads to the sensational desert finale, where the hero and his sweetheart must escape in a flying wing.

There are moments during this presentation when the audience might wonder if, just for a minute, something has gone wrong. But by revealing the tricks of the trade, the directors and stars show that what appears to be very dangerous is actually a perfectly safe, controlled piece of movie magic. It's a great show.

STAR TOURS

Having witnessed the unyielding popularity of this attraction at Disneyland in Anaheim, California, the decision was made to open a counterpart here (slated to open early in 1990). The attraction, which was inspired by George Lucas's "Star Wars" film trilogy, offers guests the chance to board Star-Speeders which are actually the same type of flight simulators that are regularly employed by the military and commercial airlines to train pilots. Synchronizing a stunning film with the virtually limitless motion of the simulator allows guests to truly feel what they see. (Note that when instructed to put on your seatbelt, do so. This is a very rough ride.)

Visitors enter an area where the famed Star Wars characters R2D2 and C3PO are working for a galactic travel agency. They spend their time in a bustling hangar area servicing the Star Tours fleet of spacecraft. Riders board the 40-passenger craft for what is intended to be a leisurely trip to the Moon of Endor, but the ride quickly develops into a harrowing flight into deep space, including encounters with giant ice crystals and laser blasting fighters. The flight is out of control from the start, as the rookie pilot proves that Murphy's Law applies to the entire universe.

The sensations are extraordinary and the technology quite advanced. Astute passengers will note that the voice of the spacecraft's captain belongs to Pee Wee Herman. (By the way, this same technology is used at the new Wonders of Life pavilion in Future World at Epcot Center. There guests take a rollicking ride through the human body, not unlike scenes from the film "Fantastic Voyage.")

Signs outside Star Tours warn that passengers must be free of back problems, heart conditions, motion sickness, and other physical limitations to ride. Pregnant women and children under 3 are not permitted to board. Children under 7 must be accompanied by an adult.

EVERYTHING ELSE IN THE WORLD

The Magic Kingdom, Epcot Center, and the Disney-MGM Studios Theme Park take up only about 460 acres of the total Walt Disney World terrain, while the total turf of the entire World comprises 43 square miles! Quite a lot of this domain is crammed with all sorts of diverse and irresistible activities of a quantity and quality seldom found anywhere else on the globe.

There is superb golf and tennis; there are beaches for sunbathing; lakes for speedboating and sailing; canoes for rent and winding streams to paddle along; bicycles for hire; campfire sites; nature trails; and picnic grounds. And that list still doesn't include River Country, Disney's own old-fashioned swimming hole; Disney Village Marketplace, an assortment of shops seldom found outside a cosmopolitan city; and the botanical garden and bird sanctuary that's called Discovery Island.

Add to all that 2 major new attractions: Pleasure Island, an after-dark entertainment complex, and a state-of-the-art water park known as Typhoon Lagoon. Among the other activities worth mentioning is the program known as Wonders of Walt Disney World, in which youngsters attending grades 5 through 10 are offered the opportunity to go behind the scenes—to meet the Disney entertainers and receive instructions from Disney cartoonists; to visit the World's extraordinary 7,500-acre conservation area; or to tour the WDW solar-powered office building (among other unique on-site ecological activities).

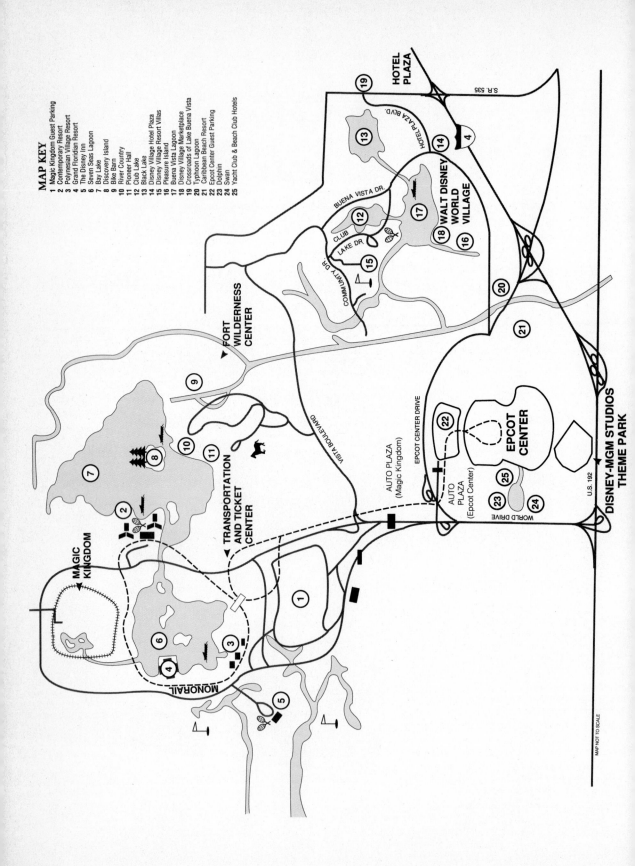

MAP KEY

1 Magic Kingdom Guest Parking
2 Contemporary Resort
3 Polynesian Village Resort
4 Grand Floridian Resort
5 The Disney Inn
6 Seven Seas Lagoon
7 Bay Lake
8 Discovery Island
9 Bike Barn
10 River Country
11 Pioneer Hall
12 Club Lake
13 Black Lake
14 Disney Village Hotel Plaza
15 Disney Village Resort Villas
16 Pleasure Island
17 Buena Vista Lagoon
18 Disney Village Marketplace
19 Crossroads of Lake Buena Vista
20 Typhoon Lagoon
21 Epcot Center Guest Parking
22 Caribbean Beach Resort
23 Dolphin
24 Swan
25 Yacht Club & Beach Club Hotels

HOTEL PLAZA

S.R. 535

HOTEL PLAZA BLVD.

WALT DISNEY WORLD VILLAGE

BUENA VISTA DR.

CLUB LAKE DR.

COMMUNITY DR.

FORT WILDERNESS CENTER

VISTA BOULEVARD

MAGIC KINGDOM

MONORAIL

TRANSPORTATION AND TICKET CENTER

AUTO PLAZA (Magic Kingdom)

AUTO PLAZA (Epcot Center)

EPCOT CENTER DRIVE

EPCOT CENTER

WORLD DRIVE

U.S. 192

DISNEY-MGM STUDIOS THEME PARK

MAP NOT TO SCALE

WDW VILLAGE

Located about 5 miles from the Magic Kingdom and only 2½ miles from Epcot Center, Walt Disney World Village comprises a number of hotel and villa-type accommodations (with and without kitchen facilities), the Village Clubhouse, the Walt Disney World Conference Center, the Disney Village Marketplace, several lakes, and a number of sports facilities—among other things. It is relatively quiet, and the pace is far more leisurely than that which exists around the Polynesian Village and Contemporary Resort. In the Buena Vista Lagoon, along whose shores the shopping area was constructed, there are even a few alligators.

But the Village is still convenient to the main activities of the World and is easily accessible from either of the two exits from I-4. The best route is the exit off the Epcot Center interchange. But it's also possible to take the exit from S.R. 535 (although this route usually is more congested and far less scenic). Buses also make the trip to and from Epcot Center, the TTC, the Disney Village Marketplace, and the Disney-MGM Studios Theme Park on a regular basis; holders of ID cards issued by WDW resorts and Disney Village Hotel Plaza establishments, as well as bearers of certain All Three Parks Passports, can ride them at no extra charge.

SHOPS

A visit to Disney Village Marketplace can involve eating in a restaurant, meeting a film star, listening to first-rate jazz over some frothy cream-and-liqueur concoction, or just sitting on a bench by the water looking at the boats zipping back and forth across Buena Vista Lagoon. But for most people, those are the extra added attractions of a complex whose real raison d'être is shopping.

Arranged in 8 low-lying, shingle-sided buildings flanking the hexagonal Captain's Tower on the shores of Buena Vista Lagoon, the Disney Village Marketplace boutiques stock everything from baby bonnets to silk dresses, thousand-dollar bottles of wine to toy soldiers and stuffed animals—and then some. There are several stores devoted to the staggering range of merchandise related to the family of Disney characters.

The best way to take it all in is simply to wander at will. Stop for lunch or a snack after a couple of hours, then go out and stroll some more. The descriptions below suggest the types of merchandise that each store offers. Particular items may not be there when you are, but comparable goods should be available. Note that weekends are fairly busy, but even then the pace tends to be leisurely. Kids who get bored by their elders' browsing can be turned loose at the marina, or at an innovative playground near the Village Stage (where the annual Christmas pageants are presented).

MICKEY'S CHARACTER SHOP: This is the largest Disney merchandise shop in all the World. As you enter, be sure to take a look up at Mickey, Minnie, and Donald flying high in a 20-foot-tall hot-air balloon. Dumbo, Jiminy Cricket, Minnie and Mickey, Chip and Dale, Tigger and Eeyore, and Tramp and his Lady are all here too—stuffed, in porcelain, and emblazoned on everything from T-shirts and back scratchers to pencils and carry-all bags. There is an enormous assortment of clothing items, plus toys, games, hats, and visors. Be sure to check out the larger-than-life stuffed Mickey.

MICKEY & CO.: Mickey Mouse gets the designer treatment at this shop where J.G. Hook fashions emblazoned with Mickey images are among the varied offerings: blouses, skirts, jogging suits, and more. There is also a variety of designer outfits for infants and kids.

YOU & ME KID: By coincidence, this new shop bears the same name as one of the Disney Channel's most popular shows. And in the same way the Disney Channel tries to offer something for every member of the family, so too does this store. It's situated in the old Pottery Chalet building, where there's plenty of room for departments for adults, boys, girls, and infants. There are toys, clothing, gift items, stuffed animals, and lots of other merchandise for each age group.

CHRISTMAS CHALET: If anything can set a mind to dreaming of white Christmases when the mercury is hitting 95° outside (and the humidity is just about the same), this lovely shop, located in the You & Me

Kid building, is it. Arranged at the edges of the rooms are small treasures in traditional reds and greens—ornaments covered with feathers, others made of wood, metal, glass, felt, and calico. The selection is one of the best of its type anywhere. In addition, there are Christmas wreaths made of velvet and calico, and other more ingenious and occasionally truly startling combinations. You even may find a Santa squirt gun, or a special Christmas jump rope.

PERSONAL MESSAGE: Also in the You & Me Kid building, this shop stocks party supplies, stationery, cards for all occasions, desk accessories, and assorted gift items. There is a special area where gifts of all kinds can be personalized. Bookworms, however, will be most grateful for its excellent selection of hardbound and paperback books, the best in all of WDW. There's something for the very serious-minded, something to tickle the funny bone, and tomes at all levels of literature in between. Stamps are available here.

CRISTAL ARTS: This shop sells roughly the same sort of cut-glass merchandise available at Main Street's Crystal Arts and Adventureland's La Princesa de Cristal in the Magic Kingdom. Large green, blue, or red cut-glass bowls and vases are available, along with clear-glass mugs, glass sculptures, and other items engraved to customers' specifications with initials, messages, or pictures. Note: If you bring a favorite photograph to this shop, the engraver can have it reproduced on a plate or other item.

GREAT SOUTHERN COUNTRY CRAFT CO.: There are fine handmade leather and silver goods, plus a boutique featuring country and folk crafts. It's a showplace of Americana gift items.

LILLIE LANGTRY'S OLD-FASHIONED PHOTO STUDIO: Main Street in the Magic Kingdom has a photo studio in the Camera Center, and Adventureland has Laffite's Portrait Deck. Lillie Langtry's is the third location where guests can pose for sepia-toned prints in Edwardian suits or flounced-and-furbelowed gowns of a degree of frilliness rarely found outside a film studio's wardrobe department.

SIR EDWARD'S HABERDASHER: Named after Edward Moriarty, a Disney executive, this shop, full of good-quality clothing for men and boys, is an oasis of traditional masculinity in a bustling village otherwise filled with trifles and treasures that seem to appeal most to the feminine heart. Located near the Captain's Tower, close to the parking lot.

GOURMET PANTRY: Not long ago, one vacationer searching for coffee and orange juice for the next day's breakfast passed up this store on the assumption that he'd find only escargots and smoked oysters. Wrong! These things can be found here, but there also are breads and pastries, meats and cheeses, cereals, yogurt, beer and soft drinks, and many more items—both mundane and exotic. Unusual teas and specially blended, freshly ground coffees are also available, and, occasionally, free

tastes are offered to passersby. Kitchen utensils, cookware, and mugs are also available. Villa guests at the Disney Village Resort take note: Purchases will be delivered to your villa at no extra charge; if you aren't going to be home, the delivery person will even stash perishables in your refrigerator. To order by phone, touch "31" on your room telephone, or, when calling from outside, dial 828-3886.

CONCHED OUT: This is the spot for Florida souvenirs and household items with a Florida theme. There are candles, plastic dishes and glasses, shells, and lots more.

CANDY SHOPPE: Adjoining the Gourmet Pantry, this small, fragrant enclave sells Godiva chocolate, fudge, chocolate bars and creams, red licorice, peppermint sticks, hard candies, and just about everything else that ever made a sweet tooth ache.

BOARD STIFF: The surf's up at this new shop. Jams (those long, flowery shorts), T-shirts, tank tops, and assorted other surfing paraphernalia are the stock in trade.

COUNTRY ADDRESS: This very good women's clothing store offers a range of merchandise from middle-priced to better coordinate leisure and professional wear. There is a collection of sophisticated daytime dresses, cocktail ensembles, plus jewelry and accessories.

RESORT WEAR UNLIMITED: This new shop features lightweight, bright, and trendy fashions. An assortment of sportswear, playwear, and swimwear is enhanced by bold jewelry, hats, and handbags.

24KT PRECIOUS ADORNMENTS: This elegant shop features a wide selection of gold fashion jewelry, ranging from unique designer items to Disney character charms and watches. Located next to Chef Mickey's Village Restaurant.

CROSSROADS OF LAKE BUENA VISTA

The shopping center located just across the road from Disney Village Hotel Plaza (constructed by the WDW folks) is a convenient dining and shopping area for both visitors and Walt Disney World employees. The 137,000-square-foot retail center is anchored by a Gooding's supermarket, which is open 24 hours a day. (Fort Wilderness, villa, and treehouse guests will find this an especially useful stop.) Other shops include Camp Beverly Hills, for California sportswear; Chico's, for casual clothing; Sunworks, which stocks women's sportswear and swimwear; McKids, for children's apparel and educational toys; MoJo's Surfin' U.S.A., for beachwear and surfboards; Foot Locker, for athletic shoes; Character Connection, the Disney merchandise shop; Beyond Electronics, which stocks stereos, tape recorders, and gadgets; White's Books; and Mitzi's Hallmark. There is also a dry cleaner, an eyeglass store, a shoe repair shop, a branch of Sun Bank, a post office, and a pharmacy. Dining options include T.G.I. Fridays, McDonalds, Taco Bell, Perkins, Rax, Red Lobster, Pebbles, Jungle Jim's, an ice cream shop, and a pizza parlor.

In addition to the shops and services, there's the Pirate's Cove Adventure Golf, an innovative miniature golf course.

TEAM MICKEY'S ATHLETIC CLUB: The locker room decor is the perfect setting for sports clothing, activewear, and sports equipment for the whole family. This is the place to find T-shirts, sweatshirts, and other items with Disney University logos.

VILLAGE SPIRITS: Located next to Country Address, this shop can expand your wine cellar with selections from a wide choice of American and imported wines. Popularly priced wines keep company with some very rare vintages bought at auction. Spirits, liqueurs, cognacs, ales, and other alcoholic potables are available, including one of the state's largest collections of miniatures. Glassware, corkscrews, ice buckets, and an abundance of other bar accessories are also featured. Wine tastings are held daily. So much for the myth that no wine or liquor is allowed at Walt Disney World.

EUROSPAIN: An array of handcrafted gifts and decorative items from prestigious Spanish artisans and designers. Presented by Arribas Brothers.

WINDJAMMER DOCK SHOP: You go through this shop on the way to Cap'n Jack's Oyster Bar. The first section is devoted to women's fashions—Javanese batik shorts; skirts and tops; cool, crinkly cotton sundresses; a fine selection of costume jewelry; and shorts in a paint store's worth of colors, in just about any style imaginable.

RESTAURANTS

For a complete listing of all Walt Disney World Village restaurants, bars, and snack shops, see *Good Meals, Great Times.*

LAKESIDE ACTIVITIES

The 35-acre Buena Vista Lagoon that borders this village of cedar-shingled shops also gives it much of its atmosphere: When the sidewalks radiate heat, the water looks cool and inviting; in the slanting rays of the late afternoon sun, it glistens like a sheet of silver.

There's always something going on. Little Water Sprites zip to and fro, speeding to the dock from feeder canals to the west, while more laid-back folks float gently along in pedal boats or V-hulled tent-topped metal-canopy boats.

It's pleasant to sit and watch all this activity from the benches at the Buena Vista Lagoon marina, centrally located in Disney Village Marketplace; over ice cream sundaes at the Ice Cream Parlor on the lake's west shore; or over frozen fresh strawberry margaritas at Cap'n Jack's Oyster Bar. Those who would rather participate need walk only a few steps to the marina, where several types of boats can be rented from morning until dusk. Opening and closing hours change from season to season; call

828-2204 for details. No swimming is allowed. (Prices subject to state tax.)

WATER SPRITES: These tiny craft are very popular. Though they don't really move very fast, they feel as if they do; and, in any event, they get up enough speed to cover quite a lot of territory on Buena Vista Lagoon. Half-hour rentals cost $11. There are usually lines of people waiting for boats between 11 A.M. and 4 P.M.; plan accordingly. The minimum age to rent or drive one of these boats (even with an adult) is 12.

CANOPY BOATS: These metal, V-hulled, 16-foot craft can accommodate up to 10 adults; some people stock up on picnic supplies at the Gourmet Pantry and turn an afternoon sail into a party. Cost is $17.50 per-half hour.

PEDAL BOATS: These 2-person craft can be rented for $5 per half-hour.

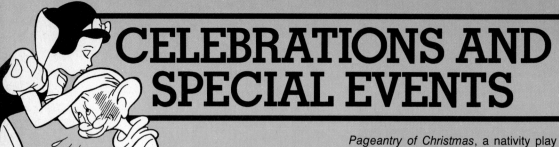

CELEBRATIONS AND SPECIAL EVENTS

There's nearly always something going on under the Captain's Tower at the Disney Village Marketplace. Some weeks the place might be stacked high with shiny new hardcover books; on another day, it might feature cruisewear and resort fashions. Crafts demonstrations and art shows are staged now and again, along with manufacturers' promotions. In the past, these have included a barnyard festival with animals from the petting farm at Fort Wilderness and birds from Discovery Island; a citrus promotion; a Trivial Pursuit promotion; and the dollmaker Madame Alexander, who was introducing a new line that had collectors lining up in the wee hours of the morning. There will also be a variety of internationally themed promotions this year. Other special activities will include presentations by cookbook authors, craft demonstrations, wine tastings, and fashion specialists.

In addition, there are a number of annual events—some in celebration of holidays.

WDW VILLAGE WINE FESTIVAL (FEBRUARY): Sixty wineries from California, other parts of the U.S., and Europe participate in this annual festival.

BOAT SHOW (OCTOBER): Because this Central Florida region has no ocean beaches, most events of this type are staged in shopping malls and exhibition halls. Here, however, boats are displayed not only throughout the Marketplace, but also in the water; and with over 200 boats from all manufacturers, this is the area's biggest in-the-water boat show.

HALLOWEEN: The Captain's Tower, made to look as spooky as a contemporary structure can be, with festoons of cobwebs and displays of Halloween merchandise, is the centerpiece of a number of activities around the Marketplace. Assorted costumed witches, ghosts, goblins, and Disney villains— *Sleeping Beauty*'s Maleficent and *Snow White*'s Wicked Witch—judge a children's costume contest for local kids (and vacationing youngsters with the foresight to bring an outfit).

FESTIVAL OF THE MASTERS: This art show, which takes place in November each year, is generally considered one of the South's best because only artists who have won an award in the past 3 years are invited to enter.

CHRISTMASTIME: Thanksgiving marks the beginning of the Christmas season here when a Christmas tree is set up in the village. Then the *Glory and Pageantry of Christmas*, a nativity play fashioned after a 13th-century pageant whose origins are in southern France, makes its annual debut. In all, there are appearances by some 3 dozen characters garbed in period costumes made from brocades, satins, silks, velvets, wool, rough homespun, and monk's cloth—a baker, butcher, candlemaker, flower seller, fruit and vegetable peddler, weaver, and others. A concert of carols precedes each evening's tableau. The Madame Alexander Doll Event offers the opportunity to meet Madame Alexander, her daughter, son-in-law, and grandson, who run the doll empire. Dolls are available for purchase at the event.

USEFUL STOPS

A Guest Services facility is located at You & Me Kid facing Lakeside Terrace. Services include reservation assistance, ticket sales, lost and found, film and stamp sales, photo processing, wheelchair and stroller rental, gift certificates, gift wrap, and general information.

BUS TRANSPORTATION: The Disney Village Marketplace bus stop and shelter is located next to Sir Edward's Haberdasher. There is bus service to the Village Clubhouse, the Disney Village Resort, the Caribbean Beach Resort, Disney Village Hotel Plaza, the Disney-MGM Studios Theme Park, Epcot Center, and the Transportation and Ticket Center. (From the latter, monorails and ferries go to the Magic Kingdom, monorails to the Contemporary Resort and Grand Floridian Resort, buses to The Disney Inn, the Polynesian Village, and Fort Wilderness.) For more information on transportation within the rest of the World, see *Transportation and Accommodations*.

FOREIGN CURRENCY EXCHANGE: This can be done at the Sun Bank during regular banking hours. See *Getting Ready To Go*.

TRAVELER'S CHECKS: These can be purchased at the Sun Bank; outside the bank, there is an American Express Cardmembers Cheque Dispenser, which cardholders (who have previously obtained a special number) may use to purchase traveler's checks.

PLEASURE ISLAND

Although Walt Disney World is not otherwise noted for its historic antecedents, a recent "discovery" may change all that. Imagineers tell us that right beside the Empress Lilly at the Disney Village Marketplace, an island was recently unearthed where an enterprising, larger-than-life 19th century ship merchant, one Merriweather Adam Pleasure held court.

Though the merchant sailing trade was in a decline at the time of his residence, the upsurge of leisure yachting assured the success of Pleasure's Canvas & Sailmaking, Inc. The booming business spawned Pleasure Island, a community developed to abet Mr. Pleasure's pursuit of adventure and excitement. So the story goes. . . and continues.

According to local legend Pleasure turned his entire operation over to his sons while he circumnavigated the globe, but he was lost at sea in 1939. Pleasure Island soon fell into disrepair due to the neglect of his lazy offspring. Enter Disney Imagineers, who have transformed the abandoned lofts, warehouses, and factories into an entertainment complex of nightclubs, restaurants, shops, and movie theaters.

The 6-acre island now fills the need for evening and late-night entertainment options for Walt Disney World guests. Pleasure Island is connected to the Disney Village Marketplace by three footbridges, and parking was greatly expanded in the area to accommodate the anticipated influx of guests. There are seven nightclubs, several restaurants

(described in detail in *Good Meals, Great Times*), an unusual variety of shops, and the AMC multiplex cinemas, featuring current films. The nightclubs open at about 7 P.M. (with the exception of the XZFR Rockin' Rollerdrome, which is open Saturdays and Sundays during the day for rollerskating) and don't close until about 2 A.M. Shops are open from 10 A.M. to midnight, and the restaurants are open from about 11:30 A.M. to midnight.

There is no fee to enter the Pleasure Island premises, its shops, or restaurants. A single ticket, which costs $14.95, allows admission to all the clubs; $7.95 for children ages 4 through 17 when accompanied by an adult. A single club ticket is also available for $6. Remember, the drinking age in Florida is 21. Guests over 18 will be admitted to the clubs (except Mannequins), but will not be served alcohol.

The clubs and shops are all described below. Restaurants within the clubs are mentioned here, but are described in more detail in the *Good Meals, Great Times* chapter.

MANNEQUINS: If a day of walking around Walt Disney World hasn't left your feet too weary, this is the place to head to dance the night away. According to local rumor, the club is housed in the warehouse once used to store Merriweather Adam Pleasure's canvas and sewing equipment. Guests enter through an elevator that rises to the third floor. Once inside, there is very little evidence of Mr. Pleasure's business. Lights, rock and roll music, live dancers, and an overall party atmosphere dominate the scene: A dance troupe has just completed a successful show and the cast and crew have decided to throw themselves a party.

The name of the club is derived from the many mannequins strategically placed all around the establishment. Each of the figures is tied to dance in some way. There are several "cats" from the musical of the same name, and wonderful recreations of Deborah Kerr and Yul Brynner dressed as Anna and the King of Siam from the "Shall We Dance" scene in the film version of *The King and I*.

The main dance floor is actually a turntable, and eight dancers perform on the rotating floor every hour, in groups of two, four, or eight. The music is provided by a deejay whose audio booth is about as high tech as they come.

The lighting is a major attraction at Mannequins. There are 70 robotically controlled lighting instruments, and a matrix of lights behind the stage has been dubbed the "toaster oven" by Disney Imagineers (because it warms the entire room when lit). There's also a machine that can cause bubbles to float in the air, hurl confetti, or even make it snow in the club.

Appetizers, specialty drinks, beer, and wine are available at a number of locations. See *Good Meals, Great Times* for details.

BATON ROUGE LOUNGE: A spacious lounge on the main deck of the *Empress Lilly* is one of the most lively spots in Walt Disney World thanks to the energetic performances by the Jazz Connection. Specialty drinks are sold by the pitcher and the chips offered by the basket are good enough to make it easy to abandon dinner plans.

NEON ARMADILLO: Once a greenhouse for exotic plants collected during Pleasure's endless world travels, the Neon Armadillo now features live country & western music nightly. Southwestern decor is highlighted by a wonderful brass chandelier in the shape of a spur and inlaid wood tabletops decorated in Navajo blanket patterns. In keeping with the Southwestern theme, two fajitas bars offer freshly made chicken, beef, or seafood fajitas. Specialty drinks, beer, and wine are also served.

ADVENTURERS CLUB: The one club devoted to keeping the legend of Merriweather Adam Pleasure alive and lively. "Explore the unknown, discover the impossible," states the credo posted at the entrance. This, the stories say, is where Pleasure stored all the treasures collected during his travels (Mrs. Pleasure apparently wouldn't allow all the stuff in their house). Incidentally, just about all of the items on display were collected at garage sales and antique shows and shops all around the world by Disney Imagineers. The place is modeled on the paneled libraries and elegant salons of similar clubs of the 19th century, and is jam-packed full of photos, furniture, trinkets, books, letters, statuettes, and other memorabilia from Pleasure's jaunts. The cozy recesses hide rooms where the masks on the walls come to life, and there are cast members portraying members of the house staff, including the maid and the curator, and several club members, prime among them an inept pilot named Hathaway Brown, the club chairperson, and a world-renowned bug expert. These players interact with guests with very amusing results.

Down the flight of stairs there is more "stuff" than anyone could ever hope to see in one visit, so just stroll around, read the captions on some of the photos, and enjoy the cool, air conditioned atmosphere. Drinks are served at the bar. If you have a seat on one of the stools, and ask the bartender to work his magic, your stool (or the one of an unsuspecting friend) may very slowly sink toward the floor leaving you, or your friend, significantly shorter. Then it's on to the library, where a player organ sets the scene for the outrageous storytellers. The show is a little corny, but nonetheless entertaining.

XZFR ROCKIN' ROLLERDROME: A novel combination of dancing, dining, and rollerskating awaits guests at this establishment, which, legend has it, was once a wind tunnel and a laboratory where Pleasure secretly developed a unique flying machine. The dance floor is located on the lowest level of the building, while a rollerskating track circles overhead on the second floor. Spinners serves up burgers, salads, chicken, and pizza on the third level.

A live band, the Time Pilots from the planet XZFR, plays during the evening hours. (On week-

ends during the day a recorded soundtrack serves as accompaniment for rollerskaters.) It seems that the band got to Pleasure Island in that secret flying machine and it is said that the Time Pilots are seven alien musicians who are viewing Walt Disney World guests from a "Mork from Ork" perspective while studying Earth culture through rock and roll. The Mother Ship, a space vehicle suspended from the ceiling, picks up band members during each set and moves them around the room above all the action. The band plays 45 to 50 minutes of each hour, and a deejay takes over during the breaks to offer uninterrupted musical entertainment. There are special music sets, including love songs and college-related tunes. The atmosphere is a little frenetic, but nonetheless exciting. Alcoholic beverages and soft drinks are available on the first level at the Orbiter Lounge. There is a $4 charge (including all-day skate rental) between 11 A.M. and 5 P.M. on weekend days. After 5 P.M. daily, skates rent for $2 per half hour with club admission.

VIDEOPOLIS EAST: Guests are required to be under 18 years of age to enter this dance club, but what's inside is anything but kid stuff. From the stainless steel dance floor to the banks of television monitors hung all around the club, this is high tech at its loftiest. Flashing lights and pulsating colored beams make the movement on the dance floor seem even more frenzied than it is, and that's just fine with the teen audience. This club was built here following the enormous success of its sister at Disneyland in Anaheim, though there are significant differences between the two installations. The video monitors display the hottest music videos, and there are several interactive television screens that allow guests a chance to play a video question and answer game. A guest who answers the questions correctly will get a chance to control the lighting or sound system for a short while. The sound, lighting, and video equipment is worth a look even if dancing like a dervish is not your thing. Only non-alcoholic beverages are served, along with snack food favored by the teen set. Guests over 18 are permitted to enter the club only if accompanied by someone under 18.

COMEDY WAREHOUSE: Set in the former plant that generated the power for all Mr. Pleasure's island enterprises, this club features a comedy troupe that performs five times each evening from 7 P.M. to 1 A.M. There are five comedians and one musician who do a Disney spoof. Guests perch on stools in a tiered arena so every seat offers a good view, even if the stools are a little tough on bad backs. Popcorn is the snack of choice, and specialty drinks, beer, wine, and soft drinks are all available.

SHOPPING AT PLEASURE ISLAND

The variety of merchandise found at Pleasure Island's shops is a little more eclectic than that found at the other Walt Disney World emporia. Some items may not, however, be available at all times.

ISLAND DEPOT: Pleasure Island souvenirs, film, rental cameras, and sundries are available at this centrally located shop. This is also the place to rent strollers and wheelchairs.

AVIGATOR'S SUPPLY: A brand label designed exclusively for Pleasure Island, the whimsical winged alligator is emblazoned on a wide variety of merchandise, including T-shirts, sweatshirts, magnets, and tote bags. There is also a broad selection of aviation-related gifts, clothing, and accessories. Leather bomber jackets, heavy duty duffle bags, airplane clocks and sculptures, and a variety of collectibles round out the offerings. There are also shirts with the Adventurers Club logo available.

CHANGING ATTITUDES: A selection of women's resortwear and accessories is sold here. The skirts, slacks, blouses, dresses, swimwear, jackets, and accessories are of a more contemporary nature than the offerings at most other Walt Disney World women's shops.

THE MOUSE HOUSE: Pleasure Island's character shop stocks the usual selection of T-shirts, sweatshirts, plush toys, gift items, hats, books, and other such merchandise.

SUSPENDED ANIMATION: Posters, prints, lithographs, cels, and original Disney animation art are sold here. It's a pleasant place to browse, even if you don't plan to buy.

FRONT PAGE: The desire to have your picture on the cover of a national magazine can be satisfied here. A wide variety of magazine titles is sold, and costumes and appropriate accessories are available at the shop.

HAMMER & FIRE: A unique outlet offering jewelry, accessories, tableware, and decorative gifts. Titanium is used in some unusual jewelry, and colorful stoneware, platters, and wall hangings round out the selections. This shop has become a favorite of local residents in search of a special gift.

DOODLES: All the merchandise here appears to have been doodled upon. Fashions from the 1950s and 1980s are offered and much of the stock reflects the atmosphere of the clubs. Neon colored T-shirts, hats, and other such items round out the stock.

YESTEREARS: The enormous surge in popularity of Disneyana collecting inspired the Walt Disney Company to reissue the line of old-time Disney merchandise found here. Dolls, puppets, posters, clothing, and figurines of Mickey, Minnie, and Donald in their earlier incarnations are on sale. Worth a stop if only for the nostalgic feelings the goods inspire.

SUPER STAR STUDIOS: Star in your own music video. Guests lip sync favorite songs for either audio or video recordings. A particular favorite with teens.

PROPELLER HEADS: Pleasure Island's arcade features the usual array of blipping and bleeping video games, and is enormously popular with younger guests. It's open from 11 A.M. to 2 A.M.

EATING AT PLEASURE ISLAND

For a complete list of Pleasure Island restaurants, fast-food emporiums, and snack spots, see *Good Meals, Great Times.*

TYPHOON LAGOON

A furious storm once roared 'cross the sea;
Catching ships in its path, helpless to flee;
Instead of a certain and watery doom;
The winds swept them here to Typhoon Lagoon!

So reads the legend guests see (looking a bit like old Burma-Shave roadside signs) as they drive into Typhoon Lagoon, a 56-acre, state-of-the-art aquatic theme park. The watery playground has been inspired by an imagined legend: a typhoon hit a small resort village years and years ago, and the storm—plus a resultant earthquake and volcanic eruption—left the village in ruins. The "local" residents, however, were very resourceful, and rebuilt their town as best they could, although the damage was severe. Trees toppled onto and into buildings, a ship was marooned atop a strangely magical mountain, and debris was strewn all around. Still they persevered, and while some structures in their resort community continue to lean, some are held up by ropes, and others have trees growing through their roofs, this is an oasis of damp fun.

Whether the typhoon, earthquake, and eruption actually ever took place doesn't really matter, since Typhoon Lagoon is a delightful place to spend a day. The assortment of visual treats is sizable, and since Typhoon Lagoon is four times the size of River Country, there's a full day's worth of activities to sample. The surf lagoon is larger than two football fields and normally kicks up 4½-foot waves; two speed slides whisk guests through a cave at 30 miles per hour; a couple of winding storm slides offer a twisting journey; whitewater routes give groups and families a chance to ride the rapids together; and much, much more.

The centerpiece of Typhoon Lagoon is the world's largest manmade watershed mountain, Mt. Mayday. Atop its peak, the Miss Tilly, a shrimp boat out of Safen Sound, Florida, is precariously perched. The smokestack atop Miss Tilly erupts every 5 or 10 minutes, shooting a 50-foot flume of water into the air. The cool water cascades down the mountain and helps to keep guests comfortable while they wait in line for the assorted slides. Guests who make the 85-foot climb up Mt. Mayday will be rewarded with a great view over the action below.

There are volleyball courts set up in several places along the beach and hammocks are strung from trees. There are also a number of thatched coverings that can provide shade or protection from an unexpected thunderstorm.

Lifeguards are on duty all over this park. There are nine at the lagoon and several more at each of the slide areas. Winding streams and waterfalls are found throughout the area, and geysers set into the walkways keep the ground wet and cool.

What follows is a description of all the specific activities available at Typhoon Lagoon. What we'll leave to your imagination is the pure pleasure of pulling up a lounge chair or stretching out on a hammock, opening a good book, and letting the watery world unfold around you.

TYPHOON LAGOON: The main swimming area spreads out over 2½ acres and contains 2.75 million gallons of water. The Caribbean blue lagoon is surrounded by a white sand beach, and its main attraction is the 4 + -foot waves that come crashing to the shore every 90 seconds. Rafts and boards are available for rent, but guests are welcome to body-surf—just ride the waves with their bodies. Water collects in 12 huge chambers above the lagoon and falls through trap doors creating the waves which are sufficiently large so that amateur and professional surfing championships are planned for the park. There are also two smaller tidal pools, Whitecap Cove and Blustery Bay, where less adventurous guests can loll about in water made for bobbing not riding.

CASTAWAY CREEK: A 2,100-foot circular river that winds through the park offers a lazy, relaxing orientation to Typhoon Lagoon. Rent a raft, or tube, or just swim along the 15-foot-wide, 3-foot-deep waterway that courses through a rain forest where guests are cooled by mists and spray; past caves and grottoes that provide welcome shade on hot summer days; and an area known as Water Works, where "broken" pipes from a water tower dump buckets of water on passersby. The 2½ feet per second current is calm and restful, and aside from a few floating props, the journey is unimpeded. There are exits along the way where guests can hop out for a while and do something else, or just to dry off a bit and then jump right back in. In the way that the Walt Disney World Railroad offers an overall perspective of the Magic Kingdom, so does Castaway Creek reveal the breadth of Typhoon Lagoon. It takes 25 to 35 minutes to ride around the park without taking a break.

HUMUNGA KOWABUNGA: These two speed slides, reported to have been carved into the landscape by the historic earthquake, will send guests zooming through caves at speeds of 30 miles per hour. The 214-foot slides offer a 51-foot drop, and

the view from the top is a little scary. But it's over before you know it, and once wary guests hurry back for another try. Disney Imagineers, when doing their research for the park, discovered that large crowds tend to gather where speed slides exist at other parks, to watch women wearing bikinis lose their bathing suit tops on the way down. Ever considerate, the Imagineers built a grandstand so that the voyeurs in the crowd have a place to sit. Modest maidens beware! A one-piece suit is far safer than a skimpy 2-piece. Guests are also warned that they should be free of back trouble, heart conditions, and other physical limitations to take the trip. Pregnant women are not permitted to ride.

SHARK REEF: For those Walt Disney World guests who have longed to jump into the tank at Epcot Center's The Living Seas, here's your chance. Guests obtain free snorkel equipment (you may not bring your own) for a swim through an artificial coral reef where they come face to face with lots of fish, even sharks. The reef is constructed around a sunken, upsidedown tanker (where guests who don't care to swim among the fish can get a close look from the portholes). There are 362,000 gallons of seawater around the reef. The sharks, by the way, are small nurse sharks and bonnethead sharks, both passive members of the species. They don't eat anything bigger than they are, and though the bonnetheads look like small hammerhead sharks, don't fret, you're safe. At any given time, there will be about 4,000 critters in the water. The colors are vibrant, and though the trip takes only about 10 to 15 minutes, it's a great introduction to the world of snorkeling. Guests must shower before entering the reef's deeps.

JIB JAMMER, RUDDER BUSTER, STERN BURNER: These three body slides send guests off at about 20 miles per hour down winding fiberglass slides, in and out of rock formations and caves, and through waterfalls. It's a somewhat tamer ride than Humunga Kowabunga, but still offers a speedy descent. The three slides are about 300 feet long, and each offers a different view and experience. It's altogether a cooling and enjoyable trip.

WHITEWATER RIDES: Three whitewater raft rides offer guests a variety of trips, all taken aboard oversize inner tubes. All the slides course through caves, waterfalls, and intricate rock work, making the scenery an attraction in itself. At **Mayday Falls**, guests ride down a 460-foot slide. The ride starts out fast, then slows down in a catch pool. But don't relax, because you'll soon be sent on a quick trip to the bottom. **Keelhall Falls** is a vortex, or spiral, ride which sends guests on a roundabout trip down a 400-foot slide. The winding nature of this trip makes it seem a little faster than Mayday Falls, but actually the speed is the same, about 10 miles per hour. At **Gangplank Falls**, groups or families have the chance to take a ride together in 6½-foot wide tubes that hold four people. The 300-foot-long slide offers a similar ride, but with the added enjoyment of sharing the experience.

KETCHAKIDDIE CREEK: Open to those four feet tall or under (unless accompanied by a small child), this kiddie area offers the same rides scaled down for pint-size visitors. There are slides, floating boats, fountains, waterfalls, squirting whales and seals, a mini-rapid ride, a grotto with a thin veil of water that kids just love to run back and forth through, and assorted floating toys to keep youngsters busy all day. There are even kid-size restrooms marked "boys" and "girls." The area is supervised at all times, so parents can feel comfortable dropping off their 4-feet-and-unders and setting off to enjoy the rest of the park.

ADMISSION: Typhoon Lagoon is a separate attraction and therefore has a separate admission. The cost is $17.50 for adults and $14 for children ages 3 to 9. A two-day pass is available for $29 for adults and $23 for children. Annual passes cost $75 for all ages. Prices are subject to change.

WHERE TO EAT: There are two restaurants at Typhoon Lagoon, both offering similar fare and outdoor seating at tables with colorful umbrellas. Leaning Palms, which was known as Placid Palms before the typhoon hit, was renamed to fit its some-

what unorthodox architecture. Burgers, hot dogs, chef's salads, and assorted snacks are sold here. Typhoon Tilly's Galley & Grog offers a similar, but somewhat more limited, menu, and also features a separate area just for ice cream and frozen yogurt. There are several food carts around the park selling lemonade, soda, ices, and snow cones. A couple of picnic areas are also available, where guests can bring their own food or enjoy a sampling from one of the restaurants. Getaway Glen is located to the left of the main entrance, past Leaning Palms, and Cascade Cove is near Shark Reef.

RESTROOMS AND CHANGING ROOMS: Restrooms equipped with showers are located at strategic points throughout the park. Dressing rooms are available to the right of the main entrance, and also farther into the park near Typhoon Tilly's. These are labeled "Buoys" and "Gulls." Coin lockers are available at most restroom and dressing room locations.

SHOPPING: Singapore Sal's, located just to the right of the main entrance, is set in a ramshackle building that was left a bit worn after the typhoon. There is an assortment of props used to lend flavor, including an old boat set upright that serves as a closet. The old wheelhouse hides four dressing rooms, and oars and other boating paraphernalia are strung from the walls and the ceiling, lending an overall cluttered look to the shop. It's a little dark, but that's because the new line of Typhoon Lagoon merchandise features bright neon colors. Women's, men's, and children's clothing, sunglasses, hats, bathing suits, towels, suntan lotion, souvenirs, thongs, beach chairs, and sweatshirts are among the wares sold here.

FIRST AID: A first aid station capable of handling minor medical problems is located just to the left of the main entrance, near Leaning Palms.

FORT WILDERNESS

In a part of the state where campgrounds tend to look like pastures—barren and very hot—the Fort Wilderness Campground, located almost due east of the Contemporary Resort, is an anomaly—a forested 650-acre wonder of tall slash pines, white-flowering bay trees, and ancient cypress hung with streamers of gray-green Spanish moss. Seminole Indians once hunted and fished here.

In all, there are some 1,190 woodsy campsites arranged in several campground loops; along some of them, Fleetwood trailers are available for rent, completely furnished and fitted out with all the comforts of home. For information about these camp-sites, see *Transportation and Accommodations.*

Scattered throughout the campground loops, there are a number of sporting facilities including 2 tennis courts and tetherball and volleyball courts. Fort Wilderness has riding stables, 2 swimming pools, a marina full of boats, a canoe livery, a beach, a jogging-and-exercise trail, electric carts and bikes for rent, and a nature trail. Some of these facilities are available for the use of campground guests only; some are open to guests at WDW-owned resort hotels and villas as well; and some can also be enjoyed by guests lodging at the establishments at the Disney Village Hotel Plaza and off the property.

There's also a petting farm where goats and ducks and other farm animals run free inside a white rail fence, and it's fun to walk through the barn that houses the large, sleek horses that pull the Magic Kingdom's Main Street trolleys.

Two stores, the Settlement and Meadow trading posts, stock campers' necessities and some Disney souvenirs. And then there's Pioneer Hall, widely known as the home of the Hoop-Dee-Doo Musical Revue and Chip and Dale's Country Morning Jamboree (described in *Good Meals, Great Times*). This rustic structure (made of western white pine shipped all the way from Montana) also has a cafeteria and lounge.

Last but not least in the Fort Wilderness catalogue, there's River Country. This 8-acre expanse of water-oriented recreational facilities embodies everyone's idea of what the perfect old-fashioned swimming hole should be like. It's a separate attraction, with its own hours and admission fees.

HOW TO GET TO FORT WILDERNESS

BY CAR: From outside the World, take the WDW exit off I-4 onto U.S. 192, go through the Magic Kingdom Auto Plaza, and, bearing to your right, follow the Fort Wilderness or River Country signs. This is the most expeditious way to go, even for WDW resort guests.

BY BUS: Take the monorail from the Contemporary Resort and the Grand Floridian Resort, the bus from the Polynesian Village, The Disney Inn, the Disney Village Marketplace, the Caribbean Beach Resort, Epcot Center, the Disney-MGM Studios, and from Disney Village Hotel Plaza establishments to the Transportation and Ticket Center. Change there to the bus to Fort Wilderness. Count on 30 to 45 minutes in transit. To ride many of these buses, you must show an ID card from one of the WDW-owned properties or a Hotel Plaza establishment; certain All Three Parks Passports will also do.

BY BOAT: Guests at WDW-owned properties, and those with admission tickets to River Country or Discovery Island, also can go by boat from Magic Kingdom marinas (about 30 minutes' ride) and from the Contemporary Resort (about 25 minutes' ride).

SOUVENIRS AND SUPPLIES

Staple food items and all sorts of other necessities of the camping life are available, along with souvenirs, at Fort Wilderness's 2 stores—the Settlement Trading Post, located not far from the beach at the north end of the campground; and the Meadow Trading Post, located near the center of Fort Wilderness.

For a complete list of places to eat in Fort Wilderness, see *Good Meals, Great Times*.

HOOP-DEE-DOO MUSICAL REVUE

Sturdy, porch-rimmed Pioneer Hall is best-known Worldwide as the home of the Pioneer Hall Players, an energetic troupe of singing-and-dancing-and-wisecracking entertainers who keep audiences chuckling and grinning and whooping it up for 2 hours, during a procession of barbecued ribs, fried chicken, corn on the cob, strawberry shortcake, and other stomach-stretching viands. If you have time for only one of the Disney dinner shows, make it this one (for more details see *Good Meals, Great Times*). Note that there is no smoking permitted in Pioneer Hall. Reservations are very hard to come by. Reservation policies are detailed on page 20.

RIVER COUNTRY

THE PERFECT SWIMMING HOLE

It's next to impossible to go through childhood reading such classics as *Huck Finn* and *Tom Sawyer* (and other such great tales of growing up) without developing a few fantasies about what it would be like to swim in a perfect swimming hole. A group of Disney Imagineers (who actually knew a commercial re-creation of such a place as kids) have concocted a Disney version on a somewhat larger scale at River Country, a water-oriented playground that occupies a corner of Bay Lake near Cypress Point at Fort Wilderness Campground.

Fred Joerger—the same Disney rock-builder who created Big Thunder Mountain, Schweitzer Falls at the Jungle Cruise, and the caves of Tom Sawyer Island (among other things) in the Magic Kingdom—has helped design scores of rocks used to landscape one of the largest swimming pools in the state; more have been piled into a small mountain for guests to climb up—and then slide down. The rocks, scattered with pebbles acquired from stream beds in Georgia and the Carolinas, look so real that it's hard to believe they aren't.

More to the point, the place is great fun. Slipping and sliding down the curvy water chutes at top speed; getting tangled up, all arms and legs, in the whirlpools of Raft Rider Ridge; and whamming into the water from the swimming pool's high slides makes even careworn grown-ups smile, grin, giggle, chortle, and roar with delight. People who climb to the top with trepidation embark on the lightning-fast journey to the bottom only because it seems too late to back out; at the bottom they rush back for more. Line-haters queue up—over and over again. Those who associate lakes with muck and weeds go into ecstasies over the way the soft sand on the River Country bottom squiggles between their toes.

WHAT TO DO: There are several basic sections of River Country—the 330,000-gallon swimming pool, one of the largest in Florida's Orange County; Bay Cove (aka the "Ol' Swimmin' Hole"), the big walled-off section of Bay Lake that most people consider the main (and best) part of River Country; an adjoining junior version of the above for small children, with its own beach; and the grassy grounds, with picnic tables and a squirting fountain in which to play. On the edge of the lake, there's also a boardwalk nature trail through a lovely cypress swamp, and a wide (if not terribly long) white-sand beach.

Heated in winter, the oversize swimming pool has a pair of water slides that begin high enough above the water to make an acrophobe climb right down again. They plunge at such an angle that it's impossible to see the bottom of the slide from the top. Daredevils who don't chicken out are shot into the water from a height of about 7 feet—hard enough,

as one commentator observed, to "slap your stomach up against the roof of your mouth." Gutsy kids adore the experience; those who like their thrills a bit tamer might prefer to watch.

The heart of River Country, Bay Cove—actually a part of Bay Lake—is fitted out with rope swings, a ship's boom for swooping and plunging, and assorted other constructions designed to put hearts into throats as swimmers plunge from air to water. The big deals, however, are the 2 flume rides—one 260 feet long (accessible by a boardwalk and stairway to the far right of the swimming hole as you face it) and a smaller one, 100 feet shorter (accessible by a stairway to the left of that) and the white-water raft ride.

The flumes, which are like overgrown, steep-sided waterslides, corkscrew through the greenery at the top of the ridge known as Whoop-'N-Holler Hollow, sending even the most stalwart shooting into the water, usually like greased lightning. Timid folk will find it easy to control their speed, however. The rule of thumb is to sit up to slow down, and lie back to speed up. Be warned that once you lie down to accelerate, getting up is virtually impossible. Reclining with arms at sides guarantees a slower ride than lying back with hands above the head. Arching your back so that only shoulders and heels are on the flume's surface increases the pace still further. Combining positions allows for braking and accelerating at will.

White Water Rapids, as the white-water raft ride mentioned above is known, involves a more leisurely trip through a series of chutes and pools in an inner tube, from the crest of Raft Rider Ridge (adjoining Whoop-'N-Holler Hollow) into Bay Cove. It's not a high-speed affair like the flumes, but some people like it better. The pools are contoured so that the water swirls through them in whirlpool fashion. You tend to get caught in the slow circling water, and when other tubers come sliding down the chutes at you, bare arms and legs get all tangled up.

ADMISSION: River Country is an attraction in its own right, with a separate admission charge that includes transportation to the site and use of all the facilities. A River Country and Discovery Island combination ticket, which includes transportation and admission to both, is also available. River Country is open from 10 A.M. to 5 P.M.; during Easter week hours are extended from 9 A.M. to 6 P.M.; and during the summer season hours are 9 A.M. to 8 P.M. The attraction is usually closed for refurbishing during January. Note that children under 10 must be accompanied by an adult. Some of the River Country adventures require swimming ability.

	Guests at WDW resorts/children 3 through 9	All other guests/children 3 through 9
River Country admission (During summer months after 3 P.M.—$2 off for all ages, or $30 family rate)	$10.75/$8.25	$11.75/$9.25
River Country/Discovery Island combination ticket	$14/$10	$15/$11

A 2-day River Country ticket is available at resort ticket locations or at the River Country ticket window. This ticket is good for any 2 days during a 7-day period; prices for resort guests are $16.75 for adults and $12.75 for children (3 through 9). Other guests pay $17.75 for adults and $13.75 for children.

Prices are subject to change and do not include a 6% tax.

WHEN TO GO: Daytime temperatures in Orlando are such that it's possible to enjoy River Country almost all year round, though it is perhaps most pleasant in spring—when the weather is getting hot but the water is still cool. In summer, the place can be very busy indeed.

Ticket windows close as the crowd approaches capacity. During WDW's busiest times of year, that may happen as early as 11:30 A.M. It's worth noting, however, that those who already have tickets will be admitted anyway. Consequently, if you plan to visit River Country in the afternoon of a summer day, it's smart to buy your combination River Country/Discovery Island ticket at the ticket booth at the entrance to the Magic Kingdom on your way into the park.

One of the World's best-kept secrets is the joy of River Country after 4 P.M. in the summer. Crowds begin to thin out dramatically then, but usually not so much that the place is empty; and a special reduced admission ticket is offered after 3 P.M. River Country closes at 8 P.M. during the summer.

HOW TO GET THERE: From the Transportation and Ticket Center, buses drop passengers off within walking distance of River Country. It's also possible to go by boat. Launches leave regularly from the dock near the gates of the Magic Kingdom. For guests arriving at River Country by car, a tram picks up at the River Country parking lot and takes guests to the entrance.

TOWELS, DRESSING ROOMS, SUPPLIES: Men's and women's dressing rooms, and coin-operated lockers are available. Quarters for these can be obtained at the concession window, but to avoid waiting in line for change, it's best to bring your own.

Towels are available for rent at 50¢ each at the concession window, but they're small, so you'll probably want to bring at least one beach towel.

FOOD: Pop's Place, the main snack stand, sells quarter-pound burgers, hot dogs, salads, beer and soda, and the like. During peak season the Waterin' Hole, a smaller stand nearby, offers a more limited selection.

Picnicking is permitted. You can eat on the beach or seek out a table on the shady lawns. (No alcoholic beverages are allowed at River Country.)

Fort Wilderness Campground is one of the liveliest spots in the World.

BEACHES: The clear waters of Bay Lake, which lap the 315-foot-long, 175-foot-wide, white-sand beach at the north end of the campground, are delightful. And swimming is allowed inside the roped-off areas. Open to guests at WDW-owned properties only.

BIKE RENTALS: Tandems, dirt bikes, surreys, and assorted other 2-wheelers can be hired at the Bike Barn for trips along Fort Wilderness's bike paths and roadways—or just for getting around. Cost is $3 per hour, or $7 per day.

BLACKSMITH SHOP: The pleasant fellow who shoes the draft horses that pull the trolleys down Main Street in the Magic Kingdom is on hand at some time every day to answer questions and talk about what he does; occasionally guests can watch him at work, fitting the big animals with the special polyurethane-covered, steel-cored horeshoes that are used here to protect the horses' hooves.

BOAT RENTALS ON BAY LAKE: Zippy little Water Sprites, sailboats, pontoon boats, and pedal boats (described in *Sports*) are available for rent at the marina, at the north end of the campground.

CAMPFIRE PROGRAM: Held nightly near the Meadow Trading Post near the center of the campground, it features Disney movies, a sing-along, and cartoons. It's free for WDW resort guests only. Chip and Dale usually put in an appearance.

CANOE RENTALS: Fort Wilderness is ribboned with tranquil canals, sometimes in full sun and sometimes canopied by tall trees, which make for delightful canoe trips of 1 to 3 hours—or longer if you take fishing gear and elect to wet your line. Rentals are available at the Bike Barn ($4 per hour, $9 per day).

ELECTRIC CART RENTALS: Available at the Bike Barn for sightseeing or transportation.

ELECTRICAL WATER PAGEANT: This twinkling cavalcade of lights (described in more detail in *Good Meals, Great Times*) can be seen from the beach here nightly at 9:45 P.M.

FISHING EXCURSIONS ON BAY LAKE: WDW's restrictive fishing policy means plenty of angling action—largemouth bass weighing 2 or 3 pounds, mainly—for those who sign up for the special 8 A.M. and 3 P.M. fishing excursions. The fee is $110 for a 2-hour excursion (each additional hour is $25) and includes gear, driver/guide, and refreshments; no license is required. Guests whose accommodations have kitchens may keep their catch. WDW has also made arrangements with a local taxidermist for guests who would like to take their catches home as souvenirs.

FISHING IN THE CANALS: Largemouth bass can be caught here as well. Those without their own gear will find cane poles and lures for sale at the trading posts; equipment is also available for rent at the Bike Barn. No license is required.

FORT WILDERNESS FUN

HAYRIDES: The hay wagon departs from Pioneer Hall and carries guests on a trip through wooded areas near Bay Lake. A ride lasts about an hour, and concludes back at Pioneer Hall. Tickets can be purchased from the hayride host. Children under 12 must be accompanied by an adult.

THE HORSE BARN: The world champion Percherons and all the draft horses that pull trolleys down Main Street in the Magic Kingdom call this corner of Fort Wilderness home. You can watch them chomping placidly on their food, and occasionally see young colts and fillies as well. The Tri Circle D insignia above the barn door is also the WDW brand; 2 small circles, Mouse ears style, atop a large one with the letter *D* inside.

JOGGING AND EXERCISE TRAIL: This 2.3-mile course, punctuated by exercise stations every quarter mile or so, is one of the Fort Wilderness attractions that draws WDW resort guests from all over the property. The weather is often steamy, but things are pleasant in the early morning—especially because most of the running trail is in the shade. You may just jog the whole length; or you can stop periodically to do the chin-ups, sit-ups, and other exercises outlined on nearby signs.

LAWN MOWER TREE: The tree that somehow, mysteriously, grew around a lawn mower is a Fort Wilderness point of interest worth hunting down. It's just off the sidewalk leading to the marina.

MARSHMALLOW MARSH EXCURSION: A nightly (during the summer months) marshmallow roast and sing-along follows a canoe trip and a short hike to the northern end of the campground, where a handful of big split logs is arranged around a fire ring. The Electrical Water Pageant, which can be seen just offshore, is part of the entertainment. Bring mosquito repellent. Cost is $6 for adults; $5 for children.

PETTING FARM: This fenced-in enclave just behind Pioneer Hall is now home to some extra-friendly goats, a miniature Brahma bull, some sheep, a few rabbits, chickens, and assorted barnyard critters. (A colony of prairie dogs didn't work out because its members persisted in burrowing out of their compound; no sooner would their Disney caretakers try to thwart them—by digging a bigger hole and installing a below-ground-level wire fence—than the little creatures would gnaw right through it.) Though mainly designed for youngsters, the Petting Farm is also a lot of fun for the adult crowd, and it's a good place to pass the time while waiting for seating at the Hoop-Dee-Doo Musical Revue in nearby Pioneer Hall. Pony rides are also available.

SWIMMING: There are two pools at Fort Wilderness.

TENNIS: Two tennis courts are available; play is on a first-come, first-served basis.

TRAIL RIDES: Offered from the middle of the campground, these trips depart 4 times daily between 9 A.M. and 3 P.M. and take riders meandering into the Florida wilderness at a walking pace, where it is not uncommon to see deer, wild birds, and even an occasional alligator. Galloping is not part of the game, so you don't need riding know-how to sign up. Cost is $10 per person for both day visitors and for guests at WDW-owned properties. No children under 9 are allowed. Reservations are recommended; phone W-DISNEY (934-7639).

VOLLEYBALL, TETHERBALL, AND BASKETBALL COURTS: Open only to guests at WDW-owned properties, these are scattered throughout the camping loops. No charge.

WATER-SKI TRIPS: Ski boats with drivers and equipment can be hired for $65 an hour at the marina, including instruction. Reservations should be made 2 to 3 days in advance. Call the Contemporary Resort (824-1000; ask for the marina).

WILDERNESS SWAMP TRAIL: A mile and a half long, this smooth footpath into the woods skirts the marshes along the shore of Bay Lake, then plunges into a forest full of tall, straight-standing cypress trees. Near Marshmallow Marsh, at the northern end of the campground.

DISCOVERY ISLAND

This 11½-acre landfall (a member of the American Association of Parks and Aquariums) on the southeast shore of Bay Lake—which is itself a natural marvel full of exotic birds and a whole United Nations of plants—is a delightful place to go for a change of pace from the Magic Kingdom. Here you're in the domain of the animals; man is just a visitor. The mood is different from anywhere else in the World, and the scenery is remarkably lush.

Before the World began, this island was flat and scrubby, just a tangle of vines. But Disney planners, thinking of Robert Louis Stevenson's classic *Treasure Island*, decided to turn it into a horticultural and zoological paradise. They cleared the vegetation, brought in 15,000 cubic yards of sandy soil, and added 500 tons each of boulders and trees. They built hills, carved out lagoons, sowed grass seed, and planted 20 types of palm trees, 10 species of bamboo, and dozens upon dozens of other plants from Argentina, Bolivia, the Canary Islands, China, Costa Rica, Formosa, the Himalayas, India, Japan, Peru, South Africa, Trinidad, and other nations around the world. Then they added winding paths, built aviaries and filled them with birds, and added a few props to carry through the Treasure Island theme. A wrecked ship salvaged from off the coast of Florida was installed on the beach, and a Jolly Roger hung from the lookout post. The creation was dubbed Treasure Island.

Since then, that theme has been abandoned and the island's name changed. But the ship is still there, as is the vegetation (lusher than ever). And the avian population is flourishing so well that the droning of the motors of the Water Sprites on Bay Lake is almost drowned out by chirps and tweets, crows and hoarse caws, cries and squeaks, and the lonely-sounding squawks of peacocks.

Now nobody makes any bones about the fact that the birds and the extraordinary vegetation constitute the island's chief attraction. Far from taking a backseat to the manmade, nature is the big deal on Discovery Island. The sweet-smelling flowers in pinks and reds and yellows that polka-dot the billowing greenery, the ferns that hang in the forests, the trees that canopy the footpaths, the butterflies, the dense thickets of bamboo, and the graceful palms—not to mention the birds themselves—are all very real; during Discovery Island hours—that is, from 10 A.M. to 6 P.M. (to 7 P.M. during the summer) every day—visitors provide (as curator Charlie Cook tells it) a good show for the birds and animals.

WHAT TO SEE: It's possible to walk the length of the paths and boardwalks that wind through the island in 45 minutes or so. But spending the better part of a day—or at least several hours—is a far better idea, since there is so much to see that it warrants more than just a rushed look. This is especially true in spring, when the birds are in breeding condition—looking their best, putting on

courting displays, and sometimes collecting materials for nests. Even during other seasons, however, each stop yields rewards. An ibis might be spotted building its nest. A sleeping tortoise—dinosaur-like, with the papery, wrinkled skin of an old woman's neck—suddenly rouses himself and creeps forward to join a clump of rocks that turns out to be other tortoises.

Many animals run free. Peacocks trail their spotted trains of iridescent green, blue, and gold around the grounds. They lose their tail feathers every September, and spend the winter growing new plumage in preparation for their springtime mating dance—a slow turning to and fro, sometimes punctuated by a quiver and a shudder of their graceful fans. A type of chicken developed in Poland, where chicken breeding is a popular hobby, occasionally chases the peacocks. The large rabbit-like animals are Patagonian cavies, members of the guinea pig family, who in the wild live in burrows to escape predators. Keeping quite calm, you can approach them slowly to examine them at close range.

In addition, there are special points of interest, which are marked on maps available on the island:

Parrots Perch: The macaws, cockatoos, and other trained birds that comprise the Discovery Island Bird Show make their home here and at a small enclosure dotted with perches nearby. One 6-year-old bird can stand on his head. Little green ones named Moe, Larry (the greenest; actually a female), and Curly (the shyest) know how to roll over. Andrew waves good-bye. Each one has his own trick, and you can stand and watch the caretakers putting them through their paces for hours.

Trumpeter Springs: The trumpeter swans who live here, the largest members of the waterfowl family, belong to a species that once was nearly extinct—as a result of hunting in the early part of the century.

Bamboo Hollow: The sturdy bamboo here was planted on the island's windward side as protection against occasional harsh weather and wind.

Crane's Roost: The small Demoiselle cranes and the striking gold-crested African crowned cranes engage in wonderfully elaborate courting dances every spring.

Avian Way: One of the largest walk-through aviaries in the world, this large enclosure, occupying close to an acre, is the home of the United States' most extensive breeding colony of scarlet ibis. Their incredible color, even richer than that of ibis in the wild, derives from a diet that is especially rich in carotenes. Even those in the forest are striking. The early South American explorers who first saw them thought that the trees were covered with blood.

Also in the aviary are white peacocks, albino animals with tails that look like the train of a lacy wedding gown, and elegant African crowned cranes, almost as common in Africa as cats and dogs are in the United States. They have a voracious appetite for insects that aids in controlling insect pests; farmers keep them for that purpose.

Pelican Bay: Brown pelicans became almost extinct because the chemical DDT, washed into rivers and absorbed by fish that the birds subsequently ate, caused their eggs to have such thin shells that even the weight of the mother pelican nesting on them broke them before hatching. It is only since Florida's 1965 ban on the chemical that the population has begun to grow again. The Discovery Island birds, though now healthy, have suffered injuries that have left them crippled in ways that would make it impossible for them to survive in the wild.

Flamingo Lagoon: Native flamingos—which nested in colonies some 20,000 strong when John James Audubon visited Florida in the early part of the 19th century—have not lived in the wild here since around 1920. The Discovery Island birds are Caribbean flamingos. They have grown accustomed to man's presence, as the early Florida flamingos could not, and are breeding.

Tortoise Beach: Early explorers used to lead Galapagos tortoises, now rare and endangered, onto their ships; because the animals can live for some time without food or water, they provided the crews with fresh meat for the duration of a trip. There are 11 here; the largest weighs some 500 pounds.

Eagle's Watch: The pair of southern bald eagles here belongs to a species that nests in the wild only in Florida. Sharp-eyed and white-headed, the birds seen here are on loan from the U.S. Department of the Interior.

HOW TO GET THERE: Watercraft from the Magic Kingdom, the Polynesian Village, the Contemporary Resort, the Grand Floridian Resort, Fort Wilderness, and River Country all call regularly at Discovery Island. To ride these, you must show a Discovery Island admission ticket or a WDW resort ID.

ADMISSION: Cost is $7.50 ($4 for children 3 through 9); combination tickets that include River Country admission as well are also available (described in this chapter's River Country section).

PHOTOS: The birds on Discovery Island offer wonderful photographic possibilities. Don't forget your camera. Film is available on the island.

BEACH: Swimming isn't allowed, but the peaceful strand flanking the shipwreck is great for sunbathing and sand castle building—or just for sitting and watching the brightly colored sails of the Hobie Cats (from the Fort Wilderness marina) go by.

FOOD: It's fun to pack a picnic, with supplies from the Gourmet Pantry at the Disney Village Marketplace or one of the Fort Wilderness Campground's trading posts, for lunch on the beach near the handsome old wreck (which is still aging gracefully along the Bay Lake shore). Ice cream sandwiches and bars, frozen juice bars, and beer and soft drinks are available at the snack bar, the Thirsty Perch.

WONDERS OF THE WORLD

There isn't a WDW visitor who wouldn't like to peek behind the scenes to see the Disney character costumes being made, or talk to a Disney character artist in person—and watch him draw Mickey or Donald Duck. Most devotees of the outdoors would give their eyeteeth to see WDW's rich 7,500-acre nature preserve, which is not normally open to the public.

Happily, there are several types of behind-the-scenes programs for both children and adults. Wonders of Walt Disney World caters to the younger set (10 to 15 years of age) and Innovation in Action and other such seminars are directed at guests age 16 and older.

Wonders of Walt Disney World, a program offered to students 10 to 15 years old, features three programs. Developed in cooperation with educational professionals, the Wonders programs are recognized nationwide as authentic learning experiences for students. Many schools grant special credit or excused absence for completing the program. Each program lasts about 6½ hours, and each student is loaned a Kodak camera to use during the session; the cost of film, as well as the cost of lunch and all the pre- and post-trip materials, is included in the $70 fee.

The highlight of the **Creative Arts** program is the visit by a Disney character artist who guides students through lessons in sketching the Disney Characters. This program is ideal for young people interested in animation and/or an art career. **Exploring Nature** begins with a discussion and film about Florida's delicate ecosystem, and includes a tour of Discovery Island and the 7,500-acre conservation area. The **Entertainment** session takes participants backstage for a look at rehearsals for actual WDW productions. Students also get to see the WDW wardrobe and costume departments, tucked underneath the Magic Kingdom.

The **Disney Learning Adventure** programs are for guests 16 and older. Each lasts about 3½ hours and costs $15, plus park admission. **Hidden Treasures of World Showcase** describes the inside story of the selection of art, architecture, costumes, and entertainment for each of Epcot Center's World Showcase pavilions. **Gardens of the World** is led by a member of the Disney horticultural staff, and is a study of the hundreds of unique plants, flowers, and trees growing in World Showcase.

Several presentations are available to groups of 15 or more people; these programs are often utilized by groups attending conventions. **Innovation in Action** is a 3½-hour seminar which begins with a presentation of Walt Disney's career and his announcement of the vacation kingdom he planned to build in Central Florida. Participants are taken to the underground tunnels beneath the Magic Kingdom, where the computers, costumes, wig rooms, wardrobes, offices, cafeterias, and utility systems that make the Magic Kingdom work are located. There is also a visit to the production center where shows and parades are rehearsed. The rest of the program is tailored to fit the needs of a particular group. Stops might include the central energy plant, where a sophisticated computer system monitors and controls the distribution of power across the vast property; the Vista United Telecommunications office, where one of the nation's most advanced telephone systems is operated; the water hyacinth project, a test area that uses plants as natural filters for waste water; the topiary garden, where trees are grown and shaped for later planting in the public areas of WDW; and the central workshops, where everything from trash cans to thrill rides is built, painted, and maintained.

The **Art and Science of Gardening at WDW** is another group program that allows visitors to go behind the scenes to study with the experts who maintain the WDW horticultural show. The session opens with a videotape of flower photography, set to classical music, and the instructor explains the philosophies of the Disney gardening and planting scheme. The group then proceeds to the WDW nursery to examine plants, flowers, trees, shrubs, foliage, and ongoing horticultural experiments. Each group may choose one subject for an in-depth presentation: tree care at Walt Disney World; flowering trees in Central Florida; big tree transplanting; pest control for ornamental landscaping; the use of annual flower beds at Walt Disney World; hanging basket production; interiorscaping; or the business of landscape maintenance. Each participant receives a copy of "Planting Ideas," a full-color guide to the gardens of Walt Disney World.

There are also several business and management seminars open to convention groups, including the **Disney Approach to People Management**, the **Disney Approach to Quality Service**, **Building Positive Images**, and **Making Magic, Communicating Your Message**.

For additional details about any of these programs, contact Walt Disney World Seminar Productions; Box 10000; Lake Buena Vista, FL 32830; 828-1500.

SPORTS

Many first-time visitors don't realize that Walt Disney World is much more than just the Magic Kingdom, Epcot Center, and the Disney-MGM Studios Theme Park. Within WDW's 27,000-odd acres there are more tennis courts than at most tennis resorts, more holes of championship-caliber golf than at most golf centers, and so many acres of other diversions—from fishing and bicycling to boating and swimming—that the quantity and variety are matched by very few other vacation destinations.

So while the golfers in the family are earnestly pursuing a perfect swing on one of the trio of first class layouts, tennis buffs can be wearing themselves out on the courts, sailors can be sailing, water-skiers can be skimming back and forth across powerboat wakes, and anglers can be dangling a cane pole in a canal—in the hopes of bringing in a big bream for dinner.

Instruction (formal or impromptu), as well as guides, drivers, and assorted leaders and supervisors (as required), make each sports offering as much fun for rank beginners as for hard-core aficionados. Moreover, the ready accessibility of all these WDW sporting activities—via an excellent system of public transportation (see *Transportation and Accommodations*)—means that no member of a visiting family or group need give up play time to chauffeur others around. By the same token, excellent supervision in all sports areas keeps to a minimum any parental fears that youngsters might get into trouble the moment they stray off without accompaniment.

Finally, staying in one of the WDW-owned hotels, at the villas of the Disney Village Resort, or in the WDW Fort Wilderness Campground is quite different from lodging off the property and visiting the World during the day, for certain sporting activities that are available to WDW resort guests are off-limits to day visitors. However, most sports facilities are available to all, and except for the potential logistical problem of coordinating a day's-end rendezvous back at the car, the functional design and convenient placement of WDW sports and recreational facilities make them as compelling for off-property lodgers as for guests at WDW's own resorts. (Prices noted herein are subject to change, and do not include applicable state tax.)

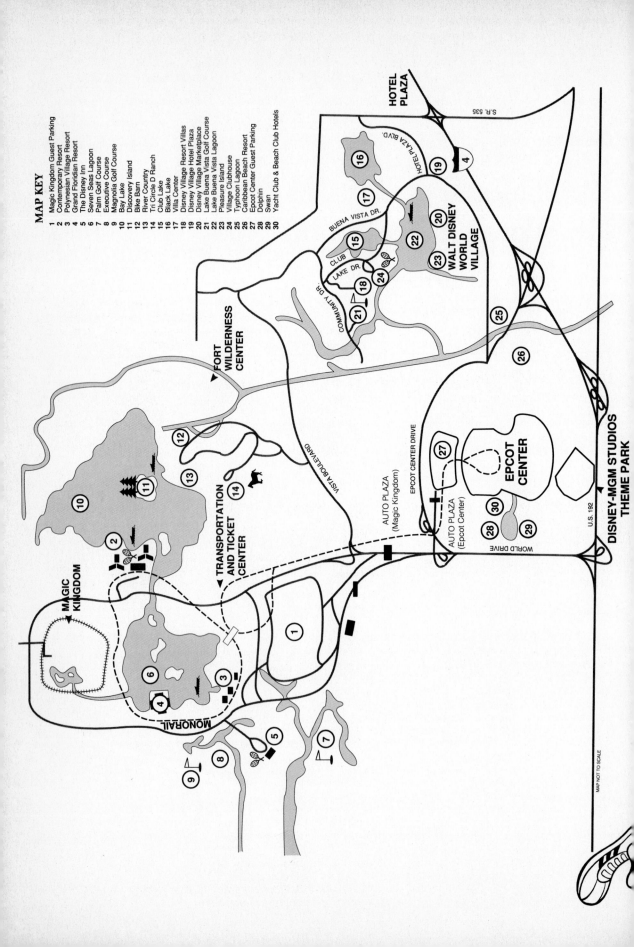

MAP KEY

1 Magic Kingdom Guest Parking
2 Contemporary Resort
3 Polynesian Village Resort
4 Grand Floridian Resort
5 The Disney Inn
6 Seven Seas Lagoon
7 Palm Golf Course
8 Executive Course
9 Magnolia Golf Course
10 Bay Lake
11 Discovery Island
12 River Country
13 Bike Barn
14 Tri Circle D Ranch
15 Club Lake
16 Black Lake
17 Villa Center
18 Disney Village Resort Villas
19 Disney Village Hotel Plaza
20 Disney Village Marketplace
21 Lake Buena Vista Golf Course
22 Lake Buena Vista Lagoon
23 Pleasure Island
24 Village Clubhouse
25 Typhoon Lagoon
26 Caribbean Beach Resort
27 Epcot Center Guest Parking
28 Dolphin
29 Swan
30 Yacht Club & Beach Club Hotels

HOTEL PLAZA

S.R. 535

HOTEL PLAZA BLVD.

BUENA VISTA DR.

CLUB LAKE DR.

COMMUNITY DR.

WALT DISNEY WORLD VILLAGE

FORT WILDERNESS CENTER

MAGIC KINGDOM

TRANSPORTATION AND TICKET CENTER

MONORAIL

VISTA BOULEVARD

AUTO PLAZA (Magic Kingdom)

AUTO PLAZA (Epcot Center)

EPCOT CENTER DRIVE

WORLD DRIVE

EPCOT CENTER

U.S. 192

DISNEY-MGM STUDIOS THEME PARK

MAP NOT TO SCALE

TENNIS EVERYONE

No one comes to Walt Disney World just for a tennis vacation; there just isn't the country-club ambience of a tennis resort, where everyone is totally immersed in the game. But the facilities and instruction program at WDW are extensive enough that such holidays are certainly within the realm of possibility. And at the very least, a couple of sets of tennis on one of the World's 13 courts is a good way to unwind after a mad morning in the Magic Kingdom, for there's seldom a problem arranging court time.

In February, March, April, June, and July the courts at the 4 separate tennis locations endure fairly heavy use, but there is usually a lull between noon and 3 P.M., and again from dinnertime until 10 P.M. Even during these busy months, however, it's usually possible to get a reservation. Of the 4 sets of courts, those at the Village Clubhouse are usually the least crowded, with those at The Disney Inn also available for play most of the time.

WHERE TO FIND THE COURTS: There are 6 tennis courts at the Contemporary Resort, just beyond the garden wing to the north of the Tower. This is WDW's major tennis facility. It boasts 3 backboards, and an automatic ball machine to work on groundstrokes and volleys. There are 2 additional courts tucked away behind The Disney Inn, and 3 cradled by adjacent woods and a section of the golf course, at the Village Clubhouse. There are also 2 courts at the Fort Wilderness Resort. All WDW tennis is played on hard courts that are open from 8 A.M. to 10 P.M. daily (hours may vary during winter months). All are lit for play after dark, and all tennis facilities are free to WDW-resort guests.

COURT RESERVATIONS: Courts may be reserved 24 hours in advance. Call 824-3578 to play at the Contemporary Resort; 824-1469 for The Disney Inn; 828-3741 for the Village Clubhouse. The Fort Wilderness courts are available on a first-come, first-served basis. The limit on the number of hours a day any single group of players can occupy a court—a restriction in effect only during very busy periods—is 2 hours on any single morning, afternoon, or evening. But that still means that you can spend up to 6 hours a day on any given court even at the busiest times, and the fact is that these restrictions on court time have never been very zealously enforced.

For players without partners, the "Tennis Anyone?" program will help find an opponent. Just call the Pro Shop at the Contemporary Resort to get your name posted.

INSTRUCTION: The tennis program at the Contemporary Resort offers clinics ($30) upon request. Video cameras are used to record players' on-court efforts for subsequent review; children as young as 3 and adults as old as 80 have participated. Nobody will try to radically change your game; the idea is to help you play better with what you have.

Private lessons are also available, by appointment, at the Contemporary Resort only. The cost is $32 per hour and $16 per half hour with a staff professional, all of whom are certified by the United States Tennis Association; $40 per hour and $20 per half hour with a head pro who supervises the entire WDW tennis program. Videotape reviews are included as part of hour-long lessons at the Contemporary Resort for an additional $10.

For more information about private lessons and group development sessions, call 824-3578.

TOURNAMENTS: Individual tournaments may be arranged by calling the Pro Shop at the Contemporary Resort. The fee for running a tournament is $40 per hour.

RACQUET RENTAL: Good-quality racquets are available for rent at $3 an hour for adults. New balls may be purchased (for $4.25 per can of 3) or used balls rented by the basket for $3. Some even boast a Mickey Mouse logo.

LOCKERS: Locker facilities are available at all tennis court areas. There is no charge for locker use.

Most people probably don't think of Walt Disney World immediately when they contemplate a golf vacation. Yet there are 3 superb courses right in the Vacation Kingdom: The Magnolia and the Palm flank The Disney Inn, and extend practically to the borders of the Magic Kingdom. In addition, just a short drive away, there's the Lake Buena Vista Golf Course, whose borders are framed by some of the villas of the Disney Village Resort.

None of these 3 Joe Lee-designed courses will set anyone's knees to knocking in terror from the regular men's or women's tees, though both the Palm and Magnolia are demanding enough to serve as the site of an annual stop on the PGA Tour tournament trail. Depending on the tee from which a golfer chooses to play, the Disney courses are challenging and/or fun, and they are constructed to be especially forgiving for the mid-handicap player. What's more, they're remarkably interesting topographically, considering that the land on which Lee started was about as hilly as a tabletop.

At all 3, the greens fees (including the required cart) are about $55 for WDW resort guests and $60 for day visitors; twilight rates, in effect beginning at 3 P.M., are $30 for each.

For tee-off times on any of the 3 courses, just phone 824-2270. Especially from February through April, it's a good idea to reserve starting times well in advance for play in the morning and early afternoon (though starting times after 3 P.M. are almost always available at the last minute). Those with confirmed reservations at the WDW resorts (which include guests at any of the 7 hotels at Disney Village Hotel Plaza) can reserve tee times 30 days in advance. Day visitors can reserve only 7 days ahead.

THE GOLF COURSES

AT THE DISNEY INN: The wide-open, tree-dotted Magnolia, which flanks the hotel to the north, plays from 5,414 (ladies) to 7,190 (championship) yards at par 72. The par-72 Palm to the south—shorter and tighter, with more wooded fairways and 9 water hazards—plays from 5,398 to 6,957 yards. The Palm was ranked among the nation's top 100 courses by *Golf Digest* magazine. Together, this pair (and the Lake Buena Vista course) hosts the big Walt Disney World/Oldsmobile Golf Classic every year, a good indication of the quality of the play to be found. Driving ranges are located near the Magnolia and Palm courses. (There's also one at the Lake Buena Vista course.)

The Executive Course: This 6-hole, 1,525-yard experimental beginner layout—a championship course-in-miniature nestled on a 25-acre corner of the Magnolia—was designed especially with the young beginner in mind. The design incorporates sand and water traps, tees and greens, just like an adult layout. But the traps are small and flat, and the water hazards are shallow enough to allow easy ball retrieval. The yardage is measured in "junior yards"—that is, only 2 feet to the yard; and the greens are made of a special low-maintenance artificial turf called Omni-Turf (which can be top-dressed to allow greater control of roll speed) instead of more-difficult-to-care-for grass. The PGA Tour, which funded the course, hopes that its ease of maintenance and low cost will encourage other communities around the country to establish similar layouts—and eventually lead to "little leagues" for young duffers.

The $10 fee for children (under 17) includes Spalding junior clubs and 12 holes of play (2 rounds). Adults pay $13 to play on the Executive Course, and it should be noted that this is a walking course only.

COURSES

AT THE VILLAGE CLUBHOUSE: Located to the south of the clubhouse and the Buena Vista Lagoon, this par-72 layout plays from 5,315 to 6,763 yards. The shortest of the trio, with the narrowest fairways, it bears less resemblance to the Magnolia than to the Palm, and it lacks the water hazards that characterize the latter.

INSTRUCTION: The Walt Disney World Golf Studio is the most compelling aspect of the golf instruction available at WDW. Each Golf Studio instructor works to help golfers develop their own styles by building on what skills they already possess. Instruction is provided via small classes with a high teacher-student ratio. Part of each lesson is recorded on videotape and then given a thorough viewing and critique. Then, to hammer in what has just been learned, the instructor repeats his suggestions and admonitions on an audiocassette tape that students can take home.

The studios, which last about 1½ hours each, are offered at 9 A.M., 11:30 A.M., and 2:30 P.M. Mondays through Saturdays at the Magnolia driving range. Call 824-2250 for reservations; the studio fee is $45, $75 including 9 holes of golf.

Private lessons: These are available at both The Disney Inn and at the Village Clubhouse at $20 per half hour with an assistant ($25 with The Disney Inn head pro Eric Fredrickson or Village Clubhouse head pro Rina Ritson, the first woman golf pro ever to hold the top position at a major golf club).

Call 824-2250 to book private lessons at The Disney Inn, 828-3741 to arrange instruction at the Village Clubhouse.

EQUIPMENT RENTAL: Titleist Pinnacle rental clubs ($15), buckets of range balls ($3.50 each), and shoes ($5) are all available at the Pro Shop—what you rent here may be better than your own gear.

TOURNAMENTS

The Walt Disney World/Oldsmobile Golf Classic, a popular spectator event that ranks as the most important on WDW's sports calendar, takes place in the fall, usually in October, and features most of the pro tour's top players. So guests who plan to play golf during their WDW vacation are advised *not* to schedule a visit for tournament week.

You can, however, play alongside the pros if you are willing to pay for it: The price of a one-year membership in the Classic Club is about $3,600. As a tourney sponsor, each member plays with 2 of the competing pros daily, for 3 of the 4 days of the tourney. While the pros are competing for cash prizes, the amateurs vie for trophies and plaques in a separate but simultaneous competition. The fee also includes lodging during the tournament, and free greens fees for a year, and admission to the Magic Kingdom, Epcot Center, and the Disney-MGM Studios Theme Park for a week. For details, phone 828-2255.

At other times of the year, smaller private competitions are held for civic, corporate, and social groups; to arrange for one (at no charge beyond the normal greens and cart fees), contact the Tournament Coordinator at 824-2275.

BOATING

Walt Disney World is the home of the country's largest fleet of pleasure boats. Most of the action is centered on 2 lakes—the 200-acre Seven Seas Lagoon, the body of water that the ferries cross and the monorails circle as they carry guests between the Transportation and Ticket Center and the Magic Kingdom; and 450-acre Bay Lake, which is connected to the Seven Seas Lagoon by the Water Bridge.

Cruising on Bay Lake and the Seven Seas Lagoon can be excellent sport, and a variety of boats are available for rent at the marinas at the Contemporary Resort, on the western shore of Bay Lake; at Fort Wilderness, to the southeast beyond Discovery Island; at the Polynesian Village, which occupies the southern edge of the Seven Seas Lagoon; at the Grand Floridian Resort; and at the Caribbean Beach Resort.

In addition, boaters can explore the lakes of Disney Village Marketplace, including 35-acre Buena Vista Lagoon.

To rent, day visitors and resort guests alike must show a resort ID, a driver's license, or a valid passport. Rental of certain craft may carry other special requirements (described below).

Note that no privately owned boats are permitted on any of the WDW waters.

SPEEDBOATS: Particularly when the weather is warm, there are always dozens of small boats zipping back and forth across the surfaces of Bay Lake, the Seven Seas Lagoon, and the lakes at Disney Village Marketplace. These are called *Water Sprites,* and they are just as much fun as they look. Though they don't go very fast, they're so small that a rider feels every bit of speed, and they zip around quickly enough so that a lot of watery terrain can be covered in a half-hour rental period ($11).

You can rent them at the Contemporary Resort, Polynesian Village, the Grand Floridian Resort, Fort Wilderness, and Disney Village Marketplace marinas. During warm weather, lines of people waiting to rent these swift little craft usually form at about 11 A.M. and remain fairly constant until about 4 P.M. The minimum rental age is 12. Even with an accompanying parent or adult, children under 12 are not allowed to drive.

SAILBOATS: The size of Bay Lake and the Seven Seas Lagoon—and their usually reliable winds—makes for good sailing, and the Contemporary Resort, Polynesian Village, Grand Floridian, and Fort Wilderness marinas rent a variety of sail craft. *Sunfish,* which can hold 2, go for $10 an hour. *Capris,* accommodating from 1 to 6—more stable because of their leaded keel, wider beam, and greater weight, and consequently better for beginners—cost $12 an hour. *Hobie Cat 14s* and *16s* cost $12 and $15 an hour respectively; catamaran experience is required. The Hobie 16, which has a mainsail and a jib, requires 2 to sail it, but cannot accommodate more than 3. Sailing conditions are usually best in March and April, and before the inevitable late-afternoon thundershowers in the summer—and that's when demand is greatest. So don't tarry. Head for the marina as soon as the urge to sail strikes.

PONTOON BOATS: *Flote Botes*—motor-powered, canopied platforms-on-pontoons, really—are perfect for families, for water lovers who aren't experienced sailors, and for older visitors more interested in serenity than thrills. They're available at the resort marinas ($35 an hour).

CANOPY BOATS: These 16-foot, V-hulled motorized boats with canopies are also good for slow cruises, and can accommodate up to six adults. They can be rented for $17.50 per half hour at the Disney Village Marketplace Marina.

PEDAL BOATS: These craft are for rent for $8 per hour at all WDW lakeside marinas for excursions on the WDW lakes. They're also available, for resort guests only, at Fort Wilderness's Bike Barn.

CANOEING: A long paddle down the glass-smooth, wooded Fort Wilderness canals is such a tranquil way to pass a misty morning that it's hard to remember that the bustle of the Magic Kingdom is just a launch ride away. Canoes are for rent at Fort Wilderness's Bike Barn ($4 per hour, $9 per day). Most

WORLD

trips last from 1 to 3 hours; those who take fishing gear can easily stay out longer. Canoes are restricted to the canals of WDW.

WATERSKIING: Ski boats with driver and full equipment ($65 an hour) are available at the Fort Wilderness, Polynesian Village, Grand Floridian, and Contemporary Resort marinas. Anyone is allowed to waterski, but there is no reduction of the posted price even if you bring along your own skis and other equipment.

FISHING

The 70,000 bass with which Bay Lake was stocked in the mid-1960s have grown and multiplied as a result of WDW's restrictive fishing policy. No angling is permitted on Bay Lake or the Seven Seas Lagoon, except on the guided 2-hour Fort Wilderness fishing expeditions. There's one leaving the campground marina each morning at around 8 A.M. and one each afternoon at around 3 P.M.; a maximum of 5 fishing persons can be accommodated on each. The fee is $110 for 2 hours ($25 for each additional hour) and includes gear, driver/guide, and coffee and pastries (in the morning) or soft drinks (in the afternoon). No license is required. Largemouth bass weighing 2 to 3 pounds each are the most common catch, though someone occasionally will reel in a bream or a bigger largemouth. Bass up to 12 pounds have been recorded.

Guests at WDW accommodations with kitchens (the villas or treehouses) may keep the contents of their creel; arrangements have been made with a local taxidermist for those guests who would like to keep their catches as souvenirs. By the way, there are no official WDW facilities for cleaning fish caught by guests. Fishing on your own is permitted in the canals in the Disney Village Resort area and at Fort Wilderness. Fort Wilderness campers can toss in their lines from any shore; villa guests can cast from the banks of the nearest canal or rent a canopy boat and chug back into remoter waters. (The waters around the Treehouses are reputed to be particularly productive.) Licenses are not required. Rods and reels are available for rent at the Bike Barn, and cane poles and lures are for sale at the Fort Wilderness trading posts.

SWIMMING

Between Bay Lake and the Seven Seas Lagoon, Walt Disney World resort guests have 5 miles of powdery white sand beach at their disposal. And that doesn't include the 11 swimming pools that come in all shapes and sizes. River Country and Typhoon Lagoon (see *Everything Else in the World*) only add to the fun.

BEACHES: When Walt Disney World was under construction during the mid-1960s, Bay Lake, with an 8-foot layer of muck on its bottom, was found to be unpolluted. It was drained and cleaned, and below the muck, engineers unearthed the pure, white sand that now edges parts of the shore, most notably at the Contemporary Resort, the Grand Floridian Resort, the Caribbean Beach Resort, and on the lake's Fort Wilderness shore. These 4 sections of beach, plus the one at the Polynesian Village, make up WDW's sandy areas. They aren't the walk-forever strands found on Florida's coasts, but they are long enough that most people don't bother to go to the end.

POOLS: There are 2 each at the Contemporary Resort, the Polynesian Village, the Disney Inn, and Fort Wilderness Resort, 7 at the Caribbean Beach Resort, and 4 at the villas of the Disney Village Resort; plus 1 each at the Village Clubhouse, the Grand Floridian Resort, Typhoon Lagoon, and at River Country. The resort pools are for registered guests only. There's no charge for admission, towels, or chairs anywhere, except at River Country and Typhoon Lagoon. One of the pair of pools at the Polynesian Village has a water slide built into great Disney-made boulders that are part of the landscaping; to get to the carved-out stairway that leads to the top, duck under a waterfall. For lap swimming, the best is the big 20-by-25-meter pool at the Contemporary Resort. When it isn't crowded (early in the morning and around dinnertime), the lifeguard is usually happy to haul in the rope that separates the deep and shallow ends. There are no diving boards at any of the pools; to practice cannonballs, head for River Country or Typhoon Lagoon, where there are large boulders made especially for leaping.

Lifeguards are on duty during most daylight hours. There is no formal swimming instruction at WDW.

In addition, each of the 7 hotels that make up Disney Village Hotel Plaza has its own pool.

DAY VISITORS: Pools and beaches at the resort hotels are not open to day guests (or to guests staying at the hotels at Disney Village Hotel Plaza). If you're just at WDW for the day and want to take a cooling break from the afternoon heat, head for River Country or Typhoon Lagoon. (See *Everything Else in the World*.)

MORE FUN STUFF

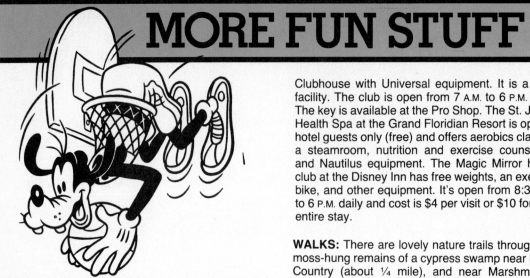

VOLLEYBALL, TETHERBALL, AND BASKET-BALL: Courts are scattered throughout the Fort Wilderness camping loops, but are open to WDW resort guests only.

JOGGING: Except in winter, late fall, and very early spring, the weather is usually too steamy in Central Florida to provide the exhilarating jogging found in cooler climes. If you run early in the morning in warm seasons, the heat is somewhat less daunting. (The scenery is also good enough to take your mind off the excess perspiration.) Guests staying at Disney Village Resort accommodations can just head out the door and run as they please along winding drives where everything is green and blessedly quiet. The 1.4-mile promenade around the Caribbean Beach Resort's lake also is perfect for jogging. Fort Wilderness offers a partially paved, 2.3-mile course that's punctuated by exercise stations.

Jogging maps that outline the Fort Wilderness route, as well as the best routes from the Contemporary Resort, the Polynesian Village, The Disney Inn, the Grand Floridian, and around the Disney Village Resort, are available at Guest Services desks in hotels and villa check-in areas; mileages range from 3.4 to 4.2 miles.

FORT WILDERNESS'S EXERCISE TRAIL: This 2.3-mile course gives joggers the chance to do chin-ups, sit-ups, and other exercises on special apparatus. Signs explain all the maneuvers—and it's almost all in the shade. There is no charge.

THE SPA: The Contemporary Resort's Olympiad Health Club (located on the hotel's 3rd floor) has Nautilus gym equipment—perfect for a good workout. Afterward, it's almost not necessary—though it's decidedly pleasant—to relax in the sauna or in individual whirlpools. For use of the facilities, the cost is $4; whirlpools are an additional $5. The hours at the health club are 9 A.M. to 6 P.M. daily, closed Sundays. Facilities are open to men and women at alternate times. Call 824-3410 for appointments and further information on hours. Note that the Spa is open to both day and resort guests. There is also a new health club at the Village

Clubhouse with Universal equipment. It is a coed facility. The club is open from 7 A.M. to 6 P.M. daily. The key is available at the Pro Shop. The St. John's Health Spa at the Grand Floridian Resort is open to hotel guests only (free) and offers aerobics classes, a steamroom, nutrition and exercise counselors, and Nautilus equipment. The Magic Mirror health club at the Disney Inn has free weights, an exercise bike, and other equipment. It's open from 8:30 A.M. to 6 P.M. daily and cost is $4 per visit or $10 for your entire stay.

WALKS: There are lovely nature trails through the moss-hung remains of a cypress swamp near River Country (about ¼ mile), and near Marshmallow Marsh at Fort Wilderness. The latter, about a mile long, leads along the reedy, sunny shores of Bay Lake, then heads into the cool woods before looping back to the starting point.

BIKING: Pedaling along the 8 miles of bike paths that weave through the Disney Village Resort and the lightly trafficked roads there and at Fort Wilderness can be a pleasant way to spend a couple of hours—especially in the winter, or in the mornings and late afternoons during the rest of the year, when it's not too hot. Both areas are sufficiently spread out that bicycles are a practical means of getting around. If you don't bring your own bike, you can rent one at Fort Wilderness's Bike Barn or at the Villa Center at the Disney Village Resort for $2.10 an hour or $5.25 per day. Tandems are available at the Bike Barn and at the Villa Center ($3 an hour or $7 a day). Anyone is allowed to ride bikes on the property.

HORSEBACK RIDING: Trail rides into the pine woods and scrubby palmetto country leave from the middle of the Fort Wilderness Campground at 9 A.M., 10:30 A.M., noon, and 2 P.M. daily. This is not for big-time gallopers—you can't ride off on your own— and the horses have been culled for gentleness, so that the trips are suitable even for non-riders. Cost is $10 a person for both day visitors and resort guests (no children under 9 are accepted). For advance reservations, which are recommended, phone W-DISNEY (934-7639).

GOOD MEALS, GREAT TIMES

In the Magic Kingdom, fast food is king: Even machines that broil 2,800 hamburgers an hour have a tough time keeping up with the demand, and in the course of just a single year, enough burgers are served to allow an individual to eat one for every inch of the 400 miles from Orlando to Atlanta.

But that is by no means all of the Walt Disney World food story. Epcot Center has added international flavors to the WDW palate—it's now possible to sample everything from maple syrup pie and bratwurst to steak and kidney pie, fettucine Alfredo, and mole poblano.

Add the numerous restaurants at the Disney Village Marketplace, the unique options at the Disney-MGM Studios Theme Park, and the first other-than-Disney-run eateries at Pleasure Island and deciding where to dine can become a confusing dilemma.

Because the number of restaurants, snack spots, cafeterias, and other miscellaneous eateries around the World is so large and so varied, this chapter presents meal information in 3 different ways. To find a specific restaurant, we've provided an alphabetized directory to all restaurants on the property—with their exact locations. So if you know the name of a desired dining place, this directory will tell you where to find it.

If you are getting hungry in a particular area of the World, and want to know what's available in the immediate vicinity, the second section of this chapter offers an area-by-area rundown of all operative eateries. Detailed data on each restaurant's atmosphere, decor, and specialties are also included.

Finally, to help in the planning of systematic programs for eating a broad swath across the World, this chapter also contains a meal-by-meal selection of eating places. These restaurants are organized by breakfast, lunch, and dinner specialties, and we've indicated certain entries for which we think it's worth going a bit out of your way. Note that menus and prices may vary during the year.

This chapter contains eating places within the boundaries of Walt Disney World only (including Hotel Plaza establishments).

The letters that conclude each restaurant entry are a key to the meals served there: breakfast (B), lunch (L), dinner (D), or snacks (S).

The list below includes all the restaurants and snack spots currently operating in Walt Disney World—at the hotels, at Fort Wilderness Resort, at the Disney Village Marketplace, at Pleasure Island, and in the Magic Kingdom, Epcot Center, and the Disney-MGM Studios Theme Park.

Adventureland Veranda: Magic Kingdom; at the east edge of Adventureland, between the bridge to the Hub and the Swiss Family Island Treehouse

Akershus: Epcot Center; in the Norway pavilion, in World Showcase

All American Sandwich Shop: Disney Village Marketplace, near the Gourmet Pantry

Aloha Isle: Magic Kingdom; in Adventureland, adjoining the Adventureland Veranda on the west

Aunt Polly's Landing: Magic Kingdom; in Frontierland, on Tom Sawyer Island

Au Petit Cafe: Epcot Center; on the World Showcase Promenade in the France pavilion, in World Showcase

Backlot Express: Disney-MGM Studios Theme Park; near the Epic Stunt Theater

Back Porch Lounge: The Disney Inn; in the Garden Gallery

Baton Rouge Lounge: Pleasure Island; on the main deck of the *Empress Lilly*

Beach Shack: Fort Wilderness Resort; near the beach

Beverage Base: Epcot Center; in CommuniCore East, near the Stargate Restaurant

Biergarten: Epcot Center; to the rear of the St. Georgsplatz in the Germany pavilion, in World Showcase

Bistro de Paris: Epcot Center; upstairs at the France pavilion, in World Showcase

Boulangerie Pâtisserie: Epcot Center; France pavilion, around the corner from Chefs de France, in World Showcase

Bratwurst Wagon: Disney-MGM Studios Theme Park; across from Min & Bill's Dockside Diner

Bridgetown Broiler: Caribbean Beach Resort; at Old Port Royale

Cantina de San Angel: Epcot Center; on the World Showcase Promenade opposite the Mexico pavilion's pyramid, in World Showcase

Cap'n Jack's Oyster Bar: Disney Village Marketplace; on the edge of Buena Vista Lagoon

Captain Cook's Snack and Ice Cream Company: Polynesian Village; on the lobby level of the Great Ceremonial House

Catwalk Bar: Disney-MGM Studios Theme Park; above the Soundstage Restaurant

Character Cafe: Contemporary Resort; adjoining the Terrace Buffeteria

Chef Mickey's Village Restaurant: Disney Village Marketplace; on the shores of Buena Vista Lagoon

Chefs de France: Epcot Center; France pavilion, in World Showcase

Churro Wagon: Magic Kingdom; at the entrance to Frontierland

Cinnamon Bay Bakery: Caribbean Beach Resort; at Old Port Royale

Columbia Harbour House: Magic Kingdom; in Liberty Square near the entrance to Fantasyland

Coral Isle Cafe: Polynesian Village; on the second floor of the Great Ceremonial House, around the corner from Papeete Bay

Coral Reef Restaurant: Epcot Center; in Future World's The Living Seas

Crockett's Tavern: Fort Wilderness Resort; in Pioneer Hall

Crystal Palace: Magic Kingdom; near the Adventureland Bridge, at the north end of Main Street

Desserts & Things: Epcot Center; in Future World's Wonders of Life

Diamond Horseshoe: Magic Kingdom; in Frontierland at the edge of Liberty Square

Diamond Mine: The Disney Inn; in Happy's Hollow

Dinosaur Gertie's: Disney-MGM Studios Theme Park; on Echo Lake

Dock Inn: Contemporary Resort; in the Marina Pavilion near the beach

D-Zertz: Pleasure Island; near Propeller Heads

Egg Roll Wagon: Magic Kingdom; in Adventureland, outside the Adventureland Veranda

El Pirata y El Perico: Magic Kingdom; in Adventureland, opposite Pirates of the Caribbean

Empress Lounge: Pleasure Island; aboard the *Empress Lilly*

Empress Room: Pleasure Island; aboard the *Empress Lilly*

Enchanted Grove: Magic Kingdom; east side of Fantasyland, opposite Tomorrowland Terrace

Fantasyland Pretzel Wagon: Magic Kingdom; between Pinocchio Village Haus and Cinderella's Golden Carrousel

Farmers Market: Epcot Center; on the first floor of Future World's The Land

Fiesta Fun Center Snack Bar: Contemporary Resort; first floor

50's Prime Time Cafe: Disney-MGM Studios Theme Park; on the south side of Echo Lake

Fireworks Factory: Pleasure Island; near the *Empress Lilly*

Fisherman's Deck: Pleasure Island; aboard the *Empress Lilly*

Flagler's: Grand Floridian; on the second floor of the main building

The Garden Gallery: The Disney Inn; off the lobby

Gasparilla Grill and Games: Grand Floridian; on the first floor of the main building

Grand Floridian Cafe: Grand Floridian; on the first floor of the main building

Gurgi's Munchies & Crunchies: Magic Kingdom; in Fantasyland, near 20,000 Leagues Under the Sea and Dumbo the Flying Elephant

Handwich Wagon: Disney-MGM Studios Theme Park; near Echo Lake

Hollywood Brown Derby: Disney-MGM Studios Theme Park; on Hollywood Boulevard

Hollywood & Vine Cafeteria: Disney-MGM Studios Theme Park; on Hollywood Boulevard

Hot Dog Wagon: Disney-MGM Studios Theme Park; near the Chinese Theater

King Stefan's Banquet Hall: Magic Kingdom; in Cinderella Castle

Kringla Bakeri og Kafe: Epcot Center; in the Norway pavilion, in World Showcase

Lakeside Terrace: Disney Village Marketplace; near Crystal Arts

The Land Grille Room: Epcot Center; on the second floor of Future World's The Land

Leaning Palms: Typhoon Lagoon; near the main entrance

Le Cellier: Epcot Center; near Victoria Gardens and the *O Canada!* film's exit in the Canada pavilion, in World Showcase

Liberty Inn: Epcot Center; alongside The American Adventure

Liberty Tree Tavern: Magic Kingdom; in Liberty Square

L'Originale Alfredo di Roma Ristorante: Epcot Center; on the east side of the piazza in the Italy pavilion, in World Showcase

Lotus Blossom Cafe: Epcot Center; China pavilion, in World Showcase

Lunching Pad: Magic Kingdom; near Mickey's Mart, in Tomorrowland

Main Street Bakery & Cookie Shop: Magic Kingdom; on the east side of Main Street, halfway between the Hub and Town Square

Marrakesh: Epcot Center; Morocco pavilion, in World Showcase

Meadow Trading Post: Fort Wilderness Resort; near the playing fields

Merriweather's Market: Pleasure Island; near Propeller Heads

Mickey's Tropical Revue: Polynesian Village Resort; Luau Cove

The Mile Long Bar: Magic Kingdom; in Frontierland, between Pecos Bill's and the Country Bear Vacation Hoedown

Min & Bill's Dockside Diner: Disney-MGM Studios Theme Park; on Echo Lake

Minnie Mia's Pizzeria: Disney Village Marketplace; near the Village Ice Cream Parlour

Mitsukoshi Restaurant: Epcot Center; on the second floor of the large building on the west side of the plaza in the Japan pavilion

Montego's Market: Caribbean Beach Resort; at Old Port Royale

Narcoossee's: Grand Floridian; at the end of the dock near the marina

Nacho Wagon: Magic Kingdom; in Frontierland, near Pecos Bill's Cafe

Nacho Wagon: Disney-MGM Studios Theme Park; near the Chinese Theater

Nine Dragons Restaurant: Epcot Center; China pavilion, in World Showcase

1900 Park Fare: Grand Floridian; on the first floor of the main building

Oasis: Magic Kingdom; in Adventureland, near the Jungle Cruise

Odyssey Restaurant: Epcot Center; astradle the Future World/World Showcase boundary, near the Mexico pavilion

Outer Rim: Contemporary Resort; on the east side of the Grand Canyon Concourse (fourth floor)

Orbiter Lounge: Pleasure Island; in the XZFR Rockin' Rollerdrome

Oriental Cargo: Caribbean Beach Resort; at Old Port Royale

Papeete Bay Verandah: Polynesian Village; second floor of the Great Ceremonial House

Pecos Bill Cafe: Magic Kingdom; near the Walt Disney World Railroad's Frontierland depot

Pinocchio Village Haus: Magic Kingdom; in Fantasyland, adjoining It's A Small World on the east

Plaza Pavilion: Magic Kingdom; east of the Plaza Restaurant, on the edge of Tomorrowland

Plaza Restaurant: Magic Kingdom; on Main Street around the corner from Sealtest Ice Cream Parlor

Polynesian Revue: Polynesian Village Resort; Luau Cove

Pompano Grill: Disney Village Resort

Portobello Yacht Club: Pleasure Island; near the *Empress Lilly*

Pop's Place: Fort Wilderness Resort; inside River Country

Port Royale Hamburger Shop: Caribbean Beach Resort; at Old Port Royale

Potato Wagon: Magic Kingdom; in Liberty Square, next to Columbia Harbour House

Pueblo Room: Contemporary Resort; south end of the Grand Canyon Concourse (fourth floor)

Refreshment Corner: Magic Kingdom; on the west side of Main Street, opposite Sealtest Ice Cream Parlor

Refreshment Outpost: Epcot Center; next to the Canada pavilion, in World Showcase

Refreshment Port: Epcot Center; between the China and Germany pavilions, in World Showcase

Rose & Crown Pub & Dining Room: Epcot Center; on the World Showcase Promenade, in the United Kingdom pavilion

Round Table: Magic Kingdom; in Fantasyland near Cinderella's Golden Carrousel

Royale Pizza & Pasta Shop: Caribbean Beach Resort; at Old Port Royale

San Angel Inn: Epcot Center; inside the Mexico pavilion's pyramid, in World Showcase

Sand Bar: Contemporary Resort; in the Marina Pavilion near the beach

Sand Trap: The Disney Inn; downstairs next to the Pro Shop

Sealtest Ice Cream Parlor: Magic Kingdom; on the east side of Main Street, opposite Refreshment Corner

Settlement Trading Post: Fort Wilderness Campground; near the Fort Wilderness marina and Pioneer Hall

Sleepy Hollow: Magic Kingdom; in Liberty Square, opposite Olde World Antiques

Soundstage Restaurant: Disney-MGM Studios Theme Park; near the Animation Building

Space Bar: Magic Kingdom; at the base of the StarJets in the center of Tomorrowland

Spinners: Pleasure Island; in the XZFR Rockin' Rollerdrome

Stargate Restaurant: Epcot Center; in Future World's CommuniCore East

Starring Rolls Bakery: Disney-MGM Studios Theme Park; on Hollywood Boulevard

Station Break: Magic Kingdom; beneath the Main Street train station

Steerman's Quarters: Pleasure Island; aboard the *Empress Lilly*

Studio Catering Company: Disney-MGM Studios Theme Park; at the Studio Tour break area

Sunrise Terrace Restaurant: Epcot Center; in Future World's CommuniCore West

Sunshine Tree Terrace: Magic Kingdom; in Adventureland, adjoining the Enchanted Tiki Room

Sweet Surrender: Pleasure Island; near Avigators Supply Company

Tambu Lounge: Polynesian Village; adjoining Papeete Bay, on the second floor of the Great Ceremonial House

Tangaroa Snack Isle: Polynesian Village; in a separate building near the east swimming pool

Tangaroa Terrace: Polynesian Village; in a separate building on the eastern edge of the property

Tempura Kiku: Epcot Center; on the second floor of the Japan Pavilion

Thirsty Perch: Discovery Island

Tomorrowland Terrace: Magic Kingdom; at the Fantasyland edge of Tomorrowland, opposite the Grand Prix Raceway

Tony's Town Square Cafe: Magic Kingdom; east side of Town Square at the south end of Main Street

Top of the World: Contemporary Resort; on the 15th floor

Tournament Tent: Magic Kingdom; in Fantasyland, near the Fantasy Faire Theater

Trails End Buffet: Fort Wilderness Resort; in Pioneer Hall

Troubadour Tavern: Magic Kingdom; in Fantasyland, next to Peter Pan's Flight

Tune In Lounge: Disney-MGM Studios Theme Park; adjacent to the 50's Prime Time Cafe; on Hollywood Boulevard

Typhoon Tilly's Galley & Grog: Typhoon Lagoon; near Shark Reef

Victoria & Albert's: Grand Floridian; on the second floor of the main building

Villa Centers: Disney Village Resort pool areas

Village Clubhouse Snack Bar: Disney Village Resort

Village Ice Cream Parlour and Bake Shop: Disney Village Marketplace

Village Lounge: Disney Village Marketplace; next to the Village Restaurant

Westward Ho: Magic Kingdom; in Frontierland, near Pecos Bill's Cafe

Yakitori House: Epcot Center; on the east side of the Japan pavilion's plaza, in World Showcase

MAIN STREET

FULL SERVICE

Tony's Town Square Cafe: This is one of the best bets for Magic Kingdom meals. The menu offers Italian specialties, steaks, and seafood. Pizza and burgers with selected toppings are perennial favorites. Other lunch specialties include fresh pasta salads, a deli platter, and a fresh fruit plate. At dinner there are grilled fresh fish, New York strip steaks, lasagna primavera, chicken with basil, and spaghetti with meatballs. For dessert: Italian pastries, orange cheesecake, and spumoni complement a cup of freshly brewed espresso or cappuccino. Children's menus and menus for guests with special dietary needs are available. The decor comes straight out of Walt Disney's film, "Lady and the Tramp." It is genteelly Victorian, with plenty of polished brass and curlicued, beautifully painted woodwork. The terrazzo-floored patio gives diners a fine view over the action in Town Square.

Full breakfasts are also served: eggs, pancakes, Mickey Mouse character waffles, cold cereals (with skim milk on request), cinnamon biscuits, and Danish pastry. B, L, D.

Plaza Restaurant: This airy, many-windowed establishment, around the corner from the Sealtest Ice Cream Parlor, is done in mirrors with sinuously curved Art Nouveau frames. The menu offers hot dishes, along with fresh salads, hamburgers, and sandwiches—plus milk shakes, floats, and the biggest sundaes in the Magic Kingdom. Cafe mocha, which combines chocolate and coffee, is another specialty. L, D, S.

CAFETERIA SERVICE

Crystal Palace: One of the Magic Kingdom's landmarks, and its only cafeteria. Modeled after a similar structure that once stood in New York State

and after another that still graces San Francisco's Golden Gate Park, it serves standard cafeteria fare. Menu offerings include prime ribs, spit-roasted chicken, baked fresh fish, pasta dishes, and healthy salads. A wide assortment of tempting desserts is also available.

This is civilized fare, and the fact that it's here at all is just more proof—as if any were needed—that the Magic Kingdom is not just for kids. The place is huge but not overwhelming, because the tables are well-spaced throughout a variety of nooks and crannies. Tables in the front look out onto flower beds and the passing throng beyond, while those at the east end have views into a secluded courtyard.

The Crystal Palace is also one of the few spots in the Magic Kingdom to serve full breakfasts—scrambled eggs and hashed brown potatoes, biscuits, sausage, bacon, ham, hotcakes, French toast, Danish pastry, and cold cereal. B, L, D, S.

VENDORS

Throughout the Magic Kingdom, there are ice cream wagons that sell Cookies 'n' Cream ice cream sandwiches, Mouse Bars, and two especially wonderful frozen treats—frozen bananas and strawberry bars.

Popcorn wagons all over the park contribute their lovely aromas all day long. The Center Street Wagons near the intersection of Main Street U.S.A. and Center Street sell hot dogs, pastries, and soft drinks.

At Epcot Center, vendors purvey soft drinks, strawberry bars, pineapple-orange-juice bars, and ice cream galore.

FAST FOOD AND SNACK SPOTS

Refreshment Corner: The small, round tables at this spacious, old-fashioned, red-and-white stop on the west side of Main Street (located near the Crystal Palace) spill out onto the sidewalk. Except when the weather is terrifically hot, it's a delightful spot for fast food—hot dogs (plain or cheese, regular and jumbo sizes), brownies, soft drinks, and coffee. During busy periods a pianist is on hand to plink away on the restaurant's white upright. L, D, S.

Main Street Bakery & Cookie Shop: This genteel little tearoom, with its small, round tables and cane chairs, is a good place for a light breakfast, a midmorning coffee break, or a mid-afternoon rest stop. Assorted pastries, cakes, and pies are the main temptations. Also offered are delicious chocolate chunk, oatmeal raisin, sugar, fudge, and peanut butter cookies baked fresh on the premises. B, S.

Sealtest Ice Cream Parlor: Ice cream lovers from all over the country converge on this corner of the Kingdom, which boasts the World's best variety of ice cream flavors. S.

ADVENTURELAND

FAST FOOD AND SNACK SPOTS

Adventureland Veranda: Bougainvillea cascades over the edges of a red tile roof that looks as if it came straight out of the tropics. Tables are clustered outside on a small patio and inside under slowly rotating fans hung from mahogany ceilings. Off to the east end of this pretty, sprawling restaurant are a couple of open-air patios with views of Cinderella Castle. Screened from the gazes of passersby, these are among the most delightful meal sites in all the Magic Kingdom. Special Adventureland Veranda hamburgers and chicken with teriyaki sauce are among the offerings. Other Americanized versions of Oriental specialties also have

their fans. For dessert: fresh fruit and assorted pies.

Note that waiting lines here usually take a few minutes longer than those of similar lengths in other fast-food establishments because of the greater number of choices. L, D, S.

Aloha Isle: Adjoining the Adventureland Veranda (on the west), this refreshment stand often sells pineapple spears and juice along with other tropical offerings including Dole Whip soft serve. S.

Egg Roll Wagon: Located just outside the Adventureland Veranda, this wagon features an assortment of eggrolls. S.

El Pirata y El Perico: In English, the Spanish name of this snack stand, directly across from Pirates of the Caribbean (outside La Princesa de Cristal), means The Pirate and The Parrot. The offerings: hot dogs with assorted toppings, including chili and cheese, and a good selection of Disney Handwiches. L, S.

The Oasis: Tucked away near the Jungle Cruise. The perfect spot for a soft drink. S.

Sunshine Tree Terrace: So close to the Enchanted Tiki Birds that you can hear the Audio-Animatronics parrot José squawking his spiel. Offerings here are some of the tastiest in the Kingdom: orange slush, shakes, frozen yogurt, soft drinks, and the excellent citrus swirl—soft-serve ice cream swirled through with a not-too-sweet frozen-orange-juice concentrate. B, S.

FRONTIERLAND

FULL SERVICE

The Diamond Horseshoe: Several times daily, from about noon until early evening, a troupe of singers and dancers presents a sometimes corny, occasionally sidesplitting, always entertaining show in this Wild West dance-hall saloon. Waitresses serve potato and corn chips, freshly baked pies, fruit punch, and cold sandwiches before the show begins. Reservations are required, and they're hard to come by. They must be made in person, at the Hospitality House on Main Street, and you can't count on getting them if you arrive much more than an hour after the Magic Kingdom opens. Those who miss the deadline can line up for possible cancellations, but with little hope of success except on days when the weather is so bad that some visitors depart early. L, S.

FAST FOOD AND SNACK SPOTS

Pecos Bill Cafe: This is not one of those Magic Kingdom eateries that is tucked away so that only those who look will find it. Sooner or later, almost every guest passing from Adventureland into Frontierland—ambling by the Frontierland depot of the Walt Disney World Railroad on the way to Big Thunder or the Country Bear Vacation Hoedown—walks by Pecos Bill. And as a sidewalk café, this establishment—fitted out with leather-seated chairs, ceilings made of twigs, and red tile floors—has few peers. There are tables indoors (in air conditioned rooms) and outdoors, under umbrellas and in an open-air courtyard. Hamburgers, cheeseburgers, barbecued chicken sandwiches, and hot dogs are the staples. L, D, S.

Mile Long Bar: The bar, a gleaming and intricately detailed beauty with a brass rail on which to lean and a set of antlers above, just goes on and on, or so it seems at first glance. Actually, it's the mirrors at either end that produce the effect that gives this relatively small refreshment stand its name. Three shaggy animal heads hang on the walls, in keeping with the Wild West theme. Guests who stand around long enough will see one animal turn to another and wink, for these are Audio-Animatronics figures just like the ones on the walls at the Country Bear Vacation Hoedown. The fare includes assorted Tex-Mex dishes like tacos, taco salads, burritos, and nachos. Definitely worth a peek. L, D, S.

Aunt Polly's Landing: The much-trumpeted sense of getting away from it all that islands always convey comes home once again out on Frontierland's Tom Sawyer Island. Though only a couple of minutes' ride across the Rivers of America via the

Tom Sawyer Island Rafts, this landfall manages to seem remote even when there are dozens of youngsters clamoring through its caves, over its hills, and across its rickety barrel bridges. Therein lies the charm of Aunt Polly's. While the adults in a party get some well-needed R&R sipping lemonade in the shade of the old-fashioned porch and watching the gleaming white riverboats docking or chugging by, the kids can go out exploring and, at nearby Fort Sam Clemens, ping the toy rifles perched on the gunholes as if there were no tomorrow—an activity as delightful for youngsters as it is dispensable for grown-ups. It doesn't even matter that Aunt Polly's offers a selection barely wider than the fare that that lady might have served her youthful nephew—peanut-butter-and-jelly and ham and cheese sandwiches, apple pies, cookies, iced tea, lemonade, and soda. An excellent choice for lunch. L, S.

Westward Ho: Soft drinks and snacks are available at this stand across from Pecos Bill Cafe. S.

LIBERTY SQUARE

FULL SERVICE

Liberty Tree Tavern: At this pillared and porticoed eatery opposite the riverboat landing, the floors are made of wide oak planks, the wallpaper

looks as if it might have come from Williamsburg, the curtains hang from cloth loops, and the venetian blinds are made of wood. Pieces of pewter and Windsor and ladder-backed chairs are scattered throughout the premises; there's a spinning wheel and a hope chest in the waiting room; and an old-fashioned writing desk and a cradle, copper bowls, and tea kettles arranged near the wide fireplace. The window glass was made using 18th-century casting methods, and most of the tables and chairs were mass-produced (for sturdiness' sake). So the Liberty Tree Tavern's charm is not of a random type.

At lunch, the staples are oversize salads and assorted sandwiches. Dinner offerings include fresh fish, shrimp, prime ribs, chicken, and lobster. Oysters and New England clam chowder are served at both meals. L, D.

FAST FOOD AND SNACK SPOTS

Columbia Harbour House: This is a fast-food shrimp house with some class. Clam chowder, salads, and assorted sandwiches, including a Monte Cristo (a batter-dipped, deep-fried turkey, ham, and swiss cheese combination), are also available. There are enough antiques and other knick-knacks decking the halls to raise this place, located near the Liberty Square entrance to Fantasyland, above the ordinary. Model ships, copper measures, harpoons, and nautical instruments, and little tie-back curtains, small-print wallpaper, and low-beamed ceilings give the place a cozy air—despite its size. L, D, S.

Sleepy Hollow: Soft drinks, brownies, Disney Handwiches, and a special Legendary Punch (fruity and not half bad) are for sale at this snack stand located opposite Olde World Antiques, near the Liberty Square bridge. Eat on the secluded brick patio outside. B, L, D, S.

MAGIC KINGDOM MEALTIME TIPS

• The hours from 11 A.M. to 2 P.M., and again from about 5 P.M. to 7 P.M., are the mealtime rush hours in Magic Kingdom restaurants. Eat earlier or later whenever possible.

• When a restaurant has more than one food-service window, don't just amble into the nearest queue. Instead, inspect them all, because the one farthest from a doorway occasionally will be almost wait-free.

• Lines at the Adventureland Veranda don't move as quickly as those at most other fast-food eateries.

• Sit-down restaurants offering full-scale meals are usually less crowded at lunch than they are at dinner.

• To avoid queues, eat at a restaurant that offers reservations—Liberty Tree Tavern in Liberty Square and King Stefan's at both lunch and dinner, and the Diamond Horseshoe, a western-style saloon in Frontierland that serves cold sandwiches and presents an amusing show at lunchtime. Reservations for the Liberty Tree Tavern and King Stefan's can be made at the restaurants; Diamond Horseshoe reservations should be made at the Hospitality House on Main Street; book them as soon as you arrive in the Magic Kingdom.

FANTASYLAND

FULL SERVICE

King Stefan's Banquet Hall: The hostesses at this establishment (named for Sleeping Beauty's father) wear 13th-century-style French head-dresses and long medieval gowns with over-skirts.

The hall itself is high-ceilinged and as majestic as the old mead hall it is supposed to represent. The delightful fruit or seafood salads or roast beef sandwiches on the noontime menu make lunch here pleasant indeed. At dinner, there are prime ribs, seafood, and chicken. There's also a children's menu and Cinderella is usually on hand to entertain children and grown-ups alike.

Reservations are required for both lunch and dinner. To make them, present yourself at the Castle door as soon after arriving in the Magic Kingdom as possible. L, D.

FAST FOOD AND SNACK SPOTS

Pinocchio Village Haus: This is another of those Magic Kingdom restaurants that seems a lot smaller from the outside than it really is, thanks to a labyrinthine arrangement of a half dozen rooms decorated with antique cuckoo clocks, European tile-fronted ovens, oak peasant chairs, and murals depicting characters from Pinocchio's story—Figaro the Cat, Cleo the Goldfish, Monstro the Whale, and Geppetto, the puppet's creator. The menu offers fried chicken strips, hot dogs, hamburgers, and cheeseburgers all served with french fries. L, D, S.

Enchanted Grove: A small stand that's the perfect spot for lemonade, lemonade slush, or a soft serve swirl. S.

Troubadour Tavern: Soft drinks and chips are available at this small refreshment stand west of Cinderella's Golden Carrousel. S.

The Round Table: Ice cream gets top billing here—soft-serve cones in chocolate, vanilla, and chocolate-vanilla swirl; hot fudge sundaes; and root beer floats. S.

Tournament Tent: Soft drinks and milk shakes are on the menu. (Open seasonally.) S.

Gurgi's Munchies & Crunchies: Located near Dumbo the Flying Elephant, catering to kids with a variety of selections to please finicky eaters. L, D, S.

TOMORROWLAND

FAST FOOD AND SNACK SHOPS

Tomorrowland Terrace: The largest fast-food spot in the Magic Kingdom, where the menu features hot and cold sandwiches and soups and salads. L, D, S.

The Lunching Pad: This small spot between the Space Port and Mickey's Mart serves natural foods, frozen yogurt, and fresh fruit. L, S.

Plaza Pavilion: Just east of the Plaza Restaurant, this sleek pink-and-purple-and-orange spot on the edge of Tomorrowland serves pan pizzas, pasta salad, and Italian specialty sandwiches. Some particularly pleasant tables look past the graceful willow trees nearby, toward the Hub Waterways and an impressive topiary sea serpent. L, D, S.

WEDway Space Bar: Located at the base of the StarJets in the center of Tomorrowland's vast concrete plaza, this small spot offers Disney Handwiches, which are bread cones with a variety of fillings that can be easily consumed using only one hand, and chips, plus assorted desserts and a variety of soft drinks. L, S.

A WORD TO THE WISE

Ride Space Mountain *before* eating, not afterward. The trip can uncomfortably jostle even the strongest stomach.

IN EPCOT CENTER

Restaurants within each area of Epcot Center are described as they would be encountered in Future World while moving counterclockwise from Space-ship Earth, and in World Showcase while walking counterclockwise around World Showcase Lagoon. **Note:** Reservations are an absolute must at certain Epcot Center restaurants, and they aren't easy to come by without following the instructions that can be found in the box on page 215.

FUTURE WORLD

FAST FOOD AND SNACK SPOTS

Sunrise Terrace Restaurant: Fried cod, fried shrimp, and boneless fried chicken strips are the specialties at this emporium located in Communi-Core West, opposite the Stargate Restaurant. This is not, however, a typically utilitarian fast-food establishment. It is a comfortable place, decorated in violet and gray shades (with touches of scarlet) and some unusually beautiful neon lights. And the food is not conventional, frozen, pre-breaded fare. It's freshly batter-dipped instead. Chef's salads and fruit salads, cornbread muffins, clam and corn chowder, peanut butter cookies, and dessert cups round out the offerings. The Sunrise Terrace stays open until one hour before Epcot Center closes, so it's a good spot to stop on your way out of the park. L, D, S.

Farmers Market: One of the most interesting of the Epcot Center eateries, and a new wrinkle on the Walt Disney World fast-food scene, this handful of very special counter service stands is located on the lower level of The Land pavilion. Each of these stands boasts a unique menu. The soup-and-salad stand offers New England fish chowder, chicken gumbo, impressive fruit salads served in half a pineapple, tuna- and chicken-salad-stuffed toma-toes, and generous vegetable salads with Swiss cheese. **The Bakery**'s morning offerings include bagels and cream cheese, sticky buns, Danish pastries, and bran, corn, and blueberry muffins. After 11 A.M., apple, pecan, Boston cream, orange

chiffon, and lemon meringue pies appear, along with cheesecake and chocolate cake, rich-looking brownies, hermit cookies with cinnamon, and loaves of date-nut bread and cheese bread (the same cheese bread served upstairs in the Land Grille Room)—plus chocolate chip cookies baked on the premises. (These are so delicious that some Disney employees make special trips to The Land just to nibble on them.)

The **barbecue store** sells barbecued beef sand-wiches, barbecued chicken-breast sandwiches, half chickens, beans, and cornbread muffins. **The Cheese Shoppe** offers cheese and fruit platters and quiche—not only the standard varieties that come with cheese or with bacon, onions, and mush-rooms, but also a widely celebrated, newly devel-oped pizza quiche. The **Picnic Fare** selections in-clude assorted cheeses, smoked sausage, and fresh fruit. A **sandwich stand** regales the hungry with several types of hefty combinations, including the Disney Handwich, while an **ice cream stand** tempts guests with cooling cones and cups. **The Potato Store** serves steaming baked potatoes stuffed with beef-in-wine sauce, cheddar cheese with bacon, or other fillings. Even the **Beverage House** here offers something special—not only chocolate, strawberry, or vanilla milk shakes, choc-olate milk, buttermilk, hot chocolate, and an array of soft drinks, but also vegetable juice, peach nectar, papaya juice, and orange juice.

Each stand has a farm-style facade done in bright colors, not unlike those that might be found in agri-cultural exhibit buildings at a midwestern state fair. With bright, umbrella-topped tables nearby, the ef-fect is cheery. Because of the wide variety of foods available here, this is one of the best bets in Epcot Center for a family that can't agree on what to eat. It's also a good spot for weight watchers. B, L, D, S.

Odyssey Restaurant: Located practically astride the Future World/World Showcase border, near the Mexico pavilion, the Odyssey is accessible via three walkways—near the Mexico pavilion, the World of

Motion, or the World Showcase Plaza's WorldKey Information System kiosk. This handsome, hexagonally shaped establishment looks less like a fast-food eatery than a moderately fancy sit-down restaurant. That's partly because of the decor, a subtle amalgam of rusts and ochres, with a carpeted floor and walls and a profusion of green plants. It's also partly because the food service lines are tucked away from the main dining area. The fact that tables are spread over several levels enhances the already pleasant ambience by making the whole place feel smaller than it really is. There's never the feeling of having arrived in a cavernous mess hall.

As for the menu, it's absolutely all-American: hamburgers, hot dogs, plus platters of chicken, tuna, and ambrosia salads. Freshly baked pies are a special treat. Best of all, the restaurant—located just a bit off the main pedestrian path—is less heavily patronized than some other more visible eating spots. L, D, S.

Desserts & Things: Located in the Wonders of Life pavilion, this snack spot offers a variety of healthy treats including frozen yogurt, yogurt shakes, oat bran waffles, muffins, and more. S.

Stargate Restaurant: This large fast-food establishment, located in CommuniCore East, is handsomely decorated in shades of blue, mauve, and magenta. It's a particularly good bet when the weather is temperate enough to allow dining at the tables on the terrace outside—or when bound for World Showcase with finicky eaters in tow. It's also one of the few Epcot Center restaurants open for breakfast. Cold cereals, Danish pastries, fruit cups, blueberry muffins, and cheese omelets served with creditable home-fried potatoes are available then. But the real specialty is the extremely satisfying, if extravagantly named, "Stellar Scramble." Made of cheese, ham, onions, green pepper, and scrambled eggs, this "breakfast pizza" might not win any prizes among connoisseurs of haute cuisine, but it's unquestionably tasty. At lunch and dinner, offerings include pepperoni or cheese pizzas, hamburgers,

steak sandwiches, fruit salads, and chef's salads. The peanut butter cookies and dessert cups are good, too. The Stargate Restaurant stays open until the park closes. B, L, D, S.

FULL SERVICE

The Land Grille Room: Sleek wood-trimmed booths, upholstered in garnet-red velvet and illuminated with handsome brass lamps, make this an exceptionally attractive restaurant. A new menu offers diners a sample-size portion and an entrée-size portion of most dishes so that they can sample more than one choice. Dinners feature roast tuna loin, mesquite-grilled boneless baby salmon served with orange walnut butter, oriental spiced chicken, broiled steak, and a special seasonal American wild game offering. There is a selection of regional pizzas with a variety of toppings. Key West pizza, for example, is topped with ginger, spiced shrimp, scallops, mushrooms, hearts of palm, and Montrachet and Monterey Jack cheeses. At lunch, the dinner entrées are available along with a variety of sandwiches, including a club sandwich of roasted turkey, Smithfield ham, lettuce, and tomato on toasted cheese bread. There is also a small children's menu available.

An added bonus is that the restaurant revolves, and as it does so it provides a fine view over the thunderstorm, sandstorm, prairie, and rain forest scenes of the "Listen to the Land" boat ride down below. The scenes were designed with diners in mind, and provide them with a peek into a farmhouse window out of viewing range of the waterborne passengers below. Reservations are suggested for lunch and dinner; those holding reservation confirmation tickets for either meal may bypass any queue that might exist at the pavilion's front entrance within half an hour of the scheduled meal seating time. L, D.

round out the selections. As a result, the place is a delight for small children, and also quite a pleasant spot for their parents. There's veranda seating, a pretty fountain, and a full complement of antique-looking decoys and chests. B, L, D, S.

Refreshment Outpost: Another good spot for a refreshing cold drink. Between the Germany and China pavilions. S.

Lotus Blossom Cafe: Adjacent to Yong Feng Shangdian shopping gallery at the China pavilion, this fast-food counter offers sweet and sour pork, egg rolls, and soup. There's a covered, outdoor seating area for about 200 people. L, D.

Coral Reef Restaurant: Decorated in cool greens and blues to complement its Living Seas surroundings, this restaurant offers diners a panoramic view of the living coral reef through large, clear viewing windows. The acrylic windows are 8 feet high and more than 8 inches thick. The dining room is constructed on several tiers, so all 264 guests have an unobstructed view. The menu features fresh fish and shellfish, including baked clams, oysters on the half shell; broiled swordfish steak served with a spicy cajun sauce, "Fishmonger's Kettle" (stocked with shrimp, scallops, lobster, clams, and more, all simmered in a tomato and white wine sauce). Landlubber selections are also available. The menu varies seasonally, and reservations are necessary for lunch and dinner. L, D.

WORLD SHOWCASE

FAST FOOD AND SNACK SPOTS

Refreshment Port: A perfect spot for a quick thirst quencher, next to the Canada pavilion. S.

Yakitori House: The nature of the food offered at this small but comfortable establishment in the Japan pavilion is representative of the pace of life in that country. The average Japanese spends about seven minutes consuming his guydon, a beef-stew-like concoction flavored with soy sauce, spices, and the Japanese rice wine known as sake—all served over rice. That, together with skewered chicken known as yakitori, which are basted with soy sauce and sesame oil as they broil, plus yakitori and teriyaki sandwiches and Japanese sweets and beverages, makes up the offerings here. Located in the Japanese gardens to the left of the plaza, the restaurant occupies a scaled-down version of the 16th-century Katsura Imperial Summer Palace in Kyoto; sliding screens, lanterns, and kimono-clad hostesses add to the atmosphere. L, D, S.

Liberty Inn: To many foreigners, American food means hamburgers, hot dogs, and french fries, and these are the staples at the Liberty Inn, located alongside The American Adventure on the far end of the World Showcase Lagoon. Chili, apple pastries, dessert cups, and chocolate chip cookies

EVERYTHING YOU NEED TO KNOW
ABOUT EPCOT CENTER RESTAURANT RESERVATIONS

Since changes in restaurant reservation procedures have changed more than once since Epcot Center opened, it's important to confirm that the procedures described below are still in effect at the time you arrive. To check, call 824-4321. Also, try to arrive 5 minutes before your reserved seating time.

For dinner reservations: Guests staying at WDW-owned hotels and Disney Village Hotel Plaza establishments can make advance reservations by telephone up to 2 days in advance. Consult your hotel's information kit for precise details. Otherwise, reservations must be made *on the day of the meal* at the WorldKey Information System screens in Earth Station—the building immediately past the waiting area for Spaceship Earth as one walks through Future World from the Entrance Plaza.

Shortly after Epcot Center opens for the day, a line of would-be reservation-makers usually develops, and those at the end have less chance of booking a table at a popular restaurant at a popular time. For this reason, and because nobody really wants to wait on an unproductive line, it's helpful to arrive at the Epcot Center turnstiles about half an hour before the published park opening. Preferred seating times (5:30 P.M. to 7:30 P.M.) are usually booked by 10 A.M., so plan your evening meal with that in mind. Decide in advance where you want to eat and when (and choose a couple of possible alternate dining times and locales), and then send the speediest member of your party on ahead to Earth Station to make reservations. (It will help if you've familiarized yourself with the location of Earth Station and the WorldKey Information System stations.) Each of the restaurants has something special about it, and there's always a good menu selection even for unadventurous eaters—even in the more exotic restaurants of World Showcase. By the same token, don't arbitrarily dismiss the idea of an early seating if you can get it: If you lunch at 11 A.M., a 5 P.M. dinner will not only be welcome, but more important, it will provide the opportunity to spend the most pleasant and uncrowded evening hours enjoying the Epcot Center attractions. And don't abandon the idea of an Epcot Center restaurant experience altogether.

For lunch reservations: This meal provides guests with another chance to enjoy the most popular Epcot Center restaurants. It also has another important appeal: With a reservation for 1 P.M., it's possible to spend some of the most crowded hours in the park consuming a pleasant meal while less fortunate visitors are waiting on some of the longest lines of the day. Reservations for lunch can also be made at the WorldKey Information System or in person at the restaurant of your choice on the day you wish to dine. Complete this chore as early in the day as possible. Also note that you may be able to walk right in—say, if the time you have in mind is not too popular (like 10:45 A.M.). Most restaurants open for lunch between 10:30 A.M. and 11 A.M.

If all else fails: It sometimes happens that someone holding a reservation does not show up at the appointed seating time (reservations are held for only 15 minutes), so it certainly doesn't hurt to stop and inquire when passing a restaurant for which you have a sudden appetite.

Boulangerie Patisserie: This bakery-and-pastry shop in the France pavilion is not hard to find: Just follow the wonderful aroma and then watch the crowds line up to consume the establishment's flaky croissants and brioches, éclairs, fruit tarts, and chocolate mousse. These are served by ladies wearing black pinafores with ruffled white blouses, under the management of the stellar trio of chefs who run the popular Chefs de France restaurant not far away—Paul Bocuse, Gaston LeNôtre, and Roger Vergé. Hint for those who hate to wait: Arrive before 10 A.M. (this has become a favorite "breakfast" stop among Epcot Center veterans) or stop here about half an hour before park closing. B, S.

Cantina de San Angel: Located along the World Showcase Promenade, just outside the entrance to Mexico's pyramid, this fast-food stand serves quick snacks like beef-filled soft tortillas; tostadas con pollo, tortillas topped with chicken and refried beans; and—perhaps best of all—churros, a sort of fried dough rolled in cinnamon and sugar. The Cantina is first rate for a tasty rest stop on a hot afternoon. Dos Equis brand Mexican beer is available, and the establishment's plant-edged terrace makes a fine grandstand for viewing the passing parade. L, D.

Kringla Bakeri og Kafe: Tucked between an ancient wooden church and a cluster of Norwegian shops, this new eating spot serves kringles, a sweet candied pretzel eaten on special occasions in Norway; vaflers, heart-shaped waffles topped with powdered sugar and jam; kransekake, almond pastry rings; and smorbrods, open-faced sandwiches of smoked salmon, beef, or ham. Ringnes Beer, brewed in Norway, is also available. There is a 55-seat outdoor eating area. B, L, S.

CAFETERIA SERVICE

Le Cellier: This low-ceilinged, stone-walled establishment tucked away on the lowest level of the Canada pavilion, just off Victoria Gardens (not far from the exit from the *O Canada!* film), looks a little like the ancient wine cellars for which it is named. It offers a full menu of Canadian foods—which are a lot more interesting than one might initially have thought. The savory, Quebec-born pork-and-potato-filled pie known as tourtière is dished out in enormous slices, each one fully 3 inches high and covered with a tempting golden crust. Tangy Canadian cheddar cheese adds zip to some appetizing fruit platters, and roast prime ribs, chicken and meatball stew, and sauteed fresh salmon complete the selection of entrées. For dessert there's maple syrup pie, a sweet cousin to pecan pie, and trifle, a traditional British treat made of layers of yellow cake, custard, strawberries, and real whipped cream—all soaked with sherry. And Canada's own Labatt's beer is on tap. The combination of all this should make Le Cellier a prime destination for those who haven't been able to get a lunch reservation at one of the more publicized World Showcase restaurants but still want something more substantial than what the fast-food eateries are offering. Queue haters should be sure to avoid the lunchtime rush hour, which runs from about 11:30 A.M. to 2 P.M. After 5 P.M. there is table service and reservations are strongly suggested. The dinner menu features beef and maple dumpling stew, poached fresh salmon topped with crabmeat and a light cream sauce, and sauteed medaillons of turkey breast. (The line is also longer right after the *O Canada!* film, but don't be deceived; it moves quickly.) L, D, S.

FULL SERVICE

Rose & Crown Pub & Dining Room: The fare here is called "pub grub"—that is, fish and chips,

WHERE TO EAT IN EPCOT CENTER IF YOU DON'T HAVE RESERVATIONS

In Future World try the Farmers Market for quiche, soups, salads, sandwiches, ice cream, and pastries. The Odyssey Restaurant, near World Showcase Plaza, is another good bet. So are Sunrise Terrace (in CommuniCore West) and the Stargate restaurant (in CommuniCore East).

In World Showcase, there's Le Cellier for lunch and dinner, a cafeteria in the Canada pavilion. France offers the informal full-service eatery known as Au Petit Café (though there are sometimes queues), and Japan has its Yakitori House, good for skewered bits of barbecued beef and chicken. Try the open-faced sandwiches at Kringla Bakeri og Kafe in Norway. The American Adventure offers the Liberty Inn, the China pavilion has the Lotus Blossom Cafe, and outside Mexico, there's the Cantina de San Angel.

steak-and-kidney pie, chicken-and-leek pie, and roast lamb. For lunch, however, it's possible to order hot roast beef with gravy and mashed potatoes, and a really delicious fresh vegetable platter served with a Stilton cheese and walnut dressing. At dinner the standard offerings are supplemented with roast prime ribs and horseradish sauce and, as appetizers, a dish known as Scotch eggs—hardboiled, covered with sausage meat and fried, then

chilled and served with mustard sauce on the side. (It's usually inedible back in Great Britain, but it's really quite tasty here in Florida.) A mixed grill of broiled pork loin, beef tenderloin, and veal kidney is also available for lunch and dinner. For dessert there's traditional sherry trifle, a confection of layered whipped cream, custard, strawberries, and sherry; and raspberry fool, strictly whipped cream and raspberry puree. Bass India Pale ale from England, Tennent's lager beer from Scotland, and Harp lager beer and Guinness stout, both from Ireland, are on tap. They're served cold, in the American fashion, or at room temperature, as Britons prefer.

The decor is really beautiful, mainly polished woods, etched glass, and brass accents. In fine weather it's pleasant to lunch under the sunny yellow umbrellas on the terrace outside and watch the sleek *FriendShip* ferries chugging across World Showcase Lagoon. On the little island just to the east, the wind ruffles the leaves of the Lombardy poplars, a species of tree that is found along roadsides all over Europe.

Horticulturally speaking, it's also interesting to note the vines on the pub's northwest wall. These Virginia creepers grow amazingly fast and, when Epcot Center opened, showed only a few tentative tendrils close to the ground. The spreading tree nearby is a laurel oak, distinguished from the southern live oaks more widely seen at Epcot Center by its upright growth and its leaves, which are shiny on both sides instead of just one.

As for the pub's architecture, it incorporates 3 separate styles. The wall facing the World Showcase Promenade is reminiscent of urban establishments popular in Britain since the 1890s, while that on the south evokes London's *Cheshire Cheese* pub, with its brick-walled flagstone terrace, slate roof, and half-timbered exterior. The canal facade, with its stone wall and clay tile roof, reminds visitors of the charming pubs so common in the British countryside.

The pub section of the Rose & Crown serves such snacks as Stilton cheese and fresh fruit platters, miniature steak-and-kidney or chicken-and-leek pies, and the above-mentioned Scotch eggs—along with all the brews noted above and traditional British mixed drinks like shandies (Bass ale and ginger beer), lager beer with lime juice, black velvets (Guinness stout and champagne), and black and tans (Bass ale and Guinness stout). This drinking-and-snacking spot is quite popular, so it's often necessary to queue up at the door. But the wait is seldom very long since few guests linger over their drinks. Reservations are not accepted in the pub area but are suggested for the adjacent dining room. L, D, S.

Chefs de France: Three-star restaurants are rare even in France (for 1988 the august Michelin guide lists only 19 of them), so it's a notable coup that WDW has somehow managed to lure 3 of France's finest cuisiniers to run this rather remarkable restaurant. Paul Bocuse and Roger Vergé each operate 3-star restaurants in France (Bocuse's is outside Lyon, Vergé's just north of the French Riviera), and together with Gaston LeNôtre (widely recognized as France's premier preparer of pastries and other delicious dessert delicacies), they form a most unusual, absolutely formidable gastronomic trio. Bocuse, Vergé, and LeNôtre operate this unique World Showcase restaurant, and they have designed a menu that features fresh ingredients readily available from Florida purveyors. One or more of the French chefs makes regular visits to WDW to supervise and adjust certain items on the menu, though there has been very little need to tinker up to now.

As you might expect, the fare here is fiercely French, but the foundation of the menu is nouvelle cuisine, which involves lighter sauces, using much less cream and butter than the classic style of French cooking. At dinner, appetizers include chilled potato, leek, and Lyon-style onion soup; salmon soufflé seasoned with tarragon and served with a white butter sauce; oysters baked with spinach and champagne sauce; and ramekins of snails in garlicky herbed butter and hazelnuts. Diners choose among entrées from grouper doused with a rich lobster sauce, roast duck with wine sauce and prunes, fillet of grouper with salmon mousse, veal with a mushroom sauce, and chicken fricassee in a mild vinegar brown sauce. At lunch the menu offers various quiches, platters of French cheeses, country-style pâtés, and a croissant stuffed with braised ham and cheese. Hot dishes are offered, such as Lyon-style sausage baked in pastry (and doused with a beef-and-wine-flavored Bordelaise sauce), and a shrimp, crab, and fish casserole in a rich lobster sauce. A beef stew redolent of wine and a rich onion soup are available at lunch and dinner, as are an array of absolutely fabulous pastries and desserts (some wonderful LeNôtre specialties) and the thick, strong coffee known as café filtre (it's the French equivalent of Italian espresso). The atmosphere is as much a delight as the food. Tablecloths are sparkling white linen, and decorative touches of brass and etched glass abound. A modest wine list accompanies both lunch and dinner menus. Note that this can be one of the most expensive of all World Showcase restaurants. Reservations necessary. L, D.

Bistro de Paris: Located above Chefs de France, this restaurant evokes early 20th-century Paris. Peach and green curlicues decorate the ceiling above brass light fixtures and sconces, large mirrors, leaded colored glass, and simple wood chairs. A traditional bistro menu (created by the same trio of French chefs responsible for the fare at Chefs de France) features steamed fillet of grouper, chicken breast in puff pastry, and braised beef. The heartiness of the fare makes it an especially good dining choice in cool weather. (There's a separate menu "for the little gourmet"—kids under 12—at reduced prices.) Reservations accepted. L, D.

Au Petit Café: Located prominently in front of the France pavilion, along the World Showcase Promenade, this sidewalk café is a delightful place to stop for a snack or light meal. Under a large canopy with small round tables and black-jacketed waiters, it's as pleasant as it can be, and it can't be beat as a people-watching headquarters. But no reservations are accepted, and long lines can develop. So don't stop if you're tired or absolutely ravenous. L, D, S.

Akershus: The Norwegian castle of Akershus, which dominates Oslo's harbor, is the most impressive of Norway's medieval fortresses. It is actually half fortress and half palace, and many of its grand halls continue to be used for elaborate state banquets. At Epcot's Akershus, guests are treated to an authentic Royal Norwegian Buffet called the *koldtbord*, literally "the cold table." The diverse mix of offerings includes both hot and cold meats and seafood, and a selection of salads, cheeses, and breads. Traditional Norwegian desserts are also seved, as are cocktails and Norwegian beer. Hosts and hostesses are on hand to answer any questions about the menu that guests may have. L, D.

Marrakesh: The tastiest part of the Kingdom of Morocco Showcase features a variety of examples of traditional and modern Moroccan cuisine. Waiters are dressed in *djellaba* (long robes) and *babouche* (pointed slippers). Moroccan menu specialties include *tagine* of veal (veal stew with vegetables), roast lamb, chicken brochette, *couscous* (coarse steamed wheat served with lamb or chicken), and *bastila* (layers of thin pastry with chicken strips, almonds, saffron, and cinnamon). Sampler platters are also available. The beautiful tilework was done by Moroccan craftsmen. Belly dancers and Moroccan musicians entertain diners at both lunch and dinner. Be aware that this food may not be to everyone's taste, particularly children's. Reservations accepted. L, D.

Mitsukoshi Restaurant: This complex of dining and drinking spots, all operated by the Japanese firm for which it is named, occupies the 2nd level of the large structure on the west side of the Japan pavilion plaza.

• Tempura Kiku: This small corner of the restaurant is devoted to the batter-dipped, deep-fried chicken, beef, seafood, and fresh vegetables that are collectively known as tempura. The individual tidbits are crisp, tasty, and delicious. L, D.

• Teppanyaki Dining Rooms: The style of these 5 rooms is not unlike that popularized by the Benihana chain all around America: Guests sit counter-style around large flat grills, while white-hatted chefs chop vegetables, meat, and fish at lightning

speed and then stir-fry it all just as quickly. Whether or not all the chopping and cooking is accompanied by a mildly comic routine depends on the sense of humor of the chef, but in any case the establishment is quite convivial. The seating arrangements make it quite natural to strike up a conversation with fellow diners; in fact, it's almost impossible to keep to yourself. Reservations necessary. L, D.

L'Originale Alfredo di Roma Ristorante: This restaurant's *trompe l'oeil* ("trick the eye") perspective paintings make diners believe they're seeing real scenes rather than mere murals, and lend real character to the decor of this popular establishment. As in the famous Roman restaurant of the same name, the specialty is fettucine Alfredo—wide, flat noodles tossed in a sauce made of butter and imported Italian Parmesan cheese. But many other sizes and shapes of pasta, all of it made right on the premises, are also available; they are significantly enhanced by tomato, meat, pesto (basil, garlic, and Parmesan), or carbonara (egg, bacon, cream, and Pecorino cheese) sauces. There are also a number of less familiar Italian preparations involving chicken, eggplant, seafood, sausage, and veal, which are all really excellent here. For dessert, choose from a number of specialties such as ricotta cheesecake, spumoni, tortoni, or gelati. Even if you don't eat here, it's fun to stop and just peer through the glass kitchen windows to watch the cooks cranking out the rigatoni, ziti, linguine, lasagna, fettucine, and spaghetti (which, the eminently readable menu reminds guests, was brought to America by Thomas Jefferson from Europe in 1786). Reservations necessary. L, D.

and jade tree (sliced steak and Chinese broccoli). Appetizers range from Chinese pickled cabbage to pan-fried dumplings and hot-and-sour soup. A selection of Chinese teas, beers, and wines is also available. The dessert menu features red bean ice cream, toffee apples, and assorted Chinese pastries. Reservations necessary. L, D.

San Angel Inn Restaurante: A corporate cousin of the famous Mexico City restaurant of the same name, the food at this establishment, located to the rear of the plaza inside the Mexico pyramid, may come as a surprise to most visitors. Although the tacos and tortillas and other specialties that usually fall under the broad umbrella of Mexican food are available, the menu also offers a wide variety of more subtly flavored fish, poultry, and meat dishes. To start, there's *queso fundido* for 2 (melted cheese and Mexican pork sausage with corn or flour tortillas) as well as guacamole (avocado dip). A compote made of sweet Mexican turnip and oranges, is also available—and delicious. As entrées, the menu offers pollo en *pipian,* chicken strips simmered in pumpkin seed sauce; *mole poblano,* chicken simmered with spices and a bit of chocolate; *huachinango à la Veracruzana,* fresh fillet of red snapper poached in wine with onions, tomatoes, and peppers; and much more that is good and tasty. Mexican desserts are largely unfamiliar to Americans, with the possible exceptions of the custard known as flan, and *arroz con leche,* best known in the United States as rice pudding. Still, such desserts as *crepas de cajeta,* thin pancakes filled with milk caramel, and *helada con cajeta,* vanilla ice cream with a milk caramel topping, are well worth trying. Dos Equis brand beer, tart lemon-flavored water, and delicious margaritas make good accompaniments. Reservations necessary. L, D.

Biergarten: Located at the rear of the St. Georgsplatz in the Germany pavilion, this huge, tiered restaurant is set in a courtyard rimmed with geranium-studded balconies and punctuated by an old mill. It's every bit as jolly as Italy's Alfredo's, especially in the evenings, partly because of the long tables that encourage a certain togetherness among guests, partly because Beck's beer is served in 33-ounce steins. But equal credit for the gemütlich atmosphere must go to the restaurant's lively half-hour-long dinner shows, in which yodelers, dancers, and other traditional southern-German musicians—each appropriately clad in lederhosen or dirndls—play accordions, cowbells, a musical saw, and a harplike stringed instrument known as the "wooden laughter." The performances are exceptional, and the Biergarten offers an extremely entertaining evening. Diners are usually invited to join in the fun on stage. The food is hearty and very German: smoked pork loin, roast chicken, the spicy marinated beef known as sauerbraten, grilled bratwurst, bauernwurst, bierwurst, and jaegerwurst, potato salad, "wine"-kraut, and potato dumplings make up the offerings. Although there's no big show at lunchtime, a few "street" entertainers are usually on hand—and the setting is pleasant nonetheless, with the big mill waterwheel slowly turning and the sound of water splashing into the millstream blending with the rousing oompah music. Reservations suggested, particularly during peak seasons. L, D.

Nine Dragons Restaurant: A recent addition to Epcot Center's varied international restaurant list offers provincial Chinese cooking styles, including Mandarin, Cantonese, Hunan, Szechuan, and Kiangche. Entrées include braised duck (served Cantonese style), Kang Bao Chicken (stir-fried chicken, peanuts, and hot dried peppers), and beef

AT THE DISNEY-MGM STUDIOS

The restaurants at the Disney-MGM Studios Theme Park are the one place in the entire complex where a hint of the present meets the Hollywood of the 1930s and 1940s. It's true that the decor and atmosphere of the Studio eateries fiercely clings to eras gone by, but the ingredients in the food have been updated and most menus offer low-fat, low-calorie items. The meatloaf at the 50's Prime Time Cafe, for example, is made with veal and shiitake mushrooms and the chili is vegetarian and served over angel hair pasta. And in a tribute to the Hollywood image, most establishments also offer a couple of "trendy" California creations.

All the Disney-MGM Studios Theme Park restaurants are described below. Reservations policies are subject to change, so be sure to call Walt Disney World Information at 824-4321 to check up-to-the-minute procedures.

FULL SERVICE

Hollywood Brown Derby: The home of the famous Cobb Salad is alive and well. This recreation of the former Vine Street mainstay is quite faithful, right down to the caricatures (lovingly reproduced from the original Derby collection) that cover the walls. Even arch rivals Louella Parsons and Hedda Hopper (portrayed by convincing actresses) still reign over the restaurant from reserved tables, just as they did when the Brown Derby was in its heyday.

The 224-seat restaurant is predominantly decorated in teak and mahogany, and the elegant chandeliers and perimeter lamps (shaped like miniature derbies) are reminiscent of the original eatery. The china is embossed with the Brown Derby logo, and hosts and hostesses are all dressed in black tie. The atmosphere is just about authentic save for the theme park clientele who show up in shorts and tennis shoes.

The menu features the famed Cobb Salad, created by owner Bob Cobb in the 1930s. It's a mixture of finely (perhaps a bit too finely) chopped fresh salad greens, tomato, bacon, turkey, egg, blue cheese, and avocado. It's tossed tableside and served with old-fashioned French dressing. The modern incarnation of the salad is also available with shrimp or lobster. Other menu selections of note include Fettuccine Derby, pasta in a parmesan sauce with chicken and red and green peppers, and filet of red snapper served with fresh buckwheat pasta. The dessert tray is tempting—try another Brown Derby institution, grapefruit cake. A children's menu is

available, although the formalish atmosphere is not likely to enchant most youngsters. Reservations are necessary. Walt Disney World resort guests can make reservations up to two days in advance (but not on the same day) by calling 828-4000. Disney Village Hotel Plaza guests can also make reservations up to two days in advance by calling 824-8800. Other visitors must make reservations in person on the same day. L, D.

50's Prime Time Cafe: The setting is straight out of the favorite sitcoms of the 1950s. Each of the plastic laminate kitchen tables is set under a pull-down lamp, and the idea is to evoke a suburban kitchenette. Video screens set all around the room show black and white clips (all related to food) from favorite 1950s TV comedies, and these nostalgic bits are visible from each of the 226 seats. The placemats pose television trivia quizzes and meals are served either on Fiesta Ware plates or TV dinner-style, on three-compartment trays. The waitresses play "Mom" with considerable enthusiasm; they make recommendations and encourage guests to clean their plates (*or no dessert!*).

The menu is packed with "comfort foods." For openers there's alphabet soup, vegetarian chili, and the French Fry Feast, served either plain or with chili and cheese. Specialties of the house include Magnificent Meat Loaf, made with fresh veal and shiitake mushrooms and served with mashed potatoes and mushroom gravy; broiled chicken and spuds; chicken pot pie; and Granny's pot roast. There are also burgers with a variety of toppings, turkey burgers, hot roast beef sandwiches, club sandwiches, Aunt Selma's chicken salad, and the Apple-A-Day TV Tray (an apple served with cottage cheese and assorted fruits). Milkshakes, ice cream sodas, and root beer floats are filling accompaniments. And when you've finished everything on your plate, "Mom" will ask if you'd like dessert.

Standouts include S'mores (you'll feel like you're back at summer camp), a graham cracker topped with chocolate and toasted marshmallows; sundaes; banana splits; and strawberry rhubarb pie. Beer and wine are served. A children's menu is available. Reservations are necessary. Walt Disney World Resort guests can make reservations up to two days in advance (but not on the same day) by calling 828-4000. Disney Village Hotel Plaza guests can also make reservations up to two days in advance by calling 824-8800. Other guests must make reservations in person on the same day. L, D, S.

CAFETERIA SERVICE

Hollywood & Vine "Cafeteria of the Stars": The distinctive art deco facade ushers guests into a contemporary version of a 1950s diner—all stainless steel with pink accents. An elaborate 42- by 8-foot wall mural depicts notable Hollywood landmarks, including the Disney Studios, Columbia Ranch, and Warner Brothers (back when they were the only studios in the San Fernando Valley). At the center of the mural is the Fox Carthay Circle Theater, where "Snow White" premiered in 1937.

The 368-seat cafeteria presents a varied menu. At breakfast, there's the Hollywood Scramble, two eggs served with bacon or sausage and a choice of potatoes or grits and a breakfast biscuit; French toast; pancakes; omelettes, lox and bagels, assorted hot and cold cereals, and fresh fruit. Muffins, danish, and croissants are also served. Lunch features a variety of salads, including the Seafood Serenade, a chilled salad of shrimp, grilled tuna, crab, and greens served with a Cajun remoulade sauce. Baby back ribs, roasted chicken, steak, and tortellini are also served midday. The dinner menu adds prime ribs, veal chops, and mesquite-grilled pork chops. Homemade pies head the dessert list. Beer and wine are available, and a children's menu is posted. No reservations. B, L, D.

FAST FOOD AND SNACK SPOTS

Soundstage Restaurant: Set up to duplicate a typical "wrap party"—a final feed celebrating the end of the shooting of a film—guests enter the 560-seat restaurant through the back of a set (inspired by Touchstone's film "Big Business") leading to a carpeted hotel lobby set, with hosts and hostesses in black and white catering costumes. This is a food court and there are three distinct areas: at the pizza and pasta shop, deep-dish pizza, linguini, tortellini, and a cold pasta salad are on the menu; the sandwich shop serves three options, including a meatball sub, chicken salad, and the Soundstage Special—thinly sliced salami, pepperoni, and bierschinken, with jarlsberg and smoked Swiss cheese; the soup and salad shop serves chef's salads, chicken salad with vegetables, New England-style clam chowder, and chicken broth with tortellini. Peanut butter and jelly sandwiches are available for kids at each stand, and dessert offerings are the same at all three stations: toffee cheesecake, chocolate chip pie, and coconut cream pie. No reservations. L, D.

Starring Rolls: Freshly baked rolls (not roles), pastries, muffins, and croissants are sold at this sweet-smelling shop. Coffee, tea, and soft drinks are also served, making this a good place for an eat-and-run breakfast. B, S.

Dinosaur Gertie's: "Ice Cream of Extinction," claims the sign at this life-size dinosaur set on Echo Lake. Ice cream bars, fruit yogurt bars, ice cream sandwiches, and frozen bananas are the staples here. S.

Backlot Express: This 600-seat counter service restaurant looks like the old crafts shops on a studio backlot. There's a paint shop, a stunt hall, a sculpture shop, and a model shop. The paint shop has paint-speckled floors, chairs, and tables; the prop shop has a delta wing kite, car engines, bumpers, and fan belts. There is outdoor seating available amidst stored streetlights, plants, and trees. Menu offerings include charbroiled chicken with flour tortillas and salsa, burgers, hot dogs, chef's salads, and chili. For dessert, there's chocolate chip cheesecake, apple pie, carrot cake, and fresh fruit. Beer and wine are available by the glass. No reservations. L, D, S.

Min & Bill's Dockside Diner: "There's good eats in our galley," proclaims the welcoming sign posted on the *S.S. Down the Hatch*, a bit of "California crazy" 1950s architecture. The little tramp steamer, complete with a cartoonlike smokestack, mast, and booms, doesn't sail. Min & Bill's sandwich offerings include sliced turkey, tuna salad, and the Santa Monica Submarine—mortadella, salami, and provolone. Specialties include the Cucamonga Cocktail, marinated gulf shrimp and fresh vegetables; San Pedro Pasta, tri-colored pasta with crab and shrimp; and fresh fruit with yogurt. Soft serve frozen yogurt is served in cups or cones with a variety of toppings. No reservations. L, D, S.

Studio Catering Co.: Guests on the Backstage Studio Tour have a break between the tram and walking portions of the tour, and this eatery offers the opportunity for a quick bite before continuing the tour. Situated just behind The Loony Bin, the menu features ham and Swiss cheese sandwiches, a Cobb Salad Handwich (served in a bread cone), and a fruit and cheese platter. There is also a choice of desserts and snacks. Beer and wine are available by the glass. No reservations. L, D, S.

IN THE HOTELS

CONTEMPORARY RESORT

Most of the hotel's restaurants are located on the Grand Canyon Concourse on the 4th floor, but there is also a restaurant on the 15th floor, and snack spots by the marina and in the first-floor Fiesta Fun Center.

Character Cafe: On the Grand Canyon Concourse. Serves a bountiful, all-you-can-eat Italian buffet—one of the World's best buys—every evening complete with characters to entertain. And each morning there's a buffet-style character breakfast. No reservations. B, D.

Pueblo Room: On the Grand Canyon Concourse, this spot is quieter than other Grand Canyon Concourse eating spots. A variety of eggs and omelettes, pancakes, and fresh fruit are on the breakfast menu. At lunch there are soups, salads, burgers, and sandwiches. Dinner entrees include chicken, fresh fish, steaks, ribs, and chops. Reservations accepted, but not required. B, L, D.

Outer Rim Cocktail and Seafood Lounge: On the Grand Canyon Concourse, opposite the Terrace Cafe, with a good view over Bay Lake. Specialty drinks, cocktails, and seafood appetizers are served. Selected sandwiches are available from 11:30 A.M. to 2:30 P.M. No reservations. L, D, S.

Top of the World: This room with a view is on the hotel's 15th floor, serving all-you-can-eat buffets for breakfast and brunch on Sunday. The lunch menu offers à la carte entrées and an unlimited salad bar. The dinner show features Broadway at the Top, a lively revue of Broadway musicals, at 6 P.M. and 9:15 P.M. nightly. The menu includes duckling, veal chops, and roast sirloin of beef jardinière. The setting, with excellent views of the Magic Kingdom, is one of the best in the World. After dark, the golden spires of Cinderella Castle glitter under floodlights, and the white lights edging the rooflines of Main Street wink and twinkle like distant fireflies. Reservations are required for the dinner shows; phone the WDW Central Reservations Office at W-DISNEY (934-7639). For Sunday brunch reservations, call 824-3611. B, L, D.

Fiesta Fun Center Snack Bar: On the first floor, serves light fare 24 hours a day. B, L, D, S.

Dock Inn: Submarines, hot dogs, frozen-juice bars, and ice cream bars are the stock-in-trade at this stand at the marina behind the hotel. L, D, S.

THE POLYNESIAN VILLAGE

Some of WDW's more interesting eating spots are located here.

Papeete Bay Verandah: Serves Minnie's Menehune character buffet breakfasts every morning, sit-down dinners daily, and brunch on Sundays. The breakfast buffet features all sorts of fresh fruit, French toast, eggs, and grits. The hot-and-cold lunch buffet is a favorite; one highlight is the coconut-spiked rice pudding for dessert. The prime ribs and red snapper are the best choices for dinner, but more adventurous diners may be tempted by some of the Polynesian-style offerings. Among the appetizers are scallops marinated in coconut milk with a touch of horseradish and sour cream; shrimp, kingfish, spinach, and cabbage steamed in ti leaves; and thin salted salmon fillets seasoned with lemon, scallions, and tomatoes. Main courses include Pua'a (sauteed pork tenderloin and oriental vegetables served in a pepper half over saffron rice) and chicken pago-pago (a marinated chicken breast glazed with a honeyed sesame sauce and served in a pineapple half). For dessert, the menu offers poached pear marinated in apricot brandy and served with a strawberry cream sauce, and macadamia nut pie with passion fruit ice cream. The room itself is large and open and offers fine views across the Seven Seas Lagoon all the way to Cinderella Castle. After dark, Polynesian dancers and a small combo entertain quietly. Reservations are requested for dinner and Minnie's Menehune breakfast; phone 824-1391. B, L, D.

Coral Isle Cafe: On the second floor of the Great Ceremonial House, around the corner from Papeete Bay. This standard coffee shop with faintly South Seas decor serves the usual assortment of eggs every morning (including an interesting shrimp-and-cheese-stuffed omelet), plus granola and other cereals, and wonderful banana-stuffed French toast, one of the best of all Walt Disney World dishes. At lunch and dinner, the house does a booming business in big fruit salads, shrimp and crabmeat salads, chef's salads, and a variety of sandwiches. The assortment of hot entrées is expanded during the evening hours. Drinks, including the special Polynesian concoctions served at the Tambu Lounge, are available. A good choice when you want a no-fuss meal. B, L, D, S.

Tangaroa Terrace: This sprawling establishment, on the eastern edge of the property near the Oahu longhouse, serves that delicious banana-stuffed French toast made with sourdough bread (eggs and other more usual breakfast selections also are available), plus dinners of prime ribs, steak, and fresh seafood, including lobster and blackened grouper. B, D.

Captain Cook's Snack and Ice Cream Company: A good spot for continental breakfasts, hamburgers, hot dogs, fruit salad, ice cream, and snacks; beer in cans is also available. The most unusual specialty: coconut hot dogs. L, D, S.

Tangaroa Snack Isle: Most guests discover this snack bar on their way to Tangaroa Terrace, the game room, or the east pool, to which it is convenient. Hamburgers and hot dogs, a variety of submarine sandwiches, chef's salad and fruit salad, and light snacks like yogurt and ice cream are all available. Canned beer is sold here, as well. L, D, S.

GRAND FLORIDIAN BEACH RESORT

There are several fine restaurants at the Grand Floridian, including one of the finest dining spots in the entire Orlando area.

Victoria & Albert's: The premier restaurant not only of the Grand Floridian, but probably of the entire Walt Disney World complex. The small dining room seats only 53, and elegant touches include Royal Doulton china, Sambonet silver, and Schott-Zweisel crystal. There is no formal, printed menu. Each night there are fish, fowl, red meat, veal, and lamb selections, which depend on the best ingredients in the market, and which are described by your waiter at the table. The chef may even make a personal appearance to accommodate special requests from patrons. There are also choices of two soups, two salads, and desserts, including the specialty souffles of fresh berries, chocolate, or Grand Marnier. There is an extensive wine list.

Once guests have selected their meal they are presented a handwritten souvenir menu. Women receive a long-stemmed rose. Jackets and ties are required. One oddity of note: Every host and hostess here is named Victoria or Albert. D.

Flagler's: There are both Italian and French influences at the hotel's largest restaurant. All meals begin with a complimentary appetizer. The specialty of the house is risotto with tuna, swordfish, and scallops. Entrees include filet of beef with four varieties of mushrooms, salmon with asparagus, and a bouillabaisse made from local seafood. The dessert specialty is zabaglione, a frothy confection of whipped egg yolks, sugar, and marsala wine served over fresh berries. The waiters and waitresses occasionally break into song when the mood suits them, and the restaurant offers a lovely view of the hotel's marina. B, D.

Grand Floridian Café: There is a character breakfast here, with Mary Poppins as the star. Southern cooking is the specialty here, and lunch and dinner selections include catfish fillet with bell pepper relish, smoked pork chops with barbecue sauce, cajun burgers, and honey-dipped fried chicken. B, L, D.

1900 Park Fare: The all-American menu takes a backseat to the decor in this 185-seat buffet restaurant. Big Bertha, a band organ built in Paris nearly a century ago, sits 15 feet above the floor in a proscenium. The bellows-powered instrument simultaneously plays pipes, drums, bells, cymbals, and xylophone. Mary Poppins, Bert, and assorted chimney sweeps join other Disney characters here during breakfast. The dinner buffet features hot and cold seafood, salads, vegetables, breads, and roasted pork, lamb, or sirloin. The offerings change weekly. B, D.

THE DISNEY INN

Garden Gallery: The open, airy spot with skylights and plants, is the resort's only full-service restaurant, and it ranks among the most pleasant spots in the World for a meal. Many Disney executives come here for lunch. The restaurant offers a pleasant away-from-it-all feel. At breakfast there is an immense all-you-can-eat buffet or you can opt for an a la carte breakfast menu. Lunch features a fresh and varied salad bar, hot sandwiches, and steaks. At dinner, there is a seafood bar with raw oysters, crab claws, shrimp, and clams, and there are also beef, veal, and fowl selections daily. French-fried ice cream, served on a peach half with vanilla sauce, is offered both at lunch (on the à la carte menu) and at dinner; it's truly scrumptious. A delicious old-fashioned strawberry shortcake is also worth a taste. B, L, D.

The Diamond Mine: A snack spot offering sandwiches, hamburgers, chicken fajitas, salads, soft drinks, coffee, and beer. B, L, S.

Sand Trap: The perfect spot for snacks—right at poolside. Early-morning coffee, juice, and cereals are available. B, L, D, S.

Narcoossee's: The open kitchen is the focal point at this casual, airy, octagon-shaped restaurant on the shore of the Grand Floridian beach. Specialties include grilled swordfish marinated in garlic, olive oil, and basil; grilled steaks; double lamb chops; veal chops; and grilled chicken. Guests who order the "Seven Seas, Seven Scoops Delight," a 48-ounce snifter filled with custard, berries, seven scoops of ice cream, and topped with whipped cream and a touch of amaretto, are served on the stage. All of this icy delight is on the house—if a single guest can finish it. Aside from the fun of watching someone devour this immense treat, there is live entertainment nightly. L, D.

Gasparilla Grill and Games: Grilled chicken, hamburgers, and hot dogs are the mainstays at this take-out, self-service restaurant near the pool. Continental breakfast is also available. B, L, D, S.

DISNEY'S CARIBBEAN BEACH RESORT

The six counter-service restaurants are located in Old Port Royale. A 500-seat common dining area serves all guests.

Cinnamon Bay Bakery: Freshly baked rolls, croissants, pastries, and other treats are available.

Port Royale Hamburger Shop: Hot sandwiches, burgers, and soft drinks are on the menu.

Oriental Cargo: A variety of Chinese items, including egg rolls, spareribs, soups, lo mein, and chicken with broccoli are available.

Montego's Market: Soups, salads, and cold sandwiches round out the offerings at this stand.

Bridgetown Broiler: Chicken fajitas, taco salads, and grilled chicken are the offerings.

Royale Pizza & Pasta Shop: Pizza by the slice or the pie and a variety of hot and cold pasta dishes are available.

PLEASURE ISLAND

The five acres of Pleasure Island, which now include the *Empress Lilly*, mostly bustle with activity during evening hours, but the restaurants are open for both lunch and dinner and offer a tempting option for WDW guests. The two largest establishments here are not operated by Walt Disney World, but rather by The Levy Restaurants of Chicago, a company known for fine eateries all over the Windy City.

Pleasure Island is particularly peaceful during the day, and it's very pleasant to take a break from the often tiring pace of the theme parks and head over for a quiet lunch. The restaurants operate from 11 A.M. to midnight; most of the snack spots are open from 10 A.M. to 2 A.M. For up-to-the-minute details on opening hours call 824-4321, or check at the Pleasure Island Depot.

Portobello Yacht Club: According to island legend, this lovely restaurant occupies the former home of Merriweather Adam Pleasure, whose business and personal adventures provide the inspiration for Pleasure Island. The elegant Bermuda-style house reflects the 19th-century ship merchant's love of leisure yachting, as well as his wife Isabella's Italian heritage. This is one of the two Levy-run Restaurants, and one of our favorites on the WDW property. The interior combines high gables and beamed ceilings, bright Mediterranean colors and earthy terra cotta tones. The 340-seat establishment is divided into several informal dining rooms, each of which displays an impressive collection of maritime memorabilia: ship models, photographs,

pennants, trophies, and navigational charts. An assortment of colorful mix-and-match dishes, utensils, and glasses adds a personal touch.

The bar, which is fitted with mahogany panelling and brass and chrome fixtures, recalls the classic details of pleasure boats of the 19th century, and the outdoor terrace evokes the mood of an elegant cruise ship.

The food, however, is the most special part of the Portobello Yacht Club. The bustling open kitchen turns out grilled meat and fish and absolutely delicious small pizzas baked in a woodburning oven. Try the *quattro formaggi*, a four-cheese pie that's a

true taste treat, and a great appetizer or drink snack. Pasta offerings include *spaghettini al cartoccio*, pasta with shrimp, scallops, clams, mussels, calamari, tomatoes, garlic, olive oil, wine, and herbs baked in parchment, and *bucatini all'amatriciana*, long pasta tubes with plum tomatoes, Italian bacon, garlic, and fresh basil. Be sure to save some room for desserts such as *cannoli modo mio*, Portobello's homemade almond cone filled with Italian chocolate chip ice cream and orange and pistachio sauces, or *cioccolato paridiso*, a rich layer cake with chocolate ganache frosting, chocolate toffee crunch filling, and warm caramel sauce. A children's menu is available.

There is also a shop at the entrance to the restaurant that stocks a variety of souvenirs, from T-shirts to caps with the Portobello Yacht Club logo. Reservations accepted for parties of 7 or more. Call 934-8888. L, D.

Fireworks Factory: The other of the duo of eateries operated by The Levy Restaurants of Chicago. Island mythology recalls that Merriweather Adam Pleasure manufactured fireworks as a hobby. In the process, he earned a reputation for creating the world's most spectacular Fourth of July fireworks displays—until his warehouse was inadvertantly blown up when a spark from his cigar went astray. The newly restored Fireworks Factory was built over the remains of the original cast iron building. The setting is true to its pyrotechnic origins, with signs of the tragic explosion throughout. Some of the props around the restaurant are on loan from the Gruccis, the famous fireworks family. The 377-seat restaurant features high ceilings juxtaposed with antique brick walls, metal stairs, and a floor stained with black gunpowder. There are two dining rooms and a bar.

Upon entering, guests are invited into a picnic-like atmosphere where they sit at bench tables topped with black-and-yellow tablecloths. Ribs are the specialty of the house: baby backs, Texas beef, and veal. They are seasoned with a blend of spices, slowly smoked over an applewood grill, and then doused in Fireworks Factory's own barbecue sauce. Food is cooked to order to insure maximum flavor and freshness.

But ribs aren't the only thing on the innovative menu. If all the appetizers sound good, try the Fireworks 3 & 3 Combo of spicy hot chicken wings, sizzling catfish, and smoked barbecue shrimp

served with a trio of sauces. Entrees include barbecued chicken, grilled filet mignon, pork chops, and porterhouse steaks. Dessert selections include Atomic Chocolate Cake, topped and filled with chocolate mousse, and coated with chocolate chips; pecan pie; key lime pie; Ben & Jerry's ice cream; and the Tollhouse Cookie Sundae, a large tollhouse cookie served on a warm cast iron skillet and topped with vanilla ice cream and hot fudge.

There is also a selection of specialty drinks including the Coconut Peach Explosion, a powerful combination of coconut, Malibu rum, and peach schnapps and the Pleasure Island Iced Tea, a mix of vodka, gin, rum, triple sec, cranberry juice, and Sprite.

A children's menu is available, as is a selection of T-shirts, sweatshirts, hats, and other items bearing the Fireworks Factory logo. Fireworks' special barbecue sauce is also available in jars to take home. Reservations accepted for parties of 7 or more. Call 934-8989. L, D.

Mannequins: Several food carts are set up around this dance club. At the seafood cart, there's shrimp salad and garlic shrimp, and other carts serve chicken and steak in appetizer-size portions, all grilled to order. A potato chip cart offers tasty chips with a variety of dips. Specialty drinks, beer, wine, and soft drinks are served at a number of bars. D, S.

Neon Armadillo: Southwestern cooking is the theme here. Two fajitas bars feature freshly made chicken fajitas, chili, and nachos with several dips. Other items on the menu include pickled eggs, sausages, and fresh pepperoni. Specialty drinks, beer, wine, and mixed drinks are available along with soda. D, S.

Adventurers Club: Foods from around the world (Mr. Pleasure developed some unusual tastes during his travels) can be found here. Shrimp Trinidad, made with shredded coconut and raisins; peppered boursin; Lebanese steak tartare; and other unique appetizers are served. Cocktails, wine, beer, and soft drinks are also available. D, S.

Spinners: Located on the top level of the XZFR Rockin' Rollerdrome, the specialty of the house is potato straws, a delicious twist on the old French fry. Pizza, burgers, and chicken wings are also on the menu. Ice cream is the dessert of choice and beer and wine are available.

Videopolis East: Mocktails, milkshakes, strawberry daquaris (without rum), and Virgin Marys are the drinks on tap at this non-alcoholic teen dance club. The food accompanying these beverages include pizza, burgers, chicken, and sandwiches, all sized to be carried around easily so no precious dancing time is lost. D, S.

Merriweather's Market: Pleasure Island's answer to the food court. Four stands offer a variety of foods prepared in a variety of ways. At the broiled and roasted stand, chicken, turkey, sausages, burgers, and fish are on the menu; at the steamed and smoked stand, try oysters, shrimp, ribs, or if you're feeling adventurous, gator; at the fried station, chicken, beef, shrimp, and spring rolls are among the offerings, and at the fresh and natural stand, chicken, tuna, and shrimp salad are the items of choice. Everything is cooked to order, so the lines tend to move slowly. There's seating for 350 diners in a common area, and beverages are available at each stand. B, L, D, S.

Sweet Surrender: And surrender you will when you pass by this wonderfully aromatic shop, located next to Avigators Supply. Frozen yogurt in a variety of flavors can be capped with toppings of your choice, and the baked-on-the-premises cookies are just too delicious to pass up—especially if you catch them hot from the oven. Fresh ice cream, served in cups or cones, rounds out the menu. S.

D-Zertz: Pastries, chocolates, and other such sweet treats are the mouth-watering fare available here. Coffee and soft drinks are also available, making it a pleasant place to stop for a quick breakfast. S.

ABOARD THE EMPRESS LILLY

Named after Walt Disney's wife, this 220-foot-long Disney version of the stern-wheelers that plied the rivers of America during the 19th century rises gleaming and white at the west edge of the Buena Vista Lagoon, ornate as a Victorian ball gown, looking perpetually ready to sail off into the sunset. She really isn't, of course. Permanently moored, she's stacked from bottom to top with restaurants and lounges, and always bursting at the seams with diners and merrymakers having a very good time.

In some very interesting ways, the *Empress Lilly*

is authentic, however. Like early riverboats, she has tall stacks like those that once allowed the sparks vented from the boiler's fire to cool off before hitting the all-wood deck or the often-flammable cargo. She also has "hog chains" strung between the two slanted poles that extend from the hull through the third deck. (Steamboats were flat-bottomed, with a superstructure light enough to allow them to draw only a few feet of water; the hog chains kept the boat from sagging in the middle from the weight of its cargo, and from "warping" at the stern from the weight of the heavy engine, boiler, and paddle wheel.) Since the *Empress* represents a cross between an excursion boat and a showboat, she has her share of jigsaw-cut gingerbread trimming, not only on the second story, or Promenade Deck, but also on the first level, the main deck. The railings on both decks are elaborate; the posts are turned and then bracketed to create an archway effect.

The hallways and public rooms are full of polished Honduran mahogany, Victorian-style flowered carpets, old-fashioned prints and brass fixtures, and tufted Victorian love seats with damask and velvet upholstery; the curtains are sheer. Each of the restaurants and lounges is a little different.

Fisherman's Deck and Steerman's Quarters: The menus in these two dining rooms are identical, it's the decor that varies. The Fisherman's Deck on the forward Promenade Deck has a huge curved expanse of window—180 degrees' worth—and in the afternoon, the sunlight that washes the pale cream-colored tongue-in-groove paneled walls and the blue tufted Victorian side chairs is as remarkable as the food. The Steerman's Quarters, on the main deck, is full of heavy red upholstery and turned mahogany spindles and paneling. It is named for the steering gear that would have occupied this area in one of the original stern-wheelers. While you're waiting for your food, you can sit by a big glass window that seems only inches away from the paddle wheel's gleaming white arms and watch it turn. Both menus offer New Orleans-style items including a spicy cajun egg roll, Bayou gumbo with duck, shrimp creole, and bouillabaisse. There's also a selection of fresh fish, including red snapper, grouper, swordfish, and catfish, all prepared to order. Meat lovers can choose prime ribs, filet mignon, or veal. A bread pudding souffle in bourbon sauce and caramel flan with orange are good dessert choices. Reservations are accepted. L, D.

The Empress Room: The most amazing thing about this restaurant (located amidships on the Promenade Deck) is not its food (though the menu is one of WDW's most ambitious), but the combination of service and atmosphere. The Louis XV decor includes painted-wood paneling, damask wallpaper, a shallow-domed ceiling with an Italian brass chandelier glittering with crystal droplets, and, between the tables-for-four along the wall, dividers fitted out with paneling and etched glass. Parts of the elaborate moldings are covered with real gold leaf (worth $8,000 when the *Empress Lilly* was constructed in 1977).

The culinary offerings include hot and curried spinach and oyster soup or chilled avocado soup, Bibb lettuce and fresh mushroom salads, country pâté, smoked duck with creamed horseradish, crabmeat sautéed in butter with brandy, Dover sole stuffed with salmon mousse and mushrooms and doused with a vermouth sauce, stuffed breast of pheasant, venison, and more. The quality of the food preparation can be erratic, but this is among the most elegant eating places in the World. The restaurant seats guests from 6 P.M. to 9:30 P.M., and a 20 percent surcharge is added to each check for service. Jackets are required for men, and reservations are a must; they are available up to 30 days in advance (828-3900). D.

DISNEY VILLAGE MARKETPLACE

Some of the World's best restaurants are located in this enclave on the southeastern edge of the property—at the Pompano Grill and among the many other eating places in the Disney Village Marketplace that are scattered among the boutiques. It's worth noting that while the restaurants hereabouts really hop at dinnertime, none is terribly crowded at lunch, except on Saturdays and Sundays, when Orlando and Kissimmee residents make the trip to the Disney Village Marketplace for a day of shopping. And these restaurants have the advantage of being just a couple hundred yards' dash from the marina, so kids can go hire a pedal boat or a Water Sprite (during lunchtime and in late afternoon) while parents linger over coffee or drinks.

Village Ice Cream Parlour and Bake Shop: This is a perfect spot for ice cream. Milkshakes and hot fudge sundaes are only a couple of the many creamy creations here. Assorted Breyer's ice cream flavors, chocolate and vanilla soft serve, and baked goods round out the menu. S.

Cap'n Jack's Oyster Bar: The menu at this waterside spot is so full of good things—seafood marinara, shrimp, ceviche, crab claws, and clams and oysters on the half shell—that it's as good for a light lunch or dinner as it is for a snack, even though the place is nominally a lounge. Cap'n Jack's is a terrific place to be, especially in late afternoon, as the sun streams through the narrow-slatted blinds and glints on the polished tables and the copper above the bar. And the house's special frozen strawberry margaritas—made with fresh fruit, strawberry tequila, and a couple of other potent ingredients—are as tasty as they are beautiful. They're served in big balloon-shaped goblets, with a slice of lime astraddle the rim: tart, slightly fruity, and altogether delightful. L, D, S.

CROSSROADS AT LAKE BUENA VISTA

WDW visitors also have several restaurants from which to choose at the Crossroads of Lake Buena Vista shopping center, across from Disney Village Hotel Plaza. These include T.G.I. Friday's, Red Lobster, McDonald's, Taco Bell, Pebbles, Perkins, Jungle Jim's, and Rax. There is also a pizza parlor and an ice cream shop.

All American Sandwich Shop: For a lighter, faster dining experience; a variety of sandwiches are available. There's always a daily special and an assortment of salads and pastries. Beer and soft drinks are available. L, D, S.

Lakeside Terrace: This is the shopping area's fast-food spot, serving hamburgers, hotdogs, fried shrimp, salads, and assorted soft drinks and beer to eat inside or out. L, D, S.

Minnie Mia's Pizzeria: Deep dish pizza by the slice, or the entire pie, is available at this window-service establishment. Beer and soft drinks are also offered.

Chef Mickey's Village Restaurant: This unassuming dining room is one of the most pleasant restaurants in Walt Disney World—and there's no waiting since reservations are accepted (828-3723). There are fine views of Buena Vista Lagoon, and the sunshine that streams through the windows keeps a whole garden's worth of house plants robust and green all year. The restaurant serves lunch and dinner, and offers fresh Florida seafood and a variety of pasta dishes. Adjoining the restaurant is the living room-like Village Lounge. Fitted out with comfortable club chairs, it's a great spot for after-dinner drinks. Valet parking is available. B, L, D.

Pompano Grill: This former country club dining room is now a family-oriented restaurant complete with a new menu and new decor. Prime ribs, chicken, New York strip steaks, and filet mignon are offered. A children's menu features 6-ounce prime ribs, fried fish, hamburgers, and grilled cheese. The dessert specialty is a layered Italian ice cream loaf. A new lighter cream-colored decor complements the natural wood tones. Ceiling fans and fern-filled planters add to the Southern feeling of the dining room. The dress is now casual, so men no longer need to wear jackets. Reservations suggested; phone 828-3735. B, L, D.

Village Clubhouse Snack Bar: The only breakfast fare is coffee and pastries; otherwise hot dogs, subs, and other snacks are available. B, L, D, S.

Villa Centers: Located at the Disney Village Resort pools. Sandwiches, sodas, and beer are served. L, D, S.

FORT WILDERNESS RESORT

Most people cook their own meals; supplies are available at the Meadow and Settlement Trading Posts (open from 8 A.M. to 10 P.M. in winter, to 11 P.M. in summer). Deli-style sandwiches can be concocted there for carry out.

Trails End Buffet: This informal, log-walled, beam-ceilinged cafeteria offers standard breakfasts (plus a 7-inch breakfast pizza, grits, biscuits and gravy, and bread pudding) every morning; and during the rest of the day serves hearty lunches and dinners featuring barbecued chicken, fish, chicken pot pie, spare ribs, and more. The Friday-night seafood buffet is very popular, and is served from 5 P.M. to 8:30 P.M. Specially priced children's portions are available. Pizza is served every night from 9:30 P.M. until midnight. Beer and sangría are available by the glass or by the pitcher. B, L, D, S.

Crockett's Tavern: Unique appetizers, steaks, ribs, and chicken are available in this Pioneer Hall establishment. A children's menu is offered and cocktails are served. L, D, S.

Beach Shack: Located near the Bay Lake beach. Potato chips and Fritos, ice cream bars and sandwiches, and grape- and orange-juice bars are available. Beer is served. L, D, S.

LATE NIGHT PIZZA

The thin-crusted variety is available from 9:30 P.M. to midnight at Trails End Buffet with nightly entertainment.

DISNEY VILLAGE HOTEL PLAZA

At the Grosvenor Resort: This newly named and renovated highrise hotel features Baskerville's, a casual restaurant serving breakfast, lunch, and dinner in an atmosphere with a Sherlock Holmes theme. B, L, D. There's also Crumpets, a lobby cafe where continental breakfast, snacks, and lighter fare are available throughout the day. B, S.

At the Howard Johnson Resort: The restaurant and adjacent coffee shop here offer the standard HoJo menu in standard HoJo style—food that is reassuringly predictable, if not outstanding. The ice cream is first rate. Open 24 hours. B, L, D, S.

At the Royal Plaza: This sprawling resort boasts a pleasant (but unremarkable) coffee shop, the Knight's Table. B, L, D, S. Pizza is available at the Giraffe Lounge from 10 P.M. to 2 A.M. The ambitious El Cid offers specialty veal dishes, as well as steaks and seafood. D.

At the Travelodge: The Palm Grill serves a hearty buffet breakfast and dinner and an à la carte lunch. B, L, D. Calypso's Palm Terrace offers breakfast, lunch, and afternoon tea. B, L, S. Chez Doughnut features donuts, pizza, croissant sandwiches, and other light snacks throughout the day. B, L, D, S.

At the Buena Vista Palace: One of the state's finest restaurants, Arthur's 27, is here. It boasts a wonderful view over Walt Disney World Village, and the food and service are both excellent. D. The Outback, decorated in an Australian theme, serves a buffet breakfast and dinner. B, D. The gardenlike Watercress Cafe offers full meals and snacks around the clock, including a character breakfast. B, L, D, S.

At the Hilton: There are 3 restaurants here. The American Vineyards offers regional American specialties, like hickory-smoked Vermont turkey, Florida stone crabs, and quail. D. The County Fair gives guests the option of serving themselves from the buffet or ordering from the menu. B, L, D. For hot dogs and hamburgers al fresco, there's the Rum Largo Pool Bar and Broiler. L, D, S.

At the Pickett Suite Resort: The Parrot Patch offers indoor and outdoor dining, with a 2-story tropical bird aviary as entertainment. B, L, D. The poolside Bar and Ice Cream Parlor is a good place for an afternoon snack or drink. S.

MEAL BY MEAL

When you're looking for something special in the way of a meal, and you're willing to go a bit out of your way to find it, the descriptions below should provide sufficient suggestions to sate your appetite. What follows are the highlights of WDW breakfasts, lunches, and dinners, as well as some suggestions for avoiding mealtime crowds at the eatery of your choice. This is a selective, not a comprehensive, list; for complete information see the preceding listings under "Restaurants of WDW."

BREAKFAST

Most people opt for eggs and bacon or something similar at their own hotel. But those who decide to go farther afield will be amazed at the choices available. For instance, the French toast served at the Polynesian Village Resort's Coral Isle Cafe and Tangaroa Terrace—made with thick slices of real sourdough bread, stuffed with bananas, deep fried, and then rolled in cinnamon and sugar—is one of the best breakfast concoctions ever.

Except during the busiest periods, restaurants in the Magic Kingdom are good choices for quick morning meals. Most fast food spots serve coffee and pastry from park opening until about 11 A.M.

At most breakfast spots in the hotels, there are likely to be lines between 8 A.M. and 10 A.M., the morning rush hour. So allow plenty of time at these hours, eat earlier or later, or stop at a snack shop for something light to stave off hunger until it's time for a lineless breakfast (or an early lunch). It's also possible to use the long card you'll find hanging from the doorknob of any WDW guestroom to order breakfast from Room Service the night before. Disney Village Resort guests will probably do best at the Pompano Grill, where breakfast begins at 7 A.M.

In Epcot Center, the Stargate Restaurant in Future World's CommuniCore East offers cheese omelets, cold cereals, Danish pastries, and the Stellar Scramble (informally known as breakfast pizza). The Farmers Market in The Land offers bagels and cream cheese, as well as eggs and delicious pastries. France's Boulangerie Patisserie, where queues can run up to 45 minutes during most of the rest of the day, is relatively uncrowded before 10:30 A.M.—despite the fact that it offers delicious brioches and croissants and excellent coffee.

At the Disney-MGM Studios Theme Park try a home-cooked breakfast at the Hollywood & Vine Cafeteria of the Stars or a quick bite at Starring Rolls Bakery.

LUNCH

Breaking up a day in the Magic Kingdom with lunch at one of the resorts can provide the energy needed to keep you going until closing time. A few of the eating spots do get crowded around midday, but the Coral Isle Cafe at the Polynesian Village and The Garden Gallery at The Disney Inn are usually particularly peaceful. The Disney Inn's special dessert—french-fried ice cream, served on a peach half and drizzled with vanilla sauce—is well worth ordering, even though it costs extra.

Lunch highlights in Disney Village Marketplace are the All American Sandwich Shop and Cap'n Jack's Oyster Bar. At Pleasure Island, there are delicious pizzas-for-one at the Portobello Yacht Club. Barbecued ribs, chicken, steaks, and pork chops are on the menu at The Fireworks Factory. Or for a lighter meal, try one of the stands at Merriweather's Market or some frozen yogurt from Sweet Surrender. If you can't tear yourself away from the Magic Kingdom for even an hour to go elsewhere for lunch, there's still no lack of selection. Hamburgers and french fries are for sale at practically every turn, and then there are Italian specialties at Tony's Town Square Cafe; the Monte Cristos (batter-dipped, deep-fried turkey, ham, and Swiss cheese sandwiches) served at the Columbia Harbour House, in Liberty Square; or the vegetable and fruit salads available at the Crystal Palace on Main Street; the clam chowder and black walnut bread served at the Liberty Tree Tavern in Liberty Square; the teriyaki-sauced beef and chicken at the Adventureland Veranda; peanut butter and jelly sandwiches at Aunt Polly's Landing on Tom Sawyer Island in Frontierland; pizza at Plaza Pavilion in Tomorrowland; chocolate crepes at King Stefan's in Cinderella Castle; and health food and salads at the Lunching Pad in Tomorrowland.

As at breakfast, crowds can be a problem; the three hours between 11 A.M. and 2 P.M. are the busiest. To avoid the rush, eat a light breakfast and a big early lunch—or have a late breakfast and a late lunch. If necessary, snatch a mid-morning snack to tide you over until things get less hectic.

Another option (especially during the summer and holiday periods) is to leave the Magic Kingdom altogether for lunch at Disney Village Marketplace or at one of the resort hotels, which are less crowded than the Magic Kingdom at noon. Except on Saturdays and Sundays, when local residents most often come out to shop, none of the Disney Village Marketplace restaurants are ever horribly crowded at lunchtime.

The hours between 11 A.M. and 2 P.M. in the Magic Kingdom are very busy, however, even though the lines usually move fairly quickly. It's generally far swifter to eat earlier or later. When there are several food service windows operating, evaluate them all before wandering into the nearest queue: Occasionally, the one farthest from the doorway will be almost (if not entirely) wait free. Note that the lines at the Adventureland Veranda generally move more slowly than those at other fast-food establishments because of the greater variety of offerings. Also, while the sit-down restaurants offering full dinners—such as Cinderella Castle's King Stefan's and Liberty Square's Liberty Tree Tavern—are crowded at lunch, they're busier still at dinnertime.

In Epcot Center, midday is a good time to sample some of the full-service restaurants offering ethnic specialties. Linger over their culinary delights, out of the heat of the midday sun, while crowds of other guests are lining up for attractions. For hamburgers

and other standard fast-food fare, try the Stargate restaurant in CommuniCore East, Liberty Inn in The American Adventure, and the sleek, attractive Odyssey restaurant near Mexico and the World of Motion. The Farmers Market, in The Land, offers a huge variety, from baked potatoes and soups and salads to barbecued sandwiches and more, and is a good choice for a family that can't arrive at a consensus. The pizza quiche offered at The Cheese Shoppe there is a favorite, and the chocolate chip cookies from the nearby Bakery make a good dessert. Ethnic fast foods are available at Japan's Yakitori House, China's Lotus Blossom Cafe, Norway's Kringla Bakeri og Kafe, and Mexico's Cantina de San Angel. Among full service eateries, The Land Grille Room is special for its imaginatively conceived regional American offerings, not to mention that delightful cheese bread. In World Showcase, meat pies and Epcot Center's best salad (the fresh vegetable platter) may be found at the Rose & Crown Pub & Dining Room; stir-fried meats and vegetables are the prime fare in the Mitsukoshi restaurants; Moroccan sampler platters are offered at Marrakesh; Chinese specialties are served at the Nine Dragons restaurant; hearty German food is offered in Germany's Biergarten; and fairly elaborate Mexican fare comprises the menu in Mexico's San Angel Inn restaurante. An enormous buffet is served at Akershus in Norway. The delightful Au Petit Cafe on the World Showcase Promenade in France is the only sit-down restaurant that doesn't require reservations, but the waiting line is often long. The most elaborate cooking is done at Italy's Alfredo's and at France's Chefs de France.

At the Disney-MGM Studios Theme Park, try the famous Cobb Salad at the Hollywood Brown Derby; a good home-cooked meal served by "Mom" at the 50's Prime Time Cafe; soups, salads, pastas, and sandwiches at the Soundstage Restaurant; salads, ribs, roasted chicken, and tortellini at the Hollywood & Vine Cafeteria of the Stars; chicken with tortillas and salsa, burgers, and chili at the Backlot Express; or sandwiches, pasta, and shrimp at Min & Bill's Dockside Diner.

SUNDAY BRUNCHES

These grand spreads take over the Pompano Grill (8 A.M. to 2 P.M.), the Top of the World at the Contemporary Resort (9 A.M. to 2:30 P.M.), and the Papeete Bay at the Polynesian Village (noon to 3 P.M.) every Sunday. All feature hot dishes along with traditional breakfast fare, fruit, and pastries. Brunches include a glass of wine or champagne. Make reservations in advance: Papeete Bay (824-1391); Pompano Grill (828-3735); and Top of the World (824-3611).

DINNER

There's an awesome choice, from the humblest snack center to the *Empress Lilly*'s ambitious Empress Room. Walt Disney World is not exactly a bastion of haute cuisine, but that doesn't mean that dinner experiences are anything less than pleasant. Service is almost unfailingly good (slipping just slightly during the busiest seasons), and the best of Walt Disney World's dinners are just fine. For a night on the World, some good choices are the Portobello Yacht Club and The Fireworks Factory at Pleasure Island; Steerman's Quarters, Fisherman's Deck, and the Empress Room, all on the adjacent *Empress Lilly*; Chef Mickey's Village Restaurant in Disney Village Marketplace; Victoria & Albert's at the Grand Floridian; the Garden Gallery at The Disney Inn; the Papeete Bay Verandah in the Polynesian Village; and the Hollywood Brown Derby at the Disney-MGM Studios Theme Park.

For family fare: Children are welcome at every WDW restaurant, but the leisurely pace of service at some places can make kids fidget. But there are plenty of choices that are well suited to dining en famille. Restaurants at the Contemporary Resort especially good for families are the Pueblo Room and the Character Cafe; the Tangaroa Terrace at the Polynesian Village is another good choice. The best choice for Disney Village Resort guests is the Pompano Grill.

The decision about where to dine may ultimately depend on the plan for the rest of the day. Especially in slack periods, the familiar long lines at the most popular attractions in the Magic Kingdom are practically nonexistent from about 6 P.M. onward. Even during the busiest times, the queues ease up a bit as the afternoon wanes. So it's a wise visitor who takes advantage of this phenomenon by having a late lunch—then dines after 9 P.M. This plan also allows time to catch the second, less-crowded run-through of the Main Street Electrical Parade.

At the Disney-MGM Studios Theme Park, enjoy a fine and leisurely meal at the Hollywood Brown Derby, or grab a quicker meal at one of the other eateries: the Soundstage Restaurant, the Hollywood & Vine Cafeteria of the Stars, Min & Bill's Dockside Diner, the Backlot Express, or the 50's Prime Time Cafe.

DINNER SHOWS

The fact that the Disney organization is the king of family entertainment is nowhere more strongly apparent than amid the whooping and hollering troupe of singers and dancers who race toward the velvet-curtained stage at Fort Wilderness Resort's Pioneer Hall. As you plow through barbecued ribs, fried chicken, corn on the cob, and strawberry shortcake, those enthusiastic performers sing, dance, and joke up a storm until your mouth is as sore from laughing as your stomach is from ingesting all the food. This is the Hoop-Dee-Doo Musical Revue, presented daily at 5 P.M., 7:30 P.M., and 10 P.M. Cost is about $29 per adult, $23 for juniors (12 through 20), and $15 for children (3 through 11); reservations can be made through the CRO (W-DISNEY—934-7639) and are required well in advance. There is no smoking permitted in Pioneer Hall.

The Polynesian Revue at the Polynesian Village (aka the Luau), presented nightly at 6:45 P.M. and 9:30 P.M., also has its moments. The performers' dancing is some of the most authentic this side of Hawaii. Many of the WDW dancers have studied at the well-respected Polynesian Cultural Center. A full Polynesian-style meal, including frozen piña coladas and a chocolate ice cream and raspberry dessert is served. Cost is about $28 for adults, $23 for juniors, and $15 for children.

Mickey's Tropical Revue, presented daily at 4:30 P.M. at the Polynesian Village Resort, is a Polynesian show aimed at the younger set. Disney characters, dressed in traditional costumes, dance along with the Polynesian performers. A full dinner including dessert is served. Cost is $24.50 for adults, $19.50 for juniors, and $11 for children.

The Top of the World at the Contemporary Resort hosts a revue of Broadway hits, Broadway at the Top—plus a view over the Magic Kingdom that will dazzle you even if the music doesn't always. A 4-course dinner is served and entrées include roast duckling, veal chops, and roast sirloin of beef. Seating is at 6 P.M. and 9:15 P.M. for the 7:45 P.M. and 11 P.M. shows, respectively; the price is $40 for adults and $18 for children (3 through 11).

The Biergarten at Epcot Center's Germany pavilion features a continuous show to entertain diners throughout the evening; it's complete with traditional German musicians, yodelers, and dancers. The fare here is hearty. Entrées range from $10.75 to $16.95.

Plan to arrive 15 minutes or so before starting time, and allow enough time for transportation and parking. (Prices are subject to change and are taxable.)

ABOUT DINNER RESERVATIONS

In most WDW restaurants, it's first come, first served. The lines that result can be avoided by eating early or late—or by choosing one of the handful of restaurants that accept dinner reservations. (Note that reservations are held for only 15 minutes.)

GRAND FLORIDIAN RESORT: Victoria & Albert's (824-2391).

POLYNESIAN VILLAGE: Papeete Bay Verandah (824-1391) and Tangaroa Terrace (824-1361).

THE DISNEY INN: The Garden Gallery (824-1484).

MAGIC KINGDOM: King Stefan's in Cinderella Castle and Liberty Tree Tavern in Liberty Square. Reservations must be made in person at the restaurants on the day of the meal; go first thing after arrival in the Magic Kingdom.

PLEASURE ISLAND: Empress Room aboard the *Empress Lilly* (828-3900); Portobello Yacht Club accepts reservations only for parties of 7 or more (934-8888; The Fireworks Factory accepts reservations for parties of 7 or more (934-8989).

DISNEY-MGM STUDIOS THEME PARK: Reservations are accepted at the Hollywood Brown Derby and the 50's Prime Time Cafe two days in advance for WDW resort guests (828-4000) and Hotel Plaza guests (824-8800) only. All other guests must make reservations in person on the same day.

DISNEY VILLAGE MARKETPLACE: Chef Mickey's Village Restaurant (828-3723); Pompano Grill in the villa area (828-3735).

Or plan to take in the dinner show at the Top of the World in the Contemporary Resort, the Luau or Mickey's Tropical Revue at the Polynesian, or the Hoop-Dee-Doo Musical Revue at Pioneer Hall—but note that *reservations for these activities must be made well in advance; some seatings sell out a year ahead!* No deposits are required, so there's no reason not to reserve early enough to avoid disappointment. (Call the CRO at W-DISNEY—934-7639—for all dinner show reservations.)

For dinner shows and supper seatings alike, you can book a table as soon as you get your confirmed reservation number, if you're staying at WDW resorts. Otherwise, you can book it 45 days ahead if you're lodging at one of the Disney Village Hotel Plaza establishments (*only* if you have made your reservation through the CRO) and 30 days if you're putting up outside Walt Disney World. Empress Room reservations may be made 30 days in advance, no matter where you're staying. In the case of dinner shows, if you can't get a place for an early performance, try for a later one (usually less heavily booked).

At Epcot Center it's important to remember every establishment offers unique delights. If you didn't get dinner reservations in advance, don't despair. Try a dinner of tourtière (a Canadian pork pie) and maple syrup pie (for dessert) at Canada's atmospheric Le Cellier. Or sample Mexican specialties at Mexico's Cantina de San Angel (whose lagoon-side tables provide a fine view of the sun setting behind Epcot Center), or the skewered, grilled meats at Japan's Yakitori House. Cravings for more conventional fast foods will be satisfied at the Stargate Restaurant in CommuniCore East, at the Odyssey Restaurant near World of Motion and Mexico, and at the Liberty Inn in The American Adventure. The Sunrise Terrace in CommuniCore West also serves more substantial, all-American dinner fare. The Farmers Market in The Land offers a little bit of everything.

Other restaurants require reservations (procedures are outlined on page 215). Try not to miss The Land Grille Room's cheese bread, the Scotch eggs in the Rose & Crown, the salmon soufflé and the pastries at Chefs de France, and the Mexican queso fundido at Mexico's San Angel Inn Restaurante. The Biergarten has lively entertainment throughout the day and evening.

SCOOPS, SUNDAES, AND SOFT SERVE

Happily it's now possible to find sugar cones at WDW. And there's something about a hot, humid summer afternoon that makes all of these cooling treats seem especially appealing.

BY THE SCOOP

IN THE HOTELS: Coral Isle Cafe at the Polynesian Village Resort, passion fruit ice cream at Papeete Bay Verandah at the Polynesian Village, and at Captain Cook's Snack and Ice Cream Company.

IN THE MAGIC KINGDOM: Liberty Tree Tavern, Liberty Square; and Tony's Town Square Cafe, Main Street; King Stefan's Banquet Hall, Fantasyland.

AT EPCOT CENTER: The ice cream stand at Farmers Market in The Land.

DISNEY VILLAGE MARKETPLACE: Village Ice Cream Parlour and Bake Shop.

PLEASURE ISLAND: Sweet Surrender.

CONES

Cone Shop, Main Street, Magic Kingdom; and the Village Ice Cream Parlour and Bake Shop, Disney Village Marketplace. Six flavors each. Farmers Market, Epcot Center. Sweet Surrender, Pleasure Island.

ASSORTED SUPER SUNDAES

IN THE HOTELS: Narcoossee's at the Grand Floridian (custard, berries, seven scoops of ice cream, whipped cream, and amaretto).

Papeete Bay Verandah (with flambéed pineapple bits, served in a pineapple half), Tangaroa Snack Isle, Tangaroa Terrace, and Coral Isle Cafe, at the Polynesian Village.

IN THE MAGIC KINGDOM: Sealtest Ice Cream Parlor and the Plaza Restaurant on Main Street.

DISNEY VILLAGE MARKETPLACE: Village Ice Cream Parlour and Bake Shop. Pompano Grill (served with a special chunky Gold Brick chocolate sauce at lunchtime, and atop bananas Foster and cherries jubilee at dinner).

PLEASURE ISLAND: Fisherman's Deck and Steerman's Quarters, *Empress Lilly* and Tollhouse Cookie Sundae at The Fireworks Factory.

DISNEY-MGM STUDIOS THEME PARK: 50's Prime Time Cafe (hot fudge, caramel, marshmallow, or the works).

SOFT SERVE

IN THE MAGIC KINGDOM: Round Table and Enchanted Grove, Fantasyland; Sunshine Tree Tavern (with a tangy frozen orange juice ripple), Adventureland.

AT EPCOT CENTER: Refreshment Port, near the Canada pavilion and Refreshment Outpost, near the China pavilion.

DISNEY VILLAGE MARKETPLACE: Village Ice Cream Parlour and Bake Shop.

IN THE HOTELS: Fiesta Fun Center at the Contemporary Resort Hotel, and at Trails End Buffet at the Fort Wilderness Resort.

FROZEN YOGURT

EPCOT CENTER: Desserts & Things.
PLEASURE ISLAND: Sweet Surrender.
DISNEY-MGM STUDIOS THEME PARK: Min & Bill's Dockside Diner.

FRENCH-FRIED ICE CREAM

THE DISNEY INN: The Garden Gallery. Ice cream served with a crispy crust offers a very unique flavor.

LEMON SHERBET PUNCH

IN THE MAGIC KINGDOM: Liberty Tree Tavern, Liberty Square.

INTERNATIONAL TREATS

AT EPCOT CENTER: Specialties at L'Originale Alfredo di Roma Ristorante include Italian concoctions like spumoni and tortoni. For a Mexican treat, visit San Angel Inn Restaurante for *helada con cajeta* (vanilla ice cream with caramel topping).

spot to watch the sunset and, when the park is open until midnight, the fireworks. Dash out onto the more easterly of the two observation decks nearby at 10:05 P.M. to see the Electrical Water Pageant blipping, bleeping, and glittering on Bay Lake below.

LOUNGES

No one ever said the Magic Kingdom's no-liquor policy means that everyone in the World is a teetotaler. Actually, some of WDW's tastiest offerings are liquid (and decidedly alcoholic), and some of its most entertaining places are its bars and lounges.

CONTEMPORARY RESORT: The watering holes here are sleek, with atmosphere aplenty.

Outer Rim Cocktail and Seafood Lounge: Overlooking Bay Lake, this lounge serves cocktails and seafood appetizers. There is entertainment in the evening.

Top of the World Lounge: Adjoining the Top of the World restaurant, this spacious room offers superb views of the Magic Kingdom. This is a good

POLYNESIAN VILLAGE: The resort's Polynesian theme has inspired a whole raft of deceptively potent potables like Seven Seas (fruit juice, grenadine, orange curaçao, and rum), Chi Chis (a standard piña colada made with vodka instead of rum), and WDW piña coladas (which include orange juice in addition to rum, pineapple, and coconut cream). There's even a special Polynesian Village nonalcoholic treat—the pink Lei-Lani, an orange juice and strawberry mixture.

Barefoot Bar: Adjoining the swimming pool lagoon, serving soda, draft beer, piña coladas, frozen daiquiris, mai tais, and various other mixed drinks. Open from 11 A.M. until 10:30 P.M. in summer (to 5 P.M. in winter).

Tambu Lounge: Cozy and clublike, this lounge adjoining the Papeete Bay Verandah is open daily beginning at 11 A.M., and offers a menu of Polynesian-style appetizers along with low-key entertainment nightly. A good spot for a quiet conversation. Open from 11 A.M. until 1:30 A.M.

GRAND FLORIDIAN: The four lounges reflect the Old Florida theme of the hotel.

The Garden View Lounge: A view of the lushly landscaped pool and garden area makes this watering hole a pleasant place to relax.

Mizner's Lounge: Named after the eccentric architect who defined much of the flavor of southeastern Florida's Gold Coast, this lounge is on the second floor of the main building.

Summerhouse: This bar serves guests at the pool and beach.

Narcoossee's: Yards of Beer, an unusual manner of service allows guests to choose from a mug, a half-yard, or a yard. And they mean a yard.

THE DISNEY INN: The Back Porch, adjoining The Garden Gallery, serves an assortment of specialty drinks and cocktails, plus sandwiches, chili, chicken salad, cheese and vegetable platters, and fresh shrimp.

CARIBBEAN BEACH RESORT: The tropical theme of the hotel carries through to the lounges here.

Captain's Hideaway: Tropical drinks, beer, wine, and cocktails are served at this 200-seat lounge at Old Port Royale.

Banana Cabana: Drinks and a variety of snacks are available at this poolside bar.

FORT WILDERNESS RESORT: Beer and sangria are served in Pioneer Hall. Crockett's Tavern serves drinks, assorted snacks, hors d'oeuvres, and full meals. For something stronger, take a blue-flagged watercraft to the Contemporary Resort. Be sure to check the operating hours before boarding so that you don't miss the last trip back. Or, if you have a car, make the short drive to the Disney Village Marketplace or Pleasure Island.

DISNEY-MGM STUDIOS THEME PARK: The settings of the lounges here are their main attraction.

Catwalk Bar: Above the Soundstage Restaurant is the 90-seat full-service cocktail lounge designed to resemble a movie prop storage area. Guests overlook the "Big Business" set below. Appetizers, specialty drinks, beer, and wine are served.

Tune In Lounge: A sitcom living room setting, with couches, chairs, and fold-up TV dinner tray tables is found at this lounge adjacent to the 50's Prime Time Cafe. Waiters in V-neck sweaters play the roles of sitcom Dads, and old television sets play scenes from beloved sitcoms. Appetizers, mixed drinks, beer, and wine are served.

DISNEY VILLAGE MARKETPLACE: Some of WDW's best lounges are here.

Cap'n Jack's Oyster Bar: Agleam with copper, right on the water, this bar serves delicious strawberry margaritas, made with strawberry tequila and real strawberries. The nibbles of steamed clams, oysters, and seafood marinara are good enough for a meal.

Village Lounge: This boîte, comfortable as a living room, is one of the World's best-kept secrets.

PLEASURE ISLAND: All the clubs (with the exception of Videopolis East) have bars that serve specialty drinks, beer, wine, and mixed drinks. The Fireworks Factory and the Portobello Yacht Club also have pleasant lounges.

Baton Rouge Lounge: This spacious lounge on the main deck of the *Empress Lilly* is one of the liveliest spots in WDW, thanks to the energetic Jazz Connection. Specialty drinks are sold by the pitcher—things like Melancholy Baby (concocted of melon liqueur, rum, and orange, lemon, and lime juices), Old Man River (made with rum, vodka, triple sec, lemon and lime juices, and a splash of coke), margaritas, and Singapore Slings. The Bayou chips—crunchy homemade potato chips sold by the basket—are delicious enough to make it easy to abandon dinner plans. Open from noon.

The Empress Lounge: Almost as elegant as the Empress Room, whose guests this mahogany-paneled bar is meant to pamper before and after a meal. The Empress Lounge features a harpist. Aboard the *Empress Lilly*.

IN EPCOT CENTER: All restaurants, including some of the counter-service establishments, offer alcoholic beverages with meals. Restaurants such as The Land Grille Room and the San Angel Inn Restaurante have small lounges at which patrons may wait for tables.

Then there are a few places that specialize in spirituous liquid refreshments:

Rose & Crown Pub & Dining Room: The pub section of this watering hole that's part of the United Kingdom pavilion is a veritable symphony of polished woods, brass, and etched glass. Beer is available along with a score of specialty drinks imported from the other side of the Atlantic.

Matsu No Ma Lounge: In addition to the exotic sake-based specialty drinks available here, this establishment offers a fine panoramic view over the whole of Epcot Center—including the World Showcase Lagoon with Spaceship Earth as a backdrop—one of the best vistas of the property available.

Biergarten: Just outside this restaurant in Germany there's a small shaded terrace where steins of beer and sausages are available.

MORE SPECIAL NIGHTTIME FUN

The Magic Kingdom, open late during several busy periods of the year, takes on additional dazzle after dark. In peak seasons, there's the Main Street Electrical Parade, a procession so spectacular that it alone is worth the trip to WDW—even though it's necessary to visit during a busy period in order to see it.

And Epcot Center is particularly lovely at night, when the lights sparkle on the Lagoon and Spaceship Earth is all aglow. But there are always a dozen or so other special happenings and events going on after dark throughout WDW.

MARSHMALLOW MARSH EXCURSION: This entertainment—offered only during the summer—consists of a trip by canoe through the winding Fort Wilderness waterways, a hike along a footpath (for a few hundred feet) to a well-hidden campfire spot on the lakeshore, a merry sing-along, a story-telling fest, and a marshmallow roast. Cost is $6 for adults, $5 for children, and reservations are required; to make them, appear in person on the day of the trip at Pioneer Hall, or call 824-2788.

RIVER COUNTRY: This archetypal, all-American swimming hole is open until 8 P.M.—under the lights—during the summer, and crowds are minimal. River Country admission is $2 less for adults and $1 less for children, after 3 P.M.

CAMPFIRE PROGRAM: This event at Fort Wilderness, held nightly near the Meadow Trading Post at the center of the campground, features a sing-along, Disney movies, and cartoons.

DISNEY MOVIES: A good choice when feet refuse to take even one more step. Full-length Walt Disney feature films are shown nightly at the Contemporary Resort for WDW guests, in the theater near the Fiesta Fun Center—usually at 4:30 P.M., 7 P.M., and 9 P.M. Movies are also shown at the Fort Wilderness Resort every evening at the campfire (for resort guests only).

TENNIS: The courts at the Contemporary Resort, The Disney Inn, Fort Wilderness, and the Lake Buena Vista Club are open until 10 P.M. year round. (See *Sports*.)

FIREWORKS: During summers and holidays when the Magic Kingdom is open late, there are fireworks at 10 P.M. nightly. The show lasts just five minutes, but packs as much dazzle as those many times its length.

ILLUMINATIONS: This nightly show is an absolutely spectacular display of music, laser lights, fireworks, and dancing water fountains that can be seen from any point on the promenade, usually at 10 P.M. Check at Earth Station for the exact time.

ELECTRICAL WATER PAGEANT: Best seen from the nearest beach, this sparkling show is composed of a 1,000-foot-long string of illuminated floating creatures. Guest Services or City Hall can tell you when and where the Electrical Water Pageant can be seen—usually at 9 P.M. from the Polynesian, 9:20 P.M. from the Grand Floridian, 9:45 P.M. from Fort Wilderness, 10:05 P.M. from the Contemporary Resort, and, during the hours when it's open late, from the Magic Kingdom at 10:20 P.M.

INDEX